Happy
Birthday
Wade
From
& Ann
'9

HISTORY OF CIVILISATION

Byzantium

Byzantium

The Empire of New Rome

CYRIL MANGO

*Bywater and Sotheby Professor of Byzantine and
Modern Greek Language and Literature in the University of Oxford*

CHARLES SCRIBNER'S SONS   NEW YORK

Copyright © 1980 Cyril A. Mango

Library of Congress Cataloging in Publication Data

Mango, Cyril A
  Byzantium, the empire of New Rome.
  Bibliography: p.
  Includes index.
  1. Byzantine Empire — Civilization. I. Title.
DF521.M36 1981 949.5 80-5870
ISBN 0-684-16768-9

1 3 5 7 9 11 13 15 17 19 I/C 20 18 16 14 12 10 8 6 4 2

Printed in the United States of America

CONTENTS

ILLUSTRATIONS

Between pages 274 and 275

Church of St John, Istanbul (courtesy of Dumbarton Oaks Center for Byzantine Studies, Washington, D.C.)

Church of Qalb-Loseh, Syria

Dome mosaic of the Rotunda, Thessalonica (by permission of Einaudi Publishers, Turin)

Mosaics, Sant'Apollinare Nuovo, Ravenna (Mansell Collection)

Studius Basilica, Istanbul, capital of porch (courtesy of Dumbarton Oaks Center for Byzantine Studies, Washington, D.C.)

St Sophia, Istanbul, capital of gallery (courtesy of Dumbarton Oaks Center for Byzantine Studies, Washington, D.C.)

San Marco, Venice, capital from St Polyeuctus, Constantinople

Piazza San Marco, Venice, one of the two 'Pilastri Acritani'

St Sophia, Istanbul, interior (courtesy of Dumbarton Oaks Center for Byzantine Studies, Washington, D.C.)

Transfiguration mosaic, Monastery of St Catherine, Mount Sinai

Abraham's Hospitality and the Sacrifice of Isaac, San Vitale, Ravenna (C. M. Dixon)

Icon of the Virgin and Saints, Monastery of St Catherine, Mount Sinai (by permission of Einaudi Publishers, Turin)

Mosaic of St Demetrius and Donors, St Demetrius, Thessalonica (by permission of Einaudi Publishers, Turin)

Great Palace pavement, Istanbul (Phaidon Press Ltd)

Plate with maenad (by permission of the Hermitage Museum, Leningrad)

Mosaic in courtyard, the Great Mosque, Damascus (courtesy of Dumbarton Oaks Center for Byzantine Studies, Washington, D.C.)

Mosaics, south-west room of gallery, St Sophia, Istanbul (courtesy of Dumbarton Oaks Center for Byzantine Studies, Washington, D.C.)

Mosaic cross in apse, St Irene, Istanbul

Mosaic in apse, Church of the Dormition, Iznik

Mosaic of the Virgin, St Sophia, Istanbul (courtesy of Dumbarton Oaks Center for Byzantine Studies, Washington, D.C.)

Church of the Myrelaion, Istanbul (courtesy of Dumbarton Oaks Center for Byzantine Studies, Washington, D.C.)

Church of St Panteleimon, Nereizi

Mosaic of the Anastasis, Hosios Loukas, Phocis (by permission of Einaudi Publishers, Turin)

Mosaic of the Washing of the Feet, Hosios Loukas (by permission of Einaudi Publishers, Turin)

Mosaic of the Nativity, Daphni (by permission of Einaudi Publishers, Turin)

The Anointing of David, Leo Bible (Vatican Library, photo by Phaidon Press Ltd)

Ivory of St John and St Paul (Museo Archaeologico, Venice, photo by Phaidon Press Ltd)

Ivory of the Forty Martyrs (Staatliche Museen Preußischer Kulturbesitz, Berlin)

The Veroli casket (Crown Copyright, Victoria and Albert Museum)

The Apostles of the Ascension, St Sophia, Ohrid (by permission of Einaudi Publishers, Turin)

The Deposition from the Cross, St Panteleimon, Nerezi (by permission of Einaudi Publishers, Turin)

Angel of Annunciation, Kurbinovo, Yugoslavia (by permission of Einaudi Publishers, Turin)

Angel of Annunciation, Panagia tou Arakos, Cyprus (courtesy of Dumbarton Oaks Center for Byzantine Studies, Washington, D.C.)

Annunciation icon, Monastery of St Catherine, Mount Sinai (reproduced through the courtesy of the Michigan–Princeton–Alexandria Expedition to Mount Sinai)

MAPS

PREFACE

The volume dedicated to the Byzantine Empire in the History of Civilization series (not to be confused with *The Byzantine Commonwealth* by Dimitri Obolensky) was originally entrusted to Romilly Jenkins (d. 1969). Had he lived to write it, he would have produced a more elegant and, I am sure, a better book than the one I am now offering to the public.

I shall refrain from mentioning the names of all the friends and colleagues, both living and dead, who have contributed so much to deepening my understanding of Byzantine civilization. I have tried to repay my debt by not asking any of them to read my typescript.

A word of explanation is perhaps required concerning the transliteration of Greek names and words. There are at least three possible systems, namely the latinized (*c* for *k*, *-us* for *-os*, *oe* for *oi*, etc.); the one that may be called the standard Greek system; and, most troublesome of all, the phonetic Modern Greek (favoured, amongst others, by the late Arnold Toynbee). I have generally followed the first in the case of proper names for the simple reason that it is the one most commonly used in the English-speaking world, but in transliterating Greek words and phrases I have adopted the second system with the addition of the circumflex accent to distinguish *eta* from *epsilon* and *omega* from *omicron*. If this leads to some confusion, I can only say that complete consistency would have produced many bizarre forms. The reader who is familiar with Procopius and St John Climacus might have had some trouble in identifying Prokopios and Ioannes ho tês klimakos.

Finally, I should like to extend my thanks to Messrs Weidenfeld and Nicolson as well as to my wife for their exemplary patience.

Oxford, November 1979   C. M.

INTRODUCTION

The Byzantine Empire, as defined by the majority of historians, is said
to have come into being when the city of Constantinople, the New
Rome, was founded in 324 AD, and to have ended when that same city
fell to the Ottoman Turks in 1453. During these eleven centuries it
underwent profound transformations; hence it is customary to divide
Byzantine history into at least three major periods – the Early, the
Middle and the Late. The Early Byzantine period may be regarded as
extending to about the middle of the seventh century, in other words to
the rise of Islam and the definitive installation of the Arabs along the
eastern and southern shores of the Mediterranean; the Middle period
either to the occupation of Asia Minor by the Turks in the 1070s or,
with less justification, to the capture of Constantinople by the Crusaders in 1204; and the Late period from either one of these two termini to
1453.

Arbitrary as the above definition may appear, there are good reasons
for maintaining it. As for the epithet 'Byzantine', serious objections
could be and have often been raised concerning its appropriateness.
For better or for worse, this term has, however, prevailed, and it would
be pedantic to reject it as long as we understand that it is merely a
convenient label. In reality, of course, there never existed such an entity
as the Byzantine Empire. There did exist a Roman State centred on
Constantinople. Its inhabitants called themselves *Romaioi* or simply
Christians; and they called their country *Romania*. A man could
describe himself as *Byzantios* if he was a native of Constantinople, not if
he hailed from another part of the Empire. To western Europeans, for
whom the word 'Roman' had an entirely different connotation, the
'Byzantines' were usually known as *Graeci*, and to the Slavs as *Greki*, but
to the Arabs and Turks as *Rum*, that is, Romans. The term *Byzantinus* as
a designation of the Empire and its inhabitants did not gain currency

I

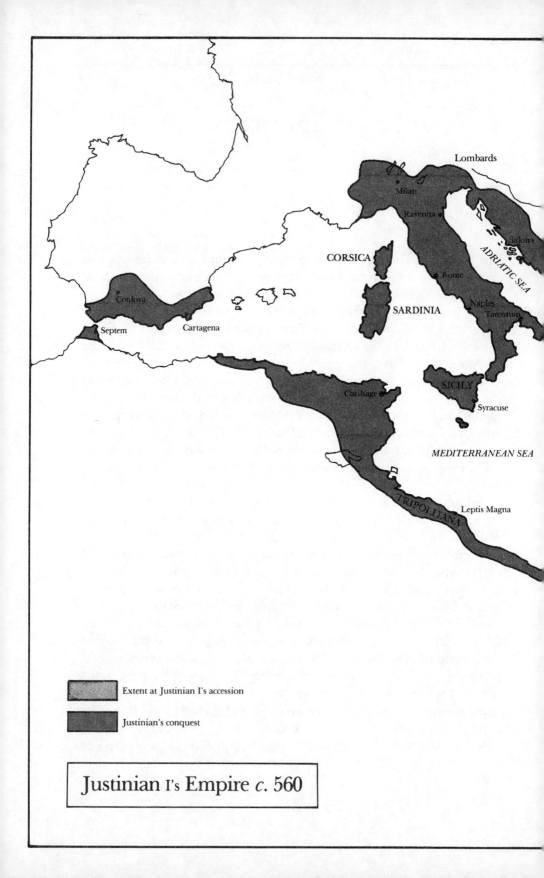

Lombards

Milan

Ravenna

CORSICA

Salona

ADRIATIC SEA

Rome

Cordova

Septem

Cartagena

SARDINIA

Naples
Tarentum

Carthage

SICILY

Syracuse

MEDITERRANEAN SEA

TRIPOLITANA

Leptis Magna

Extent at Justinian I's accession

Justinian's conquest

Justinian I's Empire *c.* 560

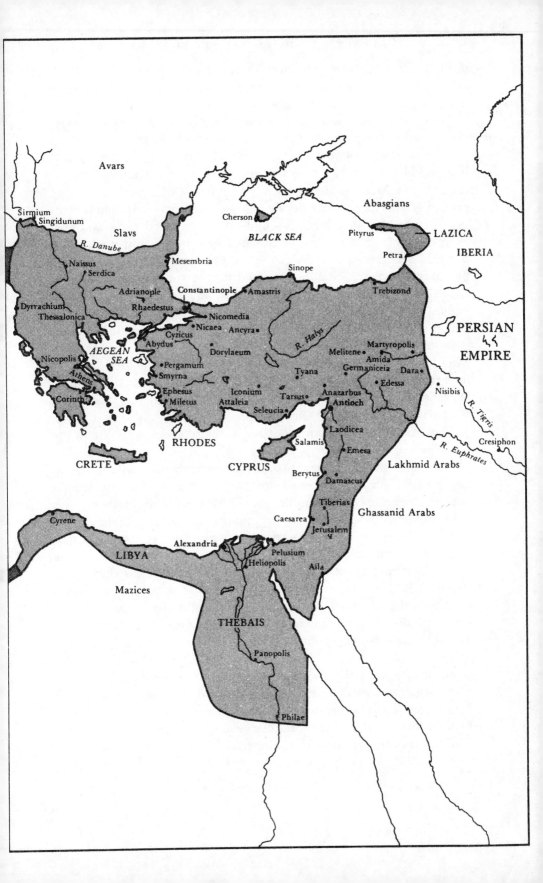

Avars

Sirmium
Singidunum

Slavs

R. Danube

Naissus
Serdica

Dyrrachium
Thessalonica

Adrianople
Rhaedestus

Nicopolis

*AEGEAN
SEA*

Athens

Corinth

CRETE

Cherson

BLACK SEA

Mesembria

Constantinople

Nicomedia
Nicaea
Cyzicus
Abydus

Amastris

Ancyra

Dorylaeum

Pergamum
Smyrna

Ephesus
Miletus

Iconium
Attaleia

Tarsus

Seleucia

RHODES

Sinope

Pityrus

Petra

LAZICA

IBERIA

Trebizond

R. Halys

Tyana

Melitene

Germaniceia

Anazarbus
Antioch

Laodicea

Emesa

Salamis

CYPRUS

Berytus

Damascus

Tiberias

Abasgians

Martyropolis
Amida

Dara

Edessa

PERSIAN

EMPIRE

Nisibis

R. Tigris

Cresiphon

R. Euphrates

Lakhmid Arabs

Ghassanid Arabs

Cyrene

Alexandria

LIBYA

Caesarea

Jerusalem

Pelusium
Heliopolis

Aila

Mazices

THEBAIS

Panopolis

Philae

until the Renaissance. Attempts to supplant it by means of more cumbersome equivalents, such as East Roman or East Christian, have not met with general acceptance.

If we take a very summary and distant view of Byzantine history (which is as much as we can do here), we may say that of the three periods we have indicated, the Early one is by far the most important. It is a period that belongs to Antiquity, whose termination it forms as regards the Mediterranean basin. The Roman Empire may have gradually shed its northern provinces, but it still extended from Gibraltar to the Euphrates, beyond whose waters it faced the traditional enemy, the Persia of the Sassanids. The confrontation and equilibrium of these two great powers was the political basis that underlay the period in question. Outside Rome and Persia, and a few minor states lying on their respective peripheries, there was nothing but a fluctuating sea of barbarism.

It is not only in terms of geographical extension and political power that the Early Byzantine State was incomparably greater than the Middle or the Late. The same applies to its cultural achievement. It integrated Christianity within the Graeco-Roman tradition; it defined Christian dogma and set up the structures of Christian life; it created a Christian literature and a Christian art. There is barely an institution or idea in the entire Byzantine panoply that did not originate in the Early period.

One can hardly overestimate the catastrophic break that occurred in the seventh century. Anyone who reads the narrative of events will not fail to be struck by the calamities that befell the Empire, starting with the Persian invasion at the very beginning of the century and going on to the Arab expansion some thirty years later – a series of reverses that deprived the Empire of some of its most prosperous provinces, namely Syria, Palestine, Egypt and, later, North Africa – and so reduced it to less than half its former size both in area and in population. But a reading of the narrative sources gives only a faint idea of the profound transformation that accompanied these events. One has to consider the archaeological evidence from a great number of sites, to understand the magnitude of the collapse. It marked for the Byzantine lands the end of a way of life – the urban civilization of Antiquity – and the beginning of a very different and distinctly medieval world. And so, in a sense, the catastrophe of the seventh century is the central event of Byzantine history. Just as the west of Europe was dominated throughout the Middle Ages by the shadow of Imperial Rome, so the mirage of the

Christian Empire of Constantine, Theodosius and Justinian remained for Byzantium an ideal to be striven for but never attained. The backward-looking nature of Byzantine civilization is largely due to these circumstances.

If the Early Byzantine period may be seen in terms of an equilibrium between two great powers, the Middle period may be likened to a triangle having one long side (Islam) and two short sides (Byzantium and western Europe respectively). The world of Islam absorbed the heritage of both Rome and Persia and, by uniting in one vast 'common market' an area extending from Spain to the confines of India, produced an urban civilization of unusual vitality. Cut off from the major routes of international commerce, constantly harassed by its enemies, the Byzantine State was nevertheless able to display great activity and recover some of the lost ground. But now it had to look in a different direction – not so much towards the 'classical lands' as towards the barbarous north and west: the Balkans, now settled by Slavs and other newcomers, the Chazar State on the north shore of the Black Sea and, beyond it, to what in the ninth century became the Russian State. New vistas were thus opened up, and Byzantine influence, spearheaded by missionary activity, radiated as far as Moravia and the Baltic. Herein lies, in the wider historical perspective, the chief contribution of the Middle Byzantine period.

The Late period may also be viewed as a triangle, but one having a different configuration. Both the Byzantine and the Arab worlds were now in disarray, while western Europe was in the ascendant. The chief developments that ushered in this last phase were the loss of the greater part of Asia Minor to the Seljuk Turks and the simultaneous cession of maritime traffic to the Italian city states. For the next hundred years Byzantium still managed to retain its unity and something of its prestige; but from about 1180 onwards the edifice began to crumble on all sides. The ensuing fragmentation – the capture of Constantinople by the knights of the Fourth Crusade, the setting up of Latin principalities in the Levant, the formation of Greek splinter states at Trebizond, Nicaea and in the Epirus, the reconstitution of a pale semblance of the Empire of Constantinople in 1261 – makes an exceedingly complex and curious story. Yet it cannot be said that this period of Byzantine history is one of universal significance; the main centres of power and civilization had moved elsewhere.

Such, in briefest outline, were the principal phases of Byzantine history. The subject of our enquiry, therefore, has both a very long extent in time and an ever-shifting geographical context. In the Early period we are concerned with almost the entire Mediterranean basin; in the Middle period the West recedes from our purview except for southern Italy and Sicily, while the focus of interest lies in Asia Minor and the Balkans; finally, we are left with Constantinople and a discontinuous scattering of lands in Asia Minor and in Greece. The diversity of locale also implies a diversity of population. It must be strongly emphasized that there never existed a Byzantine 'nation'. This topic will be more fully explored in Chapter 1, but it is worth pointing out at the very outset that any attempt to impose contemporary national categories on the Byzantine world can only lead to a misinterpretation of the facts.

One more reservation has to be made at this point. Our knowledge of any past civilization is based on records, be they written or monumental. Where written evidence is abundant, monuments assume an ancillary position: we can study the Victorian age without ever looking at the Albert Memorial, though by not doing so we may be missing some interesting insights. To the extent that written records become inadequate, monumental or archaeological evidence gains in importance. In this scheme of things the position of the Byzantine Empire is rather peculiar. At first glance, the volume of written material it has bequeathed to us appears very considerable. But then, what is the nature of this material?

The first fact that strikes the observer is the dearth of documentary or archival records. The only part of the Empire for which such evidence exists in any quantity is Egypt up to the Arab conquest, but we are often told that Egypt was by no means a representative province, and what may be deduced concerning its life thanks to the discovery of papyri does not apply to other regions. We also possess a small quantity of papyri relating to Ravenna, which was an even more marginal part of the Empire. For the rest, we are reduced to a few monastic archives, mostly pertaining to Mount Athos and southern Italy, plus two or three from Asia Minor. The archives in question are limited to land tenure and do not contain any material older than the tenth century. And that, by and large, is all. The records of the central government (and it should be remembered that the Byzantine Empire was a bureaucratic state *par excellence*), of the provincial administration, of the Church, of secular landlords, tenants, merchants and shopkeepers have all disappeared. As a result, we have no reliable population figures, no registers of births, marriages and deaths, no trade figures, no taxation figures – practically nothing, in short, that can be counted and used for statistical purposes. This means that an economic history of the Empire cannot be written in any meaningful sense. To be sure, historians, yielding to the current passion for economics and statistics, have tried to apply to the Byzantine Empire the same methods that have been so successfully used for other periods, only to founder on the same rock – the lack of evidence.

The written material at our disposal may loosely be called literary in the sense that it has been preserved in manuscript books. Counting only those in Greek, about fifty thousand manuscripts survive in various libraries, about half that number being of medieval date. Even if a large proportion of this material is liturgical, theological, devotional, and so on, the historian of the Byzantine Empire cannot complain that he does not have enough texts to read; on the contrary, he has far too many.

And yet, these texts have a strangely opaque quality; and the more elegant their diction, the more opaque they become. That is not to say that they misinform us: on the contrary, Byzantine historians and chroniclers have a reasonably good record for veracity. They give us the external husk of public events; we look in vain for the underlying realities of life. If we turn to epistolography, a genre that was assiduously cultivated throughout the existence of the Empire, we are even more disappointed: instead of personal observations, we are offered erudite clichés. Only on rare occasions is the curtain raised, and this by relatively uncultivated authors. Some Lives of saints that escaped the stylistic 'face-lift' carried out by Symeon Metaphrastes in the tenth century fall into this category; so do some *paterica*, which are collections of anecdotes about monks, and a few heterogeneous texts like the so-called *Strategicon* of Cecaumenus (eleventh century). For a brief moment we are brought face to face with the actual life in a Galatian village, in the Egyptian desert or on a gentleman's estate in central Greece. But in the great bulk of Byzantine literature reality has been strained out. I shall have more to say about this in Chapter 13.

For the historian of Byzantine civilization the limitations of his written material have serious implications. The only means of overcoming them lies, I believe, in the study of material remains, in other words in archaeology. Alas, very little has yet been done in this respect. It is true that a great number of classical cities have been excavated in the eastern provinces, and many of them exhibit a continuous pattern of occupation until the early seventh century. We are, therefore, fairly well informed concerning the material setting of urban life during the Early Byzantine period, even if a great deal still remains to be learnt. The sites in question usually reveal a dramatic rupture in the seventh century, sometimes in the form of a drastic reduction, sometimes virtual abandonment. But what came next? For the Middle and Late Byzantine periods our knowledge is still very sparse. The only type of monument that has survived in considerable numbers and has been the object of systematic study is the church. It has, however, been studied by art historians whose method of approach (though, no doubt, of interest to other art historians) is seldom relevant to the historian of civilization. We may draw some interesting deductions even from churches, but what we need – and this can hardly be achieved in the immediate future – is a systematic investigation of Byzantine cities and villages, of castles and farms, of water-works, roads and industrial installations in different provinces of the Empire. Only when this has been done shall we be in a position to speak with any assurance of the level and scale of the Byzantine civilization.

This grave lacuna has not always been perceived and has certainly not deterred a number of specialists from writing books on the civilization of Byzantium. At least a dozen such works deserve honourable mention (see the Bibliography, p. 303). Inevitably, I have had to cover much of the same ground as my predecessors, but I have adopted an arrangement that differs somewhat from the traditional one. My book has been conceived as a triptych. In its first 'leaf' I have sketched some aspects of Byzantine life – not by any means all its significant aspects, but only those which, in my opinion, have exerted a notable influence on the Byzantine cultural 'product'. In view of the enormous extent of the subject I have had to omit much that is of importance. For example, I have said little about military life, in spite of the fact that the entire course of Byzantine history was dominated by warfare. Nor have I said much about the Byzantine economy and about communications by land and sea, two interlocked topics that remain as yet very imperfectly known. In chronological terms I have laid most stress on the Early and Middle periods, often to the exclusion of the Late period. Critical readers will doubtless find other lacunae.

The second leaf of the triptych is devoted to what Norman Baynes once called 'The Thought-World of East Rome'. Here I have attempted to describe that compact and relatively stable body of belief that may properly be called Byzantinism. In so doing I have deliberately chosen the conceptual level of the 'average' Byzantine: his position, as he saw

8

it, with regard to the supernatural powers of good and evil, his place in nature, his place in history (both past and future), his attitude to other peoples, finally his notion of the good life and of the ideal man. These were not necessarily the views held by all Byzantine intellectuals, but, as will be explained more fully later, the intellectuals – at any rate after the seventh century – constituted a very small clique and exerted no appreciable influence on the thinking of the public at large.

In the last leaf of the triptych I have tried to describe what Byzantium has bequeathed to us. Setting aside, because of their highly technical nature, the subjects of Byzantine law and theology, I have limited myself to literature and art. Whatever Byzantine civilization may have been in its own day, it is on its literary and artistic expression that our appreciation of it must ultimately depend.

PART ONE

ASPECTS OF BYZANTINE LIFE

CHAPTER 1

PEOPLES AND LANGUAGES

All empires have ruled over a diversity of peoples and in this respect the Byzantine Empire was no exception. Had its constituent population been reasonably well fused, had it been united in accepting the Empire's dominant civilization, it would hardly have been necessary to devote a chapter to this topic. It so happens, however, that even before the beginning of the Byzantine period – indeed, when the grand edifice of Rome started to show its first cracks towards the end of the second century AD – the various nations under Roman sway tended to move apart and assert their individuality. The rise of the Christian religion, far from healing this rift by the introduction of a universal allegiance, only accentuated it. We must, therefore, begin with the question: Who were the 'Byzantines'? In an attempt to answer it we shall undertake a rapid tour of the Empire, noting as we proceed the populations of the various provinces and the languages spoken by them. The time I have chosen is about 560 AD, shortly after the recovery by the Emperor Justinian of large parts of Italy and North Africa and several decades before the major ethnographic changes that were to accompany the disintegration of the Early Byzantine State.

It will have been sufficient for our imaginary traveller, provided he did not intend to stray far from the cities, to know only two languages, namely Greek and Latin. The boundaries of their respective diffusion were not in all places sharply drawn. It may be said, however, as a rough approximation that the linguistic frontier ran through the Balkan peninsula along an east–west line from Odessos (Varna) on the Black Sea to Dyrrachium (Dürres) on the Adriatic; while south of the Mediterranean it divided Libya from Tripolitania. With the exception of the Balkan lands, where there was a fair amount of mingling, the western half of the Empire was solidly Latin and the eastern half solidly Greek in the sense that those were the languages of administration and

13

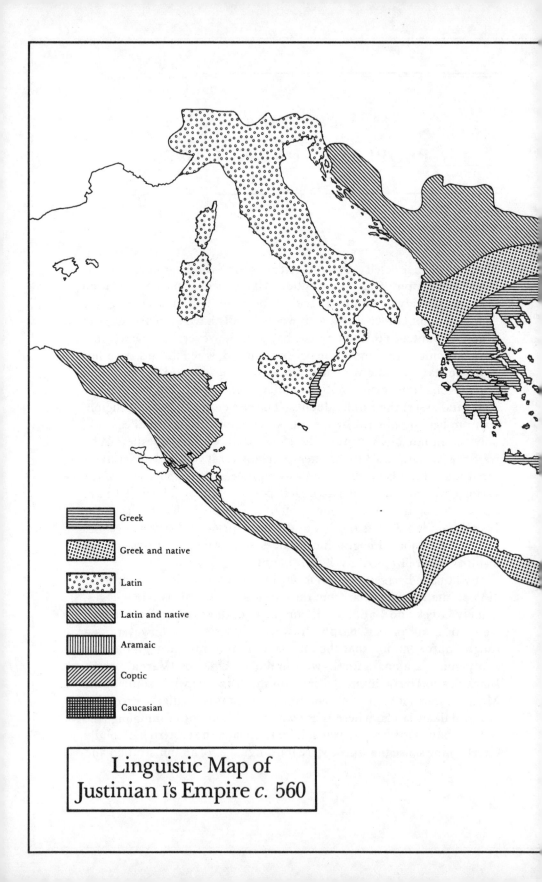

Greek

Greek and native

Latin

Latin and native

Aramaic

Coptic

Caucasian

Linguistic Map of
Justinian I's Empire *c.* 560

culture. Nearly all educated persons in the East could speak Greek, just as all educated persons in the West spoke Latin, but a great proportion of ordinary people spoke neither.

Our traveller would have had considerable difficulty in supplying himself with an up-to-date guidebook. He could have laid his hands on a bare enumeration of provinces and cities called the *Synecdemus* of Hierocles[1] as well as on a few itineraries of earlier date that gave distances between staging posts along the main roads. He might have drawn some useful but antiquated information from a little book known to us as the *Expositio totius mundi et gentium*[2] which was composed in the middle of the fourth century; but if he wanted a systematic treatise combining geography with ethnography, he would have had to pack a copy of Strabo in his luggage. If he had been able to find the geographical treatise (now lost) by the Alexandrian merchant Cosmas Indicopleustes,[3] he would probably have derived little practical benefit from it. Let us imagine that our traveller was content with such imperfect documentation and that, starting from Constantinople, he intended to travel clockwise round the Empire.

Constantinople, like all great capitals, was a melting-pot of heterogeneous elements: all seventy-two tongues known to man were represented in it, according to a contemporary source.[4] Provincials of all kinds had either settled there or would drift in and out on commercial or official business. The servile class included many barbarians. Another foreign element was provided by military units which in the sixth century consisted either of barbarians (Germans, Huns, and others) or some of the sturdier provincials like Isaurians, Illyrians and Thracians. It is said that seventy thousand soldiers were billeted on the householders of Constantinople in Justinian's reign.[5] Syrian, Mesopotamian and Egyptian monks, who spoke little or no Greek, thronged to the capital to enjoy the protection of the Empress Theodora and impress the natives with their bizarre feats of asceticism. The ubiquitous Jew earned his living as a craftsman or a merchant. Constantinople had been founded as a centre of latinity in the east and still numbered among its residents many Illyrians, Italians and Africans whose native tongue was Latin as was that of the Emperor Justinian himself. Furthermore, several works of Latin literature were produced at Constantinople, like Priscian's famous Grammar, the Chronicle of Marcellinus and the panegyric of Justin II by the African Corippus. Necessary as Latin still was for the legal profession and certain branches of the administration, the balance was inexorably tilting in favour of Greek. By the end of the sixth century, as Pope Gregory the Great avers, it was no easy matter to find a competent translator from Latin into Greek in the imperial capital.[6]

Facing Constantinople lies the huge land mass of Asia Minor which has been compared to a jetty attached to Asia and pointing towards Europe. Its most developed parts have always been the coastal edges, especially the gently shelving west face, favoured by a temperate climate and studded with famous cities. The Black Sea coastal strip is much narrower and discontinuous, while the southern shore has, with the exception of the Pamphylian plain, no low-lying edge at all. The coastal areas, save for the mountainous part of Cilicia (Isauria), where the Taurus range advances to the very edge of the sea, had been hellenized for a good thousand years and more before Justinian's reign. Along the Black Sea the limit of Greek speech corresponded to the present frontier between Turkey and the Soviet Union. To the east of Trebizond and Rizaion (Rize) dwelt various Caucasian peoples, such as the Iberians (Georgians) as well as the Laz and the Abasgians (Abkhazians), the latter two barely touched by Christian missions. The Empire also possessed a Hellenized foothold on the southern shore of the Crimea, while the high tableland of the Crimean peninsula was inhabited by Goths.

Quite different from the coastal areas of Asia Minor is the high inland plateau, where the climate is rough and much of the land unfit for agriculture. In antiquity as in the Middle Ages the plateau was sparsely populated and urban life was relatively undeveloped there. The more important cities were situated along the major highways, such as the so-called Royal Road that ran from Smyrna and Sardis, by way of Ancyra and Caesarea, to Melitene; the road connecting Constantinople to Ancyra by way of Dorylaeum; and the southern road that extended from Ephesus to Laodicea, Antioch in Pisidia, Iconium, Tyana and, through the Cilician Gates, to Tarsus and Antioch in Syria. The ethnic composition of the plateau had not undergone any notable change for some seven hundred years before Justinian's reign. It was a bewildering mosaic of native peoples as well as immigrant enclaves of long standing, such as the Celts of Galatia, the Jews who had been planted in Phrygia and elsewhere during the Hellenistic period and Persian groups of even more ancient origin. It appears that many of the indigenous languages were still spoken in the Early Byzantine period: Phrygian was probably still extant, since it appears in inscriptions as late as the third century AD, Celtic in Galatia, Cappadocian farther east. The unruly Isaurians, who had to be pacified by force of arms in about 500 AD and many of whom drifted all over the Empire as professional soldiers and itinerant masons, were a distinct people speaking their own dialect, often to the exclusion of Greek.[7] Next to them, however, in the Cilician plain, Greek had solidly taken root, except, perhaps, among the tribes of the interior.

Lying to the east of Cappadocia and straddling a series of high mountain chains were a number of Armenian provinces that had been annexed to the Empire as late as 387 AD when the Armenian kingdom was partitioned between Persia and Rome. These were strategically very important, but practically untouched by Graeco-Roman civilization, and they continued to be ruled by native satraps until Justinian imposed on them a new form of military administration. In the fifth century the Armenians acquired their own alphabet and began building up a literature of translations from the Greek and the Syriac which strengthened their feelings of national identity. Indeed, the Armenians, who were to play a crucial role in later Byzantine history, proved very resistant to assimilation as did the other Caucasian peoples.

The boundary between Armenia and Mesopotamia corresponded approximately to the river Tigris. Three centuries of Parthian occupation (from the middle of the second century BC until the Roman conquest in about 165 AD) had obliterated in Mesopotamia practically all traces of the Hellenization which the Macedonian kings had tried so hard to impose. In the period that concerns us Mesopotamia spoke and wrote Syriac. The literary form of Syriac represented the dialect of Edessa (Urfa), and it was in that 'blessed city' as well as at Amida (Diyarbakir), Nisibis (Nusaybin) and in the Tur 'Abdin that a vigorous monastic movement of Monophysite persuasion fuelled the cultivation of that language. Mesopotamia was a frontier district: the boundary between Rome and Persia lay a short distance south-east of the garrison town of Dara, while Nisibis had been ingloriously ceded to the Persians by the Emperor Jovian in 363. The cultural apartness of Mesopotamia was certainly no help to the imperial government in so sensitive an area.

The dominance of Aramaic dialects, of which Syriac is a member, extended throughout Syria and Palestine to the confines of Egypt. Here we witness a phenomenon of considerable interest. When the Hellenistic kingdoms were established following the death of Alexander the Great, Syria was divided between the Ptolemies and the Seleucids. The Ptolemies, who obtained the southern half of the country, did rather little to plant Greek colonies there. The Seleucids, on the other hand, for whom northern Syria was of crucial importance, carried out intensive colonization. They established a number of new cities, such as Antioch on the Orontes, Apamea, Seleucia and Laodicea, and injected a Greek element into existing cities, such as Aleppo. From that time onward all of Syria remained continuously under a Greek-speaking administration. Yet, some nine centuries later, we find Greek speech confined not only to cities, but largely to those very cities that had been founded by the Hellenistic kings. The countryside generally and the towns of non-Greek origin, like Emesa (Homs), clung to their native Aramaic.

It is unlikely that the use of Greek should have been more widespread in Palestine than it was in northern Syria, except for an artificial phenomenon, namely the development of the 'holy places'. Starting in the reign of Constantine the Great, practically every site of biblical fame became, as we would say today, a tourist attraction. From every corner of the Christian world people poured into Palestine: some as transient pilgrims, others on a longer-term basis. Monasteries of every nationality sprang up like mushrooms in the desert next to the Dead Sea. Palestine was thus a babel of tongues, but the native population – and we must remember that it included two distinct ethnic groups, namely the Jews and the Samaritans – spoke Aramaic as it had always done. The pilgrim Egeria, who witnessed the Easter services at Jerusalem about the year 400, has this to say:

Seeing that in that country part of the people know both Greek and Syriac, another part only Greek and yet another part only Syriac, given also that the bishop, although he knows Syriac, always speaks in Greek and never in Syriac, there is always by his side a priest who, while the bishop is speaking in Greek, translates his comments into Syriac so that everyone may understand them. Similarly for the lections that are read in church: since these must be read in Greek, there is always somebody there to translate them into Syriac for the benefit of the people, that they may receive instruction. As for the Latins who are there, i.e. those who know neither Syriac nor Greek, to them also is an interpretation given lest they be displeased; for there are some brethren and sisters, proficient in both Greek and Latin, who give explanations in Latin.[8]

Another element of the population of both Syria and Palestine consisted of Arabs who had spread as far north as Mesopotamia. Some of them, like the Nabataeans of Petra and the Palmyrenes, had become sedentary and lost their native language. Others roamed the deserts either as brigands or as vassals of the Empire whose duty it was to protect the settled areas and oversee the transhumance of the nomads. We should not, in any case, imagine that the Arab conquest of the seventh century introduced a foreign element into those provinces: the Arabs had been there all along, their numbers were increasing and, in Justinian's reign, they assumed more and more the role of keepers of the emperor's peace. When, for example, the Samaritans staged a bloody revolt in 529, it was an Arab chieftain, Abukarib, who put them down.

Closely linked with Syria by virtue of its situation was the island of Cyprus. Here Greek had been spoken since prehistoric times, but there was also a sizeable colony of Syrians as may be deduced from the prevalence of the Monophysite heresy (see Chapter 4). St Epiphanius, the most famous bishop of Salamis (d. 403), was a Palestinian and is said to have known five languages – Greek, Syriac, Hebrew, Egyptian and Latin.[9] An exaggeration perhaps, but even so an indication of the multilingualism that characterized, as it still does, the more enterprising among the Levantines.

Separated from Palestine by an area of desert lay the rich and ancient land of Egypt. Here, too, the distribution of Greek was a direct legacy of the Hellenistic age. The capital, Alexandria, was a predominantly Greek city, but it was officially described as being *ad Aegyptum*, not *in Aegypto*, an intrusion into an alien country; and the farther one travelled from Alexandria, the less Greek was spoken. Apart from the capital, only two cities had been founded by the Greeks, Naukratis in the Delta and Ptolemais in the Thebaid; nor did Hellenization make much progress under Roman administration. Setting aside the Jewish colony, which in the first century AD is said to have numbered about one million, the bulk of the population, even though they were administered in Greek, continued to speak Egyptian (Coptic), and there are signs that in the Early Byzantine period Coptic was gaining ground so that, by the sixth century, even some official acts were published in the native tongue. Above all, Coptic was the language of Egyptian Christianity, while Greek was identified with the alien hierarchy that was imposed by the imperial government.

The settled part of Egypt, which was practically limited to the Nile valley and the Delta, was threatened on all sides by barbarian tribes. From the east came raiding Saracens; in the south the black Nobadae and Blemmyes were particularly troublesome, while the west was open to Berber incursions, as was also Libya, a province that was administratively joined to Egypt. St Daniel, who was a monk at Scetis, no great distance from Alexandria, was three times kidnapped by barbarians and managed to escape only by killing his captor – a sin for which he did penance for the rest of his life.[10] When, in the second half of the sixth century, the itinerant monk John Moschus visited the Egyptian monasteries, he picked up many tales of depredations both by barbarians and by native brigands. Some monasteries had become practically deserted.[11]

With Libya we come to the limit of the Greek-speaking provinces. Farther west lay Tripolitania, a narrow coastal strip, then the important regions of Byzacena, Proconsularis and Numidia, and finally the two Mauretanias extending as far as the straits of Gibraltar. These had all been extensively romanized, and the richer areas, corresponding to modern Tunisia, had counted in better days among the most developed and prosperous parts of the Empire. How far the native population had been assimilated is a matter of uncertainty; nor it is entirely clear whether the vernacular language of the cities, which St Augustine calls Punic, was a legacy from ancient Phoenician (as appears more probable) or whether it was Berber. Our traveller in 560 would have found in any case a situation somewhat different from that which the Bishop of Hippo had known a century and a half earlier: for Africa had barely been recovered from the Vandals (in 533) who had held it for a century as an independent power. The Vandals had not been sufficiently numerous to have made a significant impact on the ethnography of the population, but their intrusion had led to the upsurge of the various Berber tribes who now seriously threatened the settled areas.

We need not concern ourselves with Spain, although part of its southern coast was recovered by Justinian from the Visigoths and remained in Byzantine hands for about seventy years. And so we may lead our traveller to Italy, where Justinian's rule had just been established on a somewhat shaky basis after a great deal of bloodshed. The whole country was then in a dreadful state. Continuous warfare between Byzantium and the Ostrogoths, lasting from 535 until 562, resulted in the destruction of Milan with a reputed loss of three hundred thousand males,[12] the virtual depopulation of Rome which suffered three sieges, and widespread starvation in the countryside. 'Italy has become everywhere even more destitute of men than Libya,' wrote Procopius,[13] perhaps without great exaggeration. As to the composition of the population, there can be little doubt that the *Italiôtai*, as Procopius called them, were basically Latin; even in the imperial capital of Ravenna, which had close ties with the East and numerous oriental settlers, Latin was the normal medium of communication. Some tiny pockets of Greek may have survived in the southern part of the peninsula and Greek certainly continued to be spoken on the east coast of

Sicily. There were other minority groups, such as the Jews and the recently arrived Ostrogoths, but the latter could hardly have numbered more than a hundred thousand. Many more waves of invaders and settlers were to come, without, however, altering the fundamentally Latin character of the population.

Crossing the Adriatic, our traveller may have disembarked at Dyrrachium and followed the Via Egnatia all the way back to Constantinople. The regions he would have to traverse were then about as desolate as Italy. To quote Procopius once again,

> Illyricum and all of Thrace, i.e. the whole country from the Ionian Gulf [the Adriatic] to the outskirts of Byzantium, including Greece and the Chersonese, was overrun almost every year by Huns, Slavs and Antae, from the time when Justinian became Roman emperor, and they wrought untold damage among the inhabitants of those parts. For I believe that in each invasion more than two hundred thousand Romans were killed or captured, so that a veritable 'Scythian wilderness' came to exist everywhere in this land.[14]

Procopius omits to mention here that some of the most destructive invasions of the Balkan peninsula had occurred before Justinian's time, in particular by the Goths in 378, by the Huns in 441–7, by the Ostrogoths in 479–82, by the Bulgars starting in 493. There can be little doubt concerning the immense amount of havoc caused by these and later incursions, but their effect on the ethnography of the regions in question is difficult to assess. The native populations were the Illyrians to the west, the Thracians and Daco-Mysians to the east and, of course, the Greeks to the south, but it would take a brave historian to state who was living where and in what numbers in the middle of the sixth century. The Slavs had already begun to settle, especially in the area between Niš and Sofia, as proved by the place names listed by Procopius,[15] and we may imagine that the prolonged presence of Gothic and other barbarian troops had left some trace. As to languages, we have already commented on the boundary between Latin and Greek. Of Illyrian (whose relation to modern Albanian is disputed) very little is known, but Thracian, in particular Bessic, was still very much alive in the sixth century.

Such, in brief outline, were the peoples and languages of Justinian's Empire; and if I have laid any stress on the native elements, it was in order to correct the bias of our literary and narrative sources. To take but one instance, the fourth-century rhetorician Libanius, who was born at Antioch and lived most of his life in that city, whose writings fill eleven printed volumes and are a mine of useful information, mentions only once the existence of the Syriac language. Yet it is an indisputable fact that Greek-speaking Antioch was an island in a sea of Syriac. Cultivated authors simply took no notice of such 'uncivilized' phenomena. Nor are inscriptions much more illuminating. Whoever set up an inscription, be it even on a tombstone, naturally used the 'prestige' language of the area. Besides, many of the vernacular dialects were not written. It is largely in the milieu of monks that we are occasionally brought face to face with ordinary illiterate folk and gain some inkling of what they spoke. Predictably, it was their native patois. Hence the custom of setting up 'national' monasteries. Others, however, were multinational: that of the Sleepless Ones (Akoimetoi) was divided by language into four groups – Latin, Greek, Syriac and Coptic.[16] The monastery founded by St Theodosius the Coenobiarch in Palestine catered for Greek, Bessic and Armenian.[17] On Mount Sinai in the sixth century one could hear Latin, Greek, Syriac, Coptic and Bessic.[18] In 518 the abbot of a monastery at Constantinople could not sign his name to a petition because he did not know Greek.[19] Similar examples could easily be multiplied.

Our survey would have been much more instructive had we been able to express in figures the relative importance of the various ethnic groups. Unfortunately, we have no reliable figures at our disposal, as has already been indicated in the Introduction. One eminent scholar has nevertheless ventured the view that Justinian's Empire, including the reconquered western provinces, had no more than 30 million inhabitants.[20] Not taking into account the losses caused by the great plague of 542, this appears to be too low an estimate: we may be nearer the truth in postulating 30 million for the eastern half of the Empire. In very approximate terms, the distribution would have been the following: 8 million in Egypt, 9 million in Syria, Palestine and Mesopotamia combined, 10 million in Asia Minor, and 3 to 4 million in the Balkans. If these figures are anywhere near the truth, it would follow that the native Greek speakers represented less than a third of the total population, say 8 million, making allowance for the unassimilated peoples of Asia Minor and for the Latin and Thracian speakers of the Balkans. The Greek, Coptic and Aramaic elements would thus have been on a footing of near parity. Compared to the spread of Latin in Gaul and Spain, it must be admitted that the Greek language had made very limited progress between the third century BC and the sixth century AD. This was no doubt due to the fact that Hellenization was largely centred on cities. About a century after the Arab conquest Greek had become practically extinct in both Syria and Egypt, which can only mean that it had not grown deep roots.

One further observation may be made on the basis of our survey, namely that in spite of mounting insecurity in nearly all parts of the Empire, most of Justinian's subjects still lived in their traditional homelands. The diaspora of the Greeks, of the Jews and, to a lesser extent, of the Syrians had occurred several centuries earlier. From the viewpoint of ethnography, as in so many other respects, Justinian's age represents, therefore, the tail end of Antiquity.

It would be wearisome to describe here all the ethnographic changes that the Empire witnessed after the sixth century, but we must say a few words about the greatest mutation of all, which started happening a few decades after Justinian's death. Its first sign was the massive installation of the Slavs in the Balkan peninsula. The Slavs came in several waves and, unlike earlier invaders, they came to stay. In an oft-quoted passage John of Amida (also known as John of Ephesus) records that in 581

an accursed people, called Slavonians, overran the whole of Greece, and the country of the Thessalonians, and all Thrace, and captured the cities, and took numerous forts, and devastated and burnt, and reduced the people to slavery, and made themselves masters of the whole country, and settled in it by main force, and dwelt in it as though it had been their own. . . . And even to this day [584 AD], they still encamp and dwell there, and live in peace in the Roman territories, free from anxiety and fear, and lead captive and slay and burn.[21]

Another source, the so-called Chronicle of Monembasia, states that in the year 587–8 the Turkic Avars (with whom the Slavs were usually allied)

captured all of Thessaly and all of Greece, Old Epirus, Attica and Euboea. Indeed, they attacked the Peloponnese and took it by war; and after expelling and destroying the native Hellenic peoples, they dwelt there. Those who were able to escape their murderous hands were scattered here and there. Thus, the citizens of Patras moved to the district of Reggio in Calabria, the Argives to the island called Orobe, the Corinthians to the island of Aegina. . . . Only the eastern part of the Peloponnese, from Corinth to Cape Maleas, was untouched by the Slavonians because of the rough and inaccessible nature of the country.[22]

There is some doubt concerning the exact date of these events, but it is undeniable that at the end of the sixth century and the beginning of the seventh, when the Danubian frontier completely collapsed, practically the entire Balkan peninsula passed out of imperial control. Only a few coastal outposts, such as Mesembria on the Black Sea, Thessalonica, Athens and Corinth, held out. Elsewhere the old population sought refuge on off-shore islands, as it did on Monembasia, or emigrated to Italy. The domain of barbarism extended as far as the outer defences of Constantinople – the so-called Anastasian Long Walls which described a wide arc from the Black Sea to Selymbria (Silivri) on the Sea of Marmora – but even these had soon to be abandoned.

The last important Slavonic settlement was that of the Serbs and Croats who in the reign of Heraclius occupied the lands where they still dwell. Then, in 680, came the Turkic Bulgars and conquered the country that bears their name, where they were eventually assimilated by the sitting Slavonic population. The barbarization of the Balkans began to be reversed only towards the end of the eighth century, but by that time its effects had become permanent.

Simultaneously with the loss of the Balkans the Empire suffered a more serious amputation by being deprived of its eastern and southern provinces. This happened in two stages. First, between the years 609 and 619, the Persians conquered all of Syria, Palestine and Egypt. They were then defeated by the emperor Heraclius and withdrew to their own country; but a few years later the same provinces were overrun by the Arabs and, this time, lost for good. The whole of the north African coast also succumbed to the invader. The Mediterranean empire of Rome simply ceased to exist, while the Byzantine State found itself limited to Asia Minor, the Aegean islands, a bit of the Crimea and Sicily.

The Persians also initiated another development that was to have important demographic consequences by striking at Constantinople through Asia Minor. In so doing they caused immense havoc. When the Arabs had succeeded to the Persians and made themselves masters of all the territories up to the Taurus mountains, they, too, struck into Asia Minor – not once or twice, but practically every year – and this went on for nearly two centuries. Many of the raids did not penetrate far from the frontier, but several of them extended as far as the Black Sea and the Aegean, and a few reached Constantinople itself. As it turned out, the Arabs never managed to gain a foothold on the Anatolian plateau. What happened instead was that every time they marched in the local population would take refuge in the inaccessible forts with which Asia Minor is so liberally provided. The Arabs would pass between the forts, taking prisoners and booty, while the Byzantines would burn the crops to deprive the enemy of supplies and keep him on the move. The consequences of this prolonged process are easy to imagine: much of Asia Minor was devastated and depopulated almost beyond repair.

In this way an enormous demographic gap was created. The Empire urgently needed farmers as it also needed soldiers. To achieve this end it had to resort to massive transfers of population. The Emperor Justinian II, in particular, applied this policy on a wide scale. He moved a good part of the population of Cyprus to the region of Cyzicus on the southern shore of the Sea of Marmora. It was, apparently, a failure: many of the immigrants perished *en route*, and those who reached their destination later asked to be repatriated.[23] Justinian II also moved 'a great multitude' of Slavs to Bithynia. Once again, he had little luck: the thirty thousand soldiers he raised from among this group to fight against the Arabs defected to the enemy, whereupon the emperor inflicted cruel reprisals on their families.[24] In the 760s, however, we are told that 208,000 Slavs came to live in Bithynia of their own accord.[25] In the eighth century we repeatedly hear of the organized settlement of Syrians in Thrace.[26]

Among the new immigrants the most prominent, however, were the Armenians, many of whom arrived without being forced to do so. The Armenians were excellent soldiers, and the Empire, deprived of its Illyrian recruiting ground, needed them badly. In fact, the immigration of Armenians had started in the sixth century, and from the reign of Maurice onwards they formed the backbone of the Byzantine army. The trickle of Armenians into the Empire was spread over many centuries. Many settled in Cappadocia and other parts of eastern Asia Minor close to their original homeland, others in Thrace, others in the region of Pergamon. It is impossible to give even a rough approximation of their numbers. Unlike the Slavs, however, the Armenians quickly rose to prominent positions, even to the imperial throne, and dominated the military establishment throughout the Middle Byzantine period.

Thus, if we place ourselves at about the time when the Empire started on the slow course of its recovery, say towards the end of the eighth century, we find a population that had been so thoroughly churned up that it is difficult to tell what ethnic groups were living where and in what numbers. It is often stated that by shedding, however painfully, its principal non-Greek-speaking elements, such as the Syrians, the Egyptians and the Illyrians, the Empire had become more homogeneous. It is also asserted that the non-Greeks were gradually assimilated or Hellenized through the agency of the Church and the army, and that this happened in particular to the indigenous populations of Asia Minor as well as to the Slavs in the Peloponnese and elsewhere in Greece. The critical reader may be advised to treat such generalizations with a measure of caution. It is true, of course, that following the eclipse of Latin, Greek became the only official language of the Empire, so that a knowledge of it was mandatory for pursuing a career or transacting business. Neither Armenian nor Slavonic ever supplanted it as a general medium of communication. It is also true that in the long run Slavonic died out in Greece and in Bithynia, and if any Armenian has been spoken in Thrace within living memory, it was not on the part of descendants of the colonists planted there in the eighth century. But then it is also known that Greek survived in Asia Minor on a continuous basis only in Pontus and a small part of Cappadocia, whereas it had become practically extinct in the western part of the subcontinent until its reintroduction there by immigrants in the eighteenth and nineteenth centuries. We would not argue from the last observation that western Asia Minor was not predominantly Greek-speaking in the Middle Ages. However illuminating it may be in some respects, the long view does not help the historian of Byzantium to solve the specific problems that confront him. Was Hellenization, for example, a conscious aim of the imperial government, and if so, how was it implemented and with what success? And if it succeeded in the Middle Ages, why had it not done so in Antiquity under conditions of a more settled life and a higher civilization?

When we look at our scanty sources, we realize that the formulation of the above questions does not correspond to the Byzantine way of thinking. First of all, the very designation 'Greek', which we use so freely today to describe those Byzantines who did not belong to any alien group, is entirely absent from the literature of the period. An inhabitant of Greece south of Thessaly would have referred to himself as a *Helladikos* (a name already current in the sixth century AD), but he could have been a Slav as well as a 'Greek'. The same holds true of other regions whose dwellers called themselves by the names of their respective provinces, for example Paphlagonians or Thrakêsians (after the Thrakêsian 'theme' in western Asia Minor). Since, therefore, there was no notion of 'Greekness', it is hard to see how there could have been one of 'hellenization'. The only passage, to my knowledge, that may

27

imply something of the kind says that the Emperor Basil I converted the Slavonic tribes from their old religion and, 'having grecized them (*graikôsas*), subjected them to governors according to Roman custom, honoured them with baptism, and delivered them from the oppression of their own rulers'.[27] It has long been, however, a matter of dispute what the term 'grecized' may mean in the present context. What we do hear about, again and again, is the conversion of various peoples to Orthodox Christianity, be they pagan Slavs or Muslim Cretans, and the setting up of an ecclesiastical organization. Here is how the Chronicle of Monembasia describes the activity of the Emperor Nicephorus I in the Peloponnese: 'He built *de novo* the town of Lacedaemon and settled in it a mixed population, namely Kafirs, Thrakêsians, Armenians and others, gathered from different places and towns, and made it into a bishopric.'[28] Surely, neither the Kafirs (possibly a generic term for converts from Islam) nor the Armenians would have contributed to the hellenization of Laconia. The emperor's purpose was simply to implant a Christian population and set up a bishopric.

There can be little doubt that the evangelization of non-Christian peoples settled in the Empire was carried out in Greek. This may cause some surprise in the case of the Slavs since the Slavonic alphabet was itself devised by a Byzantine, St Cyril, presumably in the 860s. Its invention, however, and the consequent translation of the essential Christian texts were intended for a far-away Slavonic country, Moravia; and it was entirely a matter of chance that the Cyrillo-Methodian mission, after its initial failure, should have found a fertile soil in a country for which it was not intended, namely the Bulgarian kingdom. As far as our knowledge goes, no attempt was ever made to evangelize the Slavs in Greece in their own language, just as the liturgical use of Greek was imposed on conquered Bulgaria after 1018. Clearly, this must have contributed to the spread of Greek. But was it due to deliberate policy? Is it not more likely that the absence of a linguistically qualified clergy, the relative inaccessibility of the Slavonic Scriptures, and the mixed nature of the population should have combined to make the use of Greek the easier option?

However efficacious the liturgical imposition of Greek may have proved, it has to be admitted that the assimilation of barbarian enclaves was a very slow process. In the Peloponnese the presence of pagan Slavs a short distance south of Sparta is attested in the latter part of the tenth century,[29] that is nearly two hundred years after the first attempts to bring about their conversion. Equally telling is the case of the Slavs in

Bithynia. We have seen that these were transplanted in very considerable numbers at the end of the seventh century and towards the middle of the eighth. Some two hundred years later, the Byzantine armament assembled in an effort to conquer Crete in 949 included a contingent of 'Slavonians who are established in Opsikion' (this being the administrative name of a part of Bithynia) placed under their own commanders.[30] Clearly, these Slavonians still formed a distinct group. In the next century Anna Comnena refers to a village in Bithynia 'locally called Sagoudaous',[31] presumably after the tribe of the Sagoudatai, attested in Macedonia in the seventh century. A little later the Slavonic element in Bithynia was augmented by the Emperor John II Comnenus who settled near Nicomedia a throng of Serbian captives.[32] Serbian villages are still mentioned in those parts in the thirteenth century. In other words, it is quite possible that the Slavs of Bithynia, or at any rate part of them, were assimilated by the Ottoman Turks without having ever become 'Greek'.

The obvious conclusion to be drawn from these and many other cases is that the Middle Byzantine Empire was by no means a solidly Greek state. In addition to the Armenians and the Slavs, there were many other foreign elements, such as the Georgians and the Balkan Vlachs. A massive influx of Syrians and other Christian orientals followed the eastward expansion of the Empire at the end of the tenth century; and when, in 1018, the imperial frontier was once more extended to the Danube, it comprised vast areas where Greek had never been spoken or had been extinguished a long time previously. Whether Greek speakers formed at the time the majority or a minority of the inhabitants of the Empire is a guess I should not like to hazard.

It is not altogether easy to define the feelings of solidarity, if any, that bound together the multinational inhabitants of the Empire. In the sixth century the slogan *Gloria Romanorum* still appeared from time to time on the imperial coinage, but it is not likely that there was much devotion in the eastern provinces to the idea of *Romanitas*. Besides, loyalty to Rome and admiration for her ancient greatness had been a regular theme of pagan polemic, whereas the Church maintained the position that Christians were, above all, citizens of the Heavenly Jerusalem and in so doing probably weakened the cohesion of the Empire. That is not to say that instances of loyalty to the State are absent from Byzantine history: quite the reverse is true. It is enough to recall the despair of the population of Nisibis when their city had been ceded to the Persians in 363, the demonstrations of pro-Roman sentiments at Edessa in 449 in the context of sectarian strife, and a multitude of similar cases. But then we must remember that at the time the only alternative to living under Roman rule was living under Persian rule (which was usually worse). People crushed by the burden of taxation were often tempted to desert to the enemy, even to join some barbarian tribe that levied no taxes, but that was not an option for those who enjoyed a reasonable standard of living. A feeling of *Romanitas* was hardly the determining factor.

As far as we can judge, the main links of solidarity were two: regional and religious. People identified themselves with their village, their city or their province much more than they did with the Empire. When a person was away from home he was a stranger and was often treated with suspicion. A monk from western Asia Minor who joined a monastery in Pontus was 'disparaged and mistreated by everyone as a stranger'.[33] The corollary to regional solidarity was regional hostility. We encounter many derogatory statements concerning 'the cunning Syrian' who spoke with a thick accent, the uncouth Paphlagonian, the mendacious Cretan. Alexandrians excited ridicule at Constantinople. Armenians were nearly always described in terms of abuse. Even demons, as we shall see in Chapter 7, had strong feelings of local affiliation and did not want to consort with their fellows from the next province.

Religious identity was often more strongly felt than regional identity. Had the Church been less intolerant, it may well be that different religious groups could have lived peaceably side by side, but there was usually some zealous bishop or monk who incited a pogrom, and then the fight was on. It is not surprising that Jews and the few remaining pagans should have proved the most consistently disloyal elements in the Empire. Within the Church, however, religion and regionalism overlapped to a considerable extent. And herein, perhaps, lies the key to the 'heretical' groupings that will be more fully described in Chapter 4. For what seems to have motivated the Syrian or the Egyptian Monophysite was not so much his belief in some abstruse point of doctrine as his loyalty to his own Church, his own bishop and the holy men of his neighbourhood. Whenever a Christian splinter group had a solidly established territorial base, all attempts to impose on it a uniform, imperial orthodoxy ended in failure.

If in the Early Byzantine period the idea of *Romanitas* held little potency, the same was even truer of the Middle period when the old imperial capital had receded into some 'Scythian wilderness' and the

Latin tongue had been forgotten. Even in contexts of international confrontation the emotive concept became that of Christian rather than that of Roman identity. When, in 922, Romanus I Lecapenus urged his army officers to put up a spirited defence against Symeon of Bulgaria, they vowed to die on behalf of the Christians, and this although the Bulgarians were by this time, at any rate nominally, Christian themselves.[34] Significantly, however, no new term emerged to describe the identity of the Empire as a whole. Nor was it much needed on the level of everyday life. When, in the early ninth century, St Gregory the Decapolite, a native of southern Asia Minor, landed at the port of Ainos in Thrace, he was promptly arrested by the imperial police and subjected to a bastinado. We are not told why; perhaps he looked like an Arab. He was then asked: 'Who are you, and what is your religion?' His answer was: 'I am a Christian, my parents are such and such, and I am of the Orthodox persuasion.'[35] Religion and local origin constituted his passport. It did not occur to him to describe himself as a Roman.

CHAPTER 2

SOCIETY AND ECONOMY

A sixth-century abbot is reported to have addressed these words to a novice:

If the earthly emperor intended to appoint you a patrician or a chamberlain, to give you a dignity in his palace (that palace which will vanish like a shadow or a dream), would you not scorn all your possessions and rush to him with all haste? Would you not be willing to undergo every kind of pain and toil, even to risk death for the sake of witnessing that day when the emperor, in the presence of his senate, will receive you and take you into his service?[1]

Few Byzantines, we may imagine, would have behaved differently, since the most obvious characteristic of the Byzantine polity was the overwhelming power of the central government. Short of rebellion, there was no effective counterweight to this power except in delay, inefficiency, corruption or simply distance. This remained true until the gradual disintegration of central governance which we may place approximately in the eleventh century.

In theory the emperor's authority knew no limits save those imposed by divine laws. In Chapter 12 we shall consider the ideal definition of the Byzantine emperor. Here, however, we are concerned with practice, and in practice the emperor was a man who dwelt in the imperial palace of Constantinople, far removed from the public gaze, surrounded by his court. More often than not, he owed his position to an unformulated, but generally respected, principle of heredity; alternatively, he may have been co-opted by his predecessor, chosen by an influential group or he may have owed his throne to a successful rebellion. Strangely enough, the Byzantine State never evolved a theory of imperial succession. A man became emperor by the will of God, his election was signalled by acclamation on the part of the army and the senate, and confirmed, from the fifth century onwards, by a religious coronation performed by the patriarch of Constantinople. To outside observers this system looked curiously unstable and ill-defined: some Arab authors believed that the Roman emperor owed his position to victory and was dismissed if he was unsuccessful.[2] But whatever the circumstances of the emperor's accession, he could not govern single-handed. His principal ministers were chosen at his pleasure and the effective power they wielded was not expressed by their titles. Some emperors – the more forceful ones – assumed a preponderant role in the conduct of affairs, while others were content to leave it to a relative or to one or more officials. While it was generally believed that the emperor had a duty to lead his armies in the field,[3] many emperors did not do so, either through incapacity or because they feared a rebellion during their absence from the capital. There was so much variation in practice that it may be more accurate to speak of government by the imperial palace rather than by the emperor.

The society over which the emperor presided was meant to be governed by the notion of order. Its constituent parts are variously described in our sources. We sometimes find a three-fold division into army, clergy and farmers.[4] We are further told that the army formed the head of the body politic,[5] or that the most essential occupations were farming and military service in that farmers fed the soldiers, while soldiers protected the farmers.[6] We have from the sixth century a much more elaborate classification of the civilian part of society into ten groups, namely: 1. The clergy; 2. The judiciary; 3. Counsellors (senators?); 4. Those concerned with finance; 5. Professional and technical; 6. Commercial; 7. Those concerned with the provision of raw materials; 8. Subordinates and servants; 9. The useless (in other words, the old, the infirm and the insane); 10. Entertainers (charioteers, musicians, actors).[7] Interesting as such textbook classifications may be, they do not reveal to us the functioning of Byzantine society. Before we can construct a more realistic model of it, we ought to begin with the Early period and consider briefly the State services, the municipal government, the Church, the urban trades and professions and, finally, the farmers.

All imperial service, whether military or civil, was designated by the term *militia* (*strateia* in Greek). Within it, the army formed the largest group: its total strength for both east and west towards the end of the fourth century was about 650,000. This may not strike us as an unduly big number out of a total population of probably more than 40 million, but in view of the low yield of the Late Roman economy it constituted a

33

considerable burden. Following Constantine's reforms, the army was composed of two main bodies: a mobile force of *comitatenses* and a frontier militia of *limitanei*. Their respective numbers for the eastern Empire were about 100,000 and 250,000. The *comitatenses* had no permanent camps, being usually billeted in cities, where they might also be called upon to perform police duties (the Empire had no regular police force). Some complained that as a result of this arrangement soldiers grew soft and imposed unbearable hardship on cities that had no need of protection.[8] The *limitanei*, on the other hand, were locally recruited farmers who manned the frontier forts while not busy tilling their fields. They were not regarded as being particularly effective. The historian Agathias points out that Justinian, the greatest of Byzantine conquerors, had in the latter part of his reign no more than 150,000 men under arms, scattered in various provinces, whereas the defence of the Empire required four times that many.[9] This figure, however, does not appear to include the *limitanei*, and so may represent an augmentation rather than a diminution. At the same time we have to remember that an expeditionary force was usually in the 10,000–25,000 range, and that an army of some 50,000, such as might occasionally be thrown against Persia, was considered unusually big.

Service in the army was a lifelong occupation and was meant to be well rewarded. Even so, there was little enthusiasm for it in the more civilized parts of the Empire and evasion was widespread. By Justinian's time recruitment had become voluntary and depended very largely on some of the ruder provinces, like Illyricum, Thrace and Isauria, where a military life was traditional. Much use was also made of barbarians, such as Goths, Huns and Scythians, who were either 'home grown' or taken from border tribes allied to the Empire (*foederati*). The loyalty of the latter could not always be taken for granted.

In the Early Byzantine Empire military and civil commands were generally separate, although by the second half of the sixth century they began to coalesce in some insecure provinces (notably Africa and Italy). There was thus a hierarchy of army command culminating in several *magistri militum*, and a civil hierarchy concerned with justice, finance and the running of various services, such as the public post (*cursus publicus*), the State police cum secret service (*magistriani* or *agentes in rebus*), and so on. Provincial administration was in the hands of Praetorian Prefects, now shorn of the military authority they had held earlier, and descended to the *vicarii* of dioceses and the governors of provinces. Constantinople, like Rome, had a separate administration under an urban prefect. It should be pointed out that while the middle and lower echelons of the civil service enjoyed security of tenure to the point of virtual irremovability, the higher offices were conferred for a short time only.

Some historians have spoken of a bureaucratic strangulation of the Later Roman Empire, yet by modern standards the number of civil servants was minimal: it has been calculated that in all there were no more than 30 to 40,000 of them in both east and west (c. 400 AD). The reason for this is that the cities ran their own affairs through municipal councils (curiae) composed of the more substantial local landowners. The latter, usually called decurions, formed a fairly numerous class. If we assume about 200 per city, their total number in the east would have been close to 200,000. Their importance for the history of civilization far outweighs, however, their numerical strength, since the intellectual élite of the Empire, the liberal professions, the higher echelons of the Church and a great many civil service posts, were filled by members of the decurion class. We must look at them more closely.

It is a commonplace of Late Roman history that the municipal gentry was in a state of decline. However much allowance we make for the self-interested complaints of members of their own class (Libanius being the most frequently quoted example), the fact remains that from Constantine to Justinian decurions made increasing efforts to avoid their responsibilities which were openly regarded as a servitude. From the standpoint of the law, all landowners who attained a stated property qualification were obligated to serve on councils, and their heirs after them. They were collectively responsible for all municipal works, for the repair of public buildings, aqueducts and fortifications, for keeping streets and drains clean, for providing spectacles, over-seeing the market, maintaining the post, and for all extraordinary duties imposed by the State, such as billeting soldiers, making compulsory purchases of provisions, recruiting levies for the army (when conscription was in force), and so on. The cities possessed certain resources in land and market dues to cover the necessary expenditure; even so, decurions had usually to dip into their own pockets. No wonder that they exploited every loophole to avoid such onerous, if respectable, offices. The normal way of gaining exemption was to join the civil service or the senate of Constantinople (in spite of various laws that forbade this), to enter the Church or become a public teacher. Some never married so as not to leave a legitimate heir. Some simply ran

35

away. The result of continuing pressure was that the curial class exploded: the poorer members melted away, while the rich ones grew richer at the expense of their neighbours. They became magnates who bullied their fellow-citizens and usually had enough leverage at court to win for themselves posts in the imperial administration that exempted them from municipal duties. By the middle of the sixth century councils had become practically extinct. John Lydus, born at Philadelphia in 490, could still remember the days when they administered the cities and when their members wore the toga.[10]

The gap created at provincial level was filled partly by the governors, partly (and increasingly so) by the bishops. It has been rightly pointed out that the Byzantine Church did not constitute an organization *sui juris*; in modern terms it may be described as a Department of Social Welfare. The task of providing for the indigent, for strangers, for widows and orphans was an evangelical obligation which the Church took upon itself in the fourth century. As municipal councils declined, bishops assumed, more and more, a variety of extra-religious functions. We find them dispensing justice, overseeing the market, regulating weights and measures, repairing bridges, building granaries. Where a provincial governor was in residence the bishop was his equal, while in other cities he became the top man, equivalent to a governor. The bishop was thus an administrator, and he was normally selected from the gentry because he had to be presentable and possess managerial experience. It was perfectly normal for a layman, even if he was not particularly religious, to be directly ordained bishop. Examples abound; one will have to suffice. In the early sixth century we hear of a certain Harfat who came from a family of rich landowners. When his parents died, he and a kinsman inherited the estate plus some five thousand gold pieces. Thereupon Harfat was offered the bishopric of Arsamosata in Armenia, which he declined. The offer was repeated to his kinsman 'under inducement of riches and high position', and this man, who is described as being of dishonest character, accepted it.[11] There are also many instances of laymen who made excellent bishops, like Synesius of Cyrene in the fourth century or St John the Almsgiver, patriarch of Alexandria in the early seventh.

In the early Byzantine period the Church grew extremely rich, or, to put it in another way, huge resources were channelled through it. In addition to receiving a subsidy from the State, it possessed a permanent endowment in the form of land as well as commercial property in the cities. It was constantly on the lookout for donations from the wealthy and paid particular attention to heiresses whom, if they were widows, it urged not to remarry, and if unmarried, to espouse the holy estate of virginity to the glory of God and the benefit of ecclesiastical coffers. But if receipts were large, so also were expenditures. The Church of Antioch at the end of the fourth century provided for three thousand widows and virgins in addition to invalids, strangers, prisoners and beggars. What is more, it did so without expending its capital.[12] The emoluments of the clergy and the upkeep of buildings were further charges on the ecclesiastical budget.

The Church of Alexandria, as seen through the Life of St John the Almsgiver, provides a concrete example.[13] St John was a Cypriot, a widowed layman belonging to a prominent family, and he was appointed patriarch by the emperor Heraclius in 610 to deal with a particularly troublesome situation: the Egyptian Church, in addition to its endemic upheavals, had passed almost entirely into the hands of the Monophysite party. It seems that St John proved a great success. He had a *grand seigneur*'s liberality and self-assurance; he was also, if we may believe his biographer, a man of perfect humility. Humble or not, St John found himself at the head of a vast bureaucracy. Setting aside the provincial clergy, the establishment at Alexandria numbered many hundreds of employees. There were several financial administrators (*oikonomoi*), a treasurer, a chancellor, a distributor of alms, notaries, secretaries and legal advisers. There were disciplinary officers who were empowered to inflict bodily punishment and imprisonment on clerics whose conduct was unsuitable, for example a monk who turned up in the company of a young woman. The overseers of markets and taverns were under the bishop's authority. There was an army of messengers and ushers – on one occasion twenty are mentioned – as well as gentlemen of the patriarch's bedchamber (*cubicularii*). Finally, there was the clergy proper, headed by the protopresbyter and the archdeacon and descending to the lower grades whose incumbents often practised another profession, such as that of cobbler. The patriarch held a court of justice at which he heard all kinds of grievances, by no means confined to ecclesiastical affairs. Generally, he dealt on a footing of equality with the governor of Egypt (*dux augustalis*) who happened to be the emperor's cousin.

Our document is silent about any landed property the Church might have possessed (Alexandria had no rural territory), but mentions a number of taverns from which it collected rent and other dues. Furthermore, the Church had a fleet of some fifteen large cargo vessels that carried on trade with western Europe. On one occasion, we are told, they were overtaken by a storm in the Adriatic and had to jettison their entire cargo to the value of 3,400 lb of gold. Pious donations poured in: a woman bequeathed 500 lb of gold to the Church, a twice-married layman offered during a time of famine 200,000 bushels of wheat and 180 lb of gold on condition of being made a deacon, but was turned down. In all, St John is said to have collected during his eight years in office 10,000 lb of gold from donations in addition to the 8,000 he had found in the treasury of the Church. No wonder that the Church of Alexandria acted as banker to the business community. At the same time the patriarch is said to have had 7,500 beggars in his care. He built hospices for them – elongated vaulted buildings provided with wooden benches, mats and blankets. He also built hostelries for visiting monks, and, when Jerusalem fell to the Persians in 614, he sent vast sums of money to rebuild its churches and ransom prisoners.

The three other eastern patriarchates, those of Constantinople, Antioch and Jerusalem, enjoyed resources comparable to those of Alexandria. Jerusalem, in particular, made a killing from the real estate boom in the Holy City and was, exceptionally, given leave to sell at a huge profit some of its urban holdings.[14] Provincial bishoprics were, of course, poorer, but usually did quite well. We hear, for example, of an Egyptian bishop who could afford to spend 30 lb of gold for a dinner service of tooled silver for his personal use.[15] The bishop of Anastasioupolis in Galatia, a very small town, had in about the year 600 an allowance of 365 *solidi* per year for his table, of which he spent only 40.[16]

Archaeological evidence offers striking confirmation of the wealth of the Church from the fourth to the sixth centuries. All round the Mediterranean, basilicas have been found by the score. While architecturally standardized, these were quite large buildings, often a hundred feet or more in length, and were lavishly decorated with imported marble columns, carving and mosaic. In every town more and more churches were built until about the middle of the sixth century, when this activity slackened and then ceased entirely. Was there really need for so much capacity? From the pastoral point of view the answer is surely negative. Since, however, the erection of churches was regarded as a praiseworthy act and satisfied the vanity of donors while providing additional posts for the clergy, it probably continued for a time even when it had ceased to serve any real need.

It is clear that the Church performed an important social function. It acted as a redistributor by taking from the rich and providing shelter, food and medical care to the needy. It cannot be doubted that the Church conducted these activities more efficaciously than either the State or the municipal government could have done, since it was able to appeal to the emotions of donors, to tempt them with Paradise and threaten them with Hell. Rich widows would hardly have gone with tears in their eyes to offer their gold to the *dux augustalis* or the *comes Orientis*. But as money flowed down the social scale, a good part of it (such as was not channelled into building activities) was diverted to provide for the ecclesiastical establishment. Since a career in the Church could be very comfortable in addition to the social prestige it provided, the clergy expanded in numbers. In the early seventh century, for example, the cathedral of Constantinople had an administrative staff of 88, a clergy of 525 plus 75 janitors,[17] and this after Justinian had frozen ordinations at a considerably lower level.[18] A century earlier the Church of Antioch found itself in financial straits because of the mounting number of clergy.[19]

Before we proceed to give some account of urban and rural populations, it may be helpful to consider the monetary system of the Empire and the pattern of earnings and expenditures. The basis of the coinage was the gold *solidus* (*nomisma* in Greek) which was struck at 72 to the pound. Smaller gold coins of half (*semissis*) and one third (*tremissis*) of a *solidus* also circulated, but no silver was issued until the seventh century. Small change was copper and, after the reform of the emperor Anastasius in 498, normally came in denominations of 5, 10, 20 and 40 *nummi*, the last being known as the *follis*. The relation of gold to copper tended to fluctuate, but in theory 1 *solidus* was equivalent to 180 *folles* or 7,200 *nummi*. The lack of denominations intermediate between the *follis* and the *tremissis* may strike the modern observer as inconvenient. Since the coinage was pegged to the gold standard, prices and wages remained remarkably stable, except in times of shortage caused by droughts, enemy attacks and other calamities – indeed, they did so from the fourth to the eleventh century, when the *solidus* began to be adulterated.

The information we possess on the size of personal fortunes, on incomes, on the cost of essential commodities and luxuries, on the prices paid for farm animals and slaves leads to some obvious conclusions. Firstly, there was a staggering disparity between the rich and the poor. Secondly, government service normally led to considerable riches. Thirdly, there must have been a very large number of people living on the subsistence level, since unskilled and semi-skilled workers were very poorly remunerated. Fourthly, the price of manufactured articles, especially clothing, was comparatively very high. If we may start at the bottom of the social scale, there is reasonably concordant evidence that the earnings of a labourer or semi-skilled worker were in the range of 10 to 20 *solidi* a year given steady employment. At the end of the fourth century St Gregory of Nyssa, who wished to build a church, was offered a team of workers at one thirtieth of a *solidus* per day plus food, a rate he considered exorbitant.[20] At Jerusalem in the sixth century a building worker received one twentieth of a *solidus* per day, that is 9 *folles*.[21] Roughly the same wage, namely one twenty-fourth of a *solidus*, was earned by a casual labourer at Alexandria in the early seventh century.[22] When the Emperor Anastasius was building the city of Dara in Mesopotamia as a strategic base against the Persians (505–7), he offered exceptionally high wages to the masons, namely one sixth of a *solidus* per day or one third for a workman with his own ass, with the result that 'many grew rich and wealthy'.[23] The price for an unqualified slave (about 20 *solidi*) was in line with average earnings. Now consider the price of essential commodities. A family's vegetable allowance for one day cost 5 *folles*,[24] which works out at a little over 10 *solidi* a year; a pound of fish 6 *folles*,[25] a loaf of bread as much as 3 *folles*, admittedly at a time of shortage.[26] The cheapest blanket cost one quarter of a *solidus*,[27] a second-hand cloak 1 *solidus*,[28] and a donkey roughly 3 to 4 *solidi*. It is obvious that a labourer or a mason, even if fully employed, lived just above the starvation line, unless he happened to be an ascetic who could survive on one portion of lupins per day (price 1 *follis*).

At the other end of the social scale, we find that bishop Porphyry of Gaza (late fourth century), who came of a noble family of Thessalonica, inherited on the death of his parents 3,000 *solidi*, plus another 1,400 of unspecified provenance as well as garments and silver vessels. This was only part of the estate, since Porphyry had a number of younger brothers.[29] We have already mentioned the Armenian Harfat whose parental estate amounted to 5,000 *solidi* plus land. These, it should be pointed out, were by no means exceptional fortunes, but such as might have been owned by fairly substantial decurions. An imperial magnate had immeasurably more. When Justinian's general Belisarius fell from favour, the confiscated part of his property (he was allowed to keep the remainder) amounted to 216,000 *solidi*.[30]

Let us now look at an imperial official of medium grade. John the Lydian, to whom we owe the treatise on *The Magistracies of the Roman*

State and other antiquarian works, arrived at Constantinople in 511 with a view to pursuing higher studies and then entering the administration. Luckily, a compatriot of his named Zoticus was at that very time appointed Praetorian Prefect. With the great man's help John received a post in the chancellery of the Prefecture, where a cousin of his was already employed, and in the course of one year he earned 'honestly' (as he himself says) 1,000 *solidi* by way of commissions. Delighted with such good fortune, he wrote a short panegyric of his patron and was rewarded with 1 *solidus* for each verse, naturally drawn from the public treasury. What is more, Zoticus also found a bride for his protégé, a woman of unsurpassed chastity who brought him a dowry of 100 lb of gold (7,200 *solidi*).[31] It is true that after Zoticus had been destituted, John's career suffered a setback. Nevertheless, he remained another forty years in the office of the Prefecture, worked his way to the top of his grade and retired with the title of Count, First Class. An interesting case not only of an official's earnings, but also of the importance of patronage and of geographical ties.

Unfortunately, we know next to nothing about the income of the urban middle class. Speaking at Antioch, St John Chrysostom says that one tenth of the population was rich and another tenth completely indigent.[32] We should not take these figures at face value, since the orator himself contradicts them in the next sentence. The number of the destitute, those entirely dependent on charity, was probably below 10 per cent if there is any truth in the statement quoted above that there were 7,500 beggars in the care of the Church of Alexandria, well below 5 per cent of that city's population. Nor can we conclude, I think, that 80 per cent of the inhabitants of Antioch were well-to-do. We have already seen that manual workers were extremely poor, and the same was no doubt true of other lowly occupations, such as hawkers and retailers. Craftsmen, normally organized in guilds, rated higher than retailers, and some trades, like those of the jeweller and the money-changer (*argyropratês*), could lead to substantial profits; but although we possess long lists of urban occupations, it is not possible to arrange them in ascending order. The general impression one gains is that tradesmen and craftsmen were not in a position to earn very much money. A man of this class might aspire to own his home, to buy a slave, to have a properly covered bed and a number of bronze vessels. These items established status (*schêma*) and were often acquired at the cost of stringent economies on essentials.[33]

Among occupations that could lead to a measure of wealth, that of merchant immediately comes to mind. The fourth-century *Expositio totius mundi* presents a fairly rosy picture of commercial activity. In Mesopotamia, it says, Nisibis and Edessa were very rich because the Persian trade was channelled through them. In Syria the ports of Tyre and Laodicea were particularly prosperous. Ascalon and Gaza in Palestine exported wine to Syria and Egypt. Scythopolis, Laodicea, Byblos, Tyre and Berytus were famous for their textiles. All those cities, our text says, depended on trade, and their inhabitants were rich, eloquent and virtuous. Another important centre, because of its proximity to the Persians and the Arabs, was Bostra. Egypt, of course, was renowned for its fertility. It produced everything except oil (and, we may add, wine of good quality) and Alexandria was the greatest port of the Empire. Of other parts our author seems to be informed by hearsay rather than by personal experience. He singles out the province of Asia (western Asia Minor) as a producer of wine, oil, rice, purple and spelt; other coastal regions of Asia Minor likewise for agricultural produce, while the districts of the interior contributed little more than textiles and animal skins. Concerning the Balkans he is less enthusiastic: Thrace was merely fertile; Macedonia had iron, embroideries, bacon and cheese; Greece could not even provide for its own needs, and Laconia produced only marble. Even so, Corinth had an active port.

Of course, there was a good deal of long-distance trade in the Later Roman Empire: trade in wine and oil, in salted fish and roe, in slaves, eastern spices, textiles and ready-made garments, in pottery and precious metals. Nevertheless, it did not result in the formation of great fortunes. The business tycoon was at no time a feature of Byzantine society, and perhaps the only merchant in the annals of Byzantine literature is the sixth-century Alexandrian Cosmas Indicopleustes: he certainly travelled far and wide, but we do not know whether he earned much money. The relatively low profitability of commerce was due to many interconnected causes: the weak purchasing power of the public, the self-sufficiency of most districts as regards essentials, the risks of long-distance travel. Shipwrecks were frequent and the winter months considered unfit for navigation, so that a good part of the year was dead for business. Interest rates on commercial loans were also very high. Another important factor was that the State (potentially the biggest customer) did not have recourse to private intermediaries. The provisioning of the capital cities as well as of the army was, as we would say, nationalized. The products (Egyptian corn, flax, wool, etc.) were levied directly in kind and transported by a State guild of shippers (*navicularii*) who were attached to this service on a hereditary basis. Furthermore, the State maintained factories of arms and weaving mills to produce uniforms, and held a monopoly of mining. The role of the private merchant was correspondingly diminished. In the seventh century a long-distance commercial agent, the Jew Jacob, who was entrusted with a consignment of garments worth 144 *solidi* (hardly a big sum) to sell in Africa and Gaul, received 15 *solidi* a year as commission: no wonder he defrauded his employer.[34]

The main source of wealth as well as of taxation was agriculture. There is a widely held view that the early Byzantine system was founded on large estates worked by slaves, but, strictly speaking, this is untrue. Servile labour was not much used on the land, being largely confined to domestic service. Even St John Chrysostom, who disapproved of the ostentatious accumulation of slaves, admitted that a freeborn man could not cook for himself.[35] The majority of slaves – and we have no idea what percentage they formed of the total population – consequently lived in cities. As for large estates, these certainly existed, though we should visualize them not so much as huge unbroken tracts, but rather as a great number of dispersed plots held by a single owner. In general, there was much fragmentation of land, and it was quite common for a landlord, whether an individual, the Church or the Crown, to hold estates in several provinces. Some well-known examples of very rich landowners, like the Apion family in Egypt, should not blind us to the presence of medium and small freeholders often grouped in autonomous communes. The archaeological exploration of the Limestone Massif in north Syria, a region that attained great prosperity thanks to the cultivation of the olive tree, has shown not only the co-existence of large and small holdings, but also a general trend, in the period extending from the fourth to the sixth century, towards the break-up of the bigger estates and the growth of villages composed of relatively well-to-do, independent farmers.[36] While conditions in the Limestone Massif were probably untypical of the rest of Syria, not to speak of other parts of the Empire, they serve to emphasize the danger of drawing general conclusions from literary and legislative texts.

If the slave was generally absent from the rural landscape, the tenant farmer (*colonus*) was an important feature of it. A man of degraded and anomalous status, the *colonus* was theoretically free, but in practice tied to his plot. He was, as a law of 393 puts it, 'a slave of the land'.[37] His condition was hereditary, his freedom to marry restricted, and he could not even join the army. The master of his land collected his taxes and was empowered to put him in chains if he tried to run away. It was openly admitted by the government that there was little difference between the status of a slave and that of a *colonus*.[38] The authorities, of course, were not animated by pure sadism in curbing the liberties of the tenant farmer; their primary concern was the collection of tax in accordance with the established registers. For if there was one institution that left an indelible mark on the Late Roman and Byzantine way of life, that was surely taxation. The imposition of regular and extraordinary levies – in kind upon the farmer and in money upon the merchant and artisan – was meant to be equitable; in fact, it hit the agricultural population harder than the urban, and the poor much more than the rich. The unfortunate *colonus* was deprived of about a third of his yield in tax, on top of which he had to pay rent to his landlord. It was exorbitant taxation that drove many Romans to desert to the enemy, no less so in the eleventh century[39] than in the fourth and fifth, that obliged farmers to abandon their fields, that filled the monasteries and impoverished decurions. The *indictio* or imposition of tax on a fifteen-year cycle became the most widespread form of counting years in the Byzantine Empire.

As we survey, however briefly, the social and economic history of the Early Byzantine State, we see an ever-tightening ring of interlocking constraints. The introduction of a planned economy by the Emperor Diocletian in the last decade of the third century was probably a necessary step: the State might not have survived without it. A planned economy made possible something that had not existed earlier, namely a State budget. How else could one meet the vastly increased, yet variable, cost of the army? A budget meant a rationalized system of taxation, which meant a census, which meant an expanded bureaucracy. As a result of Diocletian's reforms, the Roman world was filled with officialdom, and it could already be said in the fourth century (no doubt with considerable exaggeration) that the number of beneficiaries exceeded that of taxpayers.[40] As we all know, however, a bureaucracy generates its own momentum, and taxes have a tendency of going up rather than coming down. It is an undeniable fact that from the fourth century onwards more and more land was going out of cultivation, and it is highly likely that the main cause of this was taxation. As the tax yield diminished, the officials, armed with their registers, had no choice but to apply more repressive measures: everyone, from the lowly *colonus* to the decurion, had to be kept in his place. But the wheels of government ground slowly, distances were great, and there was plenty of scope for fraud and evasion. The figure of the patron, the 'fixer', the man of influence thus came to stand at the centre of the stage, so much so that even the cult of Christian saints was visualized in terms of patronage, as we shall see in a later chapter. We have mentioned the case of Jacob, the Jewish travelling salesman. There is a sequel to his story. When Jacob's employer at Constantinople learned that he had been defrauded, what did he do? Did he have recourse to the law? Not at all. He went to see his patron, a chamberlain in the imperial palace, and the chamberlain sent 'his own man' to Carthage to apprehend Jacob who, in the meantime, had embraced Christianity.[41]

The rigidity of the Early Byzantine social and economic structure could always be circumvented by devious means. Whatever the laws prescribed (and there is no reason to think that they were systematically applied), a resourceful man usually found a way of getting on in life. There were, of course, recognized means of social ascension, notably the army and the civil service. There are many instances of simple soldiers rising to important commands, even to the imperial throne, and of sausage-makers' sons becoming great ministers of State. And once a fortune had been made, it tended to remain in the same family for several generations, unless it was confiscated. While there was no hereditary aristocracy as an institution, officialdom brought money and money secured government posts. But then there were other ways of social mobility. The fourth-century heretic Aetius is said to have started life as a *colonus* on a vineyard. He then managed to become a smith, was apprehended for fraud, apprenticed himself to a quack doctor, emerged as a physician in his own right, came to the attention of the Caesar Gallus (Julian's brother) and ended up as a famous theologian.[42] The story may well be malicious, but it shows that this kind of career was possible. Rigidity tempered by evasion may thus be a suitable description of the Early Byzantine social structure. Perhaps it applies to other planned economies as well.

The collapse of the Early Byzantine State at the very time when the unfortunate Jacob was being bundled off from Carthage to Constantinople must have caused profound social readjustments. Unfortunately, we do not have the documentation to follow these in any detail. When the curtain of darkness begins to lift in the ninth century, we perceive that rather a different world has come into being, but we know very little about the intermediary process.

What we can see most clearly is that the entire machinery of the

imperial government was put on a different footing. The great minis-
tries of State, like the praetorian prefectures, and the great military
commands of the Masters of Soldiers were abolished. In their place we
find a greatly increased number of officials, all of them responsible
directly to the emperor and not arranged in a hierarchical pyramid.
The nature of the change, as J. B. Bury defined it,[43] was 'to substitute
the principle of co-ordination for that of subordination, and to multiply
supreme offices instead of placing immense powers in the hands of a
few'. Most striking of all was the restructuring of the provincial
administration which was initiated, it seems, by the Emperor Heraclius. The old provinces grouped into dioceses were replaced by a
number of large units called *themata* or 'themes', each governed by a
stratêgos (general) whose competence included both military and civil
affairs. This reform was first applied to Asia Minor and subsequently
extended to European provinces as the latter were gradually liberated
from the barbarians; simultaneously, the large 'themes', as originally
constituted, were split up into smaller ones. The term *thema*, whose
exact derivation still remains unclear, denoted in the first instance a
corps of soldiers and, by extension, the district in which it was
stationed. Following the first implantation of soldiers, after whom the
'theme' often received its name, recruitment seems to have been carried
on locally, so that a permanent, indigenous army came into being. The
resemblance to the old system of the *limitanei* is obvious, but now the
whole territory of the Empire became, so to speak, a frontier zone. Some
scholars believe that the salvation of the Empire during its long struggle
with the Arabs was achieved by this radical reform. They also hold that
the soldiers (*stratiôtai*) of the 'themes' received from the very beginning
grants of land on condition of hereditary military service, and that they
tilled this land while not serving on campaign. This picture of vigorous
soldier-farmers defending their hearths against the invader is contrasted with the 'effete' society of the previous age which spent its time
at the theatre and paid barbarian mercenaries to do the fighting.

There can be no doubt that the institution of the 'themes' involved a
thorough militarization of the Empire corresponding to the harsh
realities of contemporary life, but it is not at all clear how the system
worked in the first two or three centuries of its existence or what social
conditions it overlay. The accepted view is that the 'thematic' reform
was accompanied by a general fragmentation of the large estates
characteristic (or so it is claimed) of the Early Byzantine period, and
that the rural society of the Dark Ages was one in which free com-

munities of medium and smallholders predominated. To the extent that considerable numbers of immigrants were settled within the Empire at this time, as we already saw in Chapter 1, it follows that lands must have been found for them, but whether these were Crown lands or those of earlier magnates is not recorded. Nor is there any mention, as far as I know, of landowners being dispossessed in favour of immigrants or of the soldiers of the 'themes'. In any case, if there was really a trend from large to small holdings, it must have been a relative one, since, on the one hand, it is by no means certain that *latifundia* had previously been the norm in the eastern provinces, and, on the other, large estates are well attested in the eighth and ninth centuries, as will appear shortly. We may see here a change of degree rather than a revolution.

A piece of evidence that is often introduced into this context is the so-called Farmer's Law.[44] This picturesque document, which is said to date from the late seventh or the early eighth century, regulates in simple terms disputes arising in a village community. The farmers, some of whom own slaves or hire herdsmen, are represented as owners of their own fields and cattle and are free to come and go as they please. There are impoverished farmers who abandon their land, in which case the tax due on it falls on the community, but sometimes an absent farmer continues to meet his obligations *vis-à-vis* the Treasury and retains full ownership of his property, whether it is cultivated or not. There are communal lands which are divided from time to time as well as woodland within reach of the village. Orchards and vineyards are protected by ditches or fences, but fields are not, and cattle often stray into them. Herds are attacked by wolves, dogs fight and are occasionally put down, farmers pinch one another's implements. Harsh and often barbarous penalties are imposed on offenders – amputation of hands or tongue, blinding, impalement, death by fire. Despite its brevity, the Farmer's Law presents a vivid picture of village life. Can we be sure, however, that it describes a situation that was then typical of the Byzantine countryside? Can we infer from its silence on the subject of *coloni* that the latter no longer existed or were exceptional, even though they reappear under the name of *paroikoi* by the beginning of the ninth century at the latest? Or does the Farmer's Law apply to a particular kind of community whose commonness or rarity we are unable to establish? Finally, how does the Farmer's Law relate to the system of the 'themes'? It makes no mention of military service or of landholding conditional on service.

47

The continued existence of large estates is proved by a number of concrete cases. I shall not insist on one that has been often quoted, that of the Paphlagonian St Philaretos (d. 792), who is said to have possessed 48 domains, 12,000 sheep, 600 oxen, and more, all of which he distributed to the needy.[45] A more credible example is provided by St Theophanes Confessor, author of a famous chronicle, who was born in 760, the son of the governor of the 'theme' of the Aegean Sea. Left an orphan at the age of three, he grew up as a very rich young man and married a woman of equal wealth. He possessed extensive estates in Bithynia and many slaves, both male and female, including his private goldsmith. Entering imperial service with the rank of *strator* (groom), he was appointed to supervise the reconstruction of the fort of Cyzicus and acquitted himself of this task at his own expense. He would have climbed much higher in the imperial hierarchy had he not decided to become a monk and given away his property; even then he was able to raise sufficient capital for the construction of a very substantial monastery.[46] An even more extreme case is that of the widow Danelis of Patras who befriended Basil the Macedonian (the future Emperor Basil I) when the latter was as yet an obscure young man. She is described as owning 'no small part of the Peloponnese'. On her two subsequent visits to Constantinople she was carried overland in a litter by 300 vigorous young slaves who worked in relays. Her estate, which she eventually bequeathed to the Emperor Leo VI, an estate 'exceeding any private fortune and barely inferior to that of a ruler', included 80 domains and over 3,000 slaves whom the emperor sent as colonists to southern Italy.[47] It may be recalled that the Peloponnese was made into a 'theme' in about 810 following its recovery from independent Slavonic tribes. In the light of accepted theory it ought to have been settled by soldier-farmers. Yet the vast estates of Danelis were built up at this very time, since she was already a grandmother and a plutocrat when she first met Basil in the 850s.

The truth of the matter, it seems to me, is that historians have been looking in the wrong direction. Assuming a continuity of urban life in the Dark Ages, they have sought to discover an agrarian revolution. In fact, it was urban life that collapsed, as we shall see in the next chapter, whereas conditions in the countryside may not have undergone a structural change. Quite simply, the Empire was ruralized. The absence, on the one hand, of big urban populations that had to be fed, the infusion of fresh manpower into the countryside, on the other, brought about the plenty and cheapness of foodstuffs that are attested in the eighth century. At the same time the cost of maintaining the army was greatly diminished when barbarian mercenaries ceased to be recruited on a big scale. As a result of these developments, which we can discern only in the broadest outline, the complex constraints of the Early Byzantine period could be eased. If peasants regained a measure of freedom, that was probably because there were enough of them in relation to the needs of the Treasury.

The Church, too, was greatly affected by the collapse of the cities. The provincial bishop of the Middle Byzantine period was but a pale shadow of his predecessors. The Council of 869 sought to re-establish his dignity and in so doing has given us a glimpse of his social status. It ruled that a bishop ought not to go a long distance from his church to meet a *stratêgos* or any other lay dignitary; he ought not to dismount hastily from his horse or his mule and approach the said dignitary with fear and trembling; he ought not even to dine in the company of a dignitary lest he was obliged to show him undue deference.[48] If bishops were so terrified of their local governors, it is not surprising that they showed complete subservience to the emperor's wishes, even when the emperor happened to be a heretic. A hundred years later the Lombard ambassador Liudprand remarked that Byzantine bishops had few servants and lowly furnishings, that they bought and sold, and acted as their own janitors.[49] Appointment to a bishopric could be bought for a modest amount: that of Sebaste (Sivas) in eastern Asia Minor was worth 100 *solidi* in the early tenth century.[50] By way of comparison, the court title of *protospatharios*, which carried an annuity at $2\frac{1}{2}$ per cent, could be secured at the same time for a payment of 40 lb of gold, that is, close to 3,000 *solidi*. The decline in the fortunes of the Church was not due entirely to the eclipse of urban life: another contributing factor was that donations were directed more and more to monasteries, which tended to acquire an independent status, as we shall see in Chapter 5. The bishoprics were thus left with their landed properties on which they paid the basic tax, and whatever small fees they could exact from monasteries as well as for ordinations, weddings, baptisms and the like. In other words, they were on a par with private landowners and usually acted as such, abandoning the sphere of 'social welfare'. Furthermore, life in a provincial episcopal seat was extremely dreary: for an educated man who was used to the amenities of Constantinople it was equivalent to a sentence of banishment. No wonder that bishops tarried as long as possible in the capital on various excuses and often had to be pressured to return to their rustic flocks.

The development of Byzantine society during the Middle period is marked by two contradictory trends: on the one hand, a steady movement towards a kind of feudalism, on the other, a tenuous growth of an urban bourgeoisie. The former has received much more attention from historians than the latter.

The troubles of the seventh and eighth centuries appear to have pretty much obliterated the leading families of the previous period. Their ruination was probably due, above all, to economic reasons. Furthermore, a number of emperors, namely Phocas, Justinian II and Leo III, are said to have deliberately persecuted the upper classes. Whatever truth there may be in such allegations, the prominent people we meet from the eighth century onwards seem to be relative newcomers, many of them being clearly of foreign extraction. Although the prosopographic evidence at our disposal is extremely meagre, we can nevertheless quote a few cases of important families that emerged in the eighth or ninth century and survived a long time thereafter. We have said that St Theophanes Confessor (born in 760) was the son of a *stratêgos*; the latter, who was called by the name of Isaac (uncommon among Greeks), must, therefore, have been born in c. 720–30. Theophanes himself had no children, but a branch of his family must have lived on, since the Emperor Constantine VII (913–59) claimed him as a relative on the side of his mother, the Empress Zoe;[51] and we further happen to know that Zoe's great-grandfather, active in the 820s, was a *stratêgos* of the Anatolic 'theme'.[52] Another example is provided by the house of Rentakios or Rendakis. We first meet the patrician Sisinnios Rendakis in 719 somewhere in Macedonia.[53] In 867 a Rentakios was chamberlain at the imperial palace,[54] and another Rentakios, described as an uncultivated 'Helladikos', i.e. a native of Greece, was put to death for intriguing with the Bulgarians in 920.[55] The latter, incidentally, was related to the patrician Nicetas, satirized for his 'sly Slavonic face', whose daughter Sophia married Christopher Lecapenus (d. 931), son of the Emperor Romanus I.[56] In the tenth century the Rentakioi were established landowners in Boeotia.[57]

More important, however, were the great families that sprang up in eastern Asia Minor in the ninth and tenth centuries, such as the Phokades (sing. Phokas), the Sklêroi, the Maleinoi, the Doukai, and others. Partly or largely of Armenian descent and much intermarried among themselves, they held a near monopoly of high military commands. The Cappadocian Phokades, whose first known member was an obscure officer of the mid-ninth century, reached the imperial throne in the person of Nicephorus Phokas; the next emperor, the Armenian John Tzimiskes, belonged to the Kourkouas clan which had given the Empire a series of brilliant generals; the Sklêroi, enemies of the Phokades, barely missed the throne as did also the Doukai in the person of Constantine Doukas (in 913), whose relationship to the imperial Doukas family of the eleventh and twelfth centuries is unclear. These and other great clans brought to Byzantium a new aristocratic ideal. Ancient lineage was much prized among them, and fictitious genealogies were fabricated: the Phokades claimed descent from the Roman Fabii,[58] the Doukai from a non-existent cousin of Constantine the Great,[59] and even the Emperor Basil I, who came of an obscure Armenian background, was ingeniously linked with the kingly house of the Arsacids. 'We come from the Anatolic theme, from among noble Romans. Our father is descended from the Kinnamoi, our mother is a Doukas of Constantine's family. There are twelve generals (stratêgoi) among our cousins and uncles': thus speak the uncles of the epic hero Digenes Akrites whose exploits epitomize the ideals of valour and chivalry of the eastern aristocracy.[60]

The material enlargement of the great landowners is most fully documented in a collection of imperial enactments spanning the period from about 927 until 996.[61] Their immediate cause was the severe famine of 927–8 which forced many farmers to sell their lands at absurdly low prices. The plight of the 'poor' was exploited by the 'powerful' (dynatoi) who were thus able to absorb the holdings of peasants and soldiers and to infiltrate independent village communities. This was the trend that the emperors of the tenth century tried to curb; and the frequency of their enactments proves the lack of their success. But who exactly were the 'powerful'? Interestingly enough, they are defined not in economic terms, but in terms of influence and rank. The 'powerful' were those who either by themselves or through intermediaries were able to terrorize the vendors or to bribe them by promises of protection. More precisely, they were magistri and patricians, holders of other civil and military dignities, members of the imperial senate, provincial magistrates, bishops, abbots, other ecclesiastical officials, the heads of charitable institutions and imperial domains. Minor civil servants (sekretikoi) and guardsmen (scholarii) provided the upper limit of the 'poor' class. Guardsmen, however, were regarded as being more influential than soldiers (stratiôtai) and civil servants superior to those not holding any government position. There existed, therefore, in the Byzantine countryside a complex social hierarchy; and while it was possible for an ordinary person to work his way up the ladder, such ascension was viewed with disapproval. The emperors ordered that any humble people who 'in some mysterious way' had risen to a higher position would be reduced forthwith to their former estate. A particular example was made of a certain Philokales who, starting as a villager, rose to the rank of *prôtovestiarios* and in so doing had acquired all the lands of the community in which he lived. Not only was he destituted, but the splendid dwellings he had built for himself were razed to the ground. The artful Philokales may have recovered from the blow since his name was borne by a very prominent family of the eleventh and twelfth centuries.

The concern of the imperial government in repressing 'the insatiable greed' of the powerful was partly military, partly fiscal. Service in the army was at that time (we do not know exactly since when) dependent on ownership of land worth a minimum of 4 lb of gold and remained at that level until the reign of Nicephorus II Phokas who raised it to 12 lb because of the introduction of heavier armour.[62] Clearly, the army would have been depleted if soldier–farmers were forced to sell their holdings. The fiscal considerations are not quite so obvious, since lands entered in the tax registers would presumably have kept the same status whether their owners were poor or powerful. The unstated assumption, it seems, is that whereas the poor paid their taxes, the powerful had ways of evading them. Grants of immunity (*exkousseia*), which are known to have existed before the tenth century and which grew increasingly frequent in the eleventh and twelfth, were probably among the loopholes available to influential persons. Immunity from some or all taxes, applicable to land as well as to resident tenant farmers, was often awarded to monasteries and charitable establishments, but also to individuals in return for services rendered to the State and, possibly, on the strength of personal connections. Besides, Treasury inspectors were open to bribery and even provincial judges, 'out of necessity rather than inclination', could be prevailed upon to display the typically Byzantine expedient of *oikonomia*, or compromise.[63]

The consolidation of a landed aristocracy which acquired titles in the imperial hierarchy and a natural claim to great military commands, the gradual withdrawal of their vast estates from direct control by the government, the ineluctable regression of petty landholders – such appear to be the characteristics of Byzantine society in the tenth century. We are still a long way from anything that may legitimately be called feudalism, even if we interpret feudalism not in its precise institutional meaning which is only applicable to western Europe and, in particular, to the states descended from the Carolingian Empire, but in a broader sense involving a structure of personal dependence, rights over property corresponding to such dependence, and a fragmentation of political authority. Yet a trend towards 'feudalization' is unmistakably apparent in Byzantine society. We have witnessed its beginnings; its further development lies in the period of the Comneni and extends over that of the Palaeologi.

Two institutions in particular have attracted attention in this context. The first is the *pronoia* which roughly corresponds to the western benefice or tenement. First attested in the reign of Alexius I, this was the grant of an estate and resident serfs (*paroikoi*) to a knight on condition of military service. The *pronoia* was not heritable and its beneficiary was called simply a soldier (*stratiôtês*), just as in the west a vassal was sometimes designated as a *miles*. Speaking of the reign of Manuel I, and using, unfortunately, very florid language, the historian Nicetas Choniates reports that that emperor withheld the pay of soldiers and rewarded them instead 'with the so-called grants of *paroikoi*, abusing a system that had been instituted by previous emperors'. As a result, there was a great influx of applicants to the army, one man contributing a horse, another a sum of gold, and receiving in return 'imperial diplomas awarding to them acres of shady land, corn-bearing fields and Roman tributaries, the latter to serve them in the guise of slaves, so that occasionally a Roman of venerable aspect and well versed in the art of war would be paying taxes to some half-barbarian *parvenu* who did not even know the nature of a military formation'.[64] Evidently, such grants were made on a wide scale, and their consequence in the eyes of Choniates was that Byzantine lands were pillaged and appropriated by foreigners – indeed, some of the knights in question were Latins and Cumans.

The second noticeable development concerns the growth of private retinues. It may be argued that this was nothing new in Byzantium, that already in the Later Roman Empire there were private bands of soldiers called *buccellarii*, and that in the Middle Byzantine period there are scattered references to noblemen being surrounded by a circle of retainers; yet it is surely no accident that from the eleventh century onwards we hear more and more about such suites consisting not only of slaves and relatives, but also of armed guards, often in considerable numbers. It also appears that there were ties of dependence between greater and lesser nobility. Cecaumenus, in addressing advice to his son, envisages the possibility of his serving a lord (*archôn*), this being clearly distinguished from imperial service: 'If you are serving a lord, serve him not as a lord and as a man, but as an emperor and a god. Even if he is ignorant and incapable, while you have an abundance of knowledge, wisdom and skill, do not scorn him lest he ruin you.' Cecaumenus also counsels extreme reserve with regard to one's 'lady' – 'if she is playful with you, withdraw and keep your distance' – and kindness towards one's 'men', meaning retainers.[65] At about the same time the minor nobleman Eustathios Boilas speaks of serving for a period of fifteen years the Armenian Michael Apokapes (Aboukab), Duke of Edessa, from whom he received many benefits; and even if this service was in the context of the imperial government, it should be noticed that Boilas regarded Michael's two sons as his 'lords'.[66]

Our difficulty in describing the growth of Byzantine 'feudalism' stems from the fact that it never became formalized in law and did not acquire a technical vocabulary. The Byzantines were, of course, aware of the institutions of western feudalism, and in dealing with Frankish knights and princes the emperor would often extract from them an oath of fealty. The term *lizios* (liegeman) thus found its way into the Greek language, but it remained reserved to foreigners. Its Byzantine equivalent, we are told, was 'servant and subject' (*oiketês kai hypocheirios*),[67] and it may well be that these and similar Greek words, which occur very frequently in our sources, do sometimes refer to vassalage, but the context is seldom sufficiently clear to establish the distinction. While we may grant, therefore, that a coherent structure of feudal relations never developed in Byzantium, we must also admit that there did grow up a largely unformulated system that resembled feudalism in many respects. A dispersal of central authority was both its cause and its effect.

Side by side with the establishment of quasi-feudal relations, a contrary trend was occurring in the Byzantine world. As we shall explain more fully in the next chapter, urban life, which had been practically extinguished by the calamities of the seventh and eighth centuries, began picking up again. Among the possible causes of this phenomenon, one may point to increasing security and the opening of new trade routes. The Muslim threat was receding. In Asia Minor Byzantine armies were taking the offensive, an offensive that was eventually to carry them beyond the Taurus mountains into Cilicia and Syria. In the Black Sea region the newly arrived Russians, soon to be converted to Orthodox Christianity, created possibilities for long-distance trade channelled directly through Constantinople. Bulgaria adopted more peaceful ways after the death of the terrible Tsar Symeon (927) and was totally subdued by 1018. Navigation in the Aegean, still very dangerous in the first half of the tenth century, was made safe after the reduction of the Arab base on Crete (961). Little by little conditions were improving for the rebirth of an urban economy.

It cannot be said that the imperial government showed undue haste in taking advantage of the new opportunities. We possess two important documents from about the year 900 relating to economic activity, and both of them show a spirit of distrust and conservatism. The first is the text of two treaties concluded between the Byzantines and the Viking Russians.[68] We learn from them that a Russian commercial colony was established at Constantinople or, to be more exact, some distance up the Bosphorus in the suburb of St Mamas (modern Beşiktaş). The concern of the imperial authorities was mainly to keep the Russians under close surveillance rather than to derive maximum profit from the contact. The names of the Russian merchants were recorded, and they were allowed to enter the city through one gate only, in groups of fifty, escorted by a government agent. On the other hand, they received free allowances of food and wine for a period of up to six months, and were permitted to conduct their business without payment of duty. The treaties do make provision for Byzantine ships coming to grief somewhere in the neighbourhood of the Russians, in other words along the Black Sea coast, but we do not hear of any activity of Byzantine merchants at Kiev or farther north. In short, the Byzantines were content to sit at home and wait for foreign traders to come to them.

The other document we have to consider is the *Book of the Prefect* which dates from the reign of Leo VI (886–912).[69] The text we possess, which may be incomplete as it stands, regulates the activities of twenty-two professional corporations that were controlled by the prefect of Constantinople. The lawgiver's main intentions were to keep each profession within the strict bounds of its competence, concentrated in one locality where it could be easily supervised; to prohibit undue profits; and to prevent the export of certain luxury goods. Depressing as the perusal of the *Book of the Prefect* must be to anyone who believes in free enterprise, it does provide an interesting picture of the commercial life of the capital. Imported goods included raw materials such as wax for candles, but also finished products, such as unguents that came by way of Trebizond, linen cloth from the region of the Strymon and from Pontus, and Syrian silks that were brought by Syrian merchants. The latter were confined to their *mitata* (something like the Italian *fondaco* or the Turkish *han*) and could not remain longer than three months in the capital. Particular attention was devoted to the textile trade which comprised six different occupations, namely the *vestiopratai* who dealt in precious stuffs, the *prandiopratai* who specialized in Syrian imports, the *metaxopratai* who traded in raw silk, the *katartarioi* who worked the silk, the *sêrikarioi* who sewed the stuff they bought from the *metaxopratai*, and finally the *othoniopratai* or traders in linen. Each occupation was strictly confined to its own line of business; all purchases worth more than ten *solidi* had to be declared to the Prefect; and particular attention was paid so that 'prohibited goods', i.e. mainly purple cloth, should not leave the capital and find its way to the barbarian nations. It is interesting to note that the *metaxopratai* were forbidden to buy their goods outside the city, just as they were not allowed to sell them to Jewish merchants for resale abroad. Similar restrictions applied to other professions: butchers (who were limited to sheep and goats) and pork butchers had to buy live animals at designated locations in the city, slaughter and sell them on the spot. They could not go outside the city and buy the livestock directly from the herdsmen. During Lent all traffic in meat was forbidden. Fishmongers could not leave the city to buy fish from fishermen, but had to meet the latter at the city wharfs. Anyone who contravened these and a multitude of other regulations was liable to expulsion from his guild, to flogging, tonsure and banishment.

The system was clearly designed to discourage initiative and enrichment and was justified by reference to the orderly nature of the universe as established by God. It must also have resulted in a negative balance of trade. We may imagine, however, as with all other Byzantine legislation, that the provisions of the *Book of the Prefect* were flouted more than they were observed. We also find that members of the aristocracy, who were forbidden to engage in business, began investing some of their assets in buying shops from which they could expect a yield of about 5 per cent in rent. A curious document of the same period records a number of such purchases: a linen shop at the Forum, occupying the space between two columns of the portico, cost 720 *solidi* and produced a rent of 38, part of a shop selling Syrian stuffs went for 432 *solidi* and rented for 15, and so on.[70]

The opening of Byzantine society to the opportunities of trade and the parallel growth of a professional class are especially noticeable in the eleventh century. At the death of the Emperor Basil II (1025) the Empire had expanded once again to its 'ideal' boundaries, namely the Danube on one side and the Euphrates on the other; and while it was still to make some small gains (the Armenian kingdom of Ani, Edessa, the east coast of Sicily), further aggrandizement was seen to be neither necessary nor practicable. For a time no major threat appeared along the frontiers and so, at long last, society could convert from a footing of permanent military preparedness to one of peace. On the institutional level the change was reflected in the gradual dismantling of the 'themes' and, with them, of the 'thematic' armies, in the growing importance of civil magistrates in the provinces and in the centralization of army command in the hands of two Domestics of the Schools, one for the east, the other for the west, in other words more or less, in a return to the system of the Early Byzantine period. Landholding tied to military service was phased out and the obligation to serve in the army was commuted to a tax which, again as in the Early period, was used to enlist foreign mercenaries, who were now Scandinavians, Russians, Franks, Arabs, Cumans, and others. On the monetary side one notices a very slight adulteration of the gold in the reign of Constantine IX (1042–55) and an increased circulation of silver and copper, a clear sign of greater economic activity and the growth of an urban economy. On the demographic side one can probably postulate a shift of population from the country to the towns, which was not without its dangers. Finally, and perhaps most significantly, the class of traders and artisans broke out of the straitjacket of earlier restrictive regulation and assumed a role of political significance. New men, who hailed not from the entrenched families of central and eastern Asia Minor, but from the capital and the towns of the Aegean seacoast, rose to the top. Of this trend we have many indications. When, for example, the Emperor Michael V tried to rid himself of the ageing Empress Zoe (1042), he showered honours on 'the rabble of the marketplace and the practitioners of manual crafts', but in vain: the professional people were so loyal to the legitimate dynasty that they laid siege to the imperial palace and Michael was forced off the throne after 3,000 people had been killed in the fray.[71] The next emperor, Constantine IX, 'admitted to the senate practically the entire throng of the marketplace', as Psellus notes with chagrin, although he himself belonged to the class of the 'new men'.[72] Isaac Comnenus (1057) and Nicephorus Botaniates (1078) acceded to power with the help of tradesmen and professional corporations, while

Constantine x (1059–67) went so far as to abolish all distinctions between senators and ordinary citizens, and raised 'artisans' to high honours.[73] It is not for nothing that Cecaumenus delivered this piece of advice: 'Pay the closest attention to events in the capital that nothing may escape you. Have spies in all the guilds and everywhere else so you may learn anything that is being plotted.'[74]

It is one of the major tragedies of Byzantine history that the economic and social upsurge of the eleventh century was cut short before it had achieved any durable results, except perhaps in the realm of literature and the arts. The immediate cause was certainly military and political: the invasion of the Balkans by the Pechenegs, the sudden loss of most of Asia Minor to the Seljuk Turks, the war with the Normans, the negative effect of the Crusades. Would these reverses have been avoided if the Empire had retained its former, 'healthy' structure based on the 'themes' and a native army? It is easy to blame the 'civil' emperors of the eleventh century for their lack of forethought, and most historians have done so; it is more difficult to discern the deeper causes of the collapse of the 1070s. Demilitarization may have been one of them; another was surely the previously won expansion of the Empire – not to its 'national boundaries' as some scholars have put it, but well beyond any reasonable boundaries, over countries and peoples that had neither kinship nor sympathy with the government at Constantinople.

The 'saviour' who was called upon to pick up the pieces of the crumbling State, Alexius I Comnenus, faced an extremely hard task and probably did his best within his lights. Unfortunately, his vision was narrow and reactionary. Himself a member of a minor landholding family of Asia Minor, he had no sympathy with the new commercial class, and his greatest blunder was to concede to Venice (in 1082 or 1092) trading facilities at Constantinople and thirty-two other towns, from the Adriatic to the Syrian coast, with complete immunity from the payment of any duties. By this act the economic future of the Empire was sabotaged once and for all. The presence of Venetian and other Italian traders meant, of course, that Byzantine towns retained an appearance of animation, except that the major profits were siphoned off to the West. And so the centre of gravity of the Comnenian State shifted back to the land, of which there was now much less and which was to a considerable extent in the hands of big landowners. The political crisis was accompanied by a monetary collapse: the value of the Byzantine currency sank in the 1070s by more than half and never recovered again. The continued need to pay foreign mercenaries when the State coffers were empty forced Alexius I to confiscate the treasures of the churches, a temporary expedient that aroused much censure. A longer-term solution was found in the *pronoia* system of which we have spoken, but at the price of further diminishing the yield of taxes.

The partition of the Empire was becoming a distinct possibility. It was suggested to Alexius before he had become emperor by his brother-in-law Nicephorus Melissenus; it was contemplated by John II with regard to his south-eastern provinces; and it actually came to pass in the 1180s and later, when Cyprus, parts of western Asia Minor and, finally, Trebizond seceded. It is perhaps a wonder that the Comnenian State managed to survive for a century and even nourish dreams of glory, and it did so by becoming largely a family concern. Alexius I and his successors purged the old aristocracy and surrounded themselves with their relatives by birth and marriage whose pompous and newly invented titles reflected the degree of their kinship with the reigning emperor, and all of whom received ample grants of land and exemption from taxes. The Comnenian reform marks the last significant transformation of Byzantine society: what the Comnenes had done the Palaeologi continued on a smaller scale.

CHAPTER 3

THE DISAPPEARANCE AND REVIVAL OF CITIES

In the sixth century the Empire saw itself as an aggregate of cities. The handbook of Hierocles enumerates – or rather enumerated when it was complete – 935 cities. Since, however, it does not include either Italy or the reconquered provinces of North Africa, the total for Justinian's reign would have been in excess of 1,500. We must remember that in antiquity the term 'city' (*polis* or *civitas*) was not, strictly speaking, the equivalent of a town: it designated a self-administering unit, and there was all the difference in the world between a 'city' like Alexandria or Ephesus, on the one hand, and some obscure hole like Zeldepa in Scythia, on the other. Normally, however, a 'city' meant a real town provided with a rural territory and we shall so take it in the following discussion.

The cities of the sixth century were, for the most part, of ancient origin. In the East a few had been founded in the Roman period, a greater number by the Hellenistic kings, while many others had had a continuous history stretching back to remotest antiquity. While it is true to say that the area in which the urban model prevailed increased in the Early Byzantine period, the number of cities founded by Christian emperors was relatively small and none of them developed into a centre of major importance. We must not imagine that the year 324 (or whatever other date we may choose for the beginning of the Byzantine period) marked any dramatic change for the inhabitants of the cities or, for that matter, of the countryside. Life went on pretty much as before. Some gradual transformations were taking place, but they were not sufficiently sudden for anyone to think that a new era was dawning.

The physical aspect of the cities of the Early Byzantine period may readily be visualized thanks to their remains that are still dotted round the Mediterranean. Normally, they were walled: some had been fortified at a very early date, others at the time of the barbarian threat in the third century AD, others in the fourth. Inside the walls the layout of the streets was as regular as the terrain permitted. Often there were two main avenues, the Roman *cardo* and *decumanus*, meeting at right angles and terminating at the city gates. These avenues were quite wide (hence the Greek term *plateia* that was applied to them) and were bordered with covered colonnades that sheltered shops. At the junction of the main thoroughfares or elsewhere was a forum round which were grouped various public buildings: a religious centre, baths, a council chamber, a basilica used for judicial and other purposes, etc. There was normally a theatre dating from an earlier period, less often an amphitheatre (a Roman invention that did not spread very widely in the eastern provinces) and, in larger cities, a hippodrome. More basic needs were served by granaries, aqueducts and cisterns. Public buildings and places were decorated, as lavishly as circumstances permitted, with statues, paintings and fountains. Indeed, cities took great pride in their monuments: Caesarea in Palestine had a famous *tetrapylon*, as did also Bostra in Arabia; Alexandria boasted its Pharos, its Serapeum and its Caesareum; Nicaea in Bithynia was noted for the regularity of its buildings.[1]

The transition from paganism to Christianity was everywhere slow. Many pagan temples were closed at the end of the fourth and in the early fifth centuries, but elsewhere they continued to function. Their transformation into churches, whenever it occurred, was by no means immediate, the more so as the Christians regarded them as being haunted by maleficent demons. In Athens, for example (admittedly, a city of strong pagan proclivities), the temples appear to have been deconsecrated towards the end of the fifth century, and it was only in the seventh that the Parthenon, the Erechtheion and the Hephaisteion became churches. The main Christian church was usually built on a site unsullied by the old religions, often at some distance from the city centre, and was surrounded by a complex of residential and administrative buildings used by the bishop. As Christianity struck deeper roots, more and more churches were constructed to honour various martyrs or simply as a pious gesture. To take once again the case of Athens, fourteen churches of the fifth and sixth centuries are documented, and there were doubtless many more. By Justinian's time there was everywhere a glut of churches whose upkeep, as we have seen, was becoming a serious burden. Urban monasteries were exceptional, but were beginning to creep in from the surrounding countryside.

Other trends in late antique urbanism, such as the abandonment of gymnasia, were unconnected with the advent of Christianity. Outside the walls lay extensive cemeteries (since it was strictly forbidden to bury the dead *intra muros*), orchards and villas, and, sometimes, a Jewish suburb with its synagogue.

By our standards, Early Byzantine cities were quite small. Antioch, which, after Constantinople and Alexandria, was the third biggest city of the Eastern Empire, had in the sixth century an area of about 650 hectares within the walls. Laodicea in Syria, with 220 hectares, was large compared to other provincial cities. Perhaps a more typical example is provided by Nicaea whose third-century walls are still standing: the enclosed area has a maximum extent of 1,450 metres from north to south and east to west. Dara in Mesopotamia, founded by the Emperor Anastasius in 505–7 and regarded as one of the most important strongholds on the eastern frontier, measured about 1,000 by 750 metres. There is, unfortunately, no formula for converting area measurements into population figures: the amount of space covered by public buildings, streets, squares and orchards, the type of dwelling (single-storey or multi-storey), the extent of suburbs, are among the many imponderables. Nor do ancient sources yield any reliable figures. Quite exceptionally, we are given a detailed enumeration of dead bodies picked up in Jerusalem after the capture of the city by the Persians in 614: the total is 66,509.[2] We do not know, however, what relation this figure bore to the total population of Jerusalem, not to mention the fact that in times of crisis people from the surrounding countryside tended to seek the protection of a walled city. In any case, we shall not be too far from the truth in supposing that a large provincial city like Laodicea may have had a population of about 50,000, while an average provincial city may have been in the 5,000–20,000 range. Antioch, it has been surmised, had about 200,000 inhabitants and Constantinople in the fifth century probably more than 300,000.

To the ancient mind there was a fundamental distinction between urban and rural life. Procopius, writing in his most traditional manner, puts it like this with reference to the city of Caputvada founded in Africa by Justinian: 'A wall has been fashioned and a city, too, and the condition of farmland has been suddenly changed. The rustics have discarded the plough and are living in an urban fashion. Here they spend the day in the market place, they assemble to discuss the matters that are necessary to them, they traffic with one another and do all the other things that are commensurate with the dignity of a city.'[3] We may wonder how many of the new citizens of Caputvada spent their time in the assembly chamber deliberating on questions of public concern. Of one thing, however, there can be no doubt: the city and the city alone provided certain amenities that were considered an essential part of civilized life. Men, women and children (including the clergy) went regularly to public baths and spent a good deal of time on the ritual of bathing. This was normally done during working hours, for we are told that the baths were emptiest at noon and in the evening.[4] The theatre and the hippodrome were immensely popular and also occupied a good part of the day: theatrical performances started at noon and lasted until evening. For the more cultivated there were the displays put on by rhetoricians: we could call them public lectures, except that the emphasis was on literary skill rather than on information imparted. Finally, there was the pleasure of meeting friends, of chatting in the shade of colonnades or sitting in taverns. City life was very public.

The theatre, the wild beast fights and the hippodrome were the main targets of ecclesiastical invective. 'The theatre is filled,' cries John Chrysostom, 'and the entire people is seated in the upper rows. Often the roof itself is covered with men so you can see neither tiles nor stone slabs – nothing but human heads and bodies.'[5] We know very little about the content of the performances for, if any new plays were written at the time, none has survived. We are, however, told that some were of the traditional type: they were played in masks and introduced imaginary characters, such as kings, generals, physicians and sophists. In order to make his moral point, John Chrysostom emphasizes the fact that the actors were vulgar folk – rope-twisters, perchance, or vegetable vendors or even slaves.[6] Then there was the pantomime which involved dancing and music and occasionally, it seems, a certain amount of nudity: 'When you seat yourself in a theatre and feast your eyes on the naked limbs of women, you are pleased for a time, but then, what a violent fever have you generated! Once your head is filled with such sights and the songs that go with them, you think about them even in your dreams.'[7] If only, sighs our preacher, it were possible to abolish the theatre! It was the source of civil disorder, of adultery, sorcery, contempt for women; but since the theatre could not be abolished, it was, at least, possible to avoid it.[8] Manifestly, it was the devil who had built theatres in cities. People even abandoned their trades and shops to go to the theatre, and when the actors said something indecent, the senseless audience laughed instead of stoning them. 'You would not choose to see a naked woman in the marketplace, nor indeed in your own house, yet you eagerly attend the theatre. What difference does it make if the stripper is a whore? She has the same body as a free woman. Why are such things permitted when we are gathered together and shameful when we are by ourselves? Indeed, it would be better to smear our faces with mud than to behold such spectacles.'[9]

Historians have blindly followed the Church Fathers in denouncing the shameful licentiousness of the Late Antique theatre. No matter how indecent the performances were (and, perhaps, by modern standards they were fairly innocuous), the important point is that the Fathers saw in the theatre a dangerous competitor: it drew their clientele away from church and siphoned off money that might have found its way into ecclesiastical coffers. The charge of indecency was, in any case, not applicable to the hippodrome which attracted even bigger crowds and was regularly attended by the emperor. One could argue only that it led to disorders and occasioned magical practices. Besides, was it not a scandal that people should know the pedigree, the herd, the age, the names of their favourite horses, or which charioteer starting from which gate and driving which horse would win the race, when these same people were unable to name St Paul's Epistles?[10] It seems that a good part of the urban population paid little heed to such denunciations. The historian Menander Protector, in speaking of his mis-spent youth in the reign of Justin II (565–78), says that he laid aside his legal studies in favour of hippodrome races, pantomime dancing and wrestling.[11]

From the great capitals of Antioch and Constantinople, as portrayed by John Chrysostom, we may move to a provincial and barely hellenized town, namely Emesa in Syria (Homs). A glimpse of it in the middle of the sixth century is provided by the Life of St Symeon the Fool.[12] Since Symeon was a dropout, his dealings were mostly with the lower strata of society, but he did have some contacts among more respectable people: indeed, his closest friend and protector was a certain deacon John who was a man of substance. We also meet a rich man who flogged his slaves and who, on one occasion, was robbed of five hundred gold pieces by his cup-bearer, and a merchant who went on pilgrimage to Jerusalem. Manufacture is represented solely by a Jewish glass-blower round whose oven beggars would gather to keep warm. Taverns were numerous and somehow differentiated so that a publican (*kapêlos*) was not quite the same as a *phouskarios* who sold a mixture of cheap wine and water (Latin *posca*) along with lupins and chick peas by way of snacks. We also encounter a confectioner whose shop remained open even during holy week, and vendors of pastry whose platters were set up outside the main church. There were physicians in the city, but also sorceresses who made amulets. Supplies came from the surrounding countryside: we meet a muleteer who, every morning, went out of the town to buy wine directly from the farmers and who, in due course, opened a tavern of his own. People also went out of town to wash their clothes in the river Orontes which flowed about a mile to the west.

The lower strata of society included mimes and jugglers who performed in the theatre, and a great throng of prostitutes, dancing girls and beggars. The standard of morals appears to have been fairly lax: the son of the deacon John fornicated with a married woman, a rich man was unfaithful to his wife, and the saint could foretell that a group of little girls who sang songs in the street would grow up to become as licentious as any women in Syria. Standards of cleanliness were equally low: outside the city gate was a heap of refuse on which lay a dead dog, and the saint did not hesitate to ease his stomach in the middle of the marketplace. There were, however, public baths, one for men and another for women, as well as schools for boys. No establishment of higher education is mentioned.

While respectable women stayed at home, men led their lives in public. In one's neighbourhood everybody knew everybody else, but when a man moved to a different neighbourhood, he was no longer recognized. Young men would loiter in public places, dance, drink in taverns and consort with prostitutes. They also played some sort of game in an open field outside the city walls, a game that involved two opposing teams as well as 'gates', or goals. Since Emesa had no hippodrome, there is no mention of charioteers nor of the usual rivalry between the supporters of the Greens and those of the Blues. Sectarian strife also appears to have been dormant, although the population included Jacobites, orthodox Christians and Jews. We may remember that the greatest Byzantine hymnographer, Romanus the Melode, is said to have been a converted Jew of Emesa.

By and large, the kind of urban life we have been describing went on in the eastern provinces until the middle of the sixth century and, in a diminished way, until the middle of the seventh. Naturally, there were regional variations. In the Balkans urban conditions were seriously disrupted by Attila's Huns in 441–7 and again by Theodoric's Ostrogoths in 479. The biggest cities of the interior fell: Singidunum (Belgrade), Naissus (Niš), Sirmium (Sremska Mitrovica),

Marcianopolis, Serdica (Sofia). In 449 Naissus was uninhabited[13] and was still in ruins a hundred years later when Justinian re-fortified it.[14] Stobi and Heraclea Lyncestis succumbed to the Ostrogoths. To be sure, some of the damage was made good thereafter, but it was at best a partial restoration and it did not last long since everything was swept away by the Avar and Slav invasions. Elsewhere, however, no such dramatic change occurred in the fifth century. Some cities expanded while others dwindled. We know, for example, that Scythopolis in Palestine was declining, as was Pergamum in Asia Minor. So was Cyrrhus in northern Syria, where the municipal *curia* had melted away and there was not even a decent baker to be found.[15] The causes of such decline were doubtless complex. There is considerable evidence from Syria of a shift of artisanal activity to villages, so that peasants no longer needed to sell their produce and buy necessary supplies in towns. The flight of guildsmen to the countryside is well attested in imperial legislation. The growth of monasteries, which absorbed craftsmen as well as farmers, may also have contributed to this process. It is, however, premature to assert that all small cities were dwindling and all big ones becoming inflated between the fourth and the sixth centuries. We need more information before we can discern such general trends.

As we approach the year 500 certain disturbing signs begin to appear. The first was purely fortuitous: the period in question witnessed a remarkable succession of droughts, plagues of locusts, earthquakes and other calamities. Now it has to be understood that the provisioning of an ancient city was pretty finely balanced. A city normally fed on the agricultural produce of its territory. The denser the network of cities, the smaller their respective territories. Egypt was almost unique in the East in having a vast agricultural surplus which, however, was fully committed to provisioning Constantinople and the imperial armies. Furthermore, transport by road was enormously slow and expensive. A coastal town could solve a temporary shortfall in supplies, but when calamity struck an inland town and accumulated stocks became exhausted, the people had to go hungry. What this meant in practice is vividly illustrated in the case of Edessa (Urfa). After several earthquakes and the outbreak of an infectious disease, there occurred in the year 500 a plague of locusts which attacked crops in a vast area stretching from the Mediterranean, across northern Mesopotamia, to the borders of Armenia. Reduced to misery, peasants had to sell their fields and their livestock for a pittance and flocked to the cities in order to live by begging. The price of wheat rose from 30 to 4 bushels to the *solidus*, and that of barley from 50 to 6. All winter people were dying of hunger in the streets of Edessa, as many as 130 a day, so that all the available graves were soon filled up. Owing to the unsanitary conditions, a pestilence broke out and extended from Nisibis to Antioch. The harvest of 501 was poor, so that the inflated price of wheat remained almost stationary. It was only in 502 that it dropped to 12 bushels to the *solidus*, still more than double the normal rate. The catalogue of disasters recorded by the chronicler of Edessa includes the collapse by earthquake of Nicopolis (Emmaus), Ptolemais (Acre), half of Tyre and Sidon, and the capture by the Persians of Amida, where eighty thousand dead were carried out of the gates.[16] It would have taken many years, indeed several generations, to recover fully from such a combination of calamities. This respite was not granted to many eastern provinces.

Another symptom of disintegration was urban violence. It may be argued, of course, that riots were nothing new and that in the previous two centuries there had been no lack of food riots, religious riots and theatre riots. There was, however, from the reign of Anastasius onwards an escalation of violence which centred more and more on the hippodrome. The two main factions, the Blues and the Greens, regularly came to blows and then went on to commit arson. The list of these disturbances is very long and some of them resulted in enormous damage, like the great pogrom at Antioch in 507 and the famous Nika riot at Constantinople (532) which is said to have left thirty thousand corpses and reduced the centre of the city to ashes. When Antioch had been almost completely destroyed by an earthquake in 526 with an alleged death-toll of 250,000, the warring factions became reconciled, but only for a short time.[17] Especially chilling (if, doubtless, somewhat exaggerated) is the account given by Procopius of the hippodrome thugs who, he alleges, were given complete licence by the Emperor Justinian to rob and kill, rape women and extort money, with the result that respectable citizens no longer dared to go out after dark.[18] In the light of our own experience we have no trouble in visualizing those bands of youths with long beards and moustaches, with dangling hair, dressed in deliberately barbaric fashion, who engaged in gang warfare when they were not waylaying innocent people. We also have no difficulty in believing what all the Byzantine sources tell us, namely that this was mindless hooliganism and nothing more. As has recently been demonstrated,[19] the Blues and the Greens had no political objectives, no explicit class grievances or

67

religious identification. But while hooliganism has no philosophy, no one will deny that it is a symptom – be it of urban decay or a loss of values or an overly dull and regimented society.

While Byzantine cities were suffering from the combined effects of food shortages, natural calamities and factional violence, a completely unexpected blow fell on them. The bubonic plague of 541–2, the first of its kind attested in history, was by all accounts a disaster of unprecedented magnitude. Originating in Ethiopia, it spread from Egypt along the lines of maritime communication to all parts of the Mediterranean world as far as Spain in the west and Persia in the east. At Constantinople the plague broke out in the spring of 542 and raged for four months. According to Procopius, who was an eyewitness, the number of casualties rose to five thousand and then to over ten thousand each day.[20] As existing tombs became filled and there was no time to dig new ones, corpses were piled on the seashore or else flung into the towers of Sycae (Galata), whence an evil stench wafted over the city. Furthermore, the initial outbreak was followed by several others: epidemics of the plague or of other unspecified diseases are recorded in 555, 558, 561, 573–74, 591, 599 and in the early seventh century. Antioch was visited four times by the bubonic plague, roughly at fifteen-year intervals. The historian Evagrius himself caught it as a child; he later lost his wife, several children, a great number of slaves and tenant farmers and, during the fourth visitation, his daughter and grandchild.[21]

It is impossible to calculate the number of victims. When Procopius tells us that 'nearly the whole human race was annihilated',[22] or that half of those who had survived previous natural calamities were carried off by the plague,[23] he is doubtless engaging in rhetorical exaggeration. Even so, it is possible that one third to half the population of Constantinople perished in 542, and we are told that some cities became practically deserted, while others were less affected. The attested fact that young adults were particularly susceptible to the disease, coupled with the fifteen-year cycles of recrudescence, must have produced extremely damaging demographic consequences. No less serious were the economic effects: all normal occupations were interrupted, prices of goods trebled and quadrupled, starvation set in, fields were deserted and the remaining farmers were burdened with additional taxes on the non-productive land of their deceased neighbours.[24]

There can be little doubt that the plagues of the sixth century combined with an unprecedented sequence of natural disasters were a factor, perhaps the determining factor, in the collapse of urban life. For it is a fact (though some historians still refuse to recognize it) that all round the Mediterranean the cities, as they had existed in Antiquity, contracted and then practically disappeared. This happened at different times in different provinces, and the immediate cause was usually foreign invasion. The ease with which walled cities fell to an enemy who was often neither very numerous nor skilled in siege warfare, and the absence of any urban resurgence after the enemy had withdrawn show, however, that military hostilities were merely the last shock that brought down a tottering edifice. As our historical sources dwindle after the reign of Justinian and are reduced to the merest trickle after 602, it is difficult to document this process on the basis of the written word. We are reduced to laconic reports of various calamities and vague echoes of a general breakdown of law and order. After the death of the emperor Maurice (602), civil strife sprang up 'in the whole East, in Cilicia, Asia, Palestine and even Constantinople'. People killed one another in the marketplace, broke into houses, threw women, children and old men out of windows, robbed and burnt. The wave of unrest spread to the Balkan provinces and it was only thanks to the miraculous intervention of St Demetrius that Thessalonica was spared.[25] It is amidst such scenes of disorder that the curtain falls.

The evidence for the collapse of the cities is largely archaeological. It should be stressed here that although many excavations have been conducted in different parts of the Empire, relatively few have been carried out in a sufficiently methodical manner. The superimposition of modern towns on ancient sites has also hampered investigation in some centres that would be of the greatest importance to us, notably Constantinople and Thessalonica. The available information is thus still rather patchy, but it is sufficient to draw certain conclusions from it. Here are a few examples taken from different provinces.

In the Balkans, as we have already said, urban life was seriously disrupted in the middle of the fifth century. The reconstruction that took place in the first half of the sixth was not very extensive and was not destined to survive for more than a few decades. Sirmium, once an imperial capital, never recovered after the Hunnic sack and became completely deserted after its surrender to the Avars in 582. If we move south to Stobi, a provincial capital, we find considerable evidence of building in the first half of the fifth century and again after the Ostrogothic sack of 479, but no building activity whatever after the

69

sixth century and no coins later than the seventh. At Heraclea Lyncestis, only partially excavated, the picture is about the same: the episcopal church was rebuilt in the early sixth century and the latest
published coin is of Justin II. The small town of Bargala in Macedonia II
(near modern Štip) was apparently relocated to a more defensible
position in the fifth century and ceased to exist shortly after 585. If we
move east to modern Bulgaria, we find that Serdica started as a small
fortified town in the reign of Marcus Aurelius, was greatly expanded in
the early fourth century, perhaps under Constantine, and shrank to its
old nucleus (area fifteen hectares) in the sixth century, after which time
we hear no more of it. Nicopolis-ad-Istrum, founded by Trajan, was
apparently abandoned in the sixth century: some of its inhabitants may
have moved south to a hilltop at Veliko Turnovo. At Philippopolis
(Plovdiv) the urban area was cut in half in the sixth century and the city
thereafter destroyed. We hear of it again in the early twelfth century
when a population of Armenians and Bogomil heretics was dwelling
there in the midst of ancient ruins.[26]

The same panorama of abandonment is visible in Greece. At Athens
the Agora excavations have established that there was widespread
devastation in the 580s, followed by a period of makeshift existence
lasting into the second half of the seventh century. Thereafter the area
of the Agora was completely abandoned and the settlement retreated to
the Acropolis and a small fortified enclosure immediately to the north of
it. At Corinth many of the inhabitants fled in about 580 to the island of
Aegina, while Byzantine presence was maintained in the inaccessible
fortress of Acrocorinth. In the rest of the Peloponnese all cities were
wiped out. For continental Greece our evidence is very sparse. In
Boeotian Thebes there is no sign of any urban life between the sixth
century and the second half of the ninth. Phthiotid Thebes (Nea
Anchialos) on the coast of Thessaly was destroyed in the late sixth or
seventh century and probably occupied by Slav squatters: it never
revived. We may add that, with the exception of Thessalonica and the
island of Paros, not a single Early Christian church remained standing
in all of Greece, and that there is no evidence of any building activity
between about 600 and the early years of the ninth century.

Thessalonica, the seat of the prefect of Illyricum, remained in Byzantine hands throughout the dark centuries. Its walls, which may have
been built in about 450, enclosed a considerable area: roughly 1,750
metres from east to west and 2,100 metres from north to south. A mass
of Roman refugees 'from the area of the Danube, from Pannonia, Dacia,

Dardania and the other provinces',[27] sought the protection of these walls and of the city's celestial patron, St Demetrius. Besieged five times by Slavs and Avars, repeatedly visited by plague and famine, Thessalonica managed to survive as a tiny Byzantine enclave surrounded by an alien and often hostile population. Overland communication with the capital was cut off: in 698 the Emperor Justinian II had to fight his way to Thessalonica.[28] We have, unfortunately, no archaeological information on the condition of the city at this time. To judge by the few available texts, the inhabitants were reduced to a semi-rural existence, since we are told that on one occasion the advancing Avars and Slavs surprised many of them while they were tilling their fields outside the walls.[29] In the early ninth century the clergyman who was entrusted with charitable distributions to the poor received for this purpose the gift of three pigs – hardly the sign of a developed urban economy.[30] East of Thessalonica the city of Philippi appears to have been abandoned: there is, at any rate, no evidence of any activity there until the second half of the tenth century.

Of particular importance for our enquiry is the fate of the cities of Asia Minor. Incredulity has been expressed at the statement by the Arab geographer Ibn-Khordâdhbeh (c. 840) that in his time there were only five cities in Asia Minor, to wit Ephesus, Nicaea, Amorium, Ancyra and Samala (?), in addition to a considerable number of fortresses,[31] yet we can now see that he was probably not far from the truth. Let us take a few examples. In Bithynia, the Asiatic province closest to Constantinople, only Nicaea appears to have survived. Nicomedia, once a great imperial capital, lay in ruins in the ninth century. Cyzicus, the capital of the province of Hellespontus and a major city in the imperial Roman period, was half destroyed by earthquake in 543 and ceased to exist some time in the seventh century. Its imposing ruins were used as a quarry throughout the Middle Ages, while a small settlement sprang up at Artakê (Erdek) on the west side of the Cyzicene peninsula.

For western Asia Minor the archaeological evidence is fairly abundant. Ephesus, duly mentioned by Ibn-Khordâdhbeh, did survive, though greatly reduced in size. The ancient urban centre was abandoned, perhaps at the time of the Persian invasion in the early seventh century, and a new city wall was constructed enclosing an area of about nine hundred metres square between the harbour and the peak of Panayirdağ. Some distance to the east there arose a separate fortress centred on the basilica of St John the Divine (Ayasoluk). We are told

71

that in the late eighth century the fair of Ephesus produced a tax revenue of a hundred pounds of gold,[32] which, if true, indicates a considerable commercial turnover; yet the excavators have found little evidence of any building activity, save for a small church replacing the earlier and much larger basilica of St Mary. At Sardis, the capital of Lydia, the change was even more dramatic. Probably because of the Persian invasion the lower town was practically abandoned and only the hilltop fortress continued to function into the Middle Ages. At Miletus the medieval town was less than a quarter of the ancient one. At Pergamum disaster struck in the seventh century and, as at Sardis, only the acropolis remained as a fortified place. Of the fate of Smyrna nothing definite is known, but at Magnesia in the Maeander Valley the medieval town covered only a tiny fraction of the ancient one, an area of about 300 by 250 metres. Other sites that have been investigated, like Nysa and Laodicea, tell essentially the same story, while Colossae was abandoned and moved to the fortress of Chonae, famous for its shrine of St Michael.

Of the interior of Asia Minor much less is known. Amorium in Phrygia was considered in the eighth and ninth centuries as a centre of major importance, and there was widespread consternation when it was captured by the Arabs in 838 with an alleged loss of thirty thousand dead and many thousands of captives. Unfortunately, Amorium has never been investigated, but its ruins are still visible and show that it was quite a small place. At Ancyra the lower town seems to have been abandoned after it had been sacked by the Persians in about 622 and only the hilltop fortress survived. The latter was heavily fortified and consisted of a double enclosure, the inner one measuring barely 350 by 150 metres and the outer one some 500 by 300 metres. That this was considered to be the 'city' of Ancyra is suggested by the inscription set up by the emperor Michael III in about 859 over the fortress gate: 'Those who enter this gate and the city....'[33]

One more fact ought to be mentioned in this context, since it offered to some historians the initial clue to the dramatic decline of Byzantine cities, namely the sharp drop in the number of bronze coins in circulation. In sites that have been systematically excavated, such as Athens, Corinth, Sardis and others, it has been ascertained that bronze coinage, the small change used for everyday transactions, was plentiful throughout the sixth century and (depending on local circumstances) until some time in the seventh, after which it almost disappeared, then showed a slight increase in the ninth, and did not become abundant again until the latter part of the tenth. At Sardis, for example, the century and a quarter from 491 to 616 AD is represented by 1,011 bronze coins, the rest of the seventh century by about 90, and the eighth and ninth centuries combined by no more than 9.[34] *Mutatis mutandis*, similar results have been obtained from nearly all provincial Byzantine cities. It seems that only at Constantinople the decline in the volume of bronze coinage was not quite so catastrophic. It is also known that in such areas as remained under Byzantine control provincial mints ceased to function: Nicomedia after 627, Cyzicus and Thessalonica after 629. At Cherson no coins appear to have been struck between the early seventh century and the second half of the ninth.

Now it is true that the imperial government never ceased issuing coinage, in gold, silver and bronze, and we happen to know that during the dark centuries the army continued to be paid in gold, each soldier receiving twelve to eighteen *solidi* per year. The significant fact, however, is that the army was usually paid only once every three years, and occasionally every four, five or six.[35] It is difficult to see, therefore, how soldiers could meet their everyday expenses in monetary terms. More generally, the existence of an urban economy is inconceivable without an adequate supply of small change and, in view of the above considerations, one can only conclude that monetary transactions were reduced to a minimum and probably replaced by some form of barter.

If the Early Byzantine Empire was an aggregate of cities, the Middle Byzantine Empire may be described as an aggregate of *kastra* (fortresses). Even in everyday speech the term *polis* became confined more and more to Constantinople, while a place like Ancyra or Ephesus would be designated as a *kastron*. It so happens that most ancient cities in Asia Minor and Greece were built round a citadel situated on a hill. In such cases, as we have seen time and time again, the settlement could contract to the *kastron* which became the seat of whatever administrative and ecclesiastical authority may have been present. The *kastron* served as a place of temporary refuge at times of enemy invasion, but it was too cramped and often too inaccessible to provide a setting for urban life. Cities situated on flat ground were often abandoned, one of the few exceptions being Nicaea which was sufficiently far removed from the enemy. Elsewhere, as at Thessalonica, there was no physical possibility of retreating to the citadel without, at the same time, losing contact with the harbour, so that the old line of walls had to be maintained even if it was far too extensive for existing needs.

If urban life continued anywhere in the Empire, it did so at Constantinople. 'Oh, to be in the City!' was the cry of all cultivated Byzantines who for one reason or another found themselves in the provinces. Nicephorus Ouranos, governor of Antioch in about the year 1000, would gladly have exchanged life with Calypso for a whiff of the smoke of Constantinople.[36] 'Oh, land of Byzantium, Oh, thrice-happy City, eye of the universe, ornament of the world, star shining afar, beacon of this lower world, would that I were within you, enjoying you to the full! Do not part me from your maternal bosom.' So sighed in the twelfth century a Byzantine author forced to absent himself on a diplomatic mission.[37]

We must now turn our attention to the capital and trace briefly its development. Unfortunately, archaeological information is as yet rather scanty, but we do have a great mass of literary material on the basis of which a 'profile' of the city can be constructed.

The physiognomy of Constantinople was determined by the act of its foundation. In this respect it resembled other capitals that have been created by the exercise of arbitrary authority, like St Petersburg, Ankara or Brasilia; but it was not built entirely *de novo*. When, after considering other possible sites, Constantine chose to fix his residence at Byzantium (324), he had before him a sizeable town occupying the Seraglio point roughly as far as the present-day Galata bridge. Byzantium had existed a thousand years before Constantine, but its Greek past was soon forgotten, except for vague myths of the eponymous hero Byzas and his wife Phidaleia, of Io transformed into a cow and swimming across the Bosphorus to escape the gadfly that pursued her. The aspect of the town in 324 appears to have owed less to the ancient Megarians and more to the munificence of the Emperors Septimus Severus and Caracalla. Its civic centre was clustered round an agora that is represented today by the open space in front of St Sophia. Here the Romans built a hippodrome and the public baths of Zeuxippus, while a broad colonnaded street extended from the agora in a westerly direction to the city gates. The town also possessed two fortified harbours on the side of the Golden Horn, a theatre, an ampitheatre and several temples. Constantine's architects grafted the new city on to the old. The urban area was extended to about seven hundred hectares (roughly equivalent to the area of Antioch) and enclosed on the landward side by a wall. The old civic centre was retained, the hippodrome enlarged and, next to it, on a site sloping down to the Propontis, was built a vast imperial palace in which the Byzantine emperors were to reside for the next eight centuries. The old colonnaded street was extended farther west to become the main artery of the city (the Mesê) and punctuated at intervals with public places. The most important of the latter was a curved forum at whose centre was set up a column of porphyry surmounted by a statue of Constantine in the guise of the solar god Apollo Helios. Here, too, were a senate house, two arches and a monumental fountain. A quantity of antique statues, plundered from the cities of the eastern provinces, provided further adornment for the streets and squares. Contrary to common belief, Constantine laid little emphasis in his urban programme on his recently adopted Christian religion. Of the many churches that later tradition attributed to him, very few can claim to this honour: possibly the Church of Peace (St Eirene, still standing as rebuilt in the sixth and eighth centuries) and that of the local martyr Acacius, fairly certainly that of the Holy Apostles which was to serve as Constantine's mausoleum and that of his successors. In its public monuments Constantinople probably resembled other imperial capitals of the Tetrarchic period, such as Trier, Sirmium, Thessalonica or Nicomedia.

In the decades following its inauguration (330) Constantinople experienced a remarkable expansion. Attracted by free distributions of bread, by prospects of employment and the proximity of the imperial court, settlers poured in. By 359 the city was sufficiently developed to merit, like Rome, an urban prefect. The supply of drinking water had to be increased. In his new Cathedral of Holy Wisdom (completed in 360) the bishop of Constantinople was beginning to outstrip in influence and wealth the incumbents of the more ancient apostolic sees. Theodosius I and his successors undertook a further programme of urban construction: a great new harbour which must have considerably increased the commercial capacity of the city, new warehouses, the Theodosian and Arcadian fora and pompous monuments. The ladies of the reigning dynasty vied with one another in acquiring the most desirable real estate and building town mansions. In 413 the fortified circuit was again enlarged by the construction of the double land walls which made Constantinople a bastion of unparalleled strength. The potential urban space had grown to about 1,400 hectares and the population probably to 300,000 – 400,000. Constantinople was now bigger than declining Rome, bigger than either Alexandria or Antioch.

A statistical account of the city in the second quarter of the fifth century is provided by a brief document in Latin, known as the *Notitia urbis Constantinopolitanae*,[38] which tabulates the fourteen regions into

75

which, like Rome, it had been divided. Here are some of the totals: 5 imperial and 9 princely palaces; 8 public and 153 private baths; 4 fora; 5 granaries, 2 theatres in addition to the hippodrome; 322 streets; 4,388 *domus* (substantial houses); 52 porticoes; 20 public and 120 private bakeries; 14 churches. The administration and policing of the city were carried out, under the prefect's direction, by 13 *curatores* (one for each region), 65 night-watchmen, 560 firemen, and others. In all, the prefect's bureau must have numbered about a thousand employees. Although the *Notitia* was drawn up after the construction of the Theodosian land walls, it is concerned only with the Constantinian city, plus two suburbs, namely Sycae (Galata) and the Fourteenth Region farther up the Golden Horn (probably near modern Eyüp). The vast belt between the Constantinian enceinte, which was not dismantled, and the Theodosian was evidently not considered urban and remained sparsely populated throughout the Middle Ages. Here lay extensive cemeteries; here, too, some of the earlier monasteries were set up. Indeed, one may suspect that the construction of the Theodosian walls was dictated not so much by an increased population as by considerations of defence and the need to enclose vast reservoirs of water within the fortified area.

The rapid growth of the capital in the fourth and fifth centuries must have created acute problems of supply. As we have already noted, the agriculture of the ancient world was not normally geared to producing a sufficient surplus to satisfy so voracious a consumer as a new city of some three hundred thousand mouths. Neighbouring Thrace did grow a fair amount of corn and vegetables, but that was only a drop in the bucket. Besides, Thrace was chronically subject to barbarian attack, a danger which the government tried to obviate by the construction, some time in the fifth century, of the Long Walls which described a huge arc from near Selymbria (Silivri) on the Propontis to the Black Sea at a distance of about sixty-five kilometres from the capital. The west coast of Asia Minor had to feed its own, very populous cities. The only country capable of supplying Constantinople with bread was Egypt. Already under Constantine the Egyptian production was deflected from Rome to the new capital so as to form the basis of the *annona*, the free distribution of bread. The quantity in question was at first eighty thousand daily rations, which suggests a planned population of about double that number. By the time of Justinian the Egyptian contribution had grown to eight million *artabae* (a measure corresponding to three *modii* or bushels), enough to feed a population of half a million. This is not the place to discuss the many problems that are posed by these figures, but it is important to point out the complexity and potential precariousness of the system. The Egyptian crop depended, first of all, on the annual flooding of the Nile. The produce had to be collected, measured by government inspectors and conveyed to the granaries of Alexandria not later than 10 September of each year. From Alexandria the 'felicitous transport', as it was called, set sail for Constantinople. The hazards of navigation had to be taken into account, in particular the passage of the Dardanelles should a contrary wind be blowing. In order to guard against this eventuality vast granaries were constructed on the island of Tenedos, where the corn was unloaded and stockpiled, as it was at Ostia for the supply of Rome. If the Egyptian crop was inadequate or any other part of the mechanism failed to function properly, the populace of Constantinople was in danger of starving and emergency measures had to be implemented. We hear of a famine in 409 which led to a bloody uprising and a reorganization of the shipments. On another occasion a forced requisition at artificially low prices had to be made in Thrace, Bithynia and Phrygia, and, since there was no established system of transport from those regions, the producers themselves had the added burden of conveying their grain to the capital.[39] Considering how many things could go wrong, the supply of Constantinople functioned, on the whole, with commendable efficiency while receiving top government priority. It is clear, however, that the very existence of Constantinople as a big city depended on a smoothly running network of maritime supply.

It is difficult to determine the approximate date when the population of Constantinople reached its peak. This may have happened by about 500. From that time onwards we hear less and less of the construction of great public works, and more and more of the erection of churches. Justinian, of course, was a great builder, but his main effort went into the ecclesiastical and imperial sectors. Conditions in the capital may already have been declining when the plague of 542 caused the population to plummet. There is no reason to suppose that the losses were made good. The pestilence, as we have seen, kept returning at intervals for the remainder of the century and further calamities were on their way. In 619, following the conquest of Alexandria by the Persians, the importation of Egyptian corn ceased. If Constantinople was able to find other sources of supply, this was surely because there were far fewer mouths to feed. At the same time a plague is recorded. In 626 the city was besieged (and very nearly captured) by the Avars who thoroughly devastated Thrace, thus further depleting the available sources of food. In 674–8 Constantinople was blockaded by the Arabs. In 698 there was another plague. In 714–5, in expectation of another Arab attack, the then Emperor Anastasius II expelled from the city everyone who could not lay up for himself a supply of provisions to last three years – and, we may imagine, the majority could not. In 717–18 occurred the second Arab siege and another devastation of Thrace. In 747 there was a plague of extraordinary severity so that the city became, as one source puts it, 'almost uninhabited'.[40] 'Because of extreme necessity,' writes a chronicler,

a way was devised of placing planks upon saddled animals in the form of square paniers and so removing the dead, or piling them one upon the other in carts. When all the urban and suburban cemeteries had been filled as well as empty cisterns and ditches, and many vineyards had been dug up and even the orchards within the old walls [i.e. the Constantinian walls], then only was the need satisfied.[41]

The year 747 probably represents the lowest point in the medieval history of Constantinople.

We are not in a position to document in detail the impact of this steep decline on the everyday life of the capital, but it may be true to say that throughout the seventh century some semblance of urban conditions was maintained. A curious text, entitled *The Miracles of St Artemius* (compiled shortly after 659), provides us with a vivid if partial insight into the realities of life during the first half of the century.[42] Artemius was a healer saint of dubious pedigree (he had been governor of Egypt in 360) who specialized in tumours, particularly those affecting the genitals. His church was situated in a predominantly working-class area, roughly where the Grand Bazaar stands today, and his clientele was composed of ordinary people. Healing was obtained by a process of incubation, which is to say that patients slept in the church and its dependencies, sometimes for a period of several months, in the hope of being visited by the Saint in a dream or a vision. There was also an association of lay members who took part in all-night vigils and provided funds for candles, the dues being collected by a treasurer. Among the persons whose miraculous cure is recorded, several came from distant parts: we meet an African, several Alexandrians, a couple of Rhodians and a merchant from Chios. One of the Alexandrians was the guard of a granary, and we learn that he had to remain day and night on the premises, as a result of which he was unable to sleep in the church of St Artemius. 'I am an old man,' he said to the saint, 'and I cannot leave the granary and stay with you. For if I leave it, they will put another man in my place, and I shall be deprived both of my lodging and my sustenance.' Another Alexandrian – this happened in the reign of Heraclius – was a professional jester or buffoon employed in the household of a patrician, for, we are told, 'dignitaries take pleasure in exhibitions of acting'. His qualifications were a ready wit and a funny accent, like that of all Alexandrians. Other non-Constantinopolitans included a man from Amastris, a Phrygian, and a Cilician coppersmith who plied his trade near the church and had, like all his compatriots, an irascible temper. The most distant place mentioned in the text is Gaul, whither a carpenter travelled in the capacity of a repairman on a ship. Among the professions mentioned in *The Miracles of St Artemius* we find sailors, a candlemaker who kept his stall open until late at night, a bow-maker, a tanner, a wine-merchant, a female bath-keeper and several moneychangers or bankers whose trade is declared to have been dishonest. Physicians, being in competition with St Artemius, also come in for some criticism, and we are told that they charged eight to ten *solidi* to treat the child of a poor woman – a sum equivalent to the annual earnings of an unskilled worker. Public baths were very much part of daily life and were patronized, amongst others, by a deacon of St Sophia. This man, who was of some social standing (he was reluctant to sleep in the Church of St Artemius), was also the accredited poet of the Blue faction; in other words, he must have composed songs and acclamations. Interestingly enough, nothing else is said of the factions. Their role in the daily life of the citizens appears to have declined; we are even told that a stable in which the race horses had previously been kept was at the time disused. Theatres are not mentioned at all.

The impression we gain from reading *The Miracles of St Artemius* is that Constantinople remained a centre of commercial and artisanal activity (though, perhaps, on a diminished scale) at a time when urban life was, as we have seen, ceasing to exist in Asia Minor and the Balkans. The great crisis in the history of the capital occurred, I believe, in the first half of the eighth century. Of this we have several indirect indications. When, in 740, the land walls of the city were severely damaged by an earthquake, the local population was unable to rebuild them and the emperor had to impose a special tax, presumably to hire an outside labour force.[43] After the plague of 747, the Emperor Constantine v had actually to re-people the city by bringing in settlers from Greece and the Aegean islands, in other words from areas that were themselves seriously underpopulated.[44] It is interesting to note that the aqueduct of Valens, which was the principal aqueduct of the city, fell out of use in 626, when it was destroyed by the Avars, and was not repaired until 766, eleven years after the repopulation, and this only on account of a particularly severe drought. Once again, the labour force needed for this work had to be imported: 1,000 masons and 200 plasterers from Pontus, 500 pottery workers (for making clay pipes?) from Greece and the islands, 5,000 labourers and 200 brickmakers from Thrace.[45] What is striking about these figures is that even the unskilled labourers could not be found on the spot. In view of the fact that Constantinople is very deficient in nearby sources of drinking water, one can only conclude that the population must have contracted dramatically if it could live without the main aqueduct for a space of 140 years. It probably declined to well below the 50,000 mark, perhaps as little as half that number.

A dim light on the appearance of the city in about 760 is cast by a particularly muddled text entitled *Brief Historical Notes* (*Parastaseis syntomoi chronikai*).[46] The work of an ignorant and pretentious author, it purports to be a kind of guidebook to the memorable sights of the capital. The picture it evokes is one of abandonment and ruination. Time and again we are told that various monuments – statues, palaces, baths – had once existed, but were destroyed. What is more, the remaining monuments, many of which must have dated from the fourth and fifth centuries, were no longer understood for what they were. They had acquired a magical and generally ominous connotation. The disasters that were still in store for the city were foretold in the various reliefs and inscriptions that were to be seen on all sides. The 'philosophers' who were skilled in expounding them were dismayed. 'It would be a good thing', said one of them, 'if we do not live to see what is destined to happen. As for me, I would have been happier if I had not read that inscription.'

In spite of such gloomy prognostications, Constantinople started in 755 on a process of very gradual recovery that was to continue until the age of the Crusades. In the eighth century there was no building activity except for works of fortification and the repair of damage caused by earthquakes. In the ninth new buildings were undertaken, but they differed in character from those of the Early Byzantine period: civic amenities were no longer required, and the new constructions were mostly concentrated inside the imperial palace which acquired an air of the Arabian Nights. A spirit of 'renovation' – meaning the repair of what was ruined rather than the creation of something new – was cultivated by the propagandists at the courts of Michael III and Basil I. The list of the latter emperor's buildings is particularly instructive. It shows that practically all the major churches of the capital had fallen into decay, some of them to the point of 'near extinction'. So Basil proceeded to renovate over twenty-five churches in the city and another six in the suburbs. All his new buildings were in the imperial palace.[47]

In short, if one were able to draw a graph of the fortunes of Constantinople, one would find that it showed a very sharp dip at the same time when provincial cities came practically to the zero line. Nor was the pattern of recovery dissimilar in the capital and in the provinces. In the early ninth century some life returned to Corinth; Patras and Lacedaemon in the Peloponnese were resettled.[48] A little later Selymbria and Ancyra were refortified. The movement gathered momentum in the tenth century and reached a peak in the eleventh and twelfth. Archaeologically, the recovery is well documented at Corinth and Athens, less so in Asia Minor. It is important to observe, however, that the new settlements had none of the monumental character of Late Antiquity. Houses and shops were poorly built and huddled together along tortuous streets. Whenever possible standing ruins were incorporated into the new buildings, but otherwise there was no continuity of layout, which presupposes an intervening layer of total abandonment. There is little evidence as yet of urban centres such as we know them in medieval Italy, of a *piazza* bordered by a cathedral and the imposing, if castellated, palace of the local lord. Indeed, there is hardly any trace of cathedrals. Here and there a ruined Early Christian church was revamped in the eleventh century, as happened at Serres, Verria, Kalambaka and, possibly, at Ohrid. In most cases, it seems, urban life was fragmented into neighbourhoods, each one with its own tiny church. Urban monasteries sheltering behind their own enclosures were frequent and appear to have attracted more ample sources of finance than did the episcopal organization. At Athens, for example, the biggest medieval church that has survived, the Panagia Lykodêmou (the present Russian church), was monastic. The poor quality of domestic construction explains its subsequent disappearance; but where medieval Byzantine houses have been excavated and studied, it has been found that they contained capacious storage jars for agricultural produce, a sign of a life closely linked to the countryside.

The evidence of archaeology is supplemented by the written record. Perhaps the most striking feature of Middle Byzantine life in contrast to the earlier period was its privacy. Gone were the theatres, the assembly halls, the civil basilicas, the porticoes where people congregated. The hippodrome survived only at Constantinople, but functioned only a few days a year, a minutely orchestrated display of imperial ceremonial. The Life of St Basil the Younger, which gives us some idea of conditions at Constantinople in the tenth century, is remarkable in that all the action takes place indoors. Apart from the occasional fair, the only place of public assembly was now the church. Noticing that the various vendors who plied their trade at Constantine's forum had nowhere to go in times of bad weather, the Emperor Basil I built a church for them.[49] Even the church, it seems, was considered too public a place by many persons. The rich and even the not very rich built private chapels for themselves and, if they could afford it, maintained household priests – a practice that was specifically permitted by the Emperor Leo VI on the grounds that people would otherwise remain deprived of the holy mysteries and the chapels would fall into disuse. By the same token, baptism of infants in private chapels, which had been prohibited by earlier canon law, was also allowed.[50] Distrust and privacy find their most eloquent expression in the so-called *Strategicon* of the eleventh-century general Cecaumenus. Never put up a friend in your house, he advises, since the friend may seduce your wife. Let him lodge elsewhere and send him the necessary food. Lock up your daughters as if they were criminals. Avoid all parties. If you are not on the emperor's business, stay at home with your trusted servants, stockpile supplies and look after the interests of your family.[51]

As we saw in the last chapter, the upsurge of towns was accompanied by the growth of a petty bourgeoisie. For a vivid picture of the ease in which the professional classes of Constantinople lived under the Comneni we may turn to a satirical poem attributed to one Theodoros Ptochoprodromos. The author, who represents himself as an impoverished clergyman, had been urged by his father to acquire an education. 'My child,' said his father to him,

learn your letters as much as you are able. See that man over there, my child: he used to walk on foot, and now he has a fat mule with a fine harness. This one, when he was a student, used to go barefoot, and see him now in his pointed boots! This other one, when he was a student, never combed his hair, and now he is well combed and proud of his locks. That one in his student days never saw a bath door from afar, and now he bathes three times a week. That one was full of lice as big as almonds, and now his purse is full of gold pieces with the emperor Manuel's effigy.

So Ptochoprodromos learnt his letters, but to what avail? His cupboard contained nothing but piles of paper and he had nothing to eat. And so he compares his poverty to the plenty of his neighbours. The worker in gold thread has his larder full of bread and wine, of cooked tunny and dried mackerel. The shoemaker, when he wakes up in the morning, sends his boy to purchase tripe and Vlach cheese, and only after he has breakfasted on these delicacies does he start work. At dinner-time he lays aside his last and his tools and bids his wife serve a meal of three dainty courses. With obsessional attention to what everyone has to eat, Ptochoprodromos compares himself to the practitioners of other professions, even the lowliest – the tailor who happens to be a houseowner, the bakery assistant, the yogurt vendor, the itinerant seller of clothes and pepper-grinders, the butcher. All of them have a full stomach. What then is the use of Homer and Oppian?[52]

We are so accustomed to regarding the Greeks as a commercial nation that we find it hard to imagine that the Byzantines were the very opposite – people of the land, distrustful and unenterprising. And so it was not the Byzantines but foreigners who reaped the benefit of the urban development. We have already mentioned the presence of Russian and Italian merchants at Constantinople in the tenth century and the decisive importance of the granting of commercial privileges to Venice by the Emperor Alexius I. Within a short period the *basileus* discovered that he was no longer master in his own house. When, in 1126, John II Comnenus tried to suspend the privileges of the Venetians, he was constrained by force of arms to abandon his attempt. In 1148 the Venetian quarter, which lay between the two modern bridges that span the Golden Horn, was enlarged. The number of Venetians resident at Constantinople appears to have grown to about twenty thousand and their riches were immense. Being theoretically subjects of the Empire, they were at first placed under the jurisdiction of imperial officials, but, little by little, they made themselves virtually self-governing. This is not the place to recount the tortuous tale of the dealings between the Empire and Venice, the rivalries between various groups of Italians, and the vain attempts made by the emperors to play them off one against the other. It is sufficient to note that the various 'Latin' concessions occupied the best commercial real estate of the city along the Golden Horn shore and that the number of western residents

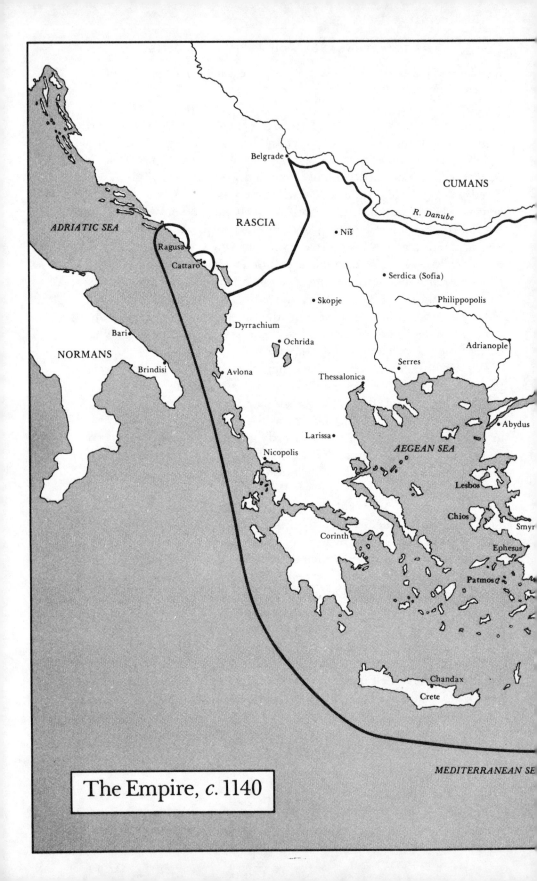

CUMANS

ADRIATIC SEA

Belgrade

R. Danube

RASCIA

Niš

Ragusa

Cattaro

Serdica (Sofia)

Philippopolis

Skopje

Dyrrachium

Bari

NORMANS

Ochrida

Adrianople

Serres

Brindisi

Avlona

Thessalonica

Larissa

AEGEAN SEA

Abydus

Nicopolis

Lesbos

Chios

Smyr

Corinth

Ephesus

Patmos

Chandax

Crete

MEDITERRANEAN SE

The Empire, *c.* 1140

Cherson

BLACK SEA

Mesembria

Mesembria
Sozopolis

Sinope

Amastris

Trebizond

Selymbria
Heraclea
Constantinople

Nicaea
Brusa

R. Halys

Dorylaeum

Sivas

SULTANATE

OF

RUM

Amorium

Kayseri

Malatya

Philadelphia

R. Tigris

Laodicea

Konya

Edessa (Urfa)

Anazarbus

Attaleia

Adana
Tarsus

Seleucia

Aleppo

Antioch

R. Euphrates

Laodicea

Nicosia
Cyprus

Homs

may have been as much as one fifth of the total population, assuming the latter to have grown to about 200,000–250,000.

A babel of foreign tongues resounded in the streets of Constantinople. Of this an amusing if, in places, obscure illustration is given by the poet John Tzetzes who wrote towards the middle of the twelfth century:

'Among Scythians,' he says, 'you will find me a Scythian [referring to one of the Turkic tribes who dwelt north of the Black Sea], a Latin among Latins, and among all other nations as if I was one of their race. When I greet a Scythian, thus do I address him: *Salamalek alti ... salamalek altuğep*. The Persians [i.e. Seljuks], too, I address in Persian: *Asan hais kourouparza hantazar harantasi*. To the Latins I speak in the Latin tongue: *Bene venesti, domine, bene venesti, frater. Unde es et de quale provincia venesti? Quomodo, frater, venesti in istan civitatem? Pedone, cavallarius, per mare, vis morari?* The Alans I address in their language: *Tapanhas mesfili hsina korthin*. ... To the Arabs I say in Arabic: '*Ala aina tamurr min, ên ente sittî maulaje sabâh*. The Russians, too, I address according to their custom: *Sdra, brate, sestrica*, and *dobra deni*. As for the Jews, I say to them fittingly in Hebrew: *Memakomene vithfaği Beelzebul timée*. ... Thus do I address proper and suitable words to everyone, knowing that this is a sign of the best conduct.[53]

Like a true Levantine, Tzetzes was able to speak a few words in several languages and, though a Ciceronian might have disapproved of his Latin, this was probably the foreign tongue he knew best.

In short, Constantinople under the Comneni was not unlike Istanbul before the First World War, when most of the economic life of the city was in the hands of foreigners as well as local Greeks, Armenians and Jews, while the Ottoman majority felt themselves to have been reduced to the status of second-class citizens. There was also a close correspondence between the privileges of the Italian colonies and the régime of 'capitulations' as it prevailed in the Ottoman Empire. In both cases the situation led to explosive tensions. But while modern Turkey has been able to eject or neutralize the alien elements of Istanbul, Byzantium proved powerless before her Italian exploiters. The arrest of all Venetian residents of the Empire and the confiscation of their property in 1171, the massacre of other Latins at Constantinople (mostly Pisans and Genoese) in 1182 served only to hasten the terrible retribution that was exacted by the West.

When the army of the Fourth Crusade stood before Constantinople in June 1203, they could hardly believe their eyes, for they had never seen a city so big and powerful, so rich, so full of palaces and churches.[54] Little did they know that their arrival would spell the ruin of the great capital. The terrible fire that broke out in August of the same year and, after raging eight days, devastated a good half of the city, was a presage of things to come. Captured by the Crusaders, systematically pillaged during a period of nearly sixty years, depleted of its inhabitants, Constantinople became but a shadow of its former self. We shall not attempt here to trace its melancholy history over the next two centuries since it repeats the colonial conditions already prevalent under the Comneni. The Spanish ambassador Clavijo, who saw Constantinople in 1403, says that the space within the walls consisted of a number of hamlets separated by cornfields and orchards. Everywhere one could see ruins of palaces and churches. Only the coastal areas had a fairly dense population, especially the trading area of the Golden Horn. By contrast, the Genoese colony of Galata, though small in area, was very populous and filled with excellent houses.[55] When it fell to the Turks in 1453, Constantinople had a population of well under fifty thousand.

Today we look in vain for traces of Byzantine houses in Istanbul. Even the layout of the city has been altered beyond all recognition. Part of the Mesê still survives as the Divanyolu, the hippodrome, the Augustaion and the forum of Theodosius are still open spaces, but the other Byzantine squares have been built over. Above all, there is no indication of any regular street grid, such as Constantine's architects would surely have traced. It is possible that the expansion of the city in Ottoman times, the frequent fires, earthquakes and rebuildings were responsible for creating that maze of tortuous streets that appear on the relatively accurate maps made in the eighteenth and nineteenth centuries. Yet it may be that the urban transformation occurred much earlier, and that Comnenian Constantinople bore the same relation to Justinian's as Comnenian Corinth did to the Corinth of the Early Byzantine period.

For a glimpse of a Late Byzantine town we have to go to Mistra in the Peloponnese. Though often called 'the Byzantine Pompeii', Mistra is actually a Frankish foundation. Its Despots' Palace is purely western, its houses closed to the outside world and often provided with crenellated towers. Even in some of the churches there are traces of Gothic influence. How much Mistra resembled other Byzantine towns of the thirteenth and fourteenth centuries is a matter of conjecture. One thing, however, is certain: it is in no way descended from a *polis* of Late Antiquity.

CHAPTER 4

DISSENTERS

'It is Our will', proclaims an imperial enactment of the year 380 that was later placed at the head of Justinian's Code,

that all the peoples who are ruled by the administration of Our Clemency shall practise that religion which the divine Peter the apostle transmitted to the Romans. . . . We shall believe in the single Deity of the Father, the Son and the Holy Spirit under the guise of equal majesty and of the Holy Trinity. We command that those persons who follow this law shall embrace the name of Catholic Christians. The rest, however, whom we adjudge demented and insane [*dementes vesanosque*], shall sustain the infamy attached to heretical dogmas. Their meeting places shall not receive the name of churches, and they shall be smitten first by divine vengeance and secondly by the retribution of Our own initiative which we shall dispense in accordance with the divine judgment.[1]

One God, one Empire, one religion – these were the cornerstones of Byzantine political thinking. Religion was defined by ecumenical councils of the Church on the basis of Holy Scripture and the exegesis of the Fathers, but it was the emperor's duty – in fact, his highest duty – to enforce its universal observance. For, to quote another imperial law, 'We are aware that Our State is sustained more by religion than by official duties and physical toil and sweat.'[2] 'If we strive by all means', wrote the Emperor Justinian, 'to enforce the civil laws, whose power God in His goodness has entrusted to Us for the security of Our subjects, how much more keenly should We endeavour to enforce the holy canons and the divine laws which have been framed for the salvation of our souls!'[3]

The literal meaning of orthodoxy was not so much the right faith as the right doctrine, and it consisted, above all, in 'confessing and glorifying aright the Father, Christ the Son of God, and the Holy Spirit.'[4] In other words, all subjects of the Empire were most emphatically urged not only to be Christians, but also to subscribe to a single and highly abstruse doctrine defining the nature and relationship of the three persons of the Trinity, for even the slightest deviation therefrom was considered to be heresy.[5] We need not, of course, imagine that the particular body of dogma that eventually became Orthodoxy with a capital O was destined from the very start to assume that position. There were times when different interpretations of Christianity enjoyed the active support of the temporal power. The Emperors Constantius II and Valens, for example, championed the cause of Arianism, Anastasius I was on the side of the Monophysites, Heraclius tried hard to impose the Monothelete compromise, and a succession of emperors in the eighth and ninth centuries were Iconoclasts. Even the great Justinian himself, the staunchest enforcer of religious uniformity, ended his life under the cloud of the Julianist heresy. It is conceivable that any one of these alternative doctrines might have triumphed. Of one thing, however, we may be sure, namely that whichever sect proved victorious, it would have been as intolerant of its rivals as was Orthodoxy. Instances of declared religious toleration during the Byzantine period may be counted on the fingers of one hand.

The fact remains, however, that by no means all subjects of the Empire were Catholic Christians. The number of those whom the government considered 'demented and insane' was extremely high in the Early Byzantine age, to the point, perhaps, of constituting the majority of the population. It was lower in the Middle period and, probably, quite small in the Late period. This chapter will be concerned with the dissenters, with those groups which for one reason or another did not accept the prevailing orthodoxy.

There were, in the first instance, the ancient pagans of whatever complexion. The disappearance of paganism was a slow process that extended from the fourth century until, in places, the end of the sixth. With the exception of a few cities like Gaza, which is said to have been predominantly pagan in about 400 AD,[6] and Carrhae (Harran), where paganism survived until well after the Arab conquest,[7] most urban centres had accepted Christianity by the fourth century. By a curious paradox the old religion maintained itself at the two opposite ends of the social scale: on the one hand among the municipal aristocracy to whom it was a matter of tradition and even loyalty to the Roman State, on the other among peasants. The teaching profession, as we shall see in Chapter 6, also offered a refuge to paganism. We shall not repeat here the oft-told story of the protracted oppression and persecution of pagans by the imperial government, by local bishops and monks, from the savage, but largely ineffectual, measures of the 340s and 350s down to the last inquisitions under Justinian. It is a melancholy story punctuated by the suppression of the temples in 391, the sacking of the Serapeum at Alexandria, the lynching of Hypatia, the closure of the philosophical schools, not to mention the destruction of countless treasures of ancient art. Yet pagans maintained themselves for a long time not only on local councils and in schools, but even in the upper echelons of the imperial administration. They did not flaunt their religion, worshipped in private (sometimes behind a false wall) and hoped no one would denounce them to the authorities.

While we know a great deal about prominent pagans, we are much less informed about rural populations. A doubtless typical case concerns the missionary activities of the Monophysite John of Amida who was made titular bishop of Ephesus in the reign of Justinian. This zealous Christian in the course of thirty-five years (542–76) converted some eighty thousand persons in the mountainous districts of Asia, Phrygia, Caria and Lydia, and destroyed their temples, in whose stead he built ninety-nine churches and twelve monasteries. The new converts were simply baptized *en masse* and each was given one third of a *solidus* from imperial funds.[8] One may well wonder what efficacy such conversions possessed. A story told by the same John may shed some light on this question. It concerns a remote mountainous area near Melitene, east of the Euphrates, whose inhabitants called themselves Christians, but used their village church to store wood, had no priests and had never heard of the Scriptures. A zealous monk called Symeon the Mountaineer (who was also a Monophysite) happened to stray into that area and was shocked by the apathy of the local population. His missionary efforts met with considerable opposition, but he established his credence by performing a miracle and then set up a school for boys and girls whom he forced to learn the Bible. He laboured at this task for twenty-six years until his disciples had become 'readers and daughters of the Covenant'.[9] Such assiduity was no doubt exceptional. It was generally recognized that rural clergy was lax and given to drunkenness. A pious boy often had to leave his native district in order to find suitable mentors.[10]

It was once fashionable to affirm that paganism was absorbed into Christianity and that the old gods re-emerged in the guise of saints, that Helios was turned into Elias (the prophet Elijah), Demeter into St Demetrius, Bacchus into St Tychon, etc.[11] While such simplistic connections no longer convince us today, it can hardly be denied that the perfunctory conversion of large segments of the population could not have changed overnight their age-old attitudes and beliefs. At the end of the seventh century men and women still danced in honour of the false gods, the name of Dionysus was still invoked at vintage time, people lit fires outside their homes at the new moon and jumped over them, and every kind of sorcery was rife.[12] One does not have to read far in the Lives of saints to discover that popular Christianity inherited and partly rationalized a vast body of pagan superstition.

Next to the pagans came the Jews. We have noted in Chapter 1 their continued presence in Palestine in the Early Byzantine period, but the majority of them were scattered throughout the Empire, largely in cities. By virtue of a long tradition in Roman law, Jews enjoyed a peculiar status: they were a licit sect, their synagogues were protected from seizure, they appointed their own clergy and had recourse in civil cases to their own courts of law. At the same time they were forbidden to proselytize, to own Christian slaves or to build new synagogues. In other words, there was a policy of containing the Jews and it was made quite plain to them that they were, of their own free choice, second-class citizens. Honours they had none: progressively barred from service in the State police, among the palatines, in the army, they were, on the other hand, bound to perform, if liable, the onerous duties of curials, but without enjoying any of the resulting privileges. 'Let them be', says a law of Justinian, 'in the same turpitude as regards their fortune as that which they have chosen for their souls' (*sint in turpitudine fortunae, in qua et animam volunt esse*).[13] The phraseology is typical and deliberate: again and again official documents refer to Jews in terms of denigration and contempt.

Why were the Jews so obdurate, why did they refuse to see the superior truths of Christianity, when these very truths were announced in their own sacred books? Justinian, who wanted to legislate on every topic, tried in this matter also to get to the heart of the problem. The Jews, he decided, should be made to read the Old Testament in such a way that they paid attention to the prophecies contained therein instead of quibbling about words. To facilitate this more fruitful approach, they were specifically allowed by the emperor to use in their synagogues the Septuagint or any other suitable translation in place of the Hebrew, while being denied the Mishna which obscured the meaning of the sacred text.[14] It was hoped by this measure to protect the Jewish congregations from the deceit of their own rabbis who, under the cloak of a hieratic and largely incomprehensible language, introduced misleading interpretations. We may suspect that Justinian had as little success in his intervention as did the Christian polemicists who produced a succession of anti-Jewish treatises always revolving round the same Old Testament passages. Some conversions may have occurred, but the bulk of the Jews remained obdurate.

The change from a policy of grudging toleration to one of forced conversion and persecution seems to have been brought about by political events. The Jews proved disloyal to the Empire. One instance of their subversion concerned developments in a distant country, namely the kingdom of the Himyarites (corresponding to present-day Yemen). The Empire had important interests in the south of the Arabian peninsula and tried, as usual, to promote them with the help of Christian missions. The Jews were also proselytizing in those parts and with greater success in that, for a time, the rulers of the Himyarites were won over to the Jewish religion. The last of these rulers, Dû-Nuwâs by name, imposed an embargo on imperial trade. The Empire intervened militarily; Dû-Nuwâs responded by ordering a massacre of Christians in the Yemen (*c.* 520). Two years later he was crushed and his country passed under the control of the Christian kingdom of Ethiopia. What concerns us here is the involvement of Byzantine Jewry in these events: Dû-Nuwâs applied his repressive measures on the grounds that 'the Christian Romans mistreat the Jews in their own country and every year kill many of them'.[15] There was also a plan of bringing pressure on him by imprisoning the rabbis of Tiberias.[16]

Then there were the Samaritan revolts starting in 484 and culminating in the terrible one of 555. It was realized, of course, that there existed a distinction between Samaritans and Jews, yet the latter did take part in the uprising of 555 whose aim was the creation of an independent state. Finally and most importantly, the Jews took the side of the enemy when Asia Minor and Palestine were invaded by the Persians. In 609–10 the Jews of Caesarea in Cappadocia submitted to the invader whereas the Christian inhabitants left the city.[17] In Jerusalem, which fell in 614, the Jews bought Christian captives and put them to death, and they burnt Christian churches.[18] Elsewhere in Palestine they joined forces with the local Saracens in looting monasteries and killing monks.[19]

When Byzantine rule had been restored, the Jews were made to pay dearly for their collaboration with the enemy. Not only were they banished from a three-mile radius of Jerusalem; in about 634 the

Emperor Heraclius is said to have ordered all the Jews in his Empire to be baptized.[20] This was the first general measure of its kind against the Jews, although it may have been preceded by others of regional applicability. It came, however, at a time when the Jewish problem was about to be solved by other means. As a result of the Arab conquests the vast majority of the Jews found themselves outside the Empire.

We do not know how many remained. The example of Heraclius was imitated by subsequent zealous emperors. Leo III ordered once again the baptism of Jews and those who complied were given the title of 'new citizens', but they did so in bad faith, while others, it seems, fled to the Arabs.[21] The failure of this measure was acknowledged by the Council of 787 which decreed that insincere converts should not be accepted; it was preferable to let them live according to their customs while remaining subject to the old disabilities.[22] A fresh attempt was made by Basil I: Jews were summoned to disputations and if they were unable to demonstrate the truth of their religion, they were to be baptized. Remission of taxes and the grant of dignities were offered as rewards; even so, after the emperor's death, most of the converts 'returned like dogs to their own vomit'.[23] The last recorded case of forced conversion was under Romanus I, but it only resulted in driving many Jews to the land of Khazaria north of the Black Sea. From then on such Jews as remained were left to live in relative peace; there was even a reverse migration of them from Egypt into the Empire in the late tenth and eleventh centuries.

The upsurge of urban life gave an impetus to Jewish communities. By 1168, when Benjamin of Tudela embarked on his long journey, he was able to make contact with groups of his correligionists at every port of call from Corfu to Cyprus and Antioch. At Thebes he found 2,000 Jewish families, 'most skilled artificers in silk and purple cloth throughout Greece', at Thessalonica 500, also silk-workers, at Constantinople 2,500, among them many rich merchants. In the capital, however, they lived in a ghetto across the Golden Horn, were often beaten up by the Christians and were not allowed to ride on horseback, except for the emperor's physician who was a Jew. While the figures given by Benjamin testify to a certain expansion of Byzantine Jewry, it must be pointed out that he quotes much higher numbers for Muslim cities like Aleppo (5,000) and Mosul (7,000).[24] Nor can it be said that Byzantine Jews, whatever their contribution to the economic life of the Empire, were ever allowed to develop a penchant for literature and scholarship.

While the Jews accounted for only a small part of the emperor's subjects, Christian heretics were extremely numerous. These are sometimes divided into two groups, on the one hand the 'sects', mostly of pre-Byzantine origin, on the other hand the followers of the 'noble' heresies, such as Arianism, who differed from Catholics only on points of definition concerning the nature of the Trinity. Such a distinction was not, however, made by the Byzantines themselves, who tended to lump together under the name of heresy all 'false' doctrines, past and present, of whatever origin. The number of these doctrines was prodigious: Epiphanius in his *Panarion* (composed in 377–80) described eighty, while St John Damascene in the eighth century went above a hundred and was at pains to show that they were all descended from four archetypal aberrations, namely Barbarism, Scythism, Hellenism and Judaism.[25] While churchmen catalogued and described, the imperial government fulminated in all directions. The Theodosian Code contains no fewer than sixty-six laws directed against heretics and prescribes various penalties: denial of the right of assembly, confiscation of their meeting houses, prohibition to appoint priests, burning of books, fines. Some heretics were to be expelled from towns and punished with *infamia*, whereby they lost the right of bequeathing property or making wills. The death penalty was reserved for Manichees alone.[26] It is true that no heretic was specifically obliged to become a Catholic, but the incentives were so powerful that it came nearly to the same thing. And even if imperial legislation was applied haphazardly (as it certainly was), it could not fail to generate an atmosphere of suspicion and distrust. Informants were encouraged, guilds were held responsible for the beliefs of their members, and masters for those of their slaves. Householders ran the risk of being heavily punished for the use to which their premises were put.

Among the sects the one that inspired the greatest fear was that of the Manichees, on the mistaken assumption that they were, in addition to their dangerous doctrines, agents of the enemy. It is true that Mani (d. 277) lived in Persian Mesopotamia, but he considered himself a Christian apostle, not to say the Paraclete in person, and was put to death at the behest of the Zoroastrian clergy. His followers were persecuted in Persia no less than in the Roman Empire. Mani's theology, with its transmigration of souls, its innumerable 'aeons', its five 'sojourns' of God and five 'archons' of Darkness, may have appeared ridiculous to some people, but it evidently exercised a wide appeal. His doctrine of the antithetical and self-subsisting principles of good and evil, his conviction that all matter was evil, that man sinned out of necessity, that salvation lay in asceticism, in abstinence from meat, wine and sexual relations – these were ideas that struck many familiar chords and seemed to find confirmation in the realities of everyday life. More radical than Christianity, untainted by the uneasy compromise which Christians had had to make with the Jewish scriptures, Manichaeism was moreover extremely vigorous in its missionary activities. By the fourth century it had already spread to practically all the Roman provinces: the first imperial measure against it dates from 297.[27] Why it subsequently lost momentum is difficult to explain, but it was still alive in the days of Justinian and it was said that the Praetorian Prefect Peter Barsymes openly supported the Manichees.[28] The area of their greatest success was, however, to be in central Asia, from Samarkand to China.

The fate of all outlawed sects was retreat to the countryside where they were not subject to the same coercion as in the towns. Some, of course, originated in the country and always remained associated with a particular geographical area. Such was Phrygian Montanism which is last recorded in the eighth century: the Emperor Leo III ordered the conversion of all remaining Montanists, but they chose to incinerate themselves in their churches, as they had previously done in the days of Justinian.[29] It is only from casual references that we are often reminded of the continued existence of this or that ancient sect. Thus the Quartodecimans (Tessareskaidekatitai), whose main fault lay in their 'Jewish' calculation of the date of Easter and who had been prominent before the First Nicene Council (325), unexpectedly reappear in 867, when the patriarch Photius rounded up a number of them and won their re-admission into the Church.[30] Given the obscurity that surrounds the Byzantine countryside, it is almost impossible to determine the prevalence of various heretical sects beyond the presumption that some areas, like Phrygia and Galatia, were particularly prone to them.

The greatest challenge to State Christianity came, however, not from the sects, but from one of the 'noble' heresies, namely Monophysitism. Some scholars even hesitate to call it a heresy, preferring the designation of schism. The Monophysites, who had overwhelming support in Egypt and Syria, opposed the Council of Chalcedon (451) for dividing, as they saw it, the person of Christ into two natures and believed in the unity of the incarnate Christ, a unity that derived from (*ek*) the two natures, human and divine. *Ek* for the Monophysites, *en* (in) for the Catholics – the difference amounted to one letter. The historian

Evagrius, who was a contemporary of the controversy, rightly remarks that the former position implied the other. Yet, he adds, people considered the issue so divisive 'out of some attachment to their notion of God' that they chose to die rather than come to an agreement.[31] If there was some deeper reason for the dispute, Evagrius was not aware of it, and he, surely, ought to have known.

The imperial government, be it said to its credit, tried several times to mediate. In 482 the Emperor Zeno issued his Edict of Union (*Henotikon*) addressed to the clergy and people of Egypt in which he appealed to the loyalty of his subjects and reminded them that victory over the foe, the blessings of peace, clement weather and abundance of produce were dependent on a concordant worship of the Godhead. He then rejected the extremists on both sides, upheld the first three ecumenical councils, barely mentioned Chalcedon and affirmed his faith in the oneness of Christ.[32] The appeal fell on deaf ears. Subsequent emperors tried different approaches: Anastasius openly favoured the Monophysites, whereas Justin I persecuted them. Justinian parleyed and persecuted by turns while his wife Theodora gave active help to the obdurate easterners. Justin II attempted a fresh compromise as did Heraclius. The net result was nil, except the creation of a new heresy, Monothelitism, born out of Heraclius' formula of conciliation.

It was not at first the intention of the Monophysites to set up a separate Church. Their first hierarchy, dating from the time of Severus, Monophysite patriarch of Antioch (512–18), consisted of regularly appointed bishops. While it was strongest in the diocese of Antioch, it also extended to eastern and southern Asia Minor. But after these bishops had been deposed and banished (519), and especially after the death of the Empress Theodora (548), there appeared no other solution but to create a distinct Church made up of titular bishops who, for the most part, were never allowed to visit their sees. This became known as the Jacobite Church after Jacob Baradaeus (d. 578), who made most of the ordinations. It is interesting to observe that Jacob's 'ghost' bishoprics were not confined to those provinces where Monophysitism was strongest, but extended to such Greek centres as Ephesus, Smyrna, Pergamum and the island of Chios, from which it may be deduced that his aim was in no sense national.

There can be little doubt that the Monophysite controversy facilitated the conquest of the eastern provinces first by the Persians and then by the Arabs. The experience of persecution, of bishops driven into exile, congregations denied their churches and monasteries broken up by armed force placed the central government in the role of an alien bully. In the words of one Syrian historian:

Heraclius did not allow the orthodox [i.e. the Monophysites] to appear in his presence and did not receive their complaints concerning the churches of which they had been robbed. That was why the God of vengeance, who alone is all-powerful ... seeing the wickedness of the Romans who, throughout their dominions cruelly pillaged our churches and our monasteries and condemned us without pity, did bring from the south the sons of Ishmael in order to deliver us from the hands of the Romans. And if, in truth, we suffered some harm in that the parish churches which had been taken from us and given to the Chalcedonians [i.e. the Catholics] remained in their possession, seeing that when the cities submitted to the Arabs, the latter granted to each confession the temples they held at the time, ... yet it was no small advantage to us to be delivered of the cruelty of the Romans, of their wickedness, their wrath, their harsh zeal with regard to us, and to find ourselves in peace.[33]

That is not to say that the Monophysites represented nationalistic tendencies or that they welcomed foreign occupation. But they could hardly be expected to fight enthusiastically on behalf of a hated and distant emperor. In Egypt, Syria and Mesopotamia the Orthodox Church was, to a large extent, imposed from the outside and when the imperial presence was removed, it either shrank or disappeared.

The débâcle of the seventh century changed drastically the configuration of dissenters in the Empire. The old pagans had become extinct except for some tiny pockets in backward areas, such as the inhabitants of Mani in the Peloponnese who were christianized as late as the reign of Basil I.[34] The great majority of Jews and Monophysites found themselves under Arab rule. There were still some communities of Jacobite Syrians along the eastern border, and some of them were settled in Thrace in the eighth century, but we do not hear much of them thereafter.[35] A more important Monophysite element consisted of the Armenians whose crucial role in the Middle Byzantine period we have already noted. Various sects continued to vegetate obscurely in Asia Minor and Muslims began to appear as prisoners of war and were even allowed to have a mosque at Constantinople. There was, however, a very large element of new pagans, namely the Slavs and Avars who had overrun practically the whole Balkan peninsula. Strangely enough, Byzantine sources tell us practically nothing about their religion, yet the presumption remains that for about two centuries and in places as long as three, vast territories that were nominally imperial reverted to paganism, and that Perun, the god of lightning, was worshipped there

97

in the place of Jesus Christ. A Sicilian text of dubious historicity (eighth century?) tells of a body of Avars, 'a foul nation completely unconversant with the Greek tongue', who dwelt in the regions of Dyrrachium and Athens, and who worshipped images of reptiles and four-legged beasts as well as fire, water and their own swords.[36] The first Byzantine expedition to penetrate continental Greece and the Peloponnese took place in 783, and those parts were treated as enemy territory.[37] Thereafter the Slavs were gradually evangelized, but it was a slow process that continued for a century and more. Nor should it be forgotten that to the north of Thrace and Macedonia lay the newly established kingdom of Bulgaria that was pagan, and even militantly pagan, until its nominal conversion to Christianity in 864. Thus, on the European side, Byzantium was faced by an expanse of primitive paganism stretching as far as the eye could see.

While these barbarians were still wallowing in their native superstitions, Byzantium was shaken by another religious storm. There may be some exaggeration in treating Iconoclasm as a heresy, but it does provide an interesting example of the emperor's decisive role in the religious sphere. It also led to the curious situation where the majority of the Empire's inhabitants found themselves to be dissenters. The issue concerned religious observance rather than dogma: Was it proper to offer veneration to images (icons) of Christ and the saints? No matter what the theologians argued, it is clear that icons had acquired a very important place in popular piety and that they were considered as numinous. The ordinary Byzantine might have had some trouble in explaining his intellectual position on this topic, but he certainly believed that an icon provided, so to speak, a locus for the saint represented. If the saint resided in his icon, he could speak through it and work miracles by its agency. The difference between an icon and a pagan idol was that the former depicted a genuine saint, an active member of God's heavenly court, whereas the latter represented not so much a non-existent entity as a demon.

It seems that the military disasters of the seventh century led many people to believe that they were being deliberately punished by God for some serious defect in their worship. What part, if any, was played in this by heretical groups is unclear. We do know, however, that there was some popular agitation before the Emperor Leo III, a Syrian from Germanicea (Marash), decreed in 730 that icons were to be removed. He wished to have the patriarch on his side, but since the patriarch refused to comply, another was appointed in his place. Those few who actively resisted the emperor were punished. No immediate need was felt of obtaining the assent of the entire Church. The emperor was within his rights in purifying the faith of his subjects, and events on the battlefront proved his orthodoxy. It was only in 754 that Leo's successor Constantine v summoned a council of 338 bishops, the entire episcopate of the Empire, and whatever they felt in their hearts, they all signed on the dotted line.

As far as we can judge, Iconoclasm never commanded much popular support. The only group that openly espoused it was the mobile army that was indoctrinated by Constantine v and bound by oath to observe it. When, in 786, the Empress Irene attempted to convene a council at Constantinople in order to reintroduce icon-worship, her plans were frustrated by the soldiers. It should also be said that the populace of the capital in the 760s joined eagerly in the persecution of iconophile monks, dragging them through the streets and spitting on them in the hippodrome; but then, Constantine v was a very popular emperor and we may imagine that the recalcitrant monks were represented as his enemies. Otherwise, we cannot point to any mass demonstrations either *pro* or *contra*. The will of the government dictated the suppression of Iconoclasm in 787, its reintroduction in 814 and its final liquidation in 843. Admittedly, there never took place any persecution of the public at large. The regular clergy generally toed the line, and it was only a number of monks (not all monks by any means) who stood up for icons and suffered the consequences. The persecution under the Emperor Theophilus in the 830s was of very limited scope.

The patriarch Photius, who presided over the liquidation of the last traces of Iconoclasm, loudly proclaimed the idea that all heresies had been defeated once and for all. The council he convened in 867 was supposed to mark 'the triumph over all the heresies', and the patriarch confidently asserted that 'no manner of impiety shall henceforth speak freely'.[38] There was no doubt in his mind – and this view came to prevail in the Orthodox Church – that religious doctrine had been defined with complete finality. Nothing could be added to it, nothing taken away, as the Photian Council of 879–80 stated at its sixth session. The Emperor Leo vi was likewise convinced that all heresies had been abolished. In olden days, he said, the celebration of baptism in private chapels was forbidden because of the fear of a heretical ritual, but no such danger existed any more.[39] It is true that no major heresy was to arise again in the Eastern Church, but sects continued to flourish at the very time when Photius and Leo vi were expressing their optimistic views.

Among these sects the one most subversive of the established order was Paulicianism whose possible links with Manichaeism have not been entirely elucidated. Its centre lay in Armenia on both sides of the Byzantine border and it appears to have sprung up in the seventh century. The Paulician doctrine, in so far as we know it, was founded on the opposition of the triune God and the evil Demiurge who created the material world. The Paulicians accepted the New Testament (except for the book of Revelation and the two epistles of Peter) and had a particular devotion to St Paul, but, like true Manichees, they rejected the Old Testament. They thought that Christ acquired his body in Heaven, so that he neither was truly born of the Virgin Mary nor died on the cross. They consequently offered no honour to the cross, just as they spurned icons and the worship of saints. Again like Manichees, they seem to have had a class of initiates, but no regular clergy or liturgy. Their indifference to the sacraments made them, however, willing to undergo baptism and other rites of outward conformity. In this way they escaped easy detection.

Although their first two leaders are said to have been killed by the emperor's order, the Paulicians do not appear to have been severely repressed until the saintly patriarch Nicephorus prevailed on the Emperor Michael I (811–13) to decree the death penalty against them. The result of this thoughtless move was that the Paulicians went over the border and sought the protection of the Arab emir of Melitene (Malatya), who granted them an operational base from which they could raid Byzantine territory. This open hostility to the Byzantine State distinguishes the Paulicians from other heretical sects, though it should be noted that their leader Sergius (renamed Tychikos), himself a Byzantine of good family, did not approve of such action.[40] After Sergius, the next two leaders of the Paulicians were simply military men: Karbeas, an ex-Byzantine officer, established his followers in the stronghold of Tephrike (Divriği), thus setting up what amounted to an independent state, while his successor Chrysocheir carried out daring raids as far as Ephesus, Nicaea and Nicomedia and proudly demanded the cession to him of all of Asia Minor. It required several difficult campaigns for the heretics to be subdued and Tephrike destroyed (878?). Much later Karbeas and Chrysocheir, their Paulician background forgotten, appear in the epic of *Digenes Akrites* as the gallant Muslim captains Karoes and Chrysocherpes (or Chrysoberges), the latter being even represented as the grandfather of Digenes himself.

The fall of Tephrike did not entail the disappearance of Paulicians in

Asia Minor. In the tenth century they were still numerous in the region of Pontus[41] and we meet them at the same time in the west of the subcontinent. Their main centre of action was, however, shifted to the Balkans where a body of them had already been settled in the eighth century. The heterogeneous and as yet incompletely evangelized population of Thrace, Macedonia and Bulgaria offered to the heresy an ideal breeding ground. It now emerged under the name of Bogomilism, so called after the priest Bogomil, of whom all we know is that he lived in Bulgaria under the Tsar Peter (927–69). The movement enjoyed a rapid success. By the middle of the tenth century the ecclesiastical authorities were worried; by the next century, if not earlier, Bogomilism was re-exported to Asia Minor, where its followers acquired the bizarre name of Phoundagiagitai. An important group was also formed at Constantinople. Some clues to the success of Bogomilism are provided by the Treatise (*Slovo*) of the priest Cosmas, believed to have been composed in about 972. It represents the sectaries as outward conformists whose most obvious distinction from the Orthodox lay in their purer and stricter life. That, however, in the eyes of Cosmas was sheer dissimulation. In addition to their gross dogmatic errors, their aversion to marriage and children, they also opposed manual labour. 'They teach their adherents not to submit to the authorities, they denigrate the rich, they hate the emperors, they rail at superiors, they insult the lords, they hold that God abhors those who work for the emperor, and they urge every servant not to labour for his master.'[42] Here, at last, we have a 'social' motive that the modern mind can understand. For Cosmas, the Bogomils were peaceful hippies who undermined the established order, and he lays the blame squarely in the court of the Orthodox. It was the Orthodox themselves who disregarded the duties of marriage, who abandoned their wives and children and drifted in and out of monasteries, alleging the difficulty of looking after a family while serving a landowner and submitting to the violence of their lords.[43] It was Orthodox monks who lived in idleness while meddling in the affairs of the laity. It was Orthodox priests and bishops who neglected their pastoral duties. Few ecclesiastics of the time paint such a vivid picture of the apathy and laxity of Christian life.

It has been noticed that Cosmas does not prescribe any violent measures against the Bogomils. Indeed, the period 950–1050 was marked by a general relaxation of persecution. But times were changing and the official attitude began to harden, especially after the installation of the Comnenian dynasty. This shift is noticeable in the history of the so-called Synodicon of Orthodoxy. The original Synodicon, which was intended to be read in all churches on the first Sunday of Lent, was composed soon after 843 and was a condemnation of Iconoclasm. For the next two centuries no additions were made to it, but from about 1050 onwards new condemnations and anathemas began to be appended. The first victim was a certain Gerontius of Lampe (otherwise unknown) who called himself the Anointed and 'vomited forth in Crete the poison of his detestable heresy'. Then it was the turn of the philosopher Italus of whom more will be said in Chapter 6. Next came the Calabrian monk Nilus who had some odd views about the divinization of Christ's human nature, then Eustratius, an ex-professor and metropolitan of Nicaea, who erred on roughly the same topic, and, in the middle of the twelfth century, the patriarch elect of Antioch, Soterichus Panteugenes, who came to grief on the question of whether the eucharistic sacrifice was offered to the Father alone or to the Trinity.[44] It is true that most of these 'errors' were of a purely academic nature and could hardly have been understood by many people; even so, the Church was eager to assert its authority and to be seen to be so doing. The emperor, too, was lending his power to this laudable end. In 1114 Alexius I came in contact with Bogomils and Paulicians at Philippopolis (Plovdiv), a town that was almost entirely 'Manichaean', and he is said to have himself disputed with the heretics for days on end, with the result that many thousands were converted to Orthodoxy.[45] The evil, however, had reached Constantinople, where a multitude of people succumbed to it, even in the best houses. Alexius apprehended the leader of the sect, a certain monk Basil, and tricked him into confessing his errors. Basil, who refused to renounce them, was condemned to be burnt, while his disciples ended their days in a dungeon. A great pyre was lit in the hippodrome and when the executioners had tossed the heretic into it, there was neither smell of burning flesh nor smoke – nothing but a thin line of vapour, for even the elements rose up to confound the impious. That was the last public act of the admirable emperor who died soon thereafter. Bogomilism, however, continued to prosper. It expanded into Serbia and Bosnia, into Italy and southern France. It even breached the defences of Mount Athos and, in the Balkans, survived the Byzantine Empire.

Nearly all Byzantine dissent assumed the form of religious heresy. Historians have searched high and low for national and social causes – the 'real' causes of which heresy was only the mask – but, on the whole, their efforts have not been rewarded. Among the examples we have reviewed, very few can be associated with break-away national tendencies: the Samaritans in the fifth and sixth centuries and the Monophysite Armenians may come under this heading. The Paulicians, too, had an independent state for the span of about twenty years, but that was the result of very particular circumstances that had nothing to do with dualism *per se*. As we have seen, the Bogomils were quite pacific in their behaviour and had no political aspirations that we know about. While the majority of them were doubtless Slavs, they attracted a following among many other nationalities.

The quest for social causes has proved equally inconclusive. In no case can we establish a clear connection between a heresy and a social class. The Manichaeans are known to have numbered many merchants, but also intellectuals, aristocrats and ordinary people. The Paulicians attracted a considerable number of soldiers. The Bogomils appear to have been largely of the peasant class, but also included minor clergy and, if Anna Comnena is to be trusted, members of some of the better families of Constantinople. Of course, it may be argued that some heresies, and the dualist ones in particular, had a social implication insofar as they discouraged marriage and procreation. Given the chronic manpower shortage of the Empire, the government might have been concerned about such doctrines, but if it was concerned for that reason, it never said so. Besides, Christian monasticism, which normally enjoyed the highest esteem, produced the same demographic effect.

The truth of the matter is that the term 'heresy' covers a diversity of phenomena that would not have been considered under the same heading were it not for the fact that State Orthodoxy lumped them all together. There were sects of a judaizing character, such as the Quartodecimans and the Athingani, whose origin went back to the earliest days of Christianity and which were content to vegetate in rural districts of Asia Minor. Their 'deviation' was largely due to questions of ritual. Then there were the 'noble' heresies which resulted from more advanced theological speculation and some of which differed from Orthodoxy only in matters of terminology. If we make allowance for the fact that certain key words such as 'nature', 'essence', 'person' were not always understood in the same sense, it is difficult to find anything that is fundamentally wrong in the doctrine of a Nestorius or a Severus of Antioch, not to mention such an eminent theologian as Theodore of Mopsuestia who was unjustly and needlessly condemned at the Fifth Council. The story of the 'noble' heresies may be full of political intrigue, but in themselves they were not intended to be subversive. And once a separate Church had been formed, attachment to it became a matter of inherited allegiance. A man who was born a Monophysite remained a Monophysite except under duress; and I know of no instance of a Catholic converting to Monophysitism as a gesture of hostility to the State.

Only in the case of the dualist heresies are we on somewhat different ground. Procopius, in describing events he knew very well, since they concerned his native city of Caesarea in Palestine, has this to say of the Samaritans who were forced by Justinian to embrace Christianity: 'Most of them, resentful of the fact that they were made to change their ancestral beliefs by law rather than of their own free will, immediately inclined to the Manichaeans and the so-called Polytheists.'[46] A later attestation concerns the soldiers who were disbanded in 786 by the empress Irene because of their support of Iconoclasm: they, too, joined the Manichaeans, or Paulicians.[47] It is not surprising that dualism should have attracted disgruntled elements since it represented itself as a movement of radical reform to regain those truths of Christianity that had been deliberately obscured by the State-sponsored clergy.[48] The appeal of such an attitude may be gauged from the fact that dualism was the only form of Byzantine heresy that spread widely across ethnic and geographical boundaries.

The real villain of the story is, of course, State Orthodoxy. 'We know', wrote Justinian, 'that nothing pleases merciful God so much as unanimity of belief on the part of all Christians in the matter of the true and stainless faith.'[49] Nor was unanimity of belief sufficient; as time went on, uniformity of liturgical practice, of feast and fast days, of dress and hair style became equally if not more important. If complete tolerance was impossible to achieve, persecution, at least, could have been avoided. Even so strict a cleric as Theodore the Studite proclaimed that the role of the Church was to instruct heretics, not to kill them.[50] The State, identified with the Orthodox Church, often thought otherwise. It was a direct result of its intolerance that millions of potentially loyal subjects of the emperor were turned into heretics and hence into enemies.

CHAPTER 5

MONASTICISM

No other aspect of Byzantine life is as amply documented as monasticism. We possess hundreds of biographies of holy monks, countless meditations, epistles, sermons, exhortations and justifications dealing with the monastic condition. We have, in addition, a number of rules, disciplinary canons, imperial edicts, even a considerable body of archival material. Yet, in spite of this overabundant harvest of literature, it is no easy matter to give an account of Byzantine monasticism in terms that would be understandable to us today.

One point has to be made at the outset: monasticism was a lay movement. It was akin to, and may have developed from, certain groupings of Christians who led a particularly austere and dedicated life, without, however, withdrawing from the world. Such men were known as *spoudaioi* (the zealous or earnest ones) or *philoponoi* (the industrious ones), while in the Syriac-speaking provinces they were called 'the sons of the Covenant'; and they possessed some form of organization of which, unfortunately, very little is known. If we consult the Life of St Antony, who is regarded as the father of monasticism, we find that he began his spiritual endeavours (in about 270 AD) by following the precepts of whatever *spoudaioi* he happened to meet and learning from them 'the advantages of zeal [*spoudê*] and training [*askêsis*]'. In those days, we are told, regular monasteries did not yet exist in Egypt, nor did solitaries live in the desert, 'but every man who wished to attend to himself would practise solitary training not far from his own village'.[1] The decisive step that Antony took – and he may not have been the first to take it – was to remove himself, initially to an empty tomb and then to the desert. Withdrawal or flight from one's village (*anachôrêsis*) had been since the first century AD a common phenomenon in Egypt in the case of impoverished people who found themselves unable to pay their taxes.[2] No such motives may be imputed to Antony who was a rich farmer and who voluntarily gave away his possessions, but it is quite possible that the rapid diffusion of the monastic movement was not unconnected with the prevalence of *anachôrêsis* as an escape from the burdens of everyday life.

Indeed, monasticism proved an immediate success. Precisely how this came about we do not know because we are very poorly informed about the first eighty or hundred years of the movement. Our earliest reliable sources date from about the middle of the fourth century, by which time it had spread to many parts of the Roman world and claimed tens of thousands of adherents. If it is true, as is generally believed, that monasticism started in Egypt, it must have reached Palestine, Syria and Mesopotamia within a very short period. We find it established in northern Asia Minor before 340 and by about 350 there were already some monks in western Europe.

At an early stage of its development in Egypt monasticism assumed the two forms that were to become classical and persist throughout the Byzantine period, namely the solitary and the communal. St Antony was the model of the former. His *askêsis* consisted essentially in isolation, prayer and fasting. While he often went without sleep, never washed and never anointed his body with oil, he did not impose on himself any of the bizarre penances that we find in later periods. His adversaries were the demons who tempted him, first with thoughts of his former comforts and family, then with lascivious desires, finally with terrifying visions of wild beasts: we must remember that to Egyptians the desert was a frightening zone peopled by monsters. When, at the age of fifty-five (*c.* 306 AD), Antony emerged victorious from his seclusion, he appeared, as it were, transfigured: he had not aged physically, while he had acquired a spiritual firmness, the gift of teaching and the ability of healing the sick. Then it was that he persuaded many persons to adopt the solitary life, 'and thus monasteries were set up in the mountains and the desert was settled by monks who had gone forth from their homes'.[3] The next fifty years of his life – he died in 356 at the age of 105 – were spent more in public. Distinguished persons came to seek his healing powers, pagan philosophers disputed with him, even the Emperor Constantine wrote him a letter which he did not wish to receive until he had been assured that the emperor was a Christian – something Antony did not seem to know. All in all, a remarkable career for an Egyptian peasant who never learnt any Greek and remained illiterate to the end of his life.

The communal (coenobitic) form of monasticism was set up in

Upper Egypt by Antony's younger contemporary Pachomius (d. 346). After serving in the imperial army and apprenticing himself to a hermit, Pachomius decided that the military model was best suited for monastic life. The establishment he set up at Tabennêsi, on the right bank of the Nile, was envisaged as a walled camp neatly divided into 'houses', each under a commanding officer. Monks were grouped in houses according to their occupation or craft and spent much of their time pursuing manual labour; they worked together, worshipped together and ate together. Particular emphasis was laid on obedience: ordinary monks were subject to the chief of their house who, in turn, reported to the abbot. By the time he died, Pachomius had become the leader of a chain of about a dozen men's monasteries and three nunneries, numbering in all several thousand inmates.

It was said that an angel of the Lord revealed to Pachomius a rule, or a set of detailed regulations, inscribed on a bronze tablet. We need not enquire whether Pachomius himself or one of his immediate successors was the author of this document which was translated from Coptic into Greek and from Greek into Latin. The fullest text that has come down to us is Jerome's Latin version made in 404.[4] It pictures a monastery surrounded by a wall and enclosing a chapel, a refectory, a room for the sick and a hostel for strangers. Monks slept in individual cells which had no locks, and were not allowed any property except a mat, two sleeveless garments, one cape and a few other essentials. Neither fasting (twice a week) nor prayer was excessive. Some knowledge of the Scriptures and a minimum of literacy were required (*etiam nolens legere compelletur*), but no need was felt for further education. Whatever they were doing, monks were required to keep a distance of one cubit from one another; they could not speak to anyone in the dark, could not leave the compound without permission (and then only in pairs) and on their return could not narrate anything they had heard outside. What, we may well wonder, was the attraction of this regimented life to which thousands of men and women flocked? Clearly, Pachomius did not impose excessive demands on entrants, and seemed to be intent on drawing as large a following as possible of ordinary people to whom he offered comradeship and a minimum standard of material security. The Rule shows awareness of the danger of admitting criminals and runaway slaves,[5] but the screening process was rudimentary and there can be little doubt that considerable numbers of robbers, debtors and misfits of every description sought anonymity behind the conventual walls.

Both in its solitary and its coenobitic form monasticism posed a threat to the established Church. The monk, it should be repeated, was a Christian layman who followed literally Christ's injunction, 'If thou wilt be perfect, go and sell that thou hast, and thou shalt have treasure in heaven' (Mt. 19. 21). He sought to be the perfect Christian, to return to the simplicity of apostolic times when 'all that believed were together, and had all things common; and sold their possessions and goods, and parted them to all men' (Acts 2. 44–5). He held that there was only one morality, one *askêsis*, namely that of the Gospel, and that, ideally speaking, all Christians would become monks. Significantly, however, he sought perfection not through the Church, but outside it. Even St Antony attained sanctity without any recourse to the clergy and felt no need during his twenty years of reclusion to take communion. His whole way of life was an implicit condemnation of the Church 'in the world'. Whereas Origen had counselled a moral rather than a physical segregation from everything that was unholy, the monk was proclaiming the virtual impossibility of winning salvation without physical withdrawal. The ministry of the Church, its liturgy, its predication appeared to be almost irrelevant.

The alarm felt by some members of the episcopacy is apparent in the Canons of the Council of Gangra (*c.* 341 AD) which constitute, incidentally, one of our earliest documents concerning monasticism. The trouble was caused by a certain Eustathius who had acquired a considerable following in the province of Pontus. The practices he encouraged, if we may believe the bishops gathered at Gangra, were the following: he broke up marriages by teaching that married persons had no hope of salvation; he held churches in contempt and organized his own services; he and his followers wore strange clothes and caused women to put on men's garments and cut off their hair (the very hair that God had given them as a reminder of their submission to men); he diverted to his own uses the offerings made by the faithful; he encouraged slaves to abandon their masters; he urged the rich to give up all their possessions; he did not recognize married priests; he disregarded the fasts of the Church and abominated the eating of flesh.[6] Clearly, Eustathius was subverting that very social order on which both the moral authority and the material livelihood of the Church depended; yet he was not branded as a heretic, was later made bishop and exerted considerable influence on St Basil who is universally regarded as a pillar of the Church.

The prestige of St Athanasius, bishop of Alexandria, contributed to gloss over the opposition between Church and monasticism. Whether from personal conviction or a shrewd calculation, he stood up as a public champion of the monastic movement.[7] His Life of Antony was a manifesto in which he laid great stress on the hermit's respect (supposed or real) for the secular clergy. He certainly used Antony as a tool in his doctrinal disputes with heretics. Many other bishops acted in the same spirit with the result that a compromise was adopted. Whereas a Eustathius would have argued that Christian perfection was unattainable in the world and even St Basil thought it was difficult to achieve,[8] there developed an acceptance of the 'two ways': monasticism was the high road to Heaven, but life in the world, if properly regulated by the Church, offered a possibility of reaching the same destination, though in a less direct fashion. Not the same *askêsis* for all Christians, but a harsher one for monks and a laxer one for laymen. Besides, it was argued, the existence of monks was highly beneficial for the public at large, even for the welfare and security of the State. For the monk by dint of self-abnegation and mourning attained a state of freedom from the passions (*apatheia*) akin to that of the angels which won for him familiarity (*parrhêsia*) with God. His prayers, therefore, were particularly efficacious. And if the Lord had been prepared to spare Sodom for the sake of ten righteous men, would he not show favour to a State that contained several thousands of holy monks?

The story of eastern monasticism after Antony and Pachomius is one of geographical expansion, local adaptation and unconscious evolution rather than one of planned reform. The solitary and coenobitic models were combined in a variety of ways. In Palestine, where monasticism is said to have been introduced at the very beginning of the fourth century by St Hilarion, a disciple of St Antony, there developed a special type of monastery known as the *lavra* grouping a number of individual cells or caves round a communal house. The cells were inhabited by semi-solitaries who gathered together for worship on Saturdays and Sundays. The prestige of the Holy Land served as a stimulus to monastic growth that assumed an international form: among the great names associated with Palestine, St Gerasimus (famous for his tame lion) was a Lycian, while both St Theodosius the Coenobiarch and St Sabas were Cappadocians. Of whatever national origin, scores of monasteries sprang up all round Jerusalem and Bethlehem, by the Jordan and the Dead Sea – at least 140 are known from textual evidence. No less successful was monasticism in Syria and Mesopotamia where, as far as we know, it first appeared in the reign of Constantine, predominantly in its anachoretic form, and was soon swept to extraordinary excesses of self-mortification. Some solitaries chose to live like wild beasts, eschewing the use of fire and feeding on whatever grew spontaneously – they were known as 'grazers' (*boskoi*). Others loaded themselves with chains or shut themselves up in cages, while St Symeon Stylites (d. 459) won international renown by standing upright on a pillar whose height was gradually raised to forty cubits, thus marking his ascension to God. The only 'dendrite' among Byzantine saints was the Mesopotamian David who betook himself to Thessalonica, to perch there on a tree like a bird.

In 357 the youthful St Basil, who was drawn to the monastic life by the example of his devout mother and sister, undertook a journey to Mesopotamia, Syria, Palestine and Egypt to observe various kinds of *askêsis* and choose the one that was most suitable. He came to the conclusion that Antonian anachoretism, while admirable in some respects, had the grave disadvantage of offering no scope for fraternal charity and no opportunity of observing all the Lord's commandments; besides, every man stood in need of correction by example or advice – something that could not be achieved in isolation. Basil decided, therefore, in favour of coenobitism, but he rightly judged the Pachomian houses to be too big for proper supervision. The community he set up at Annesi in Pontus after he had returned from his travels was a coenobium of more modest size, and that became the norm throughout the Byzantine period. As has often been observed, there never existed in the Greek Church a 'Basilian Order' or, for that matter, any other monastic 'order'; but Basil's status as one of the major Church Fathers did lead to a widespread acceptance of his monastic ideal which he set down in considerable detail in two works known as *The Longer* and *The Shorter Rules*.[9]

It was, however, from Syria that monasticism reached Constantinople. It seems to have been introduced by the Syrian Isaac who won a measure of fame by predicting to the heretical Emperor Valens his defeat at the hands of the Goths (378). The monastery he founded in *c.* 382 came to be known by the name of his successor Dalmatos, also an oriental and a former officer of the imperial guard. What appears to have been the second oldest monastery was set up by the Syrian Dios. Possibly third in seniority was that of Rufinianae, founded by the praetorian prefect Rufinus (392–5) near his suburban villa, where he established a group of Egyptian monks who, however, soon departed. The more famous monastery of the

'Sleepless Ones' (Akoimêtoi), who kept up an unceasing doxology by means of three teams that officiated in turn, was established in *c* 420, also by Syrians.

The attraction that the capital exercised on oriental monks may be perceived in an eminently curious document, the Life of St Daniel the Stylite (d. 493).[10] Daniel was born in the region of Samosata, entered a monastery near his native village at the age of twelve and eventually became its abbot. At that time Symeon the Stylite was at the height of his fame and Daniel evidently saw all the advantages he could gain by adopting this novel and spectacular type of *askêsis*. For maximum publicity there was no place like Constantinople. The idea struck Daniel while he was on a pilgrimage to Jerusalem. Callously abandoning the community he had been chosen to direct, he betook himself to 'the second Jerusalem', even though he could speak no Greek. Arriving there, he selected a suitable spot on the European side of the Bosphorus, at a village called Anaplous, close enough to the capital to attract attention. At first he had some trouble with the locals, but he established his reputation by taking on the demons in a disused pagan temple and curing the patriarch Anatolius of a disease. Then came a stroke of luck: on the death of Symeon the Stylite a Syrian monk named Sergius arrived at the capital to present to the Emperor Leo I the great ascetic's leather cowl. Unable to gain an audience, Sergius took up residence with Daniel, his fellow-countryman. The time had come to try the column trick. With the help of a palace official, a fairly low column (twice a man's height) was set up next to a vineyard belonging to another Syrian who happened to be attached to the emperor's table. In this way Daniel came to the notice of high dignitaries and the imperial family. Everyone trouped out to see the new attraction: the empress offered to set up Daniel on her own property if he agreed to move (he refused); the ex-prefect Cyrus celebrated the Syrian wonder in an elegiac inscription. Daniel, following Symeon's example, ascended a second column that was taller than the first; then a third, whose foundations were laid by the emperor himself to whom Daniel had foretold the birth of a son. A monastic complex was built with the column as a focus and a martyrium was dedicated to St Symeon whose relics were brought from Antioch and deposited with great pomp. Admittedly, Daniel's life was not a bed of roses, and in transplanting 'stylitism' from the warmer climate of Syria to the shores of the Bosphorus, he had to reckon with the winter snow: on one occasion he nearly froze to death. That, however, was a professional hazard. In his lifetime Daniel proved an enormous success and Constantinople was only too happy to have a stylite of its own.

The early monasteries were established not in the city proper, but outside the Constantinian walls, and the same was generally the case elsewhere. The presence of monks in cities was actually prohibited by a law of no less pious an emperor than Theodosius I who ordered them to inhabit 'desert places and desolate solitudes'. This law proved to be counter-productive and was repealed two years later.[11] Even so, there was a general feeling that monks had no place among the temptations and bustle of a city: at Antioch they were jeered at and dragged through the streets – and this by Christians.[12] In the countryside, on the other hand, the monk was a familiar figure and, if he happened to be a noted ascetic, he fulfilled a real social purpose: he healed diseases in people and cattle, cast out demons and disinfected, if one may say so, places made dangerous by pagan association. In short, he was a kind of witch doctor. How important he was in his rural district, how much deference he enjoyed from the local population, may vividly be seen in the Life of St Theodore of Sykeon[13] and many other texts. Was the monk, then, to be denied the same role in cities? By the sixth century it came to be accepted that a trained ascetic who was proof against all temptations of the flesh could properly undertake an urban ministry if he concealed his true identity. And so there came into being a curious category of saints, that of the 'holy fools'. The idea of simulating madness was not in itself new, but when it first appeared in the fourth century, it was in a coenobitic context, and the purpose of the exercise was to add to one's humiliations on earth so as to reap a greater reward in Heaven. A different motivation seems to have inspired the most famous 'holy fool' who acted in an urban context, St Symeon of Emesa (mid-sixth century):[14] he was bent on reforming the most despised elements of society, such as prostitutes and actors, and on converting Jews and heretics. To do so inconspicuously and , as it were, playfully, he pretended to be a harmless lunatic: he did odd jobs in taverns, consorted with loose women, misbehaved in church, deliberately violated Christian fasts, while practising in secret the strictest *askêsis*. Had not St Paul said, 'If any man seemeth to be wise in this world, let him become a fool, that he may be wise' (I Cor. 3. 18)? For obvious reasons St Symeon did not find many imitators, but the tradition of 'folly for the sake of Christ' never died out in the Byzantine world and eventually passed to Russia.

The fifth and sixth centuries marked the peak of the monastic movement in the East. Courted by the aristocracy and by emperors, encouraged by bishops, the new Christian 'philosophers' basked in the notoriety they were meant to avoid. Anecdotes about the exploits, miracles, predictions and memorable dicta of monks were collected and avidly read. For Egypt we have the *Historia monachorum* (*c.* 400) and the *Lausiac History* by Palladius (419–20), for Syria the *Historia religiosa* by Theodoret (*c.* 444). In addition to these famous works as well as individual Lives of prominent monastic saints, there circulated in all the languages of the Near East countless stories, often stereotyped and interchangeable, that eventually found their way into the collections called *paterica* (books of the Fathers). Yet, the most eloquent memorial to the prestige of monasticism is surely the huge complex of Qal'at Sim'an built by imperial initiative as the pilgrimage centre of Symeon the Stylite. What greater tribute could have been paid by civilization to bigotry?

From being willing outcasts from society the monks became, therefore, popular heroes and members of the establishment. The price they were asked to pay was regulation by and subjection to the ecclesiastical authorities. Already in the fifth century we find the monks of a diocese being controlled by a 'village bishop' (*chôrepiskopos*) or a visitor (*periodeutês*) or else placed under the authority of an exarch. Justinian tried to go even further: while recognizing the exceptional sanctity of the monastic life, he ruled that no monastery could be founded without the bishop's consent, and that the bishop, too, would appoint the abbot. He also decreed that all postulants should undergo a three-year probation, that all the monks of a given monastery, except for anchorites, should sleep in the same building so as to observe one another more closely, and that they should be severely discouraged from changing their place of residence.[15] One need not suppose that this ordinance was fully observed. Monasticism was too fluid, too dispersed and too influential to submit to such regulations. It was also beginning to acquire considerable economic wealth. Later Byzantine history proves that it retained its independence *vis-à-vis* the established Church.

As the Early Byzantine Empire was crumbling to pieces, a Cilician monk called John Moschus, who died as a refugee in Rome (634), painted a memorable picture of eastern monasticism as he had known it. He called it *The Meadow*.[16] In the tradition of earlier *paterica* it is a series of edifying anecdotes that Moschus had picked up in the course of his travels. The world he was familiar with, that of Orthodox monasticism, had already shrunk as a result of the Monophysite schism: it was centred on Palestine, extended to the south to Mount Sinai and Alexandria, but not far into Egypt, to the north and west to Cilicia, Cyprus and some of the Greek islands. A constellation of ascetics, whose fame spread by word of mouth, illuminated this world. They cultivated continence, poverty, silence, charity. Among them were a few stylites and 'grazers', but the more extreme forms of mortification were generally avoided. There was a keen spirit of competition in achieving virtue, but also a feeling that the heroic age of monasticism had passed. If Moschus shows himself intolerant, it is towards the Monophysites, but his good-natured narrative hardly allows us to suspect that next to his world, the 'internationale' of Orthodox monks, there existed a parallel world, that of the Monophysite monks who, under persecution, cultivated, perhaps with occasional excesses, much of the same virtues, who worked the same miracles and obtained the same signs from heaven. To penetrate this other world the reader may be referred to *The Lives of the Eastern Saints* by John of Ephesus.[17]

Of all social classes the monks were perhaps the least vulnerable to the catastrophe of the seventh century. Some, it is true, were massacred, while others fled to the West – to Carthage, Sicily and Rome, where we already find them well represented at the Lateran Council of 649. But even under Arab rule Orthodox monks were able to retain their principal establishments in Palestine (these were suppressed in the early ninth century) as well as Mount Sinai. St John Damascene was the most famous, but not the last representative of Orthodox monasticism in Palestine.

Unexpectedly, it was in the Byzantine Empire rather than under the infidel that monasticism was dealt its severest blow. When the Isaurian emperors made Iconoclasm the official doctrine of the realm, the secular clergy did not put up much of a fight, as we have already noted; it was the monks who organized a resistance movement. That they did so does not mean that they had a particular, 'monkish' interest in defending 'superstition' or that they derived a material benefit from the worship of icons, as some historians have suggested. It was simply that their unique authority *vis-à-vis* the people made them the natural champions of traditional religious observance. Besides, they were not quite as susceptible to government pressure as were the bishops. When driven away from one place they could go to another, even beyond the frontiers of the Empire, since the network of their connections extended both to Palestine and to Italy. However that may be, when the persecution of the iconophiles broke out in earnest in the 760s, monks were the chief victims. The Emperor Constantine v had a particular aversion to them and called them 'unmentionables'. He forced them to marry, subjected them to public derision and secularized some of the most famous monasteries of Constantinople. The persecution in western Asia Minor was, we are told, even more severe because of the zeal of the local governor, Michael Lachanodrakon. He rounded up at Ephesus all the monks and nuns in his province and said to them: 'Whoever wishes to obey the emperor and myself, let him put on a white garment and take a wife forthwith. Those who refuse to do so will be blinded and banished to Cyprus.' The order was immediately carried out and many proved to be martyrs that day, while others, our chronicler adds sadly, broke their vows and lost their souls.[18]

It was a great day for the monks when the last of the Isaurians, Leo iv, died (784) and an even greater day when Iconoclasm was officially condemned by the Seventh Ecumenical Council (787) in which they were well represented – emissaries from 132 monasteries, mostly in Constantinople and Bithynia, attended the sessions. For some thirty years thereafter there was a great surge of monastic construction, followed by a second period of tribulation when Iconoclasm was re-introduced (815–43). Once again, monks led the resistance. This time they were better organized, thanks especially to the unflagging activity of St Theodore the Studite. Descended from a prominent family of civil servants, well educated and well connected, Theodore was, above all, a practical man and a strict disciplinarian. He wished to reform monasticism by infusing it with the spirit of the early Fathers. He was interested not in mystical contemplation, but in hard work, poverty and obedience. He insisted that monks should not own slaves or any female animals (an abuse he particularly deplored); that they should not go out needlessly, should not contract any family links (such as that of godfather) with laymen, should hold everything in common and distribute to the poor any income that exceeded their needs.[19] Theodore's ideal was rather akin to that of Pachomius whom he also resembled in that he headed a confederation of monasteries numbering in all about a thousand monks. In order to achieve his aims he had to set up a hierarchy of command (assistant abbot, administrator, assistant administrator, store-keeper, disciplinary officers, and so on) and even institute a kind of gaol in which disobedient and careless monks were subjected to a diet of bread and water since correction by scourging was suitable only for laymen.[20] We may be grateful to Theodore that he laid emphasis, among other manual occupations, on the copying of books and thus helped to create a famous scriptorium at the Studius monastery.

Monasticism emerged greatly strengthened from the iconoclastic troubles. It had added a new series of martyrs and confessors to the calendar of the Eastern Church; it had also established itself as the voice of religious conscience whenever bishops were forced to compromise on matters of doctrine or discipline. The first patriarch of Constantinople after the 'triumph of Orthodoxy', Methodius (843–7), was an ex-monk; so was his successor Ignatius (847–58). There is ample evidence that the founding of new monasteries and the extension of existing ones went on apace in the ninth, tenth and following centuries, so much so that after a time the imperial government grew alarmed. In 935 Romanus I Lecapenus decreed that monasteries would be barred from acquiring the lands of peasants even by way of donation,[21] and the same prohibition was repeated by Constantine VII in 947. Nicephorus Phocas went further in 964. In a well-known constitution of that year[22] he roundly castigated the monastic establishment for their insatiable greed, for the acquisition of vast tracts of land, superb buildings and innumerable heads of cattle. This was not, he reminded them, the way in which the desert Fathers had lived. He then went on to decree that no new monasteries were to be founded. He suggested instead that old ones that had fallen into decay might be rehabilitated, but not through the donation of lands. Even ruined monasteries owned sufficient fields: what they lacked was the manpower and the animals to make the land productive. The only loopholes that Nicephorus allowed concerned monasteries which through mismanagement had lost their lands (such cases were to be investigated by government agents) and the founding of cells and *lavrai* provided these did not acquire any real estate. Now Nicephorus was a fervent admirer of the monastic life and cannot be charged with anti-clerical feelings. The main thrust of his law was to make monastic lands productive while stemming the constant erosion of peasants' holdings.

Further regulations, introduced by Basil II in 996, reveal the workings of monasticism at village level. A peasant, he says, would become a monk, build a chapel and assign his land to it. He might be joined by a couple of others. On their death the local bishop would seize the property on the pretext it was a monastery, and either keep it himself or attribute it to a lay potentate. The emperor ruled that such chapels did not have the status of monasteries and ought to revert to the village commune; the bishop's role was to be limited to supervising the conduct of the resident monks and he was forbidden to collect any dues from them. The name of monastery was to be reserved to establishments numbering a minimum of eight to ten monks. These would fall under the jurisdiction of the bishop who would be free to assign them at will, provided they did not acquire any more land.[23]

To grasp the complexity of the situation, we must bear in mind several facts. First, a Byzantine monastery was normally an agricultural concern which, if properly managed, produced a profit in addition to the contributions levied on new entrants and other donations. Secondly, a monastery's estates were, by imperial and canon law, inalienable, which meant that they could either remain static or grow. Thirdly, the ownership of monasteries was vested in a variety of bodies: some were imperial, others patriarchal or episcopal; some were privately owned through descent from the founder or some other reason; some were entirely independent. We may assume that in each case the owner drew whatever surplus the monastery produced and was in a position to exert considerable influence on the internal affairs of the establishment. The play of interests was thus extremely complex. Unless a monastery happened to be independent (*autodespoton* or *autexousion*), the monks themselves were not the main beneficiaries. Of course, they obtained a living which may have been fairly comfortable; basically, however, they were the overseers who stood between the owner and the agricultural labourers.

Towards the latter part of the tenth century we find yet another form of monastic administration. As already indicated by Basil II, a convent would be assigned to a lay patron (known as *charistikarios*) who gained complete control of its estates and revenues for the duration of his lifetime and could occasionally pass it on to his heir, but not beyond the third generation. The abuses which this system could engender were obvious: a patron could, and often did, completely despoil a monastery. Besides, monasteries became little more than assets that were exchanged and traded. The philosopher Michael Psellus, who was no less shrewd than Voltaire in his financial dealings, acquired rights over more than a dozen monasteries. And what if the patron was a man of low morals or, worse still, a foreigner? Some indignant voices rose in protest.[24] Yet the Church itself took no steps to abolish the system which, after reaching a peak in the eleventh century, appears to have declined somewhat, but remained in force until the end of the Empire. The reason may have been that the Church simply could not manage the enormous number of monasteries under its nominal jurisdiction and reckoned that, whatever abuses were perpetrated, it was better to have them administered by influential laymen than not at all.

We know a great deal about monastic properties from the eleventh century onwards and we shall know even more when the archives of Mount Athos are published in their entirety.[25] There is also the testimony of architectural monuments. It is surely no coincidence that the most splendid religious buildings of the Middle Byzantine period happen to be monastic. If we may limit ourselves to Greece, all the major surviving churches from about the year 850 onwards belonged to monasteries: Skripou, Hosios Loukas, Nea Moni on Chios, Daphni and so until the end of the Empire. No such splendour and ostentation is found in any episcopal or parish church.

Had John Moschus been allowed to rise from the dead and make a tour of Byzantine monasteries in the eleventh or twelfth century, he would surely have been surprised and not a little saddened. Yet, on the face of it, nothing had changed: the same ideals were ostensibly pursued, the same disciplinary canons were applied (or, more probably, not applied), the same definition of monastic life continued to be held up by preachers. There were, as before, solitaries, stylites, coenobia and even *lavrai* on the Palestinian model. The geography of monasticism had, of course, greatly changed. While monasteries were dotted in all Byzantine lands, including, by now, the cities, there arose a number of important centres. The most notable, from the eighth century onwards, was the Bithynian Olympus (modern Uludağ) with much of the surrounding countryside. Here lived St Platon, the uncle of Theodore the Studite, Theodore himself, St Methodius, the future patriarch, St Theophanes Confessor, St Ionnicius the Great, St Methodius, the future apostle of the Slavs, and a host of lesser saints whose hour of glory coincided with the second Iconoclastic persecution. The second great centre, from the late tenth century onwards, was Mount Athos which eventually eclipsed all other holy mountains. Mount Latmos (Latros) near Miletus rose to prominence before the tenth century and Mount Galesion near Ephesus in the eleventh. Among lesser centres we may mention Mount Kyminas, somewhere on the borders of Bithynia, and Mount Ganos in Thrace. What is rather remarkable is that central and eastern Asia Minor (except for Pontus) figure very little in the annals of Byzantine monasticism. Many monasteries doubtless existed in Cappadocia, but they have left practically no written record.

There was certainly scope for a reform of eastern monasticism, particularly in the eleventh century when the structure of society was undergoing important changes. Some ferment in monastic circles did occur and one figure, that of Symeon the New Theologian, stands out. Symeon (c. 949–1022) was a mystic, not a reformer, but he exerted considerable influence in two respects. Probably reacting against the dull materialism of contemporary monasteries, he proclaimed the purpose of spiritual life to be an inner transformation which led to a direct vision of God manifested in the guise of an ineffable light. He also insisted on the importance of total obedience to a spiritual mentor whose God-given authority of 'binding and loosing' exceeded that of any priest appointed by men. Of course, Symeon belonged to a mystical current that had distant antecedents in the Eastern Church, a current that can be traced back through St Maximus Confessor to Origen; what is, however, remarkable in the present context is the outspokenness with which he assailed the established clergy. He argued that bishops and priests had altogether lost by their unworthy conduct the gift of grace they had received from the apostles and become no better than laymen. Only the pretence and the outer garb of priesthood remained, while the spiritual gift had passed to monks – not to all monks by any means, but to those whose virtue was made visible by signs. They were the only true Christians, the successors of the apostles.[26]

Understandably, Symeon caused considerable irritation to the ecclesiastical authorities and was even banished from the capital. He had, however, the good fortune of belonging to a prominent family and living in a fairly tolerant period, otherwise he would have suffered a harsher fate, especially since his doctrine smacked of Messalianism. Had he also been less of an enthusiast, he might have realized that monasticism had become practically as inert as the secular clergy. Indeed, far from acting as the voice of Orthodox conscience, it was itself coming under the attack of bishops. We may pause to examine the case against the monks as stated by Eustathius of Thessalonica in the late twelfth century.[27]

Eustathius was no ascetic and he conceded that monks had a right to live well, provided they did so tastefully. He quotes a story concerning the Emperor Manuel i Comnenus who one night decided to prepare a banquet for a nobleman's wedding. The necessary foodstuffs being unavailable in the palace at such a late hour, an emissary was sent to the nearby monastery of St John in Petra. Although it was Tyrophagy week (the week before Lent), the good monks had no trouble in providing different kinds of bread, dry and sweet wine, fruit, olives, cheese, fresh and pickled fish as well as red and black caviar, the latter imported from the river Don. This, in the eyes of Eustathius, was a laudable example of monastic surplus. The trouble with the monks he had to deal with, possibly those of Mount Athos, was that they were both greedy and boorish. They were recruited from the lowest strata of society, among weavers, tailors, coppersmiths, leather-workers, beggars and thieves. As a result they were nearly illiterate, never read any books (indeed, they sold books from monastic libraries) and were unwilling to admit any educated postulants. Instead of 'philosophizing' in their monasteries, they spent most of their time in the market place and had a great expertise in buying cheaply and selling dearly. They drew exorbitant rents from their tenants, deliberately defrauded rich donors, faked property deeds, went hunting, carried arms. Many of them kept their personal estates and even added to them; some engaged in trade and usury. To cap it all, monks held the clergy in contempt. They continually harassed bishops and caused calculated damage to episcopal lands by closing off roads and diverting water.

While bishops and monks hurled accusations at one another, life in monasteries went on as before. To illustrate its course I have chosen two examples, very nearly contemporary and both belonging to the same province, namely Cyprus. The first, that of the monastery of Machairas, is surely the more typical of the two. The second, that of St Neophytus, reveals a remarkable personality and the fate of his endeavours.

The story of Machairas is known from the *typikon* of the monastery.[28] About the middle of the twelfth century a Palestinian hermit, Neophytus (not to be confused with his more famous namesake just mentioned), left the desert near the Jordan river and came to Cyprus where he set up a hut on a steep mountain and was fed by the peasants. He was accompanied by one disciple, Ignatius. Neophytus died and Ignatius took on another companion. The two of them began having more ambitious ideas and so they went to Constantinople to present a petition to the emperor. Manuel I granted them the mountain and its surroundings free of charge and a yearly income of fifty gold pieces. He also decreed that the monastery should be entirely independent. This enabled Ignatius to put up a chapel and a few cells and to organize a community of five or six monks. So far, a normal story.

In the year 1172 the energetic Nilus, who appears to have been also a Palestinian, joined the brotherhood. He made himself useful by fetching food supplies from Cilicia at a time of famine and eventually was made abbot. His next step was to solicit donations from the faithful in the form of real estate and farm animals. In this he was quite successful and was able to build a church, a refectory and a residential wing, the whole complex surrounded by a ditch. The monastery was consecrated by the local bishop who was made to understand that his only right was to rubber-stamp the election of the abbot. A second delegation was sent to Constantinople and received from the Emperor Isaac II (1185–95) the grant of an orchard from the Crown domains at Nicosia and a tax exemption of twelve gold pieces. This was followed by a chrysobull of the Emperor Alexius II (1195–1203) giving the monastery complete exemption from tax on its lands and on twenty-four tenant farmers (*paroikoi*) in perpetuity. Both emperors could afford to be generous since neither of them held sway in Cyprus which became an independent principality in 1185 and was conquered by Richard Lionheart in 1191. But even if Nilus drew no advantage from these privileges, the properties he had accumulated were amply sufficient. By 1210, when the final version of the *typikon* was drawn up, Nilus had also founded a nunnery in the nearby town of Tamasos which was to receive 8 per cent of the net income of the monastery. Out of these 8 per cent the priests officiating in the said nunnery were to be paid twenty-four gold pieces per annum. Supposing that the priests' salary amounted to a quarter of the endowment of the nunnery (and it was probably less than that), the total yearly income would have been 1,200 gold pieces, a pretty tidy sum in those days and a far cry from the fifty gold pieces of a few decades earlier.

The provisions of the *typikon* are particularly detailed in matters of administration. The community envisaged was a large one and was not to be increased, yet special incentives were offered for the admission of distinguished persons (*periphaneis*) who could be tonsured after a probation of six months, whereas ordinary people, in accordance with Justinianic legislation, had to wait three years while performing menial tasks. In principle, admission was free, but donations were not discouraged; once made they could not be refunded. Next to the abbot, the staff included a first and a second *oikonomos*, a sacristan, two wardrobe masters (*docheiarioi*), two or more keepers of stores, a disciplinary officer, and so on. All produce was to be carefully measured in the presence of witnesses, regular accounts were to be kept, inventories checked, new clothing issued to the monks only upon receipt of the old. It may be doubted if there existed in Cyprus at the time a more efficiently organized agricultural enterprise than the monastery of Machairas. The one topic on which Nilus has very little to say is, however, education. He specifically forbids the admittance within the enclosure of lay children for schooling. Only boys who intended to become monks were to be let in to learn the Psalter and the church service in a special cell. Clearly, the monastery of Machairas was no centre of culture.

A few decades earlier another Cypriot, named Neophytus, was inspired by stricter ideals. He came from a farmer's family and when, at the age of eighteen, he entered the monastery of St Chrysostomos near Nicosia (in 1152), he could not read or write. So for five years he was made to tend the vineyards of the community, during which time he acquired the first rudiments of literacy and learnt the Psalter by heart. Consumed by a desire for the eremitic life, he was allowed to go to Palestine with a view to finding there a suitable mentor, but he was disappointed in his quest. Back in Cyprus, he decided to proceed to Mount Latmos near Miletus. He accordingly made for Paphos in the hope of boarding a ship, but was arrested on suspicion of being a fugitive and robbed of all his money, namely two gold pieces. Being now entirely penniless, he wandered off into the hinterland and found the cave in which he was to spend the remainder of his long life (he died after 1214).

His subsequent rise to fame was largely due to the bishop of Paphos, Basil Kinnamos, who, to judge by his family name, was an aristocrat from Asia Minor or Constantinople. It was he who ordained Neophytus presbyter and persuaded him to found a community. The hermit, however, was quite unlike the astute Nilus. He endeavoured to keep his monastery small and resisted the acquisition of landed property. Only after the Latin conquest (1191), when there was scarcity of food and the brotherhood was swelled by the influx of strangers, did he consent to acquire some arable land, a vineyard and a few head of cattle, but he regarded these as necessary evils.

Sitting alone in his cave (*enkleistra*), Neophytus devoted himself to literary endeavours. His learning, of course, was not very deep: it was limited to the Bible, a few Fathers of the Church and Lives of saints. Yet, for a man of his background, he read widely and, what is more, he acquired a remarkable command of ecclesiastical Greek, if not of correct spelling. He also collected books. In one passage he tells us how for thirty-seven years he had sought throughout western Cyprus a copy of St Basil's *Hexaêmeron*, but all in vain – an interesting admission, since the

Hexaêmeron was an extremely common book. Even so, Neophytus was able to assemble a library of some fifty volumes, a respectable number for a provincial monastery. As an author, Neophytus composed sixteen works of religious content which he proudly enumerates in his *typikon*. At times he also wrote verse. Yet most of his literary production, edifying and accessible as it was to a public of moderate culture, remained unread. Several of his compositions have survived in unique copies, the very same ones that the saint deposited in the library of his monastery. There they remained gathering dust until they were bought in the seventeenth century by agents of the French government.[29]

The monastery of St Neophytus has had a continuous existence until today and it cannot be said that it suffered any hardship as a result of the Latin occupation. On the contrary, there is evidence of reasonable prosperity: at the end of the fifteenth century it had a yearly income of two hundred Venetian ducats, and new buildings, including an ambitious church, were put up. Even so, the monastery did not produce a single spiritual or literary figure. The founder's express wish that the abbot should be, like himself, a solitary was soon disregarded. Far from becoming a centre of ascetic virtue, the Enkleistra was turned into an ordinary *koinobion*, an agricultural enterprise like all the other monasteries of Cyprus.

Throughout its long existence Byzantine monasticism never broke out of its original mould. The only possibility of reform lay in a return to a stricter interpretation of the desert Fathers or else in a turning inwards, towards a mysticism that could be shared only by a few. And so the heritage of Symeon the New Theologian was picked up in the fourteenth century by the hesychasts of Mount Athos. The controversy concerning the 'uncreated light' of Mount Tabor and the method of attaining the beatific vision by holding one's breath while reciting the 'prayer of Jesus' belongs to the history of spirituality rather than to that of monasticism as an institution. We may note, however, that the manifesto of Gregory Palamas (1340) which won the formal approval of the Greek Church explicitly identified the monks as those persons of spiritual vision to whom the mysteries of the future dispensation were revealed just as the truths of Christianity had been vouchsafed to the Old Testament prophets.[30] It is hard to imagine that the good monks of Vatopedi who fought their neighbours of Esphigmenou with clubs over the possession of some fields and set fire to one another's trees[31] were the same monks who claimed for themselves such a lofty position in God's grand design.

With their long tradition of hard-headedness and financial expertise Byzantine monasteries were well prepared to survive under foreign domination. Those of Mount Athos enjoyed considerable benefits when they passed under the rule of the Serbian King Stephen Dušan. When, a few decades later, the Ottoman Turks made their first appearance in Europe, the Athonite monasteries did not even wait for Turkish domination to be established. They went straight to the Sultan, offered their submission and obtained a confirmation of the titles to their landed estates (c. 1372).[32] In the confusion that followed they were even able to extend their holdings and engage in other profitable ventures. The same cannot be said, of course, of all monasteries, but those that did survive the conquest did pretty well during the five centuries of Turkish rule. Byzantine monasticism thus outlived the Byzantine Empire.

CHAPTER 6

EDUCATION

When, in the fourth century, Christianity triumphed over paganism there existed throughout the Empire a pattern of liberal education that had undergone no fundamental change since the Hellenistic period, over a span of some five hundred years. We must begin by describing its main features.

The education of boys comprised, as it still does today, three stages: primary, secondary and higher. Starting at about the age of seven, boys (and occasionally girls, too) would be sent to an elementary teacher (*grammatistês*) who inculcated in them a knowledge of the alphabet, of reading aloud, writing and counting. It was pretty basic stuff, and the *grammatistês*, who was usually self-employed and possessed no formal qualifications, held a fairly lowly station in society – hardly better than that of an artisan. For a considerable proportion of the public education stopped at the elementary level, leaving indelible memories of the master's rod, of endless repetition and memorization. The next or secondary stage was supervised by a different (and considerably better paid) teacher, the *grammatikos*, who expounded not so much grammar in our sense of the word (he did that too) as a selected number of 'classical' authors, mostly poets and, above all, Homer. The method followed by the *grammatikos* is known to us in considerable detail for the Late Antique period and comprised for each text studied four operations, namely correction (*diorthôsis*), reading aloud (*anagnôsis*), explanation (*exêgêsis*) and criticism (*krisis*). This sounds very formal and, in fact, it was. By 'correction' was meant the confrontation of the texts held by master and students to make sure that they were identical, something that could not be taken for granted. The text was then recited with the proper intonation. This had to be done because in antiquity words were written without any separation and without punctuation. When the text had been read aloud it had to be explained, first linguistically (since the language of Homer and the other ancient poets was not generally understood), then historically, meaning that the names of various mythological personages as well as geographical names had to be identified and learnt by heart. Finally, *krisis* referred not so much to literary criticism as to pointing out the moral lessons that could be extracted from the ancient texts.

The study of the poets was supplemented by that of grammar, usually in the handbook of Dionysius the Thracian (first century BC) which retained its enormous prestige throughout the Byzantine period. This was little more than a classification of language: vowels and consonants, the quantity of vowels (in other words whether they were short, long or indifferent), diphthongs, the eight parts of speech, number, declension, conjugation, and so on. Thus equipped, the student had to tackle a number of exercises (*progymnasmata*), carefully graduated and defined, of which the first four or five kinds were done in secondary school, while the rest were reserved for the higher stage of education. In the influential handbook of Hermogenes (second century AD) the following twelve exercises are listed:

1 The fable (usually about animals).
2 The tale (*diêgêma*), defined as 'the exposition of something that happened or might have happened'.
3 The pregnant maxim (*chreia*).
4 The gnomic saying (*gnômê*) which differed from the *chreia* in that the latter could contain some action (i.e. a little anecdote), whereas the *gnômê* was limited to a general statement of a deterring or encouraging nature.
5 The confutation (*anaskeuê*) or confirmation (*kataskeuê*) of a given proposition.
6 The common-place (*koinos topos*), that is, the elaboration of a general case, for example for or against a class of people (champions of valour, criminals) whose excellence or guilt was not in question.
7 The laudation (*enkômion*) of a given person, an animal, an abstract quality, a city, and so on, or its opposite, namely the invective (*psogos*).
8 The comparison (*synkrisis*).
9 The character sketch (*êthopoiia*), normally in the form of a little speech that some well-known figure might have spoken on a given occasion, the purpose being to convey the mood (happiness/distress) and nature (man/woman, young /old) of the speaker.

10 The description (*ekphrasis*) of an object, a place, etc.

11 The discussion of a general issue (*thesis*), such as, 'Ought one to marry?' Scientific questions were to be avoided as falling within the competence of philosophers.

12 The proposal of a law or measure (*nomou eisphora*).[1]

The above exercises were minutely distinguished from one another and subdivided: for example a *thesis* was held to differ from a *koinos topos* in that it concerned a debatable point; furthermore, it could be simple ('Ought one to marry?'), simple with a particular application ('Ought a king to marry?'), double ('Should one contend in athletic games or till the earth?'), and so forth. For each exercise standard themes were set and an invariable structure laid down. In the case of the *chreia*, for example, the theme could be the saying of Isocrates, 'The root of education is bitter, but its fruit is sweet.' The pupil then had to compose his exercise in a tripartite form: 1. Praise Isocrates for his wisdom; 2. Paraphrase the maxim; 3. Justify it either positively ('The most worthwhile things can only be achieved through exertion, but once achieved bring pleasure') or negatively or by means of an illustration.

While literary studies held a preponderant place in secondary education, four scientific subjects (the medieval *quadrivium*), namely arithmetic, geometry, astronomy and musical theory were also included – or perhaps we should say that they were included in principle – making up what was called the *enkyklios paideia*, meaning general or rounded education. This term often occurs in Byzantine texts, but it is difficult to tell whether the beneficiaries of such 'rounded education' had actually studied all or any of the scientific subjects in question or whether they had merely been to a secondary school. The second alternative is the more likely, and it seems that well before the Byzantine period the sciences were relegated more and more to higher education and then only for those who wished to pursue them.

Higher education (of which we have already described in large part the curriculum) was dispensed by the rhetor or sophist and was available in the larger cities only. The rhetor/sophist, if he held an established chair, was appointed by the local council and received a salary as well as benefiting from certain exemptions. In practice he also received payments or gifts from his pupils. If, on the other hand, he was a free-lance (and many of them were), he depended entirely on fees. There was thus an in-built competition between teachers which occasionally erupted into fights and the kidnapping of students. Boys normally took up higher education at the age of fifteen and pursued it as long as their circumstances or their desires dictated: a complete course took about five years, but many left after two or three. Naturally, most of the students came from well-to-to families of decurions, government officials and lawyers. There is no way of estimating student numbers, but we may be right in saying that in the major centres they were in the hundreds rather than in the thousands. Libanius, who was the foremost sophist of Antioch in the second half of the fourth century, normally had about fifty students in his establishment whom he instructed with the help of four assistant masters. Since his teaching activity at Antioch extended over forty years, we may calculate (allowing for an average course of three years) that some seven hundred students passed through his hands. He was not, however, the only sophist of the Syrian capital.[2]

In addition to rhetoric, which formed the standard content of higher education, a few more technical subjects were available. Philosophy (including in principle what we understand today by science) flourished at Athens and Alexandria; medicine also at Alexandria, at Pergamum and elsewhere; law at Beirut. There was nothing, however, in the ancient world that corresponded to a university in the sense of a consortium of accredited teachers of various disciplines offering a syllabus of studies that led to a degree. The School of Alexandria and that of Constantinople (of which more will be said later) came closest to our concept of a university, but even there, as we shall see, the range of subjects taught was very limited. The budding scholar was, therefore, obliged to move about a great deal. After completing his secondary schooling in his local town, he would go to a larger centre, say Antioch or Smyrna or Gaza, to study with a prominent rhetor; but if he was attracted to philosophy, he would have to transfer to Alexandria or Athens. The quest for learning was synonymous with travel. It was also expensive since the young man had to maintain himself for several years in strange cities as well as paying his teachers. The mobility of students was paralleled by that of professors: Libanius, for example, had taught at Nicomedia, Nicaea and Constantinople before he settled down in his native Antioch.

Such, in brief, was the structure of education that was available in the eastern half of the Empire during the early centuries; nor was it different in the western half, except that Latin was used in the place of Greek. Setting aside for the moment the attitude of the Church, one cannot help wondering how relevant such a system was to the requirements of contemporary life. It is surely a paradox that an education largely oriented towards the art of public speaking in an assembly of citizens (and it may have been noticed that the most advanced exercise prescribed by Hermogenes was the proposal of a legal measure) should have prevailed at a time when democracy had become extinct. One can hardly imagine that the trivial issues that came up in municipal councils, such as the cleaning of sewers or the provision of public spectacles, called for flights of rhetoric as sublime as those of Demosthenes or Isocrates. Furthermore, rhetoric was taught in Attic Greek which was, to all intents and purposes, a dead language. Now it has been calculated that of the numerous identifiable students of Libanius roughly 40 per cent entered government service, 30 per cent took up liberal professions (largely court pleading which at that time did not require a legal training), 20 per cent returned to their inherited duties as decurions, and 10 per cent became teachers.[3] Only this last and smallest group can be said to have applied their education to a practical purpose; for the rest it was a training of the mind, an ability to pen an elegant epistle when circumstances demanded it, and, above all, a common stock of clichés that constituted culture.

It is not entirely anachronistic to speak of relevance, since we happen to know that the bureaucratic government as instituted by Diocletian and elaborated by his successors did create a demand for certain qualifications that liberal education was unable to supply. These concerned the study of Latin in the eastern provinces and the acquisition of notarial skills, namely stenography and accounting. The violent opposition of Libanius to these illiberal studies proves that he felt his own profession to be threatened. When he saw the throng of students making their way to the Law School of Beirut, he reacted in the same manner as would a modern professor of Classics whose students deserted him in favour of Business Administration. Latin, that barbarous tongue, was not only becoming a precondition for legal studies; its administrative use was on the increase in the fourth century (temporarily as it proved). As for notarial training, that was, in the eyes of Libanius, appropriate to slaves, not to gentlemen. Yet 'technocrats' were rising to the highest posts in the administration.

What the government desired in the field of education may be discerned in the organization of the 'University' of Constantinople in 425. Certainly, higher education had been available at Constantinople, if not from the reign of Constantine, at any rate from that of Constantius II onwards. The rewards that could be expected to result from proximity

to the court naturally attracted to the new capital a number of distinguished rhetors, including, as we have seen, Libanius, who did not
remain there very long, and Themistius (d. 388), who made for himself
a brilliant career and rose to the rank of senator, even to the post of
prefect of the city in spite of the fact that he was a pagan. The emperor
valued him because he elevated the cultural level of the capital which
became, thanks to him, 'a common lodging-house of culture'.[4] In other
words, Constantinople, in spite of its recent origins, was on its way to
becoming a 'university town'. It seems, however, that after a time the
government felt dissatisfied with the traditional pattern of education –
hence the creation of a State University. One of several constitutions
issued in 425[5] begins by regulating the status of free-lance teachers:
they may continue their courses provided they do so privately, but may
not use public auditoria. Conversely, public teachers may not give
private lessons. The composition of the State faculty is then laid down:
for Latin three *oratores* and ten *grammatici*; for Greek five sophists and ten
grammatici, while 'profounder studies' were represented by one professor of philosophy and two of law. Further constitutions concerned
the quarters assigned to the University (it was housed in the Capitol)
and the rank to which professors might aspire: after twenty years of
satisfactory service and blameless life they would be rewarded with
the title of *comes* of the first class, as would also a middle-grade civil
servant.[6]

Evidently, the University was set up not out of a disinterested wish to
foster the muses, but specifically to train State functionaries. This is
shown by the near parity of Greek and Latin, by the provision of legal
teaching and also by the fact that professors were appointed by the city
prefect acting in the emperor's name. What is, however, even more
remarkable is that the majority of the faculty (twenty out of thirty-one)
consisted of *grammatici*, or secondary-school teachers. In other words we
are dealing with an institution that combined the functions of high
school and college under direct State supervision. How well it succeeded it is difficult to say. We happen to know the names of some of its
professors: in the 470s the Egyptian Pamprepius who was a pagan and
something of a magician, in the sixth century the archetypal civil
servant John Lydus who taught Latin, a language he may not have
known very well. We cannot, however, point to any intellectual ferment, to any advance in scholarship or even to any body of learned
writing that originated in the University of Constantinople: were it not
for the ordinances of 425, we would hardly have known of its existence.

And although some historians have stated that Constantinople became, since the reign of Constantius II, the intellectual capital of the Empire, it is difficult to name in the fourth, fifth and sixth centuries any scholar or writer of note who was a native Constantinopolitan or a product of its educational establishment.

If the State made some attempt to infuse relevance into the educational system, what of the Church? That ancient education was in an ultimate sense pagan in its outlook and in a more immediate sense based on the study of pagan authors no one will deny; though it is perhaps an exaggeration to say that the heathen myths of Homer and Hesiod, worn down as they were by centuries of classroom boredom, still retained much of a 'charge'. Even so, the stricter Christians found here a source for scandal. The *Apostolic Constitutions* (fourth century) are quite uncompromising in this respect:

> Avoid all gentile books. For what need have you of alien writings, laws and false prophets which lead the frivolous away from the faith? What do you find lacking in God's Law that you should seek those gentile fables? If you wish to read histories, you have the books of Kings; if rhetorical and poetic writings, you have the Prophets, you have Job, you have the Proverbs, wherein you will find a sagacity that is greater than that of all poetry and sophistry since those are the words of our Lord who alone is wise. If you have a desire for songs, you have the Psalms, if for ancient genealogies, you have Genesis; if for legal books and precepts, you have the Lord's glorious Law. So avoid strenuously all alien and diabolical books.[7]

Similar voices were raised all through the Byzantine period. What need was there for the Christian to soil his mind with the disgusting tales of the gods who were really demons, even with the vanities of profane wisdom, when his only legitimate concern lay in salvation? Pagans leave their country and cross the sea in order to learn letters, but we do not have to go abroad to win the Kingdom of Heaven: so spoke St Antony. Besides, what came first, the mind or letters? Since the mind clearly came first, anyone who has a healthy mind has no need of letters.[8] The abolition of pagan learning by Christ, the confutation of philosophers by uneducated Christian saints are commonplaces of Byzantine literature. Take, as one example in a thousand, the Acathist Hymn which is still recited in the Orthodox Church:

> We see copious orators mute as fish before thee, O Mother of God, since they are at a loss to explain how thou remainest a virgin, yet wast able to give birth. But we, marvelling at the mystery, with faith cry out:

131

Hail, vessel of God's wisdom!
Hail, treasury of His providence!
Hail, thou who showest the wise ignorant!
Hail, thou who provest the sophists speechless!
Hail, for the skilled disputers are become foolish!
Hail, for the poets of fables are withered!
Hail, thou who rendest asunder the word-webs of Athens!
Hail, thou who fillest the nets of the fishers!
Hail, thou who drawest us from the depth of ignorance!
Hail, thou who illuminest many with knowledge![9]

The rejection of all education was not, however, a viable option even with such illumination as the Theotokos provided. Theoretically there existed a less drastic possibility, namely the institution of specifically Christian schools, just as the Jews of the diaspora had set up rabbinical schools whose curriculum was based on the Hebrew Bible and the commentaries thereon. One might even have envisaged retaining the traditional framework of education while substituting Christian texts for pagan ones. It was not an easy solution since the Bible was widely regarded, even among Christians, to be couched in particularly inelegant Greek, while there did not exist, at any rate in the fourth century, a body of Christian literature suitable to be placed before the young for their grammatical and rhetorical training. The idea of providing such material was, however, considered. In 362, when the pagan Emperor Julian forbade Christians to hold teaching appointments in secondary and higher education on the grounds that they ought not to profess things contrary to their own beliefs, the Christian *grammatikos* Apollinarius and his son, who bore the same name, transposed the Old Testament into verse using all the classical forms of metre, while they turned the New Testament into Platonic dialogues. This worthy effort came to nothing, and it is interesting to observe that its very failure was ascribed to divine Providence by a Christian historian.[10] Why so? Because, he explains, Hellenic culture had been neither condemned nor approved by Christ and the apostles. The Holy Scriptures did not teach one the art of reasoning so indispensable for defending the true faith; hence it was perfectly legitimate, even necessary, to study pagan texts in order to defeat the enemy with his own weapons, to exercise the mind and to acquire eloquence. Even so strict a moralist as St John Chrysostom does not condemn attendance at normal schools; on the contrary, he takes it for granted. He urges Christian parents to tell their children, when they are resting from their lessons, simple biblical stories, such as that of Cain and Abel; and if, he continues, a child is prepared to accept a mythical statement like 'She was made a demigod' without knowing the meaning of 'demigod', he will be equally ready to believe in the resurrection. What is more, John Chrysostom recommends that the Christian doctrine of punishment, including the story of the Flood, Sodom, the exile to Egypt, as well as all of the New Testament, should be imparted to the Christian boy only after the age of fifteen, preferably at about eighteen, in other words when he had already completed his secular studies.[11]

The best-known statement on this topic is, however, by St Basil.[12] It takes the form of a short address to his nephews who appear to have completed their secondary education at the time of writing. We may imagine that they were about to embark on their rhetoric. To safeguard their immortal souls, their uncle poses the question: How can one profit from Hellenic literature? The question is a loaded one and the argument pretty trite: One should cull from ancient literature everything that is conducive to virtue, while rejecting all examples of licentiousness and, in particular, all the tales concerning the discord and amatory adventures of the gods. The example of Moses who learnt the wisdom of the Egyptians before approaching the contemplation of the Truth provides a useful precedent. Christian youths should take advantage in the same manner of a culture that is not entirely alien. We may note the assumption that Christian writings are unsuitable for training the mind and that the deeper doctrines of Christianity are beyond the understanding of the young. More interesting than St Basil's argument is, however, the form of his address: it is a polished piece of Atticist prose sprinkled with explicit and tacit references to Plato and Plutarch, Homer and Hesiod, Solon, Theognis and several other classical authors. If he wrote in this style, it was because he loved 'fine' literature as much as any other educated man of the fourth century. The idea of rejecting the pagan heritage simply did not occur to the legislator of eastern monasticism.

Once the Cappadocian Fathers had lent their authority to the retention of classical education, the question was settled for good. The Church neither evinced pagan texts from the curriculum nor did it set up a parallel educational system. This was a development of the greatest importance. Christian boys continued to go to the same *grammatistes*, the same *grammatikos* and the same *rhêtor* as pagan boys, studied Homer and were made familiar with the stories of the old mythology. Some of them became teachers and, we may imagine, relayed the same lore to their pupils. For about two centuries Christians and pagans got on remarkably smoothly in the schools. It was no secret that the professorate was the last refuge of educated pagans, but they had a skill to impart which Christians were eager to learn. And here we may note another paradox: it was Christianity that gave rhetoric the application it lacked, namely the sermon. All the tricks of composition and persuasion learnt in the schools could now be used for a worthy purpose. There are no better examples of late antique eloquence than the sermons of the Cappadocians and St John Chrysostom.

A rare glimpse of student life in the Early Byzantine period – in the 480s to be exact – is provided by the Life of Severus, the Monophysite patriarch of Antioch, by his friend Zacharias the Rhetor.[13] Severus was a Pisidian and came from a prominent Christian family, but at first he was not particularly religious and was content to remain a catechumen, since it was the custom in his country to defer baptism until a fairly advanced age. His father, who was a curial, sent him and his two elder brothers to study grammar and rhetoric, both Greek and Latin, at Alexandria: it was there that he met Zacharias who hailed from Gaza. At the time Alexandria was probably the biggest university centre of the Empire. Our text names nine professors (grammarians, sophists and philosophers) who were then active. They appear to have taught in the same building, but on Fridays it was customary for most professors to hold forth at home, except for the philosophers who continued their regular courses at the school. The faculty was largely pagan and remained unmolested, but there were signs of tension between Christian and pagan students. Among the Christians there were activists who joined associations of lay zealots (called *philoponoi* at Alexandria), had contacts in monasteries and were ever ready to denounce to the authorities blatant cases of pagan worship. One such activist, by the name of Paralius, was so offensive in railing at paganism (his own teacher was the pagan Horapollo) that he was beaten up by his fellow students. This incident was successfully exploited by the Christians with the result that Horapollo had to go into hiding, a large cache of idols was discovered with student help and burnt publicly, and even the prefect of Egypt was placed in an embarrassing position.

From Alexandria both Severus and Zacharias proceeded to Berytus where they read law. It was a long and laborious course of four or five years, but the average young gentleman had plenty of opportunity to relax from his daily grind: he went to the theatres and the circus, played dice in the evenings or drank with prostitutes. Freshmen (*dupendii*) were, on arrival, teased by senior students. At Berytus, too, Christian activists were very much in evidence: they recruited students into religious fraternities, urged them to attend church every evening, to avoid spectacles and baths (the leader of the group washed only once a year). Several of them, including Severus (at length baptized), eventually became monks. Berytus, although traditionally pleasure-loving, was more thoroughly Christian than Alexandria, but since the students came from all parts of the Empire, there were pagans among them, and on one occasion there was a nasty scandal involving magic. Once again, the activists made the most of the incident: the chief culprit was subjected to a house search and had his grimoires confiscated, his accomplices were denounced to the bishop and there was a public burning of magical books. One of those implicated, a certain Chrysaorius of Tralles, tried to get away: he rented a ship, loaded on it his legal and magical books, his silver dinner service, his concubine and the children he had by her, but, of course, the ship sank and he perished. We do not know, incidentally, if all students were as well-heeled as Chrysaorius, but many of them were attended by slaves they had brought from their home town.

If university life at the end of the fifth century was beginning to resemble that of Nazi Germany, worse was to come. Justinian, in particular, was determined to impose uniformity of belief on all his subjects. His edict ordering the closure of the Academy of Athens (529) is widely remembered as a sign of his intolerance, though it should be pointed out that the Academy continued functioning in a diminished way for some decades after this date and that at Alexandria philosophy went on being taught by the pagan Olympiodorus until after 565, the year of Justinian's death. These, however, were surely exceptions. Even though the law of 529 forbidding pagans, heretics and Jews to teach[14] may not have been universally applied, there can be no doubt concerning the systematic persecution of pagans in the same year; again in 546 when 'a crowd of grammarians, sophists, lawyers and physicians' were hauled up before the inquisitor, John of Ephesus (who happened to be a heretic), and punished with scourging and gaol sentences;[15] and in 562 when pagan books were burnt.[16] One may readily imagine the effect of such measures on academic morale which was further undermined by the withdrawal of State subsidies from teachers.[17] We are hardly surprised to observe that by the end of the sixth century the tradition of higher education should have survived only at Constantinople, Alexandria and Berytus.

If Justinian bears a heavy responsibility for weakening the educational system, its subsequent collapse was undoubtedly due to the disappearance of the cities. All that remained in the provinces, as far as we can judge from our extremely meagre documentation, was some form of primary schooling. It seems it was during those dark centuries that the custom developed of using the Psalter as a child's first reader, a custom that remained firmly entrenched in the subsequent period. If it is true that Georgius Choeroboscus, the author of an extremely popular grammar book based on the Psalter,[18] flourished after the middle of the eighth century,[19] his effort would fit into such a development; and if it is true that he professed at Constantinople, one would have to conclude that a similar use of the Psalter had spread to the capital. Whatever remained of secondary and higher education (and it is a moot point whether they were still separate) was now concentrated at Constantinople, but it seems that the University faded out. The last attested professor is the Aristotelian commentator Stephen of Alexandria who was called to the capital by the Emperor Heraclius (hence after 610). Setting aside Choeroboscus, no further names are mentioned until the middle of the ninth century.

A little-noticed canon of the Trullan Council (692) proves that legal studies were still pursued at the time since it decrees that students of civil law ought not to follow pagan customs, frequent theatres, wear distinctive clothing or turn somersaults (if that is the meaning of the enigmatic word *kylistra*) either at the beginning or the end of term.[20] The fact that only law students are mentioned may show either that they were particularly rowdy or that no other students at university level were to be found. Yet, when the law code of the Emperors Leo III and Constantine v (the *Ecloga*) was issued, probably in 726, its composition was the work of the *quaestor sacri palatii*, two patricians and a number of State dignitaries to the exclusion of any professors; and the compilers frankly admitted that the meaning of previous legislation had become quite obscure, 'indeed, entirely incomprehensible to some, especially those outside our God-guarded Imperial City'.[21] The chronicler Theophanes, admittedly a biased witness, may not be too far from the truth when he records under the year 726 'the extinction of the schools'.[22]

An interesting insight into the decline of higher education in the seventh century is provided by the autobiography of Ananias of Shirak, the Armenian scholar who introduced into his native country the sciences of mathematics, chronological computation and cosmography. Being unable to find anyone in Armenia who would teach him 'philosophy', he betook himself to 'the country of the Greeks' and was intending to proceed to Constantinople when he was informed that a very learned teacher named Tychikos was active at Trebizond and attracted students even from the capital. To Trebizond he accordingly went and studied with Tychikos for eight years. He learnt arithmetic and other sciences and was generally able to satisfy his thirst for knowledge since his master had a rich library of both Christian and pagan books. Now this Tychikos was a native of Trebizond and had started his career as a soldier; but after being wounded in battle, he decided to become a scholar. He went to Alexandria, where he studied three years, then to Rome for one year, finally to Constantinople where he became for some time the disciple of a famous Athenian philosopher (unnamed). Pressure was brought on him to remain in the capital, but he resolved to return to Trebizond. A few years later the Athenian died and none of his students was deemed worthy to succeed him. So the emperor (it must have been Heraclius) summoned Tychikos to Constantinople, but the latter declined the invitation, and from then on students would travel from Constantinople to Trebizond to acquire knowledge, presumably in the sciences.[23] Whatever truth there may be in this story, it shows graphically the growing scarcity of qualified professors, even in the capital.

While it would be an exaggeration to say that all polite learning was interrupted in the Byzantine Empire, it was certainly reduced to a very thin trickle after the reign of Heraclius. One may even suspect that a greater reservoir of Greek learning and Greek books remained in Arab-dominated Syria and Palestine than in Constantinople. The greatest Greek-speaking scholar of the eighth century was St John Damascene (died c. 750), and two generations later the most prominent historical specialist was the Palestinian monk George Syncellus (died c. 814).

The revival of literary studies in the capital began at a very slow pace in the latter part of the eighth century. All we can say with any assurance is that there appeared at that time a group of persons, nearly all of them connected with the upper echelons of the civil service, who, without being profound scholars, possessed nevertheless a conventional rhetorical training and some acquaintance with philosophy. Such were the future patriarchs Tarasius (d. 806) and Nicephorus (758–828) and St Theodore the Studite (759–826). They seem to have acquired their instruction privately and to have passed it on to the next generation in an equally informal manner. Tarasius, for example, who was not a professional teacher, is said to have initiated his future biographer, the deacon Ignatius (d. after 843) in the rules of ancient prosody.[24] There was certainly at that time a small number of *grammatikoi* active at Constantinople, such as the future iconoclastic patriarch Antony I Kassimatas (821–?37)[25] and perhaps his successor John VII (?837–43) who was remembered by the sobriquet Grammatikos and who passed as a man of great learning, even as a magician. It was in this milieu that a momentous technical development took place: I refer to the introduction of the minuscule or cursive script in the place of the uncial (majuscule) for purposes of book production. What is perhaps most remarkable about this innovation is that it was so slow in coming – some fifty years later in Byzantium than in western Europe. The supply of Egyptian papyrus, on which books had been written in antiquity, must have been cut off or, at any rate, greatly reduced after the fall of Alexandria to the Arabs (642), and parchment, which took its place, was both scarce and expensive. The need for a more compact form of writing was, under the circumstances, obvious; besides, it did not even have to be invented since the minuscule was nothing but the notarial cursive previously used for business purposes. Yet it was only in about 790, as far as we can surmise, that minuscule books began to be produced in Byzantium and the earliest surviving example, the so-called Uspensky Gospel, dates from 834; from which we may deduce that a sufficient demand for books did not arise until the end of the eighth century.

The first real professor we meet at Constantinople as studies began to revive is Leo the Mathematician. The romantic tradition concerning this personage bears retelling because of the incidental light it sheds on the state of education at this juncture.[26] Leo received his secondary schooling (grammar and 'poetics') in the capital, but was unable to progress any further; so he moved to the island of Andros where a learned man instructed him in the rudiments of rhetoric, philosophy and arithmetic. But even this scholar was unable to satisfy Leo's curiosity. The latter wandered off into the interior of the island, visited monasteries and studied the old manuscripts preserved in them. Having thus attained the summits of knowledge – 'philosophy and her sisters, namely arithmetic, geometry and astronomy, yea even celebrated music' – he returned to Constantinople and set up a school in a humble house where he taught whatever discipline each pupil chose. Several years passed and many of Leo's students achieved success in their respective callings. One of them, a geometrician, became secretary to a military governor and was captured by the Arabs. The Caliph Mamûn (813–33), who was passionately interested in 'Hellenic studies' and especially in geometry, happened to hear of the young prisoner and brought him into the presence of his own mathematicians. Predictably, the Byzantine amazed everyone by his knowledge. When the caliph had learnt that this paragon was merely a student, he immediately sent him back to Constantinople bearing the following missive to his master: 'We have recognized the tree by its fruit, the master by his pupil. Seeing that you, who are so eminent in the sciences, remain unknown among your compatriots and have received no reward for your wisdom and knowledge, deign to come to us and give us the benefit of your teaching. If this comes to pass, the whole Saracen nation will bow before you and you will receive greater riches than any other man has ever received.' A tempting offer for an impecunious academic. Leo, however, was afraid to accept a communication from the enemy and took it to the Foreign Minister. The Emperor Theophilus was also informed of the matter and in this way Leo achieved a measure of recognition. He was given a sum of money and was set up as a public teacher in the Church of the Forty Martyrs. The disappointed caliph renewed his offer – this time two thousand pounds of gold if Leo would come even for a short visit. The emperor refused the overture on the grounds that it was senseless to communicate to foreigners that science 'on account of which the Roman nation is admired and honoured by all'. Some time thereafter Leo was ordained metropolitan of Thessalonica, but he remained in this uncongenial post only three years (840–43). Deposed as an Iconoclastic appointee, he returned to Constantinople and, at the instigation of Bardas, uncle of the young Emperor Michael III, was made head of a newly created school: Leo himself held the chair of philosophy, his ex-student Theodore that of geometry, a certain Theodegios that of astronomy and one Kometas that of grammar. We do not know when Leo died, but it was after 869.

There are some details in this story that are difficult to believe (for example the presence of scientific manuscripts in the remoter monasteries of Andros) and its chronology is not entirely satisfactory. Assuming, however, that it is true at least in outline, we should note that a State-sponsored institution of higher learning was once again established at Constantinople. Its seat was the Magnaura which was a ceremonial hall of the Imperial Palace – indeed, the hall in which emperors received foreign ambassadors. By comparison to the University of 425, its staff was smaller and the scope of its teaching heavily weighted in favour of science to the exclusion of law and, of course, Latin – hence a school for technicians rather than one for civil servants. Was this structure inspired by Leo himself or was it the government's response to the scientific progress of the Arabs? We do not know. Nor can we estimate the school's influence which could not have been insignificant since a hundred years later it was credited with having established a tradition of culture;[27] yet we cannot even be sure that it outlasted the lifetime of Bardas (d. 866) and the first generation of professors.

Among Leo's academic colleagues only Cometas is otherwise attested: we know that he prepared a new edition of Homer, probably one transliterated into the minuscule script.[28] Leo himself took some part in editing the text of Plato and possessed several scientific manuscripts including a Ptolemy and a Euclid. He appears to have dabbled in astrology and to have made predictions. One of his students, a certain Constantine the Sicilian, was so shocked by Leo's teaching that he consigned him posthumously to Hell, where he would burn for all eternity along with his fellow-pagans – Plato and Aristotle, Socrates, Epicurus, Homer, Hesiod, Aratus and the whole damned lot of them.[29]

It is undeniable that the ninth century witnessed a dramatic upsurge in scholarship. Strangely enough, however, it is difficult to connect this upsurge with the Magnaura University or any other institution of higher learning. Photius, the greatest scholar of the age, pursued a career in the civil service before he was elevated to the patriarchate of Constantinople (in 858); he never held a teaching appointment. We do not know how he acquired his education. If he was born in about 810, as some historians today believe, or even in about 820, he would have been a grown man by the time the University was established. In the next generation the most learned figure was that of Arethas, archbishop of Caesarea, born in about 850. He was a collector of classical texts (several of his beautifully copied manuscripts are still extant) and himself wrote in so precious and convoluted a style as to be practically incomprehensible. He, too, had no demonstrable connection with any university or school. All we can say is that literary culture, which had been so markedly absent from the court of the Iconoclastic emperors, regained favour in the highest circles. Though Basil I was an illiterate Armenian peasant, his son Leo VI was privately tutored by Photius and devoted himself to literary composition. He wrote a number of rather tedious homilies and tried his hand at religious hymns. It was, however, Leo's son, Constantine VII Porphyrogenitus, who embodied most fully the ideal of the scholar emperor. Of his literary activities we shall speak in Chapter 13; here we should note his intervention in the realm of higher education. We are told that, finding the liberal arts and sciences to have been neglected, he appointed a number of excellent professors: a certain Constantine, who was then *mystikos* (chief of the bureau that dealt with confidential business), was given the chair of philosophy, Alexander metropolitan of Nicaea that of rhetoric, the patrician Nicephorus that of geometry, and the imperial secretary Gregory that of astronomy. The emperor lavished attention on the students whom he often invited to share his table. When they had graduated (if we may use this term), he recruited among them judges, secretaries of the legal bureau (*antigrapheis*) and metropolitans.[30] In other words, we are dealing here with a palace school whose programme was the same as that of the Bardas University and whose explicit purpose was to train personnel for the judiciary (yet without the benefit of a chair of Law!) and the Church. Of the four professors the only one who is independently known is Alexander of Nicaea who annotated Lucian and wrote a number of extant letters. The others were dignitaries who happened to possess some scholarly competence. None appears to have been a professional scholar.

We are a little better informed about the state of secondary education at Constantinople in the first half of the tenth century thanks to the correspondence of an anonymous schoolteacher.[31] He appears to have been a somewhat cantankerous man who led a modest life, sometimes acting as scribe and editor, but who nevertheless had connections with the world of high officialdom. His pupils were all of ages and the more advanced among them tutored the beginners. The subject of instruction was ancient Greek (grammar, prosody, rhetoric), in other words the traditional repertory of the *grammatikos*, and its purpose the training of aspirants to bureaucratic and ecclesiastical posts. Fees were not fixed and were paid irregularly, if at all, to the distress of the schoolmaster who, furthermore, had to compete with rival establishments. It seems that his school, though independent, received a subsidy from the patriarchate and was subject to some sort of control by ecclesiastical and municipal authorities. At about the same time (*c.* 940) we hear of a 'president of the schools', a practising master who also supervised other teaching institutions, perhaps after the model of a trade guild.

Abraamius of Trebizond (who was to become St Athanasius the Athonite) attended at Constantinople the school directed by such a 'president' and showed so much aptitude that he was soon appointed assistant teacher and then full master in a different school.[32] It may be that the office of president denoted some reform of secondary education, but our information is too sparse to yield any firm conclusion.

We know almost nothing about the fortunes of Byzantine education from Constantine Porphyrogenitus until Constantine IX Monomachus, that is, roughly from 940 to 1040. It is a surprising lacuna considering those vast encyclopaedic enterprises that the emperor born in the purple laboriously pursued and instigated. The epithet 'academic' inevitably comes to mind in describing the *Excerpta*, the *Geoponica*, the *Hippiatrica*, and especially that enormous encyclopaedia known by the cryptic name *Souda*, yet none of these can be connected with an educational institution. Nor can it be proved that the accumulation of so much miscellaneous lore served to nourish and inspire subsequent generations of scholars. After the death of Constantine VII imperial patronage of studies lapsed, to be resumed only by Constantine IX, and then in a very different spirit.

The eleventh century was marked by a more lively intellectual climate that may be connected with the intensification of urban life and the rise of a new bourgeoisie. It was dominated by the polymath Michael Psellus and the group of scholars with whom he was linked – John Mavropous (the eldest among them), John Xiphilinus, Constantine Leichoudes, Nicetas. Did these men represent a new departure or do they loom large on our horizon because Psellus wrote so voluminously on such a wide range of subjects? On the institutional side the only obvious novelty was the setting up in about 1047 of a State-sponsored Law School under the presidency of Xiphilinus, who was entrusted with the training of future judges, advocates and notaries.[33] It is a matter of dispute whether a 'Faculty of Philosophy' was simultaneously established under the guidance of Psellus who bore the pompous title 'Consul (*hypatos*) of the Philosophers', whatever exactly that may have meant. Even if it was established, it did not last very long; neither, it seems, did the Law School. On the secondary level, we hear of many more schools in the eleventh century than in the tenth – not simply private institutions, but permanent ones that were attached to churches, probably in the same manner that a *madrasa* is attached to a mosque. These (or, at any rate, some of them) were controlled by the patriarch, although they dispensed the traditional fare of the *grammatikos*. It is difficult to tell whether this was a creation of the eleventh century. It is not, however, on the institutional level that we can discern the originality of the period, but rather in the appearance of intellectuals who were primarily teachers and who achieved great notoriety, even important positions at court and in the Church by virtue of their teaching and scholarship. We must not, of course, overstate the case. The connection between learning and public service was, as we have seen, traditional in Byzantium. Mavropous ended his life as metropolitan of Euchaita (near Amaseia), Xiphilinus became patriarch of Constantinople, and Psellus held a variety of administrative posts, including that of First Imperial Secretary (*prôtoasêkrêtis*). Yet it may be said that all three of them were teachers and intellectuals first and foremost; their scholarship was not merely a stepping stone to a career. We must also remember that the movement they represented lasted fifty years at the most. Had it been allowed to develop, Byzantium might have produced its Abelard, even a true university like those that were to spring up in the West in the following century.

As a thinker, Psellos was not a figure of great originality; indeed, it is hard to call him a philosopher in his own right. He was, however, a man of boundless curiosity who tried to embrace all the fields of knowledge. His teaching also covered a wide area, from elementary grammar and rhetoric to the natural sciences, philosophy and even law. There is no reason to think that any of this was subversive of the established order, although his researches did lead him into some grey areas. He was certainly attracted by the occult, by the so-called Chaldaean doctrines, astrology and demonology, and in philosophy his preferences went to Plato and the Neoplatonists. Let us hear him speak of his own studies:

Having found philosophy extinct in its practitioners, I revived it by my own efforts. I had not encountered any notable teachers, nor had I discovered, in spite of a thorough search, any germ of wisdom either in Greece or among barbarians. Since, however, I heard it said that Greece had achieved great things in philosophy, ... I scorned those who split hairs in such matters and sought to find something better. After reading some commentators on this science, I learned from them the road to knowledge: one referred me to another, the inferior to the superior ... and so, finally, to Aristotle and Plato. Taking them as a starting point, I made a kind of tour, going on to Plotinus, Porphyry and Iamblichus, after whom I advanced to the admirable Proclus, where I paused as in a vast harbour and drew therefrom all science and the exact knowledge of notions. Being about, after this, to ascend to the superior philosophy and to be initiated in pure science, I started with the study of incorporeal things in what is called mathematics.

From arithmetic Psellus progressed to geometry, then to music and astronomy and all the sciences that derive from them, 'not neglecting a single one of them'. On learning that there existed a wisdom that was beyond demonstration, he immersed himself in certain mystical books and profited from them as much as he was able. 'For to know such things exactly,' he admits, 'I would not boast on my own account nor would I believe anyone else who made such claims.' After explaining that his love of philosophy did not entail the neglect of rhetoric, Psellus goes on:

Inasmuch as there exists another philosophy which is superior to that one, namely the one that consists in the mystery of our religion, . . . I studied it more thoroughly than the other, in part following the pronouncements of the great Fathers, in part making my own contribution. And if anyone (I am saying this frankly and without artfulness) wishes to praise me for my culture, let him not do so . . . because I have read many books (for I am not deceived by vanity) . . . but because whatever little wisdom I have collected I did not draw from a flowing spring; nay, I found the wells obstructed. I opened them, I cleansed them and, with great toil, extracted the water that lay at a great depth.[34]

Psellus was not noted for his modesty and, in presenting this some-what embellished picture of his intellectual development, he could not forbear mentioning his excursions into the potentially dangerous fields of Neoplatonism and the occult. Had he not, indeed, conquered *all* knowledge? Yet, he took good care to make the required genuflexion before the superior philosophy of the Christian Fathers just as the Soviet scholar today seeks to placate the censor by bowing, as often as possible, before the classics of Marxism–Leninism. Although he had made many enemies, Psellus was never arraigned for impiety or for corrupting the minds of his students. That experience was reserved for his successor.

John Italus was the son of a Norman mercenary and hailed from southern Italy. He came to Constantinople in about 1050, studied philosophy under Psellus, taught for a number of years and at length became 'Consul of the Philosophers' in succession to Psellus. Although his Greek was not very elegant, he appears to have had a large following among students and he enjoyed the protection of the powerful Doukas family. In 1076–7, under the Emperor Michael vii Doukas, he was accused of impiety, but the case against him was shelved. It was revived in 1082 soon after the accession of Alexius i. This time Italus was arraigned before a tribunal composed of both ecclesiastical and lay dignitaries; his confession of faith was judged to be unsatisfactory and damaging evidence about the views he professed was provided by an informer. There was even a 'spontaneous' demonstration of popular anger against the philosopher, who barely escaped a violent death by climbing to the dome of St Sophia and hiding in a hole. He was anathematized, barred from further teaching and relegated to a monastery never to re-appear again.[35]

There is good reason to believe that the trial of Italus was politically motivated and that the charges against him were, to some extent, trumped up. There appears to have been among the higher clergy considerable sympathy for Italus, but no one dared stand up for him. Five of his students, all of them deacons, were hauled up before an assembly of bishops: they dissociated themselves from their former master and were found to be innocent. The proceedings against Italus give, therefore, the impression of having been strictly *ad personam*; and, to lend greater solemnity to his condemnation, a special chapter was added to the so-called Synodicon of Orthodoxy, wherein he was anathematized for having applied dialectics to the ineffable mystery of Christ's incarnation, for having introduced the cosmological doctrines of the pagans and, in particular, that of the eternity of the world, for admitting the transmigration of human souls and the reality of Platonic ideas, for casting doubt on the miracles of Christ and the saints, and much else besides.[36]

Not since the days of Justinian had a Byzantine academic (as distinct from a religious leader) been formally condemned and punished for the content of his teaching. In this respect the trial of Italus deserves a place in the annals of intolerance. It is still not very clear to what extent the charges against him (which are extremely incoherent) were based on opinions he actually propagated, but one thing we can say: this arrogant and contentious barbarian, as Anna Comnena describes him,[37] took his philosophy seriously. He was not, like Psellus, primarily a man of letters; he had not tasted 'the nectar of rhetoric'. He was, in short, a new phenomenon on the Byzantine intellectual scene. We can only speculate what course the educational establishment would have followed had it not been for the forceful intervention of Alexius I, but we may hazard the guess that the student body did not possess the seriousness of purpose to have made the new teaching fruitful. Italus was dismissed in student circles as an uncouth foreigner, neither a rhetorician nor a philosopher.[38]

Perhaps as a result of the Italus affair, the Church, that is the patriarchate of Constantinople, took a momentous step: it assumed direct control of education, at any rate that of prospective clergymen. There are some indications which we have noted that already in the tenth century and certainly in the eleventh the Church had some part in the running of secondary schools, but it is only from about 1100 onwards that we find an integrated system of secular and religious instruction. It consisted of a network of secondary schools at Constantinople – six, all of them attached to churches, are specifically mentioned – and culminated in a course of biblical exegesis conducted by three professors, that of the Psalter, that of the Epistles and that of the Gospel, the last bearing the title of 'Universal Teacher' (*oikoumenikos disaskalos*). The Church also maintained a 'Master of Rhetoric', first attested in the fateful year 1082. The higher teaching personnel, integrated into the patriarchal hierarchy,[39] usually ended their career as bishops of important sees. We happen to know the names of thirty-four teachers of the Patriarchal School in the twelfth century and many of their literary and pedagogic productions are preserved. One of them, the great Homeric commentator Eustathius who became archbishop of Thessalonica, stands apart. As for the rest, it is difficult to imagine a more dreary lot of pedants.

It seems that the Patriarchal School dominated the educational scene at Constantinople until 1204. Philosophy was not on its curriculum and it is not certain to what extent this discipline continued to be taught within a secular framework. We know that Italus had at least one successor, a certain Theodore of Smyrna who is chiefly remembered as a gourmet, but after him no further 'Consuls of the Philosophers' are recorded until about 1166, when Michael, nephew of the bishop of Anchialos and future patriarch (1169–77), assumed that post. Judging by his inaugural lecture,[40] he was not much of a philosopher.

In the realm of education the twelfth century represents the culmination of a conflict whose origins, as we have seen, go back to the beginning of the Christian Empire. It may be found surprising that the Church should not have asserted its authority at an earlier date. That it did not do so is perhaps due to the intermittent and generally innocuous nature of philosophical teaching. Only in the eleventh century, with the rise of a secular spirit, did the danger become acute and philosophical speculation in the schools, that 'new quest' (*nea zêtêsis*) which the Synodicon condemns, had to be stifled. We shall not follow here the later history of Byzantine education at Nicaea, Constantinople and Trebizond, a history not entirely lacking in distinction, yet confined to the traditional pattern. Instead, we shall try to formulate some general remarks.

It may have become apparent to the reader that from the seventh century onwards the distinction between secondary and higher studies tended to disappear. We have noted some isolated attempts by the government to establish a kind of university, as was done by the Caesar Bardas, by Constantine Porphyrogenitus and Constantine Monomachus, but each time these well-intentioned projects came to very little. There was thus no continuous tradition of higher studies. The recurring motif of 'the rediscovery of learning', usually thanks to the enlightened patronage of a given emperor, has to be taken with a pinch of salt, yet it did bear some relation to reality. Successive scholars like Leo the Mathematician and Psellus had some justification in believing that they had rescued learning from deep oblivion. The only continuous traditions were the teaching of law within the guild of notaries and, especially, that of grammar cum rhetoric by the *grammatikos*. Both were to be found exclusively at Constantinople.

The most obvious feature of the grammarian's teaching was its extreme conservatism. When we find Nicephorus Basilaces, a teacher in the Patriarchal School, composing in the twelfth century 'character sketches' on subjects such as 'What a sailor might have said on seeing Icarus flying in the air and Daedalus grazing the surface of the sea with the tips of his wings', or 'What Pasiphae might have said on falling in love with a bull',[41] we cannot avoid the illusion that time had stood still for a thousand years. Nor can we help asking the question: What use were Icarus and Pasiphae to the prospective civil servant, none of whose business would be conducted in Attic Greek? The most that can be said is that some acquaintance with grammar and rhetoric defined a certain professional class. Now, it has been calculated that in the tenth century the total number of boys and young men receiving grammatical training at Constantinople (hence in the whole Empire) was no more than two to three hundred.[42] It follows from this that at any given time the total number of persons who had benefited from such training was hardly in excess of one thousand. Approximate as these figures are, they give us a sense of scale without which a discussion of Byzantine education becomes meaningless. Let us imagine, then, a group of about a thousand men of respectable family, often nephews of bishops or sons of civil servants, in short, men pursuing a career that required literacy. To be able on occasion to pen an elegant epistle or to deliver an after-dinner speech in the presence of the emperor was bound to attract favourable attention. That is where Icarus and Pasiphae came in. And since the point of the exercise was to be appreciated by one's peers, what reason was there to change an educational system that marked one as a man of culture? The effects of this situation on Byzantine literature are obvious: they will be explored in a later chapter.

One final remark. Monastic education beyond the most basic level never existed in Byzantium. Since the time of Pachomius some of the larger monasteries made provision for the instruction of illiterate entrants who were often young boys. These were taught the church service, the Psalter and parts of the New Testament, preferably by an older monk who was required to use a separate room for this purpose so as to shield the brotherhood from sexual temptation. The Psalter and other essential biblical books were normally learnt by heart, thus reducing the need for literacy. The instruction of 'secular children' in monasteries, considered unsuitable by St Basil,[43] was discouraged throughout the Byzantine period.

PART TWO

THE CONCEPTUAL WORLD OF BYZANTIUM

CHAPTER 7

THE INVISIBLE WORLD OF GOOD AND EVIL

To the Byzantine man, as indeed to all men of the Middle Ages, the supernatural existed in a very real and familiar sense. Not only did that other world continually impinge upon everyday life; it also constituted that higher and timeless reality to which earthly existence was but a brief prelude. Any account of the Byzantine 'world view' must necessarily begin with the supernatural.

Since the Byzantines were Christians, their conception of this higher world was one that is still familiar to us in broad outline; yet, on the popular level (as distinct from the level of theology) it had certain distinctive features that need to be explained. Most importantly and quite naturally, the Byzantines imagined God and the Heavenly Kingdom as a vastly enlarged replica of the imperial court at Constantinople. If questioned on this point, they would probably have expressed the relation in the reverse order by saying that the emperor's court was a diminished reflection of the heavenly court. Whichever of the two was the 'archetype' and whichever the copy, their mutual resemblance was taken for granted and it explains many manifestations of Byzantine religiosity.

Before developing the consequences of this postulate, it may be useful to give an illustration of just how the Heavenly Kingdom was visualized. A number of texts, which we would be inclined to call apocryphal, provide suitable descriptions, and while the details vary from one text to another, the basic ingredients remain the same. I have chosen, because of its relative brevity, the 'Awesome and Edifying Vision of the Monk Cosmas'. This man was a chamberlain of the Emperor Alexander (912–13), but he later retired from the world and, in or about the year 933, became the abbot of a monastery on the river Sangarius in northwest Asia Minor. After a time he fell seriously ill. Five months elapsed and then, one morning, he went into a trance: his eyes stared at the ceiling of his cell, while his mouth whispered incomprehensible words. For six hours Cosmas remained in this condition; but the following day he was able to describe his vision to the brethren of his community (what follows is a paraphrase rather than a literal translation):

As I was sitting on my bed, methinks I saw on my left side a throng of little men with blackened faces [demons always appeared on the left side or in the direction of the west]. They were hideous in different ways: some had distorted countenances, others bloodshot eyes, others livid and swollen lips. The demons managed to drag me to a frightful cliff. Along its face, overhanging an abyss that reached down to Tartarus, ran a path so narrow that one could hardly gain a footing on it. The demons pushed me down this path until we came to a big gate. Here sat a frightful giant, his face all black, his nostrils emitting smoke, his tongue hanging out of his mouth to the length of one cubit. His right arm was paralysed, but with his left, which was as thick as the shaft of a column, he would seize his victims and throw them down the precipice. When the giant saw me, he cried out, 'This man is a friend of mine!' and he was about to grasp me when there appeared two old men of venerable aspect whom I recognized as the apostles Andrew and John for they resembled their representations on icons. The giant drew back in fear, and the apostles led me through the gate, past a city and into a lovely plain. In the middle of the plain was a grassy valley where an old man sat surrounded by a multitude of children. 'This,' my companions told me, 'is Abraham. You have heard of Abraham's bosom.' I did obeisance to him, and we went next to a vast olive grove. Under every tree was a tent, and in every tent a couch upon which a man rested. Among them I recognized many who had served in the palace, many from Constantinople, some peasants and some members of our monastery, all of them deceased. As I was wondering what this grove might be, the apostles reminded me of the 'many mansions' that were in the Lord's house.

We went on to a city of indescribable beauty. Its walls were built of twelve courses, each of a different precious stone, and its gates were of gold and silver. Within the gates we found a golden pavement, golden houses, golden seats. The city was filled with a strange light and a sweet smell, but as we traversed it, we did not encounter a single man or beast or bird. At the edge of the town we came to a wonderful palace, and we entered a hall as broad as a stone's throw. From one end of it to the other stretched a table of porphyry round which many guests were reclining. A spiral staircase, situated at one end of the hall, led to an internal balcony. Two eunuchs, resplendent as lightning, appeared on this balcony and they said to my companions, 'Let him also recline at the table.' I was shown a place, while the eunuchs departed to another chamber that appeared to be beyond the balcony, and they absented themselves for several hours, during which time I was able to recognize many of my fellow-guests:

some were monks of our monastery, others civil servants. At length, the eunuchs returned and they said to the two apostles: 'Take him back since his spiritual children are in great mourning for him. The Emperor has consented that he should return to the monastic life. So conduct him along a different path, and in his stead bring the monk Athanasius from Trajan's monastery.' The apostles led me away. We passed by seven lakes in which a multitude of sinners were being tormented: one was filled with darkness, another with fire, another with an evil-smelling mist, another with worms, and so forth. Soon we encountered Abraham once again who gave us a draught of sweet wine in a golden cup. Then we returned to the outer gate. The giant gnashed his teeth and said to me angrily: 'This time you have escaped me, but I shall not cease plotting against you and your monastery.' This much I remember, but I cannot explain how I regained consciousness.

When Cosmas had finished his story, a messenger was sent to the neighbouring monastery of Trajan: he found that the monk Athanasius had died at the very time when Cosmas was having his vision.[1]

Cosmas' service as a chamberlain may account for the vividness of his vision of the heavenly palace. The great hall or *triclinium*, the *cubicula*, the spiral staircase (*kochlias*), the balcony (*hêliakon*), the table of porphyry, the attendant eunuchs – all these were familiar features of the imperial palace. The only difference was that in Heaven everything was much bigger and more splendid. The equivalence of the earthly and heavenly palaces is, indeed, a commonplace of Byzantine thought. Among the many texts that could be quoted in support of this statement, one will suffice. When the eleventh-century man of letters John Mavropous was first introduced at court in the reign of Michael IV (1034–41), he composed a complimentary poem in which he expressed the wish that he would continue to be received with favour. He feigned fear of being turned away at the gates of the palace by the emperor's 'winged angels'. But if he overcame this obstacle and was able to draw close to the throne, would not the Cherubim strike him with their flaming sword? John did not have the bad taste of comparing to Christ the uncouth Michael IV. He suggested, nevertheless, that Christ might be present in the palace: for just as he had joined the three Hebrews in the furnace, so now, too, he could add his presence to that of the imperial threesome – Michael, his wife Zoe, and the latter's sister Theodora.[2]

God's retinue consisted, in the first place, of the angelic host which was, in theory, rigorously stratified and differentiated. The angels, infinite in number, constituted God's army or regulars, officers and generals; they also served as special emissaries, much as the *magistriani* did on earth, in addition to forming the heavenly *cubiculum* or body of chamberlains. On earth they performed various functions according to their rank: they guarded individuals, churches, altars, cities, even nations. It cannot be said, however, that the Byzantines ever worked out a consistent and generally accepted system of angelology. The teaching of the Bible on this score is notoriously confusing; as for the *Celestial Hierarchy* by pseudo-Dionysius (*c.* 500 AD), it was indeed considered an authoritative work because of its attribution to the apostolic age, but it was far too abstruse to be comprehended by the general public. The Byzantines were sufficiently familiar with the seraphim and the cherubim such as they are described in the visions of Isaiah and Ezekiel. They were often invoked in the liturgy and represented in church decorations, though it must be admitted that their distinctive features were often confused. Of the Thrones, Powers, Dominions and Principalities they had no clear conception. As for the archangels, only two, namely Michael and Gabriel, had a firm place in popular devotion; the others, including Raphael and Uriel, appear mostly in prayers and incantations of an occult character. St Michael was the commander-in-chief, the *archistratêgos*, of the celestial host, and had several cult centres in Asia Minor, the most famous being at Chonai (Colossai) in Phrygia, where he was believed to have split a rock and diverted the course of a torrent.

The early Church had resolutely opposed the cult of angels. Already St Paul, writing – significantly enough – to the Colossians, had issued this warning: 'Let no man beguile you of your reward in a voluntary humility and the worshipping of angels' (Coloss. 2. 18). The Council of Laodicea in Phrygia, which met some time in the fourth century, went even further: 'Christians ought not to abandon the Church of God and go forth, and call upon the angels by name, and organize their worship, which is forbidden. Anyone who is apprehended devoting himself to this concealed idolatry, let him be anathema.'[3] In the next century Theodoret of Cyrrhus noted that 'this disease has remained for a long time in Phrygia and Pisidia', and that 'until this day one may see churches of St Michael among these peoples and their neighbours'.[4] The condemnations proved of little avail: St Michael continued to be worshipped, not only in western Asia Minor, but throughout the Empire. At Constantinople he had no fewer than twenty-four churches.

Concerning the nature of the angels two slightly divergent views were held. The first, which appears to have been the earlier one, was that they were not pure spirit, but consisted of a very fine matter that could be seen by men of particular sanctity, 'those whose eyes God has opened'.[5] The more usual view, however, was that the angels were immaterial, but capable of assuming bodily form which, incidentally, rendered them fit subjects for representation. When they made themselves visible, it was usually in the guise of youthful eunuchs. One popular text describes the angel who remained as the permanent guardian of St Sophia as 'a eunuch clad in a white garment, beautiful of appearance, like one who had been sent from the palace'.[6] In the *Life of St Andrew the Fool* an angel comes to cook a pot of beans for one Epiphanius, a young man of great sanctity. The celestial being is represented as 'a beautiful youth, wonderfully tall, his face shining brighter than the sun, clad in divine garments – white blended with gold from his neck down to his breast, and from his breast down to his hips and his knees shining like green grass and citron'.[7] Elsewhere St Michael appears 'with a numerous retinue, himself clad in the garments of a *praepositus*'.[8]

All of this, of course, makes perfect sense. The angels, being sexless and acting as God's attendants, had their closest earthly analogy in the eunuchs of the imperial palace. The chief of the eunuchs was the *praepositus sacri cubiculi*, whose position was, therefore, analagous to that of St Michael. Furthermore, the Byzantine mind saw no incongruity in a eunuch's occupying the position of a military commander: this was common practice. To cite but one example, Narses, one of Justinian's most successful generals, was a eunuch.

In addition to the angels, God's court also included the saints. An altogether outstanding place, comparable to that of the emperor's family, was held by the Mother of God – the *Theotokos*, as she was usually called – and John the Baptist. These two personages appear alongside Christ on one of the most widespread types of Byzantine icon which we refer to as the *Deêsis*: Christ stands or sits enthroned in the middle, while his Mother and the Forerunner stand on either side, their heads slightly bowed, their hands extended in a gesture of intercession on behalf of the human race. In the same position they also appear at the Last Judgement.[9]

It would be superfluous to describe here the pre-eminence of the Virgin Mary in the Christian pantheon; to the Byzantines, moreover, she had the particularly important role of being the patron and protectress of Constantinople.[10] She assumed this part by virtue of two highly venerated relics which found their way to the capital – the Girdle and the Veil. The Girdle (*zônê*) was kept as the Basilica of St Mary of the Coppermarket (*Chalkoprateia*), said to have been built by the Empress Pulcheria in 450: its ruined apse is still preserved a short distance west of St Sophia. The relic itself, according to one tradition, was brought by Justinian from Zela, a place south of Amaseia in eastern Asia Minor; according to another, it was translated from Jerusalem by the Emperor Arcadius.[11]

More famous than the Girdle was the Veil (*maphorion*) which was kept in a special chapel next to the Basilica of St Mary of Blachernae in the northern corner of the capital. It was said that this relic was discovered at Capernaum by the patricians Galbius and Candidus during the reign of Leo I (457–74). It belonged to a Jewish woman who kept it in a wooden chest. The patricians were able, however, to purloin it by substituting another chest of exactly the same size, and brought the Veil to Constantinople. Its miraculous powers were manifested at some of the gravest moments of the capital's history: it was the *maphorion* that saved Constantinople from the Avars and the Persians in 626 and from the Russians in 860.[12]

Apart from St John the Baptist who spans the transition from Law to Grace (and who, in Constantinople alone, had thirty-five churches dedicated to him), the prophets, priests and patriarchs of the Old Testament played a minor part in Byzantine piety. Among the saints of the New Dispensation, the Apostles were, if one may say so, at the hierarchical summit; they did enjoy a considerable cult, yet cannot be described as the most popular of saints. Those that were the most popular constitute at first sight a strange band: many, indeed most of them, were shadowy figures concerning whom nothing very definite was known; and if one searches into the reasons of their popularity, one discovers them not in any trait of each saint's historical character or activity, but rather in the existence of a local cult which achieved a measure of fame.

Take the case of St Nicholas of Myra.[13] Nothing definite is known concerning this bishop who is supposed to have lived in the fourth century and to have taken part in the Council of Nicaea in 325 (the latter, however, being highly doubtful). By the sixth century some stories came to be associated with him: he had rescued from execution three citizens of Myra and then repeated the same feat by delivering three generals of the Emperor Constantine. A church in honour of St Nicholas was built at Constantinople by Justinian. Some time thereafter the bishop of Myra was confused with a local homonym, Nicholas of Sion (a monastery in Lycia) who died in 564, and a number of miracles that were credited to the latter (including the stilling of storms) were transferred to the former. By the ninth century the 'conflated' St Nicholas emerges as a major doctor of the Orthodox Church, and his representation in mosaic is set up in St Sophia on a par with those of St John Chrysostom, St Basil and other great Fathers. It is difficult to tell why this elevation took place. In any case, Nicholas had the advantage of a well-established local cult and of a miraculous tomb which exuded a holy oil. It may be that his fame first spread among Byzantine seamen who put in at the port of Myra, and so was disseminated to other parts of the Empire, until the figure of this kindly old man with a short round beard became one of the most familiar in the iconographic repertory. The translation of his relics to Bari in 1087 contributed to an even wider diffusion of his cult throughout Christendom.

Or take the case of St Demetrius of Thessalonica.[14] He, too, was a shadowy figure, supposedly a victim of the Diocletianic persecution. Moreover, he did not originally belong to Thessalonica, but to Sirmium. When, in 442–3, the capital of the prefecture of Illyricum was moved to Thessalonica so as to be protected from the attacks of the Huns, the cult of Demetrius also migrated. Shortly thereafter a magnificent basilica was built in his honour: it is still standing, though it was severely damaged by fire in 1917. The absence of relics – in the seventh century they still did not exist – was gradually forgotten or glossed over. Not only did a tomb appear, but it was made, by means of a fraudulent arrangement of concealed pipes, to emit a holy oil, so that Demetrius shared with Nicholas the enviable epithet of *myroblêtês*. Transformed into a military saint (he was originally a deacon), a youthful figure with curly hair, he repeatedly 'defended' his city against barbarian attack.

Much the same observations could be made concerning other popular saints, such as St Theodore, St George, St Mamas, St Spyridon. The medieval mind, unlike the modern mind, was not concerned with their historicity: what mattered was the existence of a local cult which provided the saint with a 'power base'. To a Thessalonican, St Demetrius was his countryman who stood in close proximity to the Almighty and who would pay particular attention to a petition coming from his own city; to have him in Heaven was rather better than to have a fellow Thessalonican occupying a high position in the imperial service. The saint's nebulous character was no obstacle to this role; indeed, it was an advantage: for thus he could become endowed with every conceivable virtue, which would not have been possible had he possessed a well-defined historical personality.

The ordinary Byzantine regarded each saint as dwelling, in the first instance, in his principal church; to a lesser extent (or perhaps more intermittently) in other churches dedicated to him and, furthermore, in his relics and icons wherever these might be. Hence the desirability of pilgrimage. John Moschus (c. 600 AD) tells us of an anchorite who lived close to Jerusalem and who had such great affection for the martyrs that he would undertake long journeys to St John's at Ephesus, St Theodore's at Euchaita (in Pontus), St Thecla's at Seleucia (in Cilicia) and St Sergius's at Resafa (in Syria).[15] In the words of our author, the anchorite did not visit the churches of these martyrs; he simply went to St John's, St Theodore's, and so on, as if for a personal meeting. An even more revealing example is provided by a certain Gregory, the biographer of St Basil the Younger (tenth century). This man owned a farm at Rhaedestus in Thrace (modern Tekirdağ) to which he used to go in the summer to collect the harvest. On one occasion, before setting out from Constantinople, where he normally resided, he repaired to the Church of St Stephen in his neighbourhood and prayed for a safe journey by sea and land. However, once he had reached Rhaedestus, he fell into the clutches of a young woman who happened to be a witch. He resisted her blandishments; she revenged herself by inflicting on him a fever. As Gregory lay in a coma, he remembered to call on St Stephen: 'Holy, first martyr Stephen, apostle of Christ, have I not implored you to help me as I was departing from the City? Behold, I am gone, and you will see me no longer; nor will I continue to serve you – this I know for sure, for I have come close to the gates of death.' – 'What is the trouble with you, my friend?' replied St Stephen. 'I have not been here. I have churches all over the world, and I have been visiting them as all saints do. Do not, therefore, blame me. I have just arrived.' St Stephen made Gregory recite a prayer – one of those old magical prayers containing invocations to the seraphim, the cherubim and all the heavenly host – and the witch's spell was broken.[16]

We have seen that Gregory performed 'services' that were agreeable to St Stephen and so made himself a *persona grata*. The institution of patronage provided the exact model for such practices and some texts are perfectly explicit on this point. In the seventh century an elderly man who had belonged all his life to the lay brotherhood of St Artemius (a healer saint) and who, nevertheless, developed an ulcer, bitterly remarked: 'If I had placed myself in the service of a man on earth, I would have been deemed worthy of more support and solicitude.' Another disappointed customer of St Artemius cried out: 'What sort of patronage is this? The saint is an impostor!'[17] For just as the human patron had influence among persons of authority, so the saint was supposed to have a direct pipeline to celestial power. The key word in this connection was *parrhêsia*. In ancient Greece this meant 'freedom of speech', the citizen's prerogative of frankly expressing his opinions. By the Byzantine period, however, *parrhêsia* had acquired a different spectrum of connotations: while occasionally retaining the meaning of 'free speech' or 'boldness' (usually in a bad sense), it came to stand more and more for the kind of familiarity or 'access' which the favourite courtier enjoyed with regard to his master.[18] Similarly, the saint had *parrhêsia* in God's presence and, in this capacity, he could obtain favours for his clients. The same Gregory expresses it quite blatantly. 'We often observe this', he says, 'with respect to the earthly emperor as well, namely that through the mediation of his closest friends he forgives the penalty that is due to the gravest crimes and faults.' Salvation, of course, could be won the hard way, through fasting and deprivation, but not everyone was capable of this. Hence, continues our author, the importance of winning over several holy men, or, if not several, then a few, and if not a few, at least one. If the holy man is alive, use your resources to contribute to his needs and well-being; if you are indigent, propitiate him by means of physical service, obedience and humility. If he has died, make whatever contribution you can to his church in the way of oil, candles and incense or, if you are sufficiently rich, by feeding the poor and clothing the naked. In this manner, when you depart this life, the saint will receive you over there and intercede on your behalf at the Lord's judgement. For did not Christ himself say, 'He that receiveth a righteous man in the name of a righteous man shall receive a righteous man's reward' (Mt. 10. 41)?[19]

Locked in continuous, if unequal, combat with the forces of light were the forces of darkness, the innumerable host of the demons. It would be a mistake to dismiss these as a product of superstition, unworthy of the historian's consideration. To the Byzantine man demons were a reality, and he saw his whole life as a battleground between the battalions of good and evil; especially so the monk who became accustomed to using a military phraseology in this respect: the words *polemos* (war) and *polemeisthai* (to be under attack) constantly recur to denote the spiritual struggle against demons.

Under the category of demons the Byzantines included a wide

variety of spirits, each one of whom had a defined function or location. At the most primitive level we find the maleficent spirits of nature who hardly belong to the Christian view of things. A particularly detailed prayer of exorcism falsely attributed to St Basil gives the following enumeration of them:

> Take fright, leave, flee, depart, O unclean demon ... wherever you happen to be, ... whether you have the form of a serpent or the face of a beast or are like a vapor or like a bird, ... whether you appear in the morning or at noon or at midnight or at some other untimely hour or at dawn, ... whether you are in the sea or in a river or under the earth or in a well or by a cliff or in a ditch or in a lake or in a bed of reeds or in a forest ... or in a grove or in a thicket or in a tree or in a bird or in thunder or on the roof of a bath or in a pool of water, whether we know or do not know whence you have come ... depart to a waterless, desert and untilled land where no man dwells.[20]

The Lives of saints are full of references to demons that haunted the out-of-doors, as a few examples will show. In the sixth century St Nicholas of Sion, whom we have already mentioned, was called upon to deal with a huge cypress tree inhabited by a demon who terrified the surrounding region and killed anyone that drew near. The saint, before a large assembly, began chopping the tree down with an axe; it wavered and began falling into the crowd (naturally at the devil's instigation), but Nicholas caught it single-handed and made it fall in the opposite direction. Thereupon the demon admitted defeat and departed.[21] Demons lurked in deserted places, kept watch at the crossing of rivers and torrents, and were particularly numerous underground. A man who walked abroad after dark ran the risk of becoming possessed. An injudicious excavation, especially of a spot marked by the remains of pagan antiquity, was apt to release a multitude of demons who would then take possession of human beings and farm animals.

The Life of St Theodore of Sykeon (in Galatia), who died in 613, offers a particularly varied assortment of demon tales. When the saint was still a boy, he would get up in the middle of the night and make his way to a Church of St George that stood on a hilltop near the village of Sykeon. As he was walking in the dark, he would be attacked by demons who took the shape of wolves and other wild beasts. A spot eight miles distant from Sykeon was haunted, especially at noon, by 'Artemis, as she is called, with a multitude of demons', so that no one could draw near. Another spot was so infested with unclean spirits that neither man nor animal could approach it, especially at noon and after sunset. The saint had a cave dug there, and stayed in it from Christmas until Palm Sunday, fasting and praying. Visitors could hear sounds of lamentation as the spirits were being driven away by the holy man's presence. At length, not only was the spot cleansed, but it even acquired a peculiar sanctity so that a handful of earth picked from there and mixed into food and drink cured diseases in men and animals. In a village, situated in the territory of Gordiane, the inhabitants were building a bridge over a stream. The project was nearly complete when the workmen ran out of stones, and they proceeded to extract some slabs from a nearby hill. As they did so, there issued forth a throng of unclean spirits who entered the men and women of the village, while others occupied places along the public road and on the boundaries of the village territory where they molested the animals and passers-by. St Theodore was sent for, and as he approached, the demons began crying out: 'Why have you come from Galatia to Gordiane? You ought not to cross boundaries. We know why you have come, but we shall not obey you like the demons of Galatia, for we are hardier than they are.' It was to no avail: Theodore expelled the demons from the men and women they had possessed; he then rounded up the spirits lurking in the countryside and along the roads (they could be seen in the form of flies, hares and dormice), and drove them back into the excavation, which was then covered up.[22]

On another occasion, a rich man at Heracleia Pontica (now Karadeniz Ereğlisi) dug a trench near his house; out of it came unclean spirits that attacked members of his household and other inhabitants of the city. In a village of the region of Lagantine stood a marble sarcophagus containing the remains of ancient pagans who were guarded by demons. The peasants removed the lid of the sarcophagus to use as a water-trough, thereby releasing the demons. A similar incident that took place at Germia in Galatia caused a considerable stir. The local bishop made a large excavation with a view to building a cistern. In so doing, he struck an ancient cemetery and the demons who were lurking in the tombs came out and possessed the inhabitants, both rich and poor. And whereas the rich, out of a sense of shame, shut up the affected members of their households, the poor flocked to the church. Theodore was fetched, and he began by interrogating the demons. The latter laid the blame on the bishop. They had been quite content to dwell in their tombs, but when the bishop, stirred on by ambition, drove them out of their humble quarters, they were filled with rage – something they would not normally have done in the days of such a renowned exorcist as St Theodore. In the presence of a great concourse of clergymen, even of Jews and heretics, Theodore performed his ritual. The demons that had possessed the poor were herded together, but then they began protesting. 'There are many of our company', they cried, 'that are in bodies hidden in the houses of the rich and in hostels. Let them come, too, before you confine us.' Theodore did not consent. 'If respectable citizens have done this out of shame, why make a public spectacle of them? All the hidden spirits, be they in houses or hostels, will be driven out by the angelic host and brought here.' And so it came to pass. There were, however, two women who had been possessed from an earlier time, and whose demons complained with some reason: 'Do not shut us up here. . . . We are not of this company, but came from the region of Cappadocia before the excavation was made.' Theodore agreed to deal with them on another occasion. On the rest of the demons he enjoined, for the sake of decency, not to tear completely the clothes of their victims as they departed from their bodies, so that the men would be left in their drawers and the women in their tunics. And so the demons were driven back into their hole which was covered up with earth. As each victim recovered, he would relate his experiences: one had seen a snake coming out of his mouth, another a dormouse, another a lizard.[23]

These naïvely reported incidents prompt a number of observations. We may note, first, the strong local feeling exhibited by the demons: those of Gordiane considered themselves tougher than those of Galatia; the demons that hailed from Cappadocia refused to let themselves be confined at Germia, and their plea was considered reasonable by St Theodore. Secondly, demons were associated with the memorials of ancient paganism. The identification of the pagan gods with demons is a commonplace of Early Christian thought; indeed, in the examples we have quoted Artemis does appear with an escort of demons. But the old gods were already dead; they had left only a vague memory, a maleficent aura. All the same, the countryside was still covered with remains of Graeco–Roman antiquity. The great marble sarcophagi carved with funerary banquets and other strange figures were too valuable not to be occasionally re-used as water-troughs and fountains, yet they also appeared ominous. Rather than release the demons that guarded them, it was often thought wiser not to touch them – a circumstance for which archaeologists may be grateful.

Demons were always ready to enter the bodies of humans and domesticated animals where, attracted by the warmth and moisture, they could dwell, like parasites, for long years. In so doing they caused various diseases and a derangement of the senses. Not all diseases, of course, were due to demons, and some would respond to medical treatment or to curative waters; yet a great many were the result of possession and lay, therefore, beyond the physician's competence. Only an exorcist could help, and his methods were rough. He would often strike the patient in the chest or throw him to the ground and step upon his neck. The demon, always unwilling to depart, could cause levitation; when forced out, he convulsed the patient, made him tear his clothes, and then left him unconscious. But the cure, once effected, was complete.

In addition to 'rank and file' demons, there was also an officer class with specialized functions. We often hear of the demon of fornication and the demon of boredom or despondency (akêdia), to whose attacks monks were particularly vulnerable. The demon of somnolence and yawning busied himself with putting to sleep the faithful who were attending service in church.[24] Some of these demons held a military rank in the infernal hierarchy – captain of a hundred or captain of a thousand. The demon of the hippodrome belonged to the latter category and was still active in the tenth century when the hippodrome games had sunk to the level of an infrequent ritual.[25]

Unlike Milton's Satan, the Byzantine devil was not a proud rebel; instead, he was rather seedy, as Dostoevsky, too, imagined him. He usually appeared as a Negro of small stature or as a serpent, a black dog, an ape, a crow or a mouse. He could, however, assume other disguises, for example, that of an Arab merchant or of an old woman. He was a coward and a liar and he emitted a bad smell. As every monk knew, his favourite tactic was to inspire dirty thoughts or feelings of boredom. When he failed in this approach, he terrified his victim by taking on the form of a wild beast or of a giant and he would occasionally inflict physical violence on him. Quite often he made predictions, not because he knew the future, but because he was able to move very fast (being a spirit) and so could either announce events that had taken place afar or draw from them a likely inference. For example, if it rained heavily near the source of the Nile, the devil was on pretty safe ground in foretelling a flood in Egypt. The holier a man was, the more the devil envied him and tried to entrap him. But the holy man usually possessed 'the gift of the discernment of spirits'. He could, so to speak, smell the devil out and could then put him to flight by the sign of the cross or by reciting Psalm 68: 'Let God arise, let his enemies be scattered; let them also that hate him flee before him.' For, at bottom, the demons were powerless: as St Antony pointed out, they even had to ask the Lord's permission to enter the Gadarene swine. And for what other reason did they assume the form of lowly animals?[26]

Life on earth was thus lived on two levels, the visible and the invisible, of which the latter was by far the more significant. Ordinary mortals were not aware of the contest that was continually taking place on account of their salvation, but men of holiness could actually see and smell the spiritual beings, both good and evil. The final act of the contest occurred at the time of a man's death and shortly thereafter. For when a human being was about to expire, a throng of demons would hasten to his deathbed in the expectation of gaining possession of his soul and would be opposed in so doing by the guardian angel. Once the soul had been parted from the body, it had to journey through the air and stop at a number of 'customs posts' or 'toll houses' (telônia) manned by demons who examined it on its deeds on earth and either let it proceed upon payment of the appropriate due, calculated in good works, or seized it there and then. This curious belief, probably of Egyptian origin, is already alluded to in the Life of St Antony.[27] Some two or three centuries later we read of St Symeon, the saintly fool of Emesa, praying in these words for the salvation of his recently deceased mother: 'Grant her, O Lord, an escort of angels to protect her soul from the evil spirits and pitiless beasts of the air who attempt to swallow all that go by.'[28]

According to a tenth-century text,[29] there were twenty-one 'toll houses', each representing one of the following sins: slander, abuse, envy, falsehood, wrath, pride, inane speech (including laughter, jokes, obscenity, provocative gait and licentious song), usury coupled with deceit, despondency coupled with vanity, avarice (this one was covered by a particularly thick cloud of darkness), drunkenness, remembrance of evil, sorcery and magic, gluttony (including prohibited eating during fasts), idolatry and heresy, homosexuality male and female, adultery, murder, theft, fornication and, finally, hardness of heart. It is explained that the great majority of souls failed in the toll houses of adultery and fornication – an interesting commentary on Byzantine life. What is particularly remarkable, however, is that the presiding demons were in possession of detailed ledgers (kôdikes) in which every particular transgression was entered with its exact date and the names of witnesses. Only when a person had fully confessed a sin on earth and made expiation for it was the relevant entry erased from the ledger. The burden of the imperial bureaucracy and the fear of the tax-collector could not have been represented more graphically.

It is fair to say that the Orthodox Church never officially endorsed the bizarre notion of the *telônia*. The destiny of the departed soul prior to the Last Judgement was a question that remained in suspense. The custom of praying for the deceased and of making offerings in church on the third, ninth and fortieth day after death presupposed the possibility of changing or, at any rate, alleviating the verdict. In some quarters it was believed that for forty days after death the disembodied soul revisited the places of his earthly life, was shown the delights of paradise and the torments of hell and, after making obeisance to the Lord, was assigned a place of sojourn.[30] When Gennadius Scholarius, the first patriarch of Constantinople after the Turkish conquest, was consulted on this topic, he gave the following guarded answer. The souls of the righteous went straight up to Heaven after death just as the souls of unrepentant sinners went to Hell or to some other dark and unpleasant place. As for the middling, there were three possibilities: these 'average' souls were either temporarily relegated to the earthly paradise or, as the Latins thought, to a purgatory situated somewhere near the convex boundary of the air or, thirdly, were subjected to the *telônia*. Scholarius regarded the third alternative as the most likely, the more so as it was confirmed by a considerable body of tradition. It seems, however, that he had in mind not so much a direct passage of the souls through the toll houses as a lengthy sojourn or 'shunting up and down' which served to remind the soul of its misdeeds and so purified it.[31]

The role of the demons in each man's existence was concluded by the posthumous examination of the soul. As on earth so in the suprasensible sphere a man's fate was decided by the bureaucracy of angels and demons. Divided according to classes, the departed souls now awaited the Last Judgement, which was no judgement at all, but a kind of grand imperial pageant in the course of which the existing sentences were made permanent. Of this we shall speak in a later chapter.

CHAPTER 8

THE PHYSICAL UNIVERSE

We must not be misled by the proposition, true though it may be to some extent, that the Byzantines inherited the scientific speculation of the ancient Greeks. It is a fact that in some periods more than in others a few members of the intellectual élite of Byzantium devoted themselves to the study of ancient cosmology and geography. Texts of Aristotle, of Ptolemy, of Strabo and other authors were copied and commented; and while we must be eternally grateful to the Byzantine scholars who have preserved this heritage for us, we would be wrong in supposing that their efforts had any appreciable impact on the general public. The ordinary Byzantine did not, of course, lack all interest in the world around him, but in his eyes problems of natural science were part of biblical exegesis and were solved in authoritative discussions of the Six Days of Creation (*hexaêmeron*). The key text was the first chapter of Genesis which, in spite of its brevity, contains a fair number of incongruities. A few other biblical passages, especially in the books of Psalms and Isaiah, had to be taken into account, but the chief task was the interpretation of Genesis which posed many difficulties both by its statements and its omissions. We must begin by gaining some understanding of these difficulties.

On the first day, we are told, God created the heaven and the earth, the latter being as yet invisible and without form. Darkness was upon the abyss, and the Spirit of God moved upon the face of the water. God also created light which He divided from darkness, and He called the light 'day'. On the second day He created the firmament so as to separate the waters that were above it from those that were below it, and He called the firmament 'heaven'.

From the very start the candid reader is puzzled. Seeing that the sun and the moon were created on the fourth day, how is it that there had been three prior days, each with its morning and evening? Which was this light that did not come from the sun, and which was the darkness that does not appear to have been created? Was the abyss the same thing as the water? Most important, what exactly was the firmament which was different from the heaven and yet was called 'heaven', and what were the waters above the firmament?

On the third day God said, 'Let the waters under the heaven be gathered in one place and let the dry land appear.' And He called the dry land 'earth', and the bodies of water He called 'seas'. Since water naturally flows downward, how is it that it did not behave in this manner on the first day, instead of awaiting God's command? Why does the Bible sometimes refer to one sea that occupies a single space, and at other times to several seas? Finally, why did God create grass and fruit trees on the third day when the sun did not yet exist?

The two great luminaries and the stars were created on the fourth day. The text says clearly that they were 'in the firmament' or 'in the firmament of the heaven'. It is not specified whether the moon was created full, but this minor point concerned chronology rather than the structure of the universe.

The creation of fishes, birds and terrestrial animals did not cause any particular difficulty. But how was one to interpret God's words when He was creating man? Why did He say, 'Let *us* make man in our image, after our likeness'? Whom was He addressing, and what is the meaning of 'in our image'?

Further puzzles, this time of a geographical nature, were posed by the description of Paradise in Chapter 2 of Genesis. Paradise was situated somewhere to the east and gave rise to four rivers, namely the Pison, 'which compasseth the whole land of Havilah, where there is gold', the Gihon, which 'compasseth the whole land of Ethiopia', the Tigris (so in the Septuagint) which flows opposite Assyria, and the Euphrates. Even if the Byzantines had no clear notion concerning the Pison and the land of Havilah, the three other rivers were well known: the Gihon could only be the Nile, while the Tigris and the Euphrates were called by their own names. It was also generally realized that the latter two arose in Persian Armenia, while the sources of the Nile lay very far from that country, somewhere in Ethiopia. How was it, then, that these three rivers, not to mention the enigmatic Pison, all started at the same spot, namely in Paradise?[1] Could one not reach Paradise by following these rivers upstream? And if the earthly Paradise still existed, as the Bible implies, where exactly was it, and why had it not been seen by anyone since the expulsion of Adam from it?

These were some of the principal difficulties connected with the text of Genesis. There was also one important omission: nothing is said about the creation of angels, whereas the book of Job (38. 7) affirms – and these are the very words of the Lord as He spoke out of the whirlwind – that 'when the stars were born, all my angels praised me in a loud voice'. Hence the angels were already in existence on the fourth day. And if the serpent that tempted Eve was the devil, when had the fall of Satan occurred?

The almost impossible task of reconciling the biblical text with the notions of the world that were generally accepted in antiquity was undertaken before the beginning of the Byzantine period, and may be traced from Philo Judaeus in the first century AD to Theophilus of Antioch in the second, to Origen in the third and to St Basil in the fourth. We shall not follow it here in detail, except to note that the earliest exegetes provided certain answers that were to become definitive. Thus Philo solved the puzzle of the creation of grass and trees before that of the sun. This was done, he says, in order that men might not ascribe the growth of vegetation to the action of the sun, in other words as an argument against idolatry. Philo also interpreted 'correctly' the reference in Gen. 1. 14 to the heavenly bodies serving 'for signs and for seasons' by saying that they were meant to announce changes of weather and enable men to make certain necessary predictions, not to vindicate astrology. On the other hand, Philo's most ingenious suggestion, that of interpreting the first day of Creation as referring to an ideal world illuminated by an intelligible light, did not win acceptance.[2]

The contribution of Theophilus of Antioch[3] proved more durable because it was more down-to-earth. He explained that the heaven made on the first day was not the heaven visible to us, but another one higher up, and that it was fashioned like a roof or a vault – this with reference to Isaiah 40. 22, 'It is God who made heaven as a vault and spread it out as a tent to dwell in' (so in the Septuagint). The earth he explained as a base and foundation; the abyss as being the multitude of waters. One half of the waters, he says, was raised above the firmament to provide rain, showers and dew, the other half being left on the earth for rivers, springs and seas. Theophilus was rather silly in connecting rain with the waters above the firmament, and this part of his theory was later abandoned, but his explanation of dew, which occurs without the agency of clouds, was retained. Theophilus also introduced a number of symbolical comparisons that were to become standard: the moon that waned and was reborn referred to man; great fishes and carnivorous birds to greedy men and transgressors; quadrupeds to men who were ignorant of God. More importantly, he explained the plural form of 'Let us make man' as being addressed to the Logos, that is, the Son.

Setting aside Origen, whose subtle interpretation fell by the wayside, we come to St Basil's homilies on the *hexaêmeron*, a text that was to prove extremely popular and influential throughout the Byzantine period.[4] His position may be defined as follows:

1. He rejects all pagan theories of the universe on the grounds that one contradicts the other. There is no need, therefore, to disprove them: they suffice for their own refutation. What is the purpose of all this arithmetic and geometry, the study of solids, even renowned astronomy? It is all 'laborious vanity'. As St Paul says (a key text in this connection), 'They became vain in their imaginations, and their foolish heart was darkened. Professing themselves to be wise, they became fools' (Rom. 1. 21–2).

2. The certitude, so sadly lacking among the pagans, is provided by Moses (the reputed author of Genesis) whose academic qualifications were excellent, since he was educated by the Egyptian sages and spent forty years in contemplation. Thus equipped, he saw God face to face and was told the truth directly. What need, then, to listen to human arguments?

3. The Bible must be understood literally, not allegorically. If it is silent on certain matters it is because these matters do not concern us.

4. The universe has a moral purpose; it is a school wherein reasonable souls are instructed and guided upward to the contemplation of the invisible. Consequently, the study of the world ought to be conducted by a spirit cleansed of carnal passions, free from everyday cares and always questing after an adequate notion of God.

So much for principles; we now come down to particulars. First, Basil establishes that the world is not eternal: it had a beginning and it shall have an end, for 'heaven and earth shall pass away' (Mt. 24. 35). It seems that before the creation of the world there was an 'older condition', illuminated by a spiritual light and not contained in time, but Basil is not very specific about this. Temporal creation started with that of the upper heaven which is made of a light substance, something like smoke. This is stated by Isaiah (51. 6), and there is no need to enquire any further. The same prophet also explains, as we have seen, that heaven was set up like a vault. As for the earth, it is equally useless to ask what it is that it rests on. If it rests on air, why is it that the air does not recede under the weight? If on water, why does not the earth sink? And furthermore, what does the water rest on? The argument becomes endless: the best answer is provided by the Psalmist – 'In the hand of God are the ends of the earth' (Ps. 94. 4 in the Septuagint). So far, Basil has been discussing a universe that has a top and a bottom. He adds, however, that some naturalists have a different theory: in their view the earth is immobile because it is in the exact centre of the universe. Basil himself is unwilling to take a position on this doctrine. If the reader finds it plausible, he should convey his admiration to God's wisdom; if not, may the simplicity of his faith prevail over logical arguments.

The firmament, according to Basil, should be distinguished from the heaven that was created on the first day. As its name implies, it is composed of some fairly firm and resistant substance, but he refuses to specify whether this is like ice, rock crystal or mica. He is even willing to admit the existence of a third heaven, attested by St Paul (II Cor. 12. 2), or of several heavens (Ps. 148. 4). But what of the waters above the firmament? Some critics had objected that if the firmament had a domical shape, the waters would necessarily have flowed down its convex exterior. Not at all, replies St Basil; for if the interior is concave, it does not follow that the exterior is convex. The latter may well be flat, as it often happens in baths that have domical vaults on the inside and a flat roof on the outside. As for the waters, they are there, so to speak, as a cooling agent. For fire is a necessity of life, yet fire consumes water. In the end fire will prevail (as attested by Isaiah 44. 27), but God has wisely calculated the duration of the world and has provided a sufficiency of water to counteract the action of fire.

We have already mentioned the difficulties arising from the 'gathering in' of the waters on the third day. In answer to the first objection, namely why the water did not of its own accord flow down to its assigned place, Basil replies that we are acquainted with the properties of water as they are today; but how do we know that water had the same property, namely of flowing downward, prior to the third day of Creation? God's order determined the nature or propensity of water which, presumably, it had previously lacked. As to the existence of one or several seas, Basil is prepared to admit that there are indeed many lakes, but for him there is only one sea. The Caspian, which some authorities believed to be land-locked, must, therefore, communicate with the ocean. Furthermore, the sea has its assigned place. No matter how agitated it becomes, it always breaks on the shore, and a substance as soft as sand is sufficient to contain it. The Red Sea could easily have flooded Egypt which lies on a lower level,[5] had it not been kept in check by the Creator.

These examples are sufficient to illustrate Basil's approach. In spite of his search for certitude, a certitude provided only by the Bible, he was content to bypass some of the great problems of cosmology. He was much more at ease when he described the moral lessons that might be drawn from the observation of animals – a topic to which we shall return in the next chapter. Perhaps he was too cultivated a man to adopt the simple-minded conclusions that followed inescapably from a literal interpretation of the biblical text, and so took refuge in a kind of indifferentism. Nor did St John Chrysostom, who followed an allegorical approach in this respect, entirely satisfy a public that wanted simple answers to fundamental questions. This public accordingly turned to another school of exegesis, usually called the School of Antioch, which had the courage to construct a system that was entirely biblical. Its masters, after Theophilus of Antioch, were Diodorus of Tarsus, Theodore of Mopsuestia, Severianus of Gabala and, finally, Cosmas Indicopleustes.

Diodorus was a contemporary of St Basil's. His work, entitled *Against Destiny*, is unfortunately lost, but we have a lengthy analysis of it by the patriarch Photius.[6] It is evident from this résumé that Diodorus had a good reason for denying a spherical universe as it was conceived by naturalist philosophers; for if one admitted the celestial spheres composed of a fifth element and endowed with perpetual motion, one was half-way to astrology and paganism. It was with a view to subverting the very basis of astrology that Diodorus delineated the 'true' nature of the universe. According to him, 'there exist two heavens; one of them, higher than the visible sky, came into existence at the same time as the earth [in the sense that they were both created on the first day], while the other is the visible one. The first of the two fulfils the function of a roof; the second does the same with regard to the earth, while also serving as a foundation and a base for the one above. The earth is one. The heavenly space has been assigned to the superior powers and the space under the heaven to visible beings. The heaven is not spherical, but has the form of a tent or a vault. In support of this idea,' says Photius, 'he thinks he can present scriptural testimony, not only concerning the form of the universe, but also concerning the setting and the rising of the sun. He also explains the variable length of days and nights and inquires closely into other matters of the same kind which, in my opinion, do not necessarily follow, even if they are in accord with Holy Writ.' We easily recognize here the system of Theophilus.

Some twenty years after Diodorus we meet Severianus of Gabala, a preacher greatly appreciated at the court of Constantinople in spite of his thick Syrian accent. In his homilies on the *hexaêmeron*[7] the same Antiochene ideas are expounded with a number of slight variants. The universe is compared by Severianus to a two-storied house, the in-between floor being the visible sky or firmament. This is composed of ice and upholds one half of the waters so as to counteract the fire of the luminaries. So abundant is this water that part of it falls down to earth in the form of dew. On the Day of Judgement the upper water will be withdrawn, as a result of which the firmament will melt and the stars fall down. The same water serves the further purpose of reflecting downward the light of the sun and the moon which would otherwise have mounted up. The structure of the universe is repeated in that of the human body. The upper portion, above the firmament, is similar to the brain whose working is invisible and which is separated from the mouth by the palate (*ouraniskos*) whose name appropriately resembles that of the sky (*ouranos*).

The gathering of the waters is expounded by Severianus in a manner more ingenious than St Basil's. The earth, he says, was created flat on the first day and was, therefore, entirely covered with water. On the third day, however, the Lord fashioned the earth into mountains and depressions so that the water flowed down to form the sea. The observation of mountains and rocky islands proves that they were at one time joined together.

The luminaries were created independently of the sky and were then attached to it, much as an artist paints a picture and then hangs it on the wall. The sun was fixed to the east, the moon to the west. The pagan idea according to which the sun passes under the earth during the night is rejected. In fact, it traverses the northern regions, hidden by a kind of wall, and its course is obscured by the waters. This is confirmed by Ecclesiastes 1. 5–6: 'The sun rises and the sun sets, and hastens to his place. Rising there, he goes toward the south and turns to the north' (so in the Septuagint). The variable duration of the day depends on the length of the sun's journey, seeing that it does not always rise at the same spot. The moon which wanes, dies and is reborn is the symbol of human life and a guarantor of our resurrection.

Along the way Severianus explains various difficulties of the sacred text. The creation of angels is not mentioned in Genesis because this book was composed by Moses after the exodus, at a time when the Jews were still accustomed to the idolatry they had learnt in Egypt: the legislator did not wish to give them an excuse for reverting to their errors. As for the silence of the Bible concerning the four elements, this is not surprising since the heaven and the earth imply the existence of water, fire and air. Furthermore, fire and air are closely linked. The superior powers are of fire – a heavenly and immaterial fire, yet related to ours as shown by the fact that we are able to 'borrow' the fire of the sun, something that would not have been possible if the two were of a different nature. Besides, if there had been no fire in the earth, how is it that we can obtain a spark from a stone or a piece of wood?

It seems that the audience of Severianus was rather bored by his lectures on natural science. 'We wish to learn theology,' they cried, 'not physiology!' The preacher retorted that this criticism was misguided, since, next to theology, it was the study of nature that provided the surest foundation for piety. If one were to banish 'physiology', one would have to banish the prophets and the apostles who spoke of it. St Paul, nay, the Saviour Himself pursued physiology.

The ideas of Severianus, along with a few of St Basil, Diodorus and others were picked up in the sixth century by an anonymous author whom we call pseudo-Caesarius.[8] His work, entitled *Dialogues*, assumed the common form of questions and answers and constituted a little summa of useful knowledge, both theological and scientific. In spite of its difficult style, it enjoyed a wide popularity. Quoted in florilegia and in Byzantine chronicles, it was translated into Slavonic in the tenth century and into Arabic in the eleventh. By and large, pseudo-Caesarius reproduces the system of Severianus, but he introduces a number of reflections that may be his own. He accepts the form of the universe similar to a two-storied house and a firmament made of ice which supports one half of the waters. Here he adds an interesting illustration. The Pison, he says, one of the four rivers of Paradise, is the one called the Danube (elsewhere he affirms that the Danube and the Indus were one and the same!). In the winter this river is covered with a layer of ice so resistant that it can uphold tens of thousands of mounted barbarians who invade the Roman territory in the direction of Illyricum and Thrace. This layer is bathed by the water beneath it, and sometimes it rains upon the ice, yet the water that is above the ice is not mingled with the water that is below. The firmament does not melt from the heat of the sun, because the latter is very small in comparison, like a tiny lamp in a big house. If one takes a very large platter and places a lamp beneath it, the platter is not going to melt. This, incidentally, is also the reason why the sun moves continually: had it remained stationary, it would have damaged the firmament. Pseudo-Caesarius disagrees with Severianus in affirming that the sun is not attached to the firmament; instead, it is suspended in mid-air thanks to the lightness of its substance. In that case, asks his interlocutor, why is it not tossed by the wind? Because, he replies, the wind blows farther down, near the surface of the earth. Besides, the wind is powerless to move a stone or a house; how could it shift a body as big as the sun? If the sun and the moon had been attached to the firmament, they would, furthermore, have scratched by their movement the surface of the celestial vault. As to the trajectory of the sun, the author specifies that during the night it is hidden by the rising ground of Cappadocia, or the Taurus range; which implies, incidentally, that he was writing south of Asia Minor. In that northern region beyond Cappadocia the rays of the sun are shaded by waters and vegetation and are reflected sideways under pressure of the firmament as it happens when a lamp is placed under a screen.

Pseudo-Caesarius must have lived at about the same time as the retired Alexandrian merchant whom we call Cosmas Indicopleustes, author of the *Christian Topography*.[9] The main ideas that he expressed in this book with all the zeal of the autodidact were the ones we have been describing, but he had the merit of systematizing them, illustrating them with diagrams and enlivening them with his personal recollections. Although he does not appear to have gone as far as India, he certainly travelled down the Red Sea, visited Ethiopia and the island of Socotra as well as other countries. It is unfortunate that an earlier geographical work of Cosmas happens to be lost; for in it he 'described more fully the whole earth, both the one beyond the ocean, and this one, and all its countries, together with the southern parts from Alexandria to the Southern Ocean, namely the River Nile and the countries adjacent, and all the races of Egypt and Ethiopia; the Arabian Gulf besides, with the countries adjoining and their inhabitants as far as the same ocean, and likewise the middle country between the river and the gulf, with the cities, districts and tribes therein contained.'[10] If I am not mistaken, this was the only work of geography based on personal experience that was produced during the Byzantine period.

The universe of Cosmas had the shape of a rectangular box with a vaulted lid and resembled, as one Victorian commentator put it, 'one of the huge receptacles in which female travellers of our day carry their dresses'. The earth, likewise rectangular, formed the base of the box and was surrounded on all sides by the ocean which was not navigable. Beyond the ocean, however, was a narrow strip of land whose eastern portion contained the earthly paradise. It was to this strip that the four walls of the universe were welded. Half-way up, the walls supported a ceiling, namely the firmament with the waters above it. The walls then curved inward to enclose the Heavenly Kingdom. The surface of the earth was inclined from north to south with the result that one had to go uphill when travelling towards the north. Cosmas does not explain, however, why it was that the waters of the ocean did not all flow to the south. Somewhere in the north was also a huge mountain (the same we have encountered in pseudo-Caesarius) behind which the sun hid during the night. A fundamental postulate of Cosmas' system is that the universe was exactly reproduced by the Tabernacle of Moses, which was likewise divided into two spaces by means of the veil, while the table of shew-bread, which was twice as long as it was broad and was placed lengthwise from east to west, typified the earth. Ridiculous as this notion may appear to us, we must remember that the theory of a rectangular earth had antecedents in Greek science and tended to be confirmed by the experience of ancient travellers who knew that one could traverse a much longer distance from east to west than from north to south. Cosmas himself calculated the distance from China to Gibraltar as approximately twelve thousand miles, while the north–south dimension of the earth was only half that figure.

The system of Cosmas had some weaknesses even within his terms of reference. His notion, for example, that the luminaries of the sky were propelled by angels has no authority in the Bible. He was also unable to give a satisfactory account of the rivers of Paradise which he forced to somehow flow under the eastern arm of the ocean before they emerged out of the ground. In spite of such blemishes, we must grant that Cosmas managed to construct a remarkably coherent system which satisfied the requirements of the Bible, the claims of symbolism and the first-hand experience of the traveller. What is more, his ideas had a considerable diffusion in later centuries, in spite of the fact that the *Christian Topography*, containing as it did nearly a hundred illustrations that were necessary for the understanding of the text, could not have been copied very often. In the ninth century it was read by Photius (who, as an intellectual, found it ridiculous)[11] and reproduced in a splendid manuscript that still exists today (*Vaticanus graecus* 699). It was also translated into Slavonic, perhaps in the tenth century, and continued to be read in Russia as an authoritative textbook down to the seventeenth century.[12]

There can be little doubt that the Antiochene conception of the universe, as exemplified by Cosmas, reflected the views of the average Byzantine on this subject. Whenever a Byzantine saint had a vision of the Heavenly Kingdom or of the Last Judgement, he thought in terms of a four-cornered universe covered by a ceiling, above which God held His court and where the elect would eventually enjoy everlasting bliss.[13] The illustrations of Creation in manuscripts of the Old Testament followed, more or less, the same model; and to the extent that a Byzantine church was a symbolical copy of the *kosmos*, it, too, presupposed a world of box-like shape.[14]

It seems it was only in the eleventh century that an attempt was made to diffuse once again the cosmological doctrines of the ancients. In his encyclopaedic opuscule *De omnifaria doctrina*[15] Michael Psellus dealt at some length with the structure of the universe. He made a few concessions to traditional Christianity by acknowledging that the world was not eternal (this was a very important point) and that earthquakes were caused by God as stated in Psalm 103. 32; for the rest, however, while denouncing 'the vain wisdom of the Hellenes', he simply returned to the spherical universe. The *De omnifaria doctrina* was dedicated first to the Emperor Constantine IX and, in a revised form, to Michael VII Doukas and, to judge by the number of extant manuscripts, enjoyed a fair amount of popularity in the later Byzantine centuries. It was not, however, a work that the ordinary person was capable of understanding and we may doubt that it had much of an impact on the consciousness of the public. The average Byzantine listened to his preachers and looked at the paintings that adorned the walls of his church. All the cosmology he needed had been set down by the greatest of all scientists, the prophet Moses.

CHAPTER 9

THE INHABITANTS OF THE EARTH

The earth is inhabited by animals and human beings. The difference between the two is that humans possess a rational soul, while animals do not. This is indicated by Leviticus 17. 11, 'The soul of all flesh is in the blood,' that is to say the vital principle of all animals is of a material nature. The same distinction is established in the book of Genesis, for in creating the animals of the sea and of the air God said, 'Let the waters bring forth the moving creatures that have life and fowl that fly' (Gen. 1. 20), which means that the life is contained in the animal, while in the case of man God first formed his body and then 'breathed into his nostrils the breath of life' (Gen. 2. 7), thus indicating the difference between body and soul. The spirit of the animal dies with his body, while the human soul will live forever.

God first created aquatic animals to show that life begins with baptism. Birds are grouped with the fishes in Genesis because they swim in the air more than they walk.[1] There is also a slight distinction between God's command concerning fishes, namely, 'Let the waters bring forth the moving creatures that have life,' and His command concerning terrestrial animals, 'Let the earth bring forth the living creature after his kind.' Aquatic animals have an imperfect existence: their sight and hearing are feeble, they have no memory or imagination, they do not recognize any familiar being, whereas terrestrial animals have keener senses.[2] The nature of each animal species has been established by God's command and no length of time will alter it. Each kind has his peculiar characteristic: the lion is proud, the ox is calm, the wolf is savage. The animals that are easiest to capture are also the most prolific (rabbits, wild goats, and so on).

Animals have been created to be subject to man. This is indicated by their name (*ktênos* = beast, fancifully derived from *ktêma* = possession)

177

and the fact that it was Adam who named them, thus establishing his authority over them, just as when one is enrolled in the imperial army one is marked by the imperial seal.[3] The thousands of names that Adam was able to invent proves his great intelligence before the Fall. The purpose of animals was threefold. Some were created to be eaten, the same that are slaughtered today; others to transport burdens, like horses and camels. The third kind consists of 'imitative' animals that were made to amuse man who was alone in Paradise. Some of these, like apes, imitate gestures, others, like parrots, imitate sounds. Originally the serpent was very friendly to man, which is why the devil chose him as his instrument. At that time he walked upright thanks to a rapid whirling of his tail. Even today, when he is angered, he tries to lift up his head, but soon reverts to a crawling posture because he cannot resist the force of God's condemnation. One should not imagine, however, that the animals lived in Paradise any more than servants live in the imperial palace. They were summoned only when their lord had need of them.[4]

Another reason for the creation of animals was to teach us moral lessons and to provide theological symbols. Big fishes feed on little fishes: we do the same when we oppress the weak. The cunning crab waits for the oyster to open in the sun, then tosses in a pebble to prevent the valves from shutting and so devours his prey. We, too, act like the crab when we pounce on the goods of our neighbour. The dissimulation of polyps which assume the colour of their surroundings is imitated by the hangers-on of the rich and powerful, for these men are temperate or libertine as circumstances require. We may also draw some admirable lessons by observing the denizens of the deep. They are not separated by any natural boundaries, yet each kind is content to dwell within its own territory. Thus, whales, which are as big as mountains, have been naturally assigned to the Atlantic Ocean which has no islands and is not bounded by any continent on the other side. Not so with us: we are constantly moving 'the ancient landmarks which our fathers have set' (Prov. 22. 28); we keep dividing land, we add house to house and field to field by defrauding our neighbours. The loathsome viper unites with the eel, and the latter submits, if not very willingly. In like manner wives should endure their husbands, even if the latter are violent, drunken and disagreeable. Husbands, too, should take this lesson to heart. The viper spits out his poison before entering on this union; the husband should likewise renounce his harsh ways. Or, to put it differently, the union of the viper and the eel is adulterous. Men who are invading other people's marriages should recognize what kind of a reptile they are imitating.[5]

Animals also teach us more exalted lessons of governance and religion. Bees are ruled by a king (we would say a queen) who exercises a natural ascendancy and who, though armed with a sting, does not use this weapon. The king is not appointed by his subjects, he is not elected by lot, nor does he come to power by the rule of heredity – three principles that often lead to the worst results; his superiority is due to nature. The transformation which the silkworm undergoes from caterpillar to larva to butterfly teaches us to believe in the change which our own bodies will experience at the time of the Resurrection. So also the vulture, which reproduces without copulation, gives us reason to accept the virgin birth of Christ.[6] It was especially a work called *Physiologus*, equally popular in the East and in the West, that served to disseminate the theological interpretation of alleged animal behaviour: the lion who sleeps with his eyes open typifies the crucified Christ whose divinity remains awake, the young pelican who is killed by his parents and returns to life on the third day is also a symbol of Christ, and so on.[7]

Like all medieval men, the Byzantines had a keen interest in exotic animals, both real and imaginary. The ecclesiastical historian Philostorgius,[8] apropos of the earthly Paradise, affirms that the biggest animals were to be found in the eastern and southern regions of the earth in spite of the heat that prevailed there. He enumerates the elephant, the Indian buffalo which he had seen on Roman territory, dragons ninety feet long and as thick as a beam of which he had seen the skin, the giraffe, the zebra, the phoenix, the parrot and certain spotted birds called Garamantes. He had beheld at Constantinople the picture of a unicorn: it had the head of a dragon, a twisted horn, a beard, a long neck, a body like that of a deer and the feet of a lion. As for monkeys, there were thousands of different varieties, many of which were brought to the Roman Empire. One was called Pan: it had the head and legs of a goat, but for the rest was pure ape. A specimen was once sent to Constantine the Great by the King of India, but it died on the way and arrived at Constantinople in a mummified condition. Philostorgius thinks that this monkey was deified by the Hellenes, as were also the satyr and the sphinx. The latter he had seen himself: it had bare breasts like a woman's, a rounded face and a voice resembling the human, but inarticulate and peevish. This beast was very savage. One such must have been brought to Thebes in ancient times. Legend represented him as winged because he jumped swiftly and as uttering enigmas because of his indistinct voice. Cosmas Indicopleustes, too, devotes an excursus to exotic animals.[9] He describes quite soberly the rhinoceros, which he had seen in Ethiopia, the buffalo, the giraffe, the yak, the musk, the 'hog-deer' of which he had tasted the flesh and the hippopotamus whose teeth he had sold at Alexandria. He admits not having seen a unicorn, but he delineates it after four statues he had observed in Ethiopia. The unicorn, he explains, is difficult to catch. When pursued, it leaps from a rock, turns a somersault in the air and lands on its horn which acts as a shock-absorber. Its existence is, moreover, confirmed by Holy Scripture.

Since God created only two rational species, namely angels and men, one ought not to believe in dragons who assume human form and carry away women. Dragons do exist, but they are merely serpents. It is not true that they rise up in the air and are killed by thunder as some ignorant people say.[10] The same argument is applied to satyrs by the eleventh-century general Cecaumenus.[11] If, he says, they existed, as stated in the Life of St Paul the Theban,[12] and were rational beings, how is it that Christ did not come to them? What prophet, what apostle was sent to instruct them? Why is there no gospel addressed to satyrs? The Fathers of the desert, he continues, did see various strange animals that live in those parts, such as dragons, asps, basilisks and unicorns, whose existence may be admitted, but not that of satyrs.

Indeed, holy monks stood in a special relation to the animal kingdom. Many of them showed particular kindness to animals. A monk of Alexandria, we are told,[13] fed every day the dogs that were in his monastery, gave flour to the smallest ants, grain to the bigger ones, and biscuits soaked in water to the birds. St Stephen the Sabaite (d. 794) even fed the harmless black worms that lived in the desert.[14] The most famous and instructive animal story, however, is that of the lion of St Gerasimus, later transferred to St Jerome. This lion, out of whose paw the saint had extracted a thorn, remained to serve him and even carried burdens for him in lieu of a donkey. When Gerasimus died, the lion, too, expired of grief. 'This came to pass,' says John Moschus, 'not because the lion had a rational soul, but because God wished to glorify those who glorify Him and demonstrate the obedience which animals had shown towards Adam.'[15] The power over the animals which Adam had lost because of the Fall could thus be regained by the saint.

The idea that different animal species had their distinctive and immutable characteristics – characteristics that were not only physical, but also moral, such as the pride of the lion and the equanimity of the ox – was also applied to human races and peoples. This formed part of an old argument against astrology that we find in Diodorus of Tarsus[16] and later in pseudo-Caesarius.[17] The point of the argument was to prove that peoples having very different customs and institutions lived in the same geographical areas, so that their peculiarities could not be ascribed to astral influence. Thus, the Brahmans and the Indians live in the same astral region, yet the Brahmans are the most virtuous of men, while the Indians live like pigs. The Chaldaeans and Babylonians practise incest and they do so not only in their own country, but also when they live abroad – which 'they still do' among the Medes, the Parthians, the Elamites, the Egyptians, the Phrygians and the Gala-tians, 'living their foul life in certain villages'. Similar examples of sexual depravity may also be observed in other parts of the earth, such as Britain, where many men lie with one woman and many women with one man. The Slavs, who are also called Danubians, devour the breasts of nursing women and dash their infants against rocks, while other tribes living in the same region abstain from all meat. And while some of them are unruly, massacre their leaders, eat foxes, wild cats and boars, and call one another by howling like wolves, others are abstemi-ous and docile. If our character was determined by the position of the stars at the moment of our birth, and if it were true that the conjunction of Mercury and Venus in the house of Mercury produced sculptors and painters, while the same conjunction in the house of Venus produced perfumers, actors and poets, why is it that these occupations are entirely absent among the Saracens, the Libyans, the Moors, the Germans, the Sarmatians, the Scythians and, in general, all those who live to the north of the Black Sea?

The diversity of the peoples was explained by the division of the earth among Noah's sons and the subsequent multiplication of tongues during the building of the Tower of Babel; for, prior to that event, all humanity was one and spoke the same language, namely Hebrew. The basic list of peoples was provided by Chapter 10 of Genesis. In the Septuagint version this list contains a number of names that may be interpreted in an ethnic sense and others that are clearly ethnic. Thus, among the eight sons of Japheth we find Iouan, who makes one think of the Ionians, Tharsis who bears some resemblance to the Thracians as well as the Ketians (recalling Citium, a city of Cyprus) and the Rho-dians. Among the four sons of Ham, Mizraim clearly refers to Egypt

181

(Misr), while Canaan begat Sidon, the Jebusite, the Amorite, Aradios (from Arados in Syria), the Samarian and Amathi (from the city of Amathus in Cyprus), and so on.

The identification of these outlandish names was undertaken by Flavius Josephus[18] who was concerned to show the priority of the Bible to the pagan traditions. Of the various peoples, he says, some have kept their original Hebrew names, while others lost them on account of the Greeks (the Macedonians). For when the latter rose to power, they gave to the nations names they could understand, thus creating the false impression that these nations were of Greek descent. Josephus is also responsible for a geographical division of the earth among Noah's sons, a division that was later adopted by the Christian tradition. The descendants of Japheth, he says, began by inhabiting the Taurus and the Amanus (the mountain range between Syria and Cilicia), then advanced into Asia up to the River Tanais (the Don) and in Europe all the way to the straits of Gibraltar, that whole country being then uninhabited. The sons of Ham held the coast of Phoenicia and Palestine down to Egypt and thence all of North Africa as far as the Atlantic Ocean. Finally, the sons of Shem received most of Asia as far as the Indian Ocean.

At some time after Josephus but before the fourth century was composed a more systematic list known as *The Division of the Earth*.[19] This text, which has not come down to us in its original form, enjoyed a wide diffusion in the Middle Ages, not only in the Greek-speaking world (it appears in all Byzantine chronicles), but also in the West, in Syria, Armenia, and so on. It is a little treatise of geography and ethnography comprising seventy-two nations, this being the number of languages that came into being at the time of the construction of the Tower of Babel. The division of the earth among Noah's sons ran, more or less, in three parallel zones from east to west: the progeny of Japheth had all the north along a line running from Media to Gibraltar, that of Shem the middle zone, and that of Ham the south along a line running through the point of juncture between Palestine and Egypt. The anonymous author also added a list of peoples who possessed an alphabet, and of principal rivers, islands and big cities.

This, the fullest list of peoples known to the Byzantine tradition, did not extend any farther east than the Persian Empire. While the existence of India was generally known, the other countries of central and eastern Asia were shrouded in mystery. The ever-popular Alexander romance gave some wonderful details about the peoples and animals that inhabited those exotic parts. Among the many texts connected with the Alexander legend there circulated an *Itinerary from Paradise to the Country of the Romans*.[20] This text informs us that next to the earthly Paradise lay the country of the Macarini or Camarini whence flows a mighty river that splits into four branches. The Macarini are good and pious. They have no fire and do not cook any food, but are sustained by manna that falls down from the sky, and they drink a mixture of wild honey and pepper. Their clothes are so pure that they are never stained. There is no illness among them and they live to an age of between 118 and 120 years. They know in advance the time of their death and prepare for it by lying down in a sarcophagus of aromatic wood. They also have no government since they live in perfect concord. All the precious stones come from their country. Next to the Macarini live the Brahmans who are also exceedingly virtuous, but as one moves farther west there is a gradual deterioration. The sowing of crops starts in the country of Nebus, the fifth from the east, which is also the first country that has a government of elders. War-riors are first encountered in Axoum, the tenth country, then comes India Minor which breeds a multitude of elephants, and finally Per-sia, which is prosperous but very wicked. Little attempt appears to have been made by the Byzantines to integrate these eastern peoples into a biblical framework, but it was claimed that the virtuous nations of the Far East were Christian.

The main problem that occurred to the Byzantine mind with regard to the peoples of the earth concerned their status in the plan of divine Providence. The equality of men is proclaimed in the Gospel, since God 'hath made of one blood all nations of men for to dwell on all the face of the earth, and hath determined the times before appointed, and the bounds of their habitation; that they should seek the Lord, if haply they might feel after him, and find him, though he be not far from every one of us' (Acts 17. 26–7). Yet it seemed as if these various peoples had not been the object of equal solicitude on the Lord's part. There was no difficulty about the initial period, the 2,900 years or so that extended from Creation to the division of the tongues. But what of the following 2,600 years to the Incarnation? The prophets were sent only to the Israelites, whereas the other nations remained in ignorance of God. And what of the period after the Incarnation? No matter how far-flung was the predication of the Gospel, it did not extend to the whole earth. Finally, what was, in the scheme of divine Providence, the role of the pagan nations?

To these questions we find only sporadic and partial answers. Granted that all men were 'of one blood', Noah's ancient curse weighed upon the descendants of Canaan, son of Ham: 'Cursed be Canaan; a servant of servants shall he be unto his brethren. Blessed be the Lord God of Shem; and Canaan shall be his servant. God shall enlarge Japheth, and he shall dwell in the tents of Shem; and Canaan shall be his servant' (Gen. 9. 25–7). This curse, it was believed, was delivered not only because Ham had seen his father's nakedness, but also in anticipation of Canaan's cupidity in invading Palestine and Phoenicia, lands that belonged to Shem. While thus downgrading the Africans because of their ancestral sin, Noah also foretold the glorious destiny of Japheth's offspring, since it was among the latter that Christianity was to make the greatest progress.[21]

Another avenue of giving some satisfaction to the non-believers who had lived prior to Christ's advent was provided by St Peter's statement that the Lord 'also went and preached unto the spirits in prison which sometime were disobedient' (I Pet. 3. 19). It was even said that St John the Baptist, who had died before Christ, had begun to preach to the spirits in Hades and that this predication was completed at the time of the Lord's Descent. In confirmation of which it was related that a lawyer had once cursed Plato. The following night the philosopher appeared to him in a dream and said: 'Stop cursing me. I do not deny that I lived as a sinner, but when Christ came down to Hades, I was the first to believe in him.' It does not follow from this that the dead will have another chance to repent, for that was a unique occasion.[22]

If a net could thus be cast round all those who had died before the Crucifixion, the next difficulty concerned the universality of the Christian preaching. This involved a point of considerable importance. When St Peter said that 'in every nation he that feareth Him, and worketh righteousness, is accepted with Him' (Acts 10. 35), he was speaking at a time when the Gospel had not yet been disseminated everywhere, but this was no longer the case.[23] Had it been otherwise, the members of 'the nations' (*ethnikoi*), that is, non-Christians, could expect to be saved by good works alone. Hence the necessity of proving that the Good Tidings had, in fact, been carried to all countries – a myth that was bolstered up by the apocryphal Acts of the Apostles. It was alleged that before setting out on their respective missions, the apostles gathered at Jerusalem and allotted to each other all the regions of the inhabited world. St Peter assumed responsibility for the circumcised Jews, James and John for the East, Philip for Samaria and Asia,

Matthew for Parthia, Thomas for Armenia and India, Andrew for Bithynia, Lacedaemonia and Achaea, and so on. The geographical area of each apostle's activity shows great variation from one text to another. We even find Matthew in the land of the Man-Eaters, Philip and Bartholomew in 'the land of the Ophians and the desert of the she-dragons'.[24] Next to Thomas, who was active in faraway India, Andrew proved a great traveller, since he evangelized Scythia, founded churches along the south shore of the Black Sea (including that of Byzantium) and finally took in Achaea as well, where he suffered martyrdom.[25]

These legends conceal a reality that remains but dimly known, namely the progress of Christian missions. In the Early Byzantine period the domain of Christianity showed a notable expansion. The ecclesiastical historian Sozomenus, writing in the fifth century, noted the conversion of all the western peoples between the Rhine and the Atlantic Ocean, that of the Armenians and the Georgians, and described the progress of the true faith among the Persians.[26] A century later the continuator of Zachariah of Mitylene spoke of the mission that had been sent among the eastern Huns, beyond the Caspian Gates, and of the translation of the Scriptures into the local dialect.[27] Had not Christ said, 'Be of good cheer, I have overcome the world' (Jn 16. 33)? And again, 'The gates of hell shall not prevail against my church' (Mt. 16. 18). The fulfilment of these prophecies was clearly seen by Cosmas Indicopleustes. There were Christian churches, he writes, as far away as Ceylon, Malabar and the isle of Socotra.

'And so likewise among the Bactrians and Huns and Persians, and the rest of the Indians, Persarmenians, and Medes and Elamites, and throughout the whole land of Persia there is no limit to the number of churches with bishops and very large communities of Christian people, as well as many martyrs, and monks also living as hermits. So too in Ethiopia and Axôm, and in all the country about it; among the people of Happy Arabia – who are now called Homerites – through all Arabia and Palestine, Phoenicia, and all Syria and Antioch as far as Mesopotamia; among the Nubians and the Garamantes, in Egypt, Libya, Pentapolis, Africa and Mauretania, as far as southern Gadeira [Gades in Africa], there are everywhere churches of the Christians, and bishops, martyrs, monks and recluses, where the Gospel of Christ is proclaimed. So likewise again in Cilicia, Asia, Cappadocia, Lazica and Pontus, and in the northern countries occupied by the Scythians, Hyrcanians, Heruli, Bulgarians, Helladikoi [Greeks] and Illyrians, Dalmatians, Goths, Spaniards, Romans, Franks, and other nations, as far as Gadeira on the ocean towards the northern parts, there are believers and preachers of the Gospel confessing the resurrection from the dead; and so we see the prophecies being fulfilled over the whole world.[28]

Indeed, to an observer living in the sixth century, it might well have appeared that not much additional territory remained to be won. The only big obstacle was Persia, where Christianity had already made very notable progress. It was reported, however, that the king of Persia himself, under the influence of his Christian physician and the Nestorian Catholicos, had ceased eating the flesh of impure animals and had built a hospice for strangers, something that had been quite unheard of before.[29]

The dream of an entirely Christian *oikoumenê* came close to being realized when Heraclius subdued the Persian Empire and may, indeed, have formed an important part of that emperor's policy. The catastrophic reverse that Christianity suffered immediately afterwards was totally unexpected, and it may be said that Byzantine thinking never adjusted to it. In the seventh century in particular the success of the *ethnikoi* posed an agonizing problem. Was it by God's will that the impious enemy was inflicting so much harm on the Christians? Churchmen could only reply that those calamities were indeed occurring by God's will so as to chastise the Christians for their sins. The good fortune of the godless was not, however, due to their virtue. 'The lawless and impious enemy, subservient as they are to their inherent wickedness, inflict upon us these calamities that are displeasing to God, in return for which they will certainly suffer eternal punishment.'[30] It even appeared to some observers that the *ethnikoi* were healthier, physically superior to the Christians, among whom there was a great deal of gout, leprosy, epilepsy and other diseases. The argument that God visited illness upon the Christians because He loved them carried little conviction. Accordingly, Anastasius of Sinai attempted a different explanation. Diseases, he says, occur *also* (that is in addition to God's will) for hereditary reasons, or because of the air, a variable and humid climate or excessive eating and drinking. That the quality of air possesses this effect is proved by the fact that the inhabitants of Aila (Aqaba) never suffer from gout. The importance of a proper diet is demonstrated by the Jews who originate in a dry, hence healthy region, but who are addicted to an excessive consumption of meat, wine and sauces and, consequently, have as many diseases as the Christians. The idea that epilepsy or demoniac possession could be due to physical causes was quite foreign to the Byzantine way of thinking, yet Christ Himself had said of the demon, 'This kind can come forth by nothing, but by prayer and fasting' (Mk. 9. 29). If, then, the demon could be cast out by fasting, he might also – of course, by God's permission – enter a body on account of gluttony. Nor should one be surprised if godless foreigners appear on occasion to possess certain supernatural faculties, for example the Saracens, who are able to predict who is going to be killed on the field of battle. They do so by observing certain physical signs – a fact confirmed by experts in medicine who affirm that Providence has placed in the human body, especially in the eyes, some secret signals that announce the approach of death, and that these signals are observed by demons who then deceive people by making correct predictions. Besides, it is a known fact that pagans and heretics can perform miracles with the help of demons. For example, says Anastasius, there was once a heretical bishop of Cyzicus who, by reciting a prayer, was able to uproot an olive tree that obstructed the window of his church and, on another occasion, caused a corpse to speak. When he died various apparitions and hallucinations took place over his tomb – all through the agency of demons. The only means of distinguishing between a true and a false miracle, between the Christian and the godless, is by the results they achieve, for 'by their fruits ye shall know them'.[31]

The prevalence of apostasy after the Arab conquest was perhaps an indication that the arguments of the Church did not meet with general acceptance. Yet throughout the Byzantine period the success of the *ethnikoi* was explained in precisely the same way as it had been by Anastasius. This reasoning was applied to the Avars, to the Arabs, to the Bulgarians, to the Russians, to the Latins, finally to the Turks. In 860, during the siege of Constantinople by the Russians, the patriarch Photius publicly declared that 'While God's people waxes strong and triumphs over its enemies by His alliance, the rest of the nations, whose religion is at fault, are not increased in strength on account of their own good deeds, but on account of our bad ones'.[32] In the fifteenth century, as many times before, the same question was asked: Why is it that the Turks are victorious, while we are in disarray? Is it perhaps because we have not accepted the superior revelation of Mohammed, just as the Jews have been punished for not accepting that of Christ? – No, replies the Emperor Manuel II Palaeologus. First, we cannot be compared to the Jews who, since the fall of Jerusalem, have had neither king nor city nor temple. Secondly, many empires have come and gone whose success cannot be attributed to their religious superiority – for example, that of the Assyrians, that of the Persians, or that of Alexander of

Macedon, who was manifestly impious since he sacrificed to demons. Furthermore – and here, at last, we encounter a new thought – there exist in the West several Christian states that are more powerful than that of the Turks. A little time still remains before the end of the world: who knows what changes may take place in it?[33]

CHAPTER 10

THE PAST OF MANKIND

The average Byzantine, like all other simple folk, had but a limited awareness of the succession of years. When he thought about such matters at all, he reckoned by the system of indictions. An indiction was a fifteen-year cycle initially introduced for the purpose of tax assessments, but when one referred, for example, to the fifth indiction, one meant the fifth year (starting on 1 September) of any given cycle, not the fifth cycle. In his *Spiritual Meadow* John Moschus relates the following characteristic story. In Cilicia, in the foothills of the Amanus mountain range, he had met two elderly laymen. They told him that seven years earlier they had observed that a fire was lit at night on the mountain top. They went up in daytime to investigate, but found nothing. The fire continued to shine in the darkness for a period of three months. At length they decided to carry out the ascent at night. They located the light and remained at that spot until morning, when they discovered a cave containing a dead anchorite who was clutching a Gospel book. Next to him was a tablet inscribed with the following words: 'I, the humble John, died in the fifteenth indiction.' And then the two men started to compute the years, probably on their fingers, and realized with a shock that seven years had passed since the anchorite's demise, although he looked as if he had died that very day.[1]

The record which the monk made of his own death was, in fact, typical of Byzantine epitaphs of the Early period. To us this may seem surprising, for we regard a tombstone as a memorial that is intended to survive for several centuries if not forever; but a Byzantine was usually content to engrave on the stone an inscription of this nature: 'The servant of God Theodore died on the 13th of the month of August, a Sunday, indiction 13.' It was as if the information conveyed by the epitaph would be of interest for only a few years, one or two indiction cycles at most.

The main reason for this disregard of absolute dates lay in the lack of a generally recognized form of chronology. At the time when Moschus was writing (about 600 AD) official documents were still dated, as in the Roman period, by consulship; but since this institution had become an empty formula and the consulship was assumed by the emperor at irregular intervals and at different times of the year, one had to be something of a specialist to make sense of the system.[2] The regnal year, with which the consulship was often identified, was less confusing, except that one had to know not only the year of an emperor's accession, but also the day and the month. Then there was a multitude of local eras, especially in the eastern provinces. Syrians usually reckoned by the Seleucid era (also known as the era of the Greeks) which started on 1 October 312 BC. At Antioch, however, there was an era starting in 49 BC, at Bostra another from 106 AD, while Gaza in Palestine counted from 61 BC. At Alexandria they used the era of Augustus from 30 August 30 BC, but also that of Diocletian (the era of the Martyrs) from 284 AD, and so on. The *annus mundi* was not yet used as an ordinary system of dating and there was, as we shall see, considerable disagreement concerning the method of its computation. It began to appear sporadically in the eighth century and slowly gained ground; but even in the Middle and Late Byzantine periods, when the *annus mundi* was solidly entrenched, the use of dates in inscriptions, manuscripts, buildings, and so on remained the exception rather than the rule.

The interest of the *annus mundi* for our purpose is that it reflected the entire conception of the human past that was held by Christians in the Late Antique and Byzantine periods, a conception that was both 'historical' and symbolic and also had to take account of certain astronomical factors. This system was enshrined in a type of book known as the 'universal chronicle' or, as the Byzantines usually called it, the 'chronicle from Adam'. When the average Byzantine wished to inform himself on the course of past history, it was to this type of book that he turned. As a result, the universal chronicle enjoyed a wide circulation, and since it was meant for the ordinary reader, it was couched in simple language. As time went on, chronicles were supplemented with an account of recent events. They were treated, in fact, not as literary works, but as handbooks or almanacs that called for periodic revision. This circumstance has caused much difficulty to scholars desirous of identifying the successive layers of such compilations. Here, however, we are concerned not with particular problems of attribution, but with the genre as a whole and the ideas it contains.

The first impression that Byzantine chronicles produce on the reader is one of naïveté, but the triviality of much of their content should not blind us to the extreme complexity of their conceptual framework. They are, in fact, the product of a long evolution and of much scholarly endeavour, and we must pause briefly to examine their ancestry. The story they tell is not that of one nation, but of the whole world as it was then known. The principal strand of that story is provided by the Bible, but several other threads – Assyrian, Egyptian, Greek and Roman – have been intertwined with it. The synchronization of these separate histories required an overall chronological framework. More importantly, the chronicles set out to explain the working of divine Providence and, since God acts in an orderly fashion, history, too, must express not only His moral purpose, but also the symmetry of His design. By what process, then, was this vast panorama built up?

To start with the chronological element, we may note that long before the birth of Christian historiography, the hellenized Jews were much preoccupied with demonstrating the antiquity, hence the respectability, of their religion as contrasted with the confused and unhistorical nature of the Greek and Roman traditions. Already in the first century AD Josephus wrote at length on this topic and demonstrated not only that Jewish historical records extended over a period of some five thousand years, but also that they were more reliable than the contradictory stories told by the Greek historians.[3] The legacy of the Jewish apologists was eagerly seized by the Christians who had to face the same criticism from their pagan adversaries and who, a little later, had the added task of fighting the Jews with the latter's own weapons. As far as we know, the earliest Christian author to have made a detailed chronological computation on the basis of the Old Testament was Theophilus of Antioch (end of the second century AD). Using the Septuagint version (which differs markedly from the Hebrew with regard to chronology), he calculated that Creation took place in about 5515 BC.[4] He himself admitted that his figures were approximate, within a maximum range of error of some two hundred years. What is rather more interesting for us, however, is that he was able to link biblical chronology to that of the Graeco-Roman world, for at II Chronicles 36. 21–2 it is stated that the end of the Babylonian captivity (4954 after Creation according to his reckoning) coincided with the first year of King Cyrus of Persia. From there it was plain sailing, for it was known that Cyrus reigned 28 years and that his death occurred contemporaneously with the accession in Rome of Tarquin the Proud, from which time, according to chronological handbooks, 713 years elapsed until the death of Marcus Aurelius (180 AD). In this reckoning the Incarnation of Christ plays no part, nor was Theophilus concerned to establish a relative chronology of biblical and gentile history, a task that was left to later Christian scholars, especially Africanus (third century AD) and Eusebius of Caesarea.

To this 'historical' evidence was added a mystical consideration. The early Christians believed, on the analogy of the Six Days of Creation, that the world would last six thousand years, for it was written that a thousand years were like a day in the sight of God (Ps. 90. 4). If so, it would have been particularly satisfying if the Incarnation had taken place exactly in the year 5500, the mid-point of the sixth cosmic day, the more so as the combined dimensions of the Ark of the Covenant amounted to five and a half cubits (Exodus 25. 10). All the early Christian and Byzantine systems, except that of Eusebius, attempt to come as closely as possible to this figure.

The third aspect of the problem had to do with the adjustment of the solar and lunar calendars. Since Christ rose from the dead at about the time of Passover (the fourteenth day of the month Nisan), it was believed that the first day of Creation must have fallen close to the same date, also a Sunday, which, furthermore, ought to have been 25 March, the date of the spring equinox according to the Julian calendar. It was, in fact, the same kind of calculation as that involved in determining the date of Easter, a problem that greatly preoccupied the early Church. By that time the Jews had already abandoned a purely lunar calendar and had adopted a soli-lunar year of 354 days (12 months of 29½ days), that is, 11 days shorter than the solar year, but every three years they inserted an additional (embolic) month. In this way the date of Passover, instead of travelling all through the solar year as do Mohammedan feasts, could remain in the spring. The Christians, for their part, who were on the Julian calendar, had by the third century chosen a cycle of 8 years for the purpose of computing the date of Easter. The reason for this was that 8 solar years (including 2 leap years) = 2,922 days, which is pretty close to 99 lunar months (5 years of 12 months plus 3 years of 13 months) = 2,923½ days. This cycle gave eight possible dates for Passover, so that in the ninth year one returned to the same day of the month as in the first; but it did not yield the same days of the week. To take account of both factors, one had to multiply 8 × 7 = 56. After 56 years Passover would thus return to the same day of the month and the same day of the week. The earliest preserved Paschal table, that of Hippolytus, actually uses a cycle of 112 years (56 × 2). There was still, of course, a gap of one and a half days every 8 years, a deficiency that was later remedied by more accurate cycles.

The table of Hippolytus is, however, sufficient to illustrate the principle involved. The first day of Creation fell, as we have said, on a Sunday 25 March. Seeing that the moon was created on the fourth day and was created full (all of God's works being perfect), the first 14 Nisan would have been on Wednesday, 28 March, if the moon was created in the morning, or Thursday, 29 March, if it was created in the evening. According to the canon of Hippolytus, the possible dates for 14 Nisan were: 18, 21, 25, 29 March; and 2, 5, 9, 13 April. The choice fell, therefore, on Thursday 29 March, a synchronism which, according to the same canon, occurred in 266 AD and 322. Counting back, the date of Creation plus the AD date minus 1 (since there is no year 0) had to be a multiple of 112. The result, if it was to fall as closely as possible to 5500 BC, was 5503 (5,503 + 322 − 1 = 5,824 = 112 × 52).

The discrepancy in Hippolytus of one and a half days every 8 years between the solar and the soli-lunar calendars led, as we have said, to the invention of more accurate cycles. The one that prevailed in the East was a cycle of 19 years, and this necessitated a re-calculation of the date of Creation which was now thought to have occurred in 5492 BC. This is the so-called Alexandrian era which was still used by the chroniclers George Syncellus and Theophanes in the early ninth century. By that time, however, the normal Byzantine era of 5508 BC had already been introduced so as to take also account of the indiction cycle, and it was this Byzantine era that prevailed until the end of the Empire.[5]

The foregoing, somewhat arid, discussion was necessary to explain the chronological skeleton of the Byzantine view of history. The main structure of the universal chronicle was erected in the third century, perfected by Eusebius at the beginning of the fourth and further systematized in the fifth by the Alexandrians Panodorus and Annianus. The work of these pioneers has come down to us only in fragments. The earliest preserved Byzantine chronicle, that by the Antiochene John Malalas, dates from the sixth century, and is followed by the Paschal Chronicle in the seventh, George Syncellus and Theophanes at the beginning of the ninth, George the Monk towards the middle of the ninth, the several versions of Symeon Logothete in the tenth and so forth. The tradition of the universal chronicle was continued even after the fall of Constantinople to the Turks and supplied the historical reading matter of the Greek people until the revolution of 1821.

In broad outline the content of the world chronicle was the following.[6] The account of the antediluvian age raised no particular difficulties since it was based on the Bible and Old Testament apocrypha. We may note, however, that this long period (2,362 years according to some reckonings) was marked by a process of nomenclature and practical invention, even if much of this knowledge was later lost as a result of the Flood. Adam gave names to all the animals; Cain invented the measurements of the earth, while Lamech's three sons discovered, respectively, cattle-breeding, musical instruments and the forging of brass and iron. The greatest sage of that remote period was, however, Seth, who devised the Hebrew alphabet, discovered the succession of years, months and weeks, and gave names to the stars and to the five planets. The names he bestowed on the planets (the sun and the moon having already received theirs from God) were, curiously enough, Kronos, Zeus, Ares, Aphrodite and Hermes, so it was not the planets that were named after the pagan gods, but the gods (who were really men) that were named, much later, after the planets. Seth, who had been divinely forewarned of the Flood, was thoughtful enough to write down the names of the stars on a stone slab which survived the catastrophe and enabled Canaan to compile an astronomy. It also seems that certain Chaldaean letters were contrived before the Flood by the so-called Wakeful Ones, the same as the mysterious sons of God who married the daughters of men in Genesis 6. 2, and that these letters were used to express some magical lore. They were later discovered by Salah who became versed in this dangerous knowledge and passed it on to others.

The Flood, which destroyed all humanity except for Noah and his family, played an important part in establishing a relative chronology of Jewish and gentile history. Among the various national traditions current in Late Antiquity, only the Assyrian (or so it was thought) mentioned a universal deluge. The Flood of Deucalion of Greek mythology was considered to have been local rather than universal; as for the Egyptians, they had never heard of a flood at all. It followed from this that only the Assyrians or Chaldaeans had a history stretching further back than the Flood. According to their records there had been ten antediluvian kings, the last of them, Xisuthrus, being saved from the Flood. It followed that Xisuthrus was the same as Noah and that Chaldaean and Jewish histories were one. As for the Egyptians, who had no recollection of a flood, yet claimed a history stretching back nearly thirty thousand years, one could only conclude that they did not know how to count. Evidently, Egyptian history began after the Flood, and their first ruler was Mizraim, Noah's grandson.

The division of the earth among Noah's sons (of which we have already spoken) and the subsequent multiplication of the tongues provided the natural starting points for the history of various gentile peoples. Now one of Ham's descendants was Nimrod, the mighty hunter, who ruled something called the land of Shinar (Genesis 10. 10), evidently in Assyria or Persia, even though that part of the world appears to have been assigned to Shem. The Bible neglects to say that Nimrod also invented magic and astrology which he taught to the Persians, and that when he died he was deified and became a star in the sky, the same as Orion. Nimrod, therefore, was some sort of a giant, and it was not unnatural that he should have been succeeded by another giant named Kronos, the son of a certain Ouranos and Aphrodite. This Kronos subdued all of Syria and Persia and became the first ruler of men. He married Semiramis (whom the Assyrians called Rhea) and had two sons, Ninos and Zeus (also called Picos) and one daughter, Hera, whom Zeus married. To make matters worse, when Kronos died, he was succeeded by Ninos who married his own mother Semiramis, and so this foul custom of incest became implanted among the Persians. In spite of their sins, the progeny of Kronos were now launched on their historic course. Ninos, appropriately enough, built Nineveh. After him reigned a certain Thouras who was renamed Ares and was worshipped by the Assyrians under the Persian [sic] name of Baal. As for Picos Zeus, he somehow became King of Italy, a part of the world that had at that time neither cities nor government, being simply inhabited by the tribe of Japheth. This Zeus was an amorous fellow and begat a numerous progeny by his concubines. His successor, Faunus (renamed Hermes), had to contend with the plots of his seventy-odd half-brothers and, at length, fled to Egypt where he was received with great honour because he had brought with him a large quantity of gold and was also able to foretell the future. Eventually, Hermes became King of Egypt. He was succeeded by the lame Hephaistos who came to be remembered for two achievements: first, he introduced a law requiring the women of Egypt to practise monogamy and, second, he received, thanks to a mystical prayer, a pair of tongs from heaven and this enabled him to forge weapons of iron: for previously men had fought with clubs and stones. We may note in passing that while certain characteristics of the Olympian gods are still dimly discernible in this farrago of nonsense, their Greek origin has been forgotten. The progeny of Kronos is represented as either Assyrian or Persian; Zeus ruled in Italy, while Hermes and Hephaistos are associated with Egypt.

The pagan gods and their descendants were thus inserted into the period of some five centuries that stretched from the construction of the Tower of Babel to Abraham, a period concerning which the Bible has nearly nothing to say save for a bare genealogy (Genesis 11). This was the time of the 'old idolatry', invented by one Seruch of the tribe of Japheth, and it lasted down to Terah, Abraham's father, who was a sculptor. Idolatry (*hellênismos*) derived from the custom of setting up statues of prominent men, became popular in Egypt, Babylonia and Phrygia and then spread to Greece, where it received its name after one Hellên, a son of Picos Zeus.

With Abraham we reach one of the nodal points that marked the course of universal history, for it was he who introduced the true knowledge of God and broke his father's idols. Himself a Chaldaean, he inaugurated the history of the Hebrew people. He was also an important figure in the history of science: being versed in astronomy by virtue of his Chaldaean background, he taught this discipline to the Egyptians. It was from the Chaldaeans, too, that he learnt the use of letters and passed it on to the Phoenicians from whom, at a later time, the Greeks derived their own alphabet. Moreover, he was contemporary with Melchizedek, the gentile priest-king who founded Jerusalem and was the prototype of Christ. The kingdom of Sicyon, the oldest in Greece, was set up at about the same time.

The next stage of the historical process was provided by Moses, the greatest of all prophets before John the Baptist and, incidentally, the first historian. The importance of Moses had to do not so much with the fact that he led his people out of captivity as with the superior revelation that was granted to him and the 'signs' that accompanied his entire career. Like Christ, the infant Moses was saved from being killed along with the other newly born males of his people; like Christ, too, he withdrew into the desert – not for forty days, but for forty years. When he parted the Red Sea, he struck it with a cruciform motion, and when he cast a tree into the bitter waters of Marah, that, too, pointed to the life-giving cross. The twelve wells of water and seventy palm trees at Elim stood for the twelve major and seventy minor apostles. The manna that was gathered on the sixth day of the week and remained uncorrupted on the sabbath prefigured Christ's body. Finally, though Moses died and was buried, no one was able to see his tomb. The religious code that Moses set down was, of course, a provisional one, geared to the imperfect understanding and idolatrous customs of his people – a shadow of the reality that was to come. By comparison, however, with the gentile peoples of his time – he was generally thought to have been contemporary with Inachus, first King of the Argives – Moses was a figure of towering learning, an observation that served to prove once again that all pagan and especially Greek knowledge was a much later and derivative development.

The next great sage of the Israelites was King Solomon who, in spite of his regrettable weakness for women, acquired knowledge of all natural things and wrote books about plants and animals. He also set down various remedies and incantations against demons. These books, which were plagiarized by Greek 'iatrosophists', were later destroyed by order of Hezekiah who saw that people used them for medical purposes instead of praying to God for healing. Considerable interest also attached to Solomon's Temple which was especially venerable because it was at the time the only temple of the true God. The carved figures of cherubim it contained were often cited as a justification of the use of icons. As for the ark of the covenant that was placed in the holy of holies, it not only denoted the form of the universe, but also imitated the shape of a mysterious temple that had been shown to Moses on the summit of Mount Sinai – a temple, we may imagine, that resembled the Christian church. Solomon lived a few years after the Trojan War whose story, as told in Byzantine chronicles, was derived not from Homer, but from the fables of Dictys.

After Solomon, the history of the Israelites was all downhill and merited little attention save for the prophets who strove in vain to correct the ways of the Chosen People. The focus of interest now shifts to the gentile kingdoms, first that of the Assyrians who captured Jerusalem and destroyed the Temple, then that of the Persians under whom the Jews were not allowed to return home. The tempo of universal history is now quickening and the exact time of the Incarnation is revealed by the prophet Daniel. The Persian kingdom is undone by Alexander who comes close to worshipping the true God and, after making offerings at Jerusalem, sets out on his eastward march. India appears on the distant horizon, with the 'river Ocean' that surrounds the whole earth and the virtuous Brahmans. Alexander's Empire is divided; Antiochus Epiphanes profanes the restored Temple and sets up 'the abomination of desolation' in accordance with Daniel's prophecy. The successor kingdoms make war on each other until they are conquered by Rome.

The Incarnation of Christ, which is the central event of the entire historical process, corresponds to the reign of Augustus, the first ruler to hold sway over the whole earth and bringer of universal peace. Moreover, since the Roman Empire is the fourth kingdom prophesied by Daniel, it fittingly ushers in the advent of the Creator of the four elements. The expiration of Daniel's seven 'weeks' is, furthermore, connected with the suppression of the anointed high priests of the Jews. The Roman emperors after Augustus are largely seen from the viewpoint of Christianity. Under Tiberius Christ is crucified. The Crucifixion falls on a Friday because man was created on the sixth day and Adam ate the fruit of the forbidden tree at the sixth hour of the day. The resurrection repeats the Creation. Christ's miracles are reported by Pilate to Tiberius who allows complete freedom to Christian predication so that the whole earth is filled with it. The reign of the wicked Caius witnesses the conversion of St Paul and the martyrdom of Stephen, that of Claudius the institution of monasticism by St Mark. Under Nero, the first persecutor of the Christians, Peter, Paul, James and Luke are put to death. Meanwhile, the Jews had been allowed forty years, counting from the Ascension, to repent. Their failure to do so results in the sack of Jerusalem and the destruction of the Temple. This is the fourth captivity of the Jews and it shall have no end, nor will the Jews have any more prophets. Their subsequent attempts to rebuild the Temple are supernaturally frustrated.

As Christianity spreads, the first heresies begin to appear – those of Basilides, Valentinus, Tatian and Bardesanes. Even the learned and abstemious Origen falls into error – an error that is later to be revived by Arius. Then a false Christ appears in the person of Mani, a follower of a certain Buddha. He rejects the Old Testament and teaches that Jesus Christ was a ghost. His dreadful doctrine inspires a multitude of Christian heresies. By now we are towards the end of the third century AD, and a last stand against Christianity is made by the Emperors Diocletian and Maximian, but both meet a violent death [sic]. At last, Constantine becomes emperor. He falls ill, sees St Peter and St Paul in a dream, is cured by Pope Sylvester and accepts baptism along with his mother Helena. Christianity triumphs, the First Council is convened at Nicaea and the seat of Empire is moved to the New Rome which is also the New Jerusalem. The last stage of universal history is thus inaugurated. All that remains to be done before the Second Coming is to eliminate heresies and to carry the Christian message to the ends of the earth.

Such, in brief, is the view of the past that we find in Byzantine chronicles, a panorama both vast and obscure. We look in vain for any coherent development of the story or any sign of God's concern for the salvation of all mankind. The scope of providentially guided history is universal down to the Flood and the Tower of Babel, but is then reduced to the merest trickle down to Pentecost when, in theory, it becomes universal again. The intervening period of some 2,700 years, that is roughly half of history before the Incarnation, remains in the shade save for the fortunes of the Jews. But what of the other peoples whose succinct annals were given by Eusebius in parallel columns? They were, apparently, entrusted by God to 'the angels of the nations' who, because of their inefficiency rather than their wickedness (for they had to bear the brunt of furious attack on the part of the demons), could do no better than introduce astral worship; that, in turn, degenerated into crass idolatry.[7]

The working of divine Providence was manifested in the fulfilment of prophecies and, more mysteriously, in numerical correspondences like some abstract pattern in an oriental rug. More obscurely still, the doctrine of the Trinity and of the virgin birth was, it seems, proclaimed in riddles by the oracle of Apollo and by the Sibyls, and was written down, here and there, on stone slabs. When, for example, a very ancient pagan temple at Cyzicus was being converted into a Church of the Virgin Mary in the reign of Leo I (457–74), an oracle was found inscribed on the side of it and an identical one at Athens. Both were replies to the following question posed by the citizens: 'Prophesy to us, O prophet Phoebus Apollo, whose house this shall be.' The god answered: 'Whatever leads to virtue and order, that you may do. For my part, I proclaim one triune God ruling on high whose eternal Word will be conceived by a simple maiden. Like a fiery arrow he will traverse the whole world, capture it, and offer it as a gift to his Father. Her house this shall be, and Mary is her name.'[8] While we may feel justifiable doubt concerning the authenticity of such inscriptions, the fact remains that some Byzantines tried, however clumsily, to show that the pagans, too, had been given in remote Antiquity a chance to hear the Christian message.

Degraded as it became in the process of constant retelling, the Byzantine outline of universal history never lost the characteristics that were built into it between the second and fifth centuries AD. The fabulousness and inaccuracy of the 'profane' content was due to the fact that the early compilers of Christian chronicles had perforce to rely on whatever popular compendia they could lay their hands on, especially those which gave lists and dates of the rulers of various countries – Berosus for Assyria, Manetho for Egypt, Castor for Assyria, Greece and Rome, and so on. The serious historians of Antiquity did not lend themselves to such use. By modern standards, the historical research carried out by Africanus, Eusebius and their successors may indeed appear rather shoddy, but we cannot deny that it constituted a very considerable effort. Furthermore, it was an effort that could not be repeated in the later Byzantine period since much of the necessary documentation had in the meantime been lost. In historiography as in most other areas of knowledge the ordinary Byzantine remained limited to the legacy of the Early Christian period.

CHAPTER 11

THE FUTURE OF MANKIND

'Little children, it is the last time: and as ye have heard that Antichrist shall come, even now are there many antichrists; whereby we know that it is the last time.' So wrote the apostle John (I Jo. 2. 18) who himself half believed that he would live to see the Second Coming, for had not the Lord said of him to Peter, 'If I will that he tarry till I come, what is that to thee?' (Jo. 21. 22–3)

The belief in the impending end of the world was a cornerstone of Early Christianity and, though by the beginning of the Byzantine era three centuries had already elapsed since Christ's Ascension to Heaven, it was not a belief that could be lightly discarded. For, without the Second Coming, the Christian view of history is reduced to nonsense. Furthermore – and this point needs stressing – there was no theological, symbolic or numerical reason why this event should have been postponed to some indefinitely distant future. Not only would such a delay have spoilt the balance and symmetry of the divine dispensation; there was also, to put it bluntly, insufficient 'stuff' to fill an unduly long waiting period.

The 'stuff' in question, the basic elements of the eschatological vision, was borrowed from the Bible and the apocrypha. Particularly authoritative, since it came from Christ's own lips, was the 'synoptic apocalypse' (Mt. 24; Mk. 13; Lk. 21). This foresaw, first, a period of warfare between kingdoms and nations, of 'famines and pestilences and earthquakes in divers places', which would announce 'the beginning of sorrows' (or, more literally, of the birth pains). All manner of iniquity would then be rife and many false prophets would arise; even so, 'the gospel of the kingdom' would be preached to the whole world, 'and then shall the end come'. 'The abomination of desolation spoken of by Daniel the prophet' would stand in the holy place and there would be great distress and lamentation, but, for the sake of the elect, those days would be shortened. Then the sun and the moon would lose their light, the stars would fall from heaven, and the Son of Man would appear in the clouds with power and glory. The elect ought to watch for the appropriate signs; for, though the exact time of the Second Coming was not known even to angels, save to the Father alone, yet 'this generation shall not pass till all these things be fulfilled'.

Christ's apocalypse was part and parcel of the great wave of eschatological speculation that swept over the Jewish world between the second century BC and the first AD. This is not the place to examine in detail the various ideas that were expressed at that time, but we may isolate a few of the motifs that were to play an important part in the Byzantine period. Particularly potent was the myth of the Antichrist mentioned in the Johannine passage we have quoted at the beginning of this chapter. Already adumbrated in the book of Daniel, 'the man of sin' or 'son of perdition' assumes a more concrete form in the teaching of St Paul. He is to appear during the time of 'falling away', shortly before the Second Coming, and would sit in the temple of God, posing as God and working miracles, but the true Lord would destroy him 'with the spirit of his mouth' (II Thess. 2). It was also believed that the Antichrist would belong to the tribe of Dan, that he would be resisted by Elijah (or Elijah and Enoch, these being presumably the two witnesses mentioned in the book of Revelation) whom he would kill, that his reign would last three and a half years, and so forth. Also from the book of Daniel came the notion of the four kingdoms or beasts, the last of which – the one with iron teeth and ten horns, the beast that 'shall devour the whole earth, and shall tread it down, and break it in pieces' – was generally identified with the Roman Empire in spite of the fact that in the author's mind it had clearly denoted that of the Seleucids. The reign of the fourth beast would be directly followed by the Last Judgement (Dan. 7). Of even earlier origin, namely the book of Ezekiel (ch. 38–9), was the notion of Gog and Magog (or, more correctly, Gog from the land of Magog), the northern nations that were to do battle with Israel in the last days. This was picked up in the book of Revelation and associated with the 'little season' when Satan would be 'loosed out of his prison' wherein he had been confined for a thousand years (Rev. 20. 8). For the later Byzantines there was an additional clue here, for Gog is described as being 'prince of Rosh', which in the Septuagint version is rendered by 'Rhos' – the same name as that borne by the Russians.

When the confused body of these and other biblical and para-biblical beliefs was passed on to the Byzantines, it had already undergone a significant transformation: instead of applying, as it had done at the beginning, to the future of the Jewish nation alone, its meaning was extended to embrace all men and, particularly, the Christians. The role of the Roman Empire in the pattern of 'the last things' was acknowledged, whether Rome was regarded as the enemy (as in the book of Revelation) or, on the contrary, as the power that staved off the advent of the Antichrist. Furthermore, the pagan belief in the eternity of Rome was confirmed by the identification of Rome with the Fourth Kingdom which was destined to last until the end of time. Even the conversion of the Empire to Christianity could be made to fit into the apocalyptic scheme since Christ himself had prophesied that the Gospel would be preached to all the world as a necessary prelude to the final catastrophe. One circumstance, however, that was not foreseen was the transfer of the capital to Constantinople. The Byzantine contribution was to adapt the scheme once again so as to place Constantinople at the centre of the universal stage.

Given the fragmentary nature of the evidence, it is difficult to determine the process of this adaptation. A Sibylline text of the late fourth century, whose contents may be reconstructed with some certainty, not only does not assign any particular importance to Constantinople, but even foretells that the new capital would not last sixty years. When the same text was revised in the very first years of the sixth century by an author writing in Syria, the figure 60 was altered to 180, but the sneering tone of the remark was retained: 'Do not be arrogant, city of Byzantium, for thou shalt not reign thrice sixty years!'[1] In another text of the same date (c. 500 AD), namely the Seventh Vision of Daniel, which survives only in an Armenian version, Constantinople plays a more crucial, yet distinctly maleficent, role. It is represented as 'the Babylon of seven hills' which has enriched itself at the expense of other lands and is filled with all manner of injustice. The author takes a positive pleasure in detailing the calamities that would shortly fall on the wicked capital: its walls would collapse, its inhabitants would slowly perish until, at the very end of time, no trace of it would be left. People would then point to its site and exclaim, 'Was that, indeed, a city?'[2]

The reign of the Emperor Anastasius, when these oracles were composed, appears to have been a time of intense eschatological speculation. The reason for this is easy to discern. Ever since the third century, if not earlier, the view had prevailed that the world was destined to last six thousand years on the analogy of the Six Days of Creation. For had not the Psalmist expressly said that a thousand years were like a day in the sight of God (Ps. 90. 4)? Since, as we have seen, Creation was dated to approximately 5,500 BC, it followed that the incarnation of Christ occurred precisely in the middle of the last 'day', and the end would come in about 500 AD. The exact date depended, of course, on the system of computation that was adopted. Assuming the use of the so-called Alexandrian era (that of Annianus), the end of the world would have been expected in 508. When this did not occur, some leeway was left to fiddle with the figures. That this was done in some quarters is suggested by the following curious anecdote that gained a wide currency at the time. It was said that shortly before his death (518) Anastasius had a dream: an angel appeared before him holding a book and, after turning over five leaves, read out the emperor's name and said to him, 'Behold, because of your greed, I am erasing fourteen [years].' Terrified by this vision, Anastasius called in his diviner and was informed that he would soon die. Indeed, he fell ill shortly thereafter and expired in the midst of a terrible thunderstorm.[3] Since Anastasius was either eighty-eight or ninety at the time of his death, it is hard to imagine that any rational observer expected him to live another fourteen years. The point of the story is probably that he would have survived, were it not for his fiscal exactions, until the end of the world in 532, but it is hard to explain how the latter figure was arrived at. It might, perhaps, have been reckoned from the time of Christ's passion.

In spite of the hardship he may have caused by his financial measures and the opposition he may have aroused by supporting the Monophysite cause, it was surely difficult to regard Anastasius, an extremely competent ruler, in the role of an apocalyptic king. It was different, however, with Justinian, whose limitless ambition resulted in so much human loss. This inscrutable man who, in his physical appearance, resembled the infamous Emperor Domitian, who was allegedly observed to turn late at night into a headless phantom, whose face was sometimes transformed into a mass of featureless flesh, could surely be regarded as the Prince of Demons or the Antichrist himself. Such, at any rate, was the inference that Procopius drew in his *Secret History*.[4] Besides, Justinian's reign was filled with ceaseless wars, with earthquakes, pestilences and every other form of calamity. On one such occasion, when Constantinople was shaken by a terrible earthquake in 557, the rumour that the world was coming to an end gained wide currency and was particularly fanned by the 'holy fools' who alleged that they had received supernatural intimation of the future. The population panicked: some fled to the mountains and became monks, others gave money to churches, the rich distributed alms to the poor, and even magistrates abandoned for a time their dishonest ways.[5]

The ever-deepening crisis of the late sixth and seventh centuries could not but have exerted a similar influence on people's minds. Tiberius II, a virtuous emperor, was assured by an angel of the Lord that the time of apocalyptic impiety would not occur during his reign. Thus comforted, he died in peace.[6] The expectation of dreadful calamities was indeed fulfilled during the reign of the tyrant Phocas (602–10), followed by the desperate war between the Roman and Persian Empires and the siege of Constantinople by the Avars (626). All the signs were pointing to the final catastrophe. A prophecy attributed to the Persian King Chosroes II proclaimed that the 'Babylonian' supremacy over the Romans would last for three 'hebdomads' from the year 591 (in other words until 612), after which, in the fifth 'hebdomad' (619–26), the Romans would vanquish the Persians; 'and when these things have been accomplished, the day without evening will dawn upon men'.[7] By a further coincidence, the campaigns of Heraclius against Persia lasted six years, like the Six Days of Creation. His triumphal return to the capital (628) corresponded to the divine sabbath[8] and was followed by what can only be interpreted as a deliberately apocalyptic act: Heraclius journeyed to Jerusalem to give thanks to God and restored to Mount Golgotha the miraculously 'invented' relic of the True Cross. It was not to remain there for long.

Whoever circulated the prophecy of Chosroes II was unaware of the fact that his fifth 'hebdomad' did in fact correspond to an event of cosmic magnitude, the year of the Hegira. The victorious advent of the Arabs had not been explicitly foreseen in earlier apocalyptic literature, but when the Caliph 'Umar entered Jerusalem in his filthy cloak of camel hair and asked to be conducted to the site of Solomon's Temple that he might build upon it a prayer house of his own 'blasphemy', the patriarch Sophronius could not help exclaiming: 'Truly, this is the abomination of desolation standing in the holy place as affirmed by the prophet Daniel!'[9] The Antichrist had appeared; and if he was not of the tribe of Dan, he was, at any rate, a descendant of Ishmael. The Arabs were a biblical people sent by God to enact the calamities of the 'last days'. It is true that their dominion was seen to last longer than the expected three and a half years, but it could not be long-lasting. The only question was: How long?

Not very long, because the end is near 'and there does not remain a length of time'. So wrote in the third quarter of the seventh century a Mesopotamian monk, the author of the so-called *Revelation of Methodius of Patara*.[10] This text, originally composed in Syriac, soon translated into Greek and into Latin, was destined to exert a profound influence on the eschatological thinking of the Middle Ages – indeed, its impact may be traced down to the nineteenth century; and this in spite of the fact that the *Revelation* was concocted in a remote part of the world in response to the plight of the Jacobite Church under Muslim domination. The author was scandalized by the attitude of many of his co-religionists who had sought an accommodation with the Arabs and had even denied their faith. Some of them, it seems, pinned their hopes on the King of Ethiopia who was, at the time, the only independent ruler of the Monophysite faith, and this with reference to Psalm 68..31, 'Ethiopia shall soon stretch out her hands unto God.' The possibility of an Ethiopian intervention in Mesopotamia was, admittedly, very remote; rather than wait for this to happen, our author strove to show that salvation would come from Byzantium which was, so to speak, the same thing as Ethiopia. This surprising view he justified by the following considerations. Philip of Macedon had married Chuseth (alias Olympias), daughter of Phol, King of Ethiopia. After Philip's death, Chuseth returned home and was given in marriage to Byzas, King of Byzantium. They had one daughter, named Byzantia, who married Romulus Archelaos (or Armaleios), King of Rome, and received that city as a wedding gift. Romulus and Byzantia had three sons: Archelaos (or Armaleios) who reigned in Rome, Urbanus who reigned in Byzantium, and Claudius who reigned in Alexandria. Thus, the Empire of the Romans and the Greeks was proved to be of Ethiopian origin, and it was that Empire that would manifestly 'stretch out her hands unto God'.

After providing this demonstration and a few other facts of universal history, our author proceeds to describe the devastation caused by the Arab conquest and equates the miseries of his time with the 'falling away' that had been foretold by St Paul. But, after the Arab dominion had lasted 77 years (or is it 7 times 7?), there shall arise 'an emperor of the Greeks, that is of the Romans' who 'shall awake as one out of sleep and like a man who had drunk wine' (Ps. 78. 65), and he shall smite the

Arabs and impose on them a heavy yoke. Everyone will then return to his home, be it Cilicia, Isauria, Africa, Greece or Sicily; Arabia will be devastated and Egypt burnt. Then peace will reign: cities will be rebuilt; people will eat and drink, marry and give in marriage. But not for long: for now Gog and Magog will break out of the Caspian Gates and overrun the eastern lands all the way to Joppa, where the archangel of the Lord will smite them down. Then the Roman Emperor will proceed to Jerusalem and dwell there ten and a half years; and the Antichrist will appear, a man born at Chorazin and brought up at Bethsaida (cf. Mt. 11. 21). The emperor will ascend the rock of Golgotha and place his crown on the True Cross, and the Cross will rise to heaven. The Antichrist will be opposed by Enoch and Elijah whom he will kill, and will be himself destroyed by the Lord. Finally, the Son of Man will appear in judgement.

The hope that the Arab Empire would collapse in the seventh century appeared for a time to be nearing fulfilment. The Arab civil war (661–5), the unsuccessful attack on Constantinople (674–8) and the destructive incursions of the Mardaites into Syria and Palestine could be construed as confirming this view. The Arabs had to accept peace on unfavourable terms from the Emperor Constantine IV and, as one chronicler puts it, 'there was great tranquillity in both East and West'.[11] Soon, however, the Arabs were again on the offensive. We do not know in detail how this new situation was made to fit the apocalyptic vision, except that the anticipated duration of the Arab Empire was gradually extended: in the late eight century the period of its prosperity and power was assigned a total span of 152 years.[12] In about 820 a Sicilian prophet was content to adapt Pseudo-Methodius, but introduced a new touch, namely that the last emperor would be revealed in Syracuse. He would send his emissaries 'to the inner regions of Rome and tame the fair-haired nations, and together they will pursue Ishmael'. In Rome the emperor would find buried treasure, enough to pay his troops, and then he would march by land to Constantinople. Then the Antichrist would appear, etc.[13] An interesting feature of this prophecy is that it assigns to the Germanic peoples a role in the eschatological scheme. The 'fair-haired nations' were destined to play an important part in later Byzantine prophecy, sometimes identified with the westerners, at other times with the Russians.

The provincial apocalypses we have been discussing do not fully reflect the enhanced status of Constantinople on the mystical plane. This change in emphasis, confirmed by the transfer of the True Cross to

the capital, must have occurred during the dark centuries: Constantinople now appeared as the New Jerusalem, the repository of the most
precious relics of Christendom. For an exposition of this altered view we
must turn to the Life of St Andrew the Fool which I would be inclined to
attribute to the early eighth century, although it is usually dated to the
ninth or tenth. St Andrew, who belonged to the class of the saintly
insane, is alleged to have lived in the fifth century, but it is highly
unlikely that he ever existed; nor is it clear what intention inspired the
composition of his lengthy Life. In any case, this text came to enjoy
immense popularity, largely because of the eschatological section it
contains. The latter is presented in the form of a conversation between
Andrew and his disciple Epiphanius. Without giving a literal translation, we shall summarize its main points.[14]

The disciple opened the conversation by asking: 'Tell me, please,
how will the end of this world come about? By what sign will men know
that the consummation is at hand? How will this city, the New
Jerusalem, pass away, and what will happen to the holy churches that
are here, to the crosses and the venerable icons, the books and the relics
of the saints?'

The Holy man replied:

Concerning our city you should know that until the end of time it shall not
fear any enemy. No one shall capture it – far from it. For it has been entrusted
to the Mother of God and no one shall snatch it away from her hands. Many
nations shall smite its walls, but they shall break their horns and depart in
shame, while we gain much wealth from them.

Hear now about 'the beginnings of the sorrows' and the end of the world. In
the last days the Lord shall raise up an emperor from poverty and he shall walk
in righteousness: he shall put an end to all wars, enrich the poor, and it shall be
as in the days of Noah. For men shall be rich, living in peace, eating and
drinking, marrying and giving in marriage. Thereafter the emperor shall turn
his face towards the East and shall humble the sons of Hagar [the Arabs], for
the Lord shall be much angered by their blasphemy. The emperor shall
annihilate them and consume their children with fire. And he shall regain
Illyricum for the Roman Empire, and Egypt shall bring her tribute once more.
And he shall set his right hand upon the sea and subdue the fair-haired nations
and humble all his enemies. And his reign will last thirty-two years. In those
days all the hidden gold will be revealed by God's wish and the emperor will
scatter it among his subjects by the spadeful, and all his nobles will become like
emperors in wealth, and the poor like the nobles. With great zeal he will
persecute the Jews, and no Ishmaelite will be found in this city. No one will
play the lyre or the cither or sing songs or commit any other shameful act; for

he will abominate all such men and will eradicate them from the City of the Lord. And there will be great rejoicing as in the days of Noah before the flood.

When his reign has ended, 'the beginnings of sorrows' will set in. Then the Son of Iniquity will arise and reign in this city three and a half years, and cause such wickedness to be done as has not been committed since the beginning of the world. He will decree that fathers should lie with their daughters and mothers with their sons and brothers with their sisters, and whoever refuses to do so will be punished with death. The stench and abomination will rise up before the Lord who will be bitterly angered, and He will command His thunder and lightning to smite the earth. Many cities will be burnt down and men will be paralysed with fear.

Thereafter another emperor will reign over this city and he will abjure Jesus Christ. He will read the writings of the pagans and will be converted to paganism. He will burn the churches and call the life-giving Cross a gallows. In those days there will be most fearful thunder in the heavens and violent earthquakes which will cause cities to fall down. Nation will rise up against nation, and kings against kings, and there will be tribulation and sorrow on earth.

When this impious reign has ended, an emperor will come from Ethiopia and rule twelve years in peace, and he will rebuild the ruined churches of the saints. And then another emperor will come from Arabia and rule one year. During his rule the fragments of the True Cross will be joined together and will be given to him. He will go to Jerusalem and deposit there the Cross and place his crown upon it, and then will surrender his soul.

Thereupon three foolish youths will arise in this city and they will rule in peace a hundred and fifty days, after which they will be angered at one another and make civil war. The first will go to Thessalonica and conscript its inhabitants from the age of seven upward, even priests and monks. He will build big ships and go to Rome, and he will enlist the fair-haired nations. The second youth will go to Mesopotamia and to the Cyclades and he, too, will conscript the priests and the monks. And then he will go to the navel of the earth or, as others say, to Alexandria, and there he will await his companions. The third will raise an army in Phrygia, Caria, Galatia, Asia, Armenia and Arabia, and he will enter the town of Sylaion [on the south coast of Asia Minor] which will not be captured by anyone until the end of time. When all three meet, they will fight a great battle against one another, and they will cut each other to pieces, like sheep in a butchery. All three kings will be killed, and the blood of the Romans will run in streams, and none of them shall survive. Now every woman will be a widow; seven women will seek one man and find him not. Blessed will be those serving the Lord on mountains and in caves who will not see these evils.

Since no man of the nobility will have remained, a base woman will arise in Pontus and rule this city. In those days there will be conspiracies and slaughter in every street and in every house: sons will murder their fathers and daughters their mothers. In the churches there will be turpitude and bloodshed, music, dances and games, such as no man has seen before. This impure queen will make herself into a goddess and fight against the Lord. She will befoul the altars with dung, and gather together all the holy vessels and the icons of the saints and the crosses and the gospels and every written book, and will make a great heap and burn them. She will seek the relics of the saints so as to destroy them, but she will not find them; for the Lord will invisibly remove them from this city. She will destroy the altar table of St Sophia and, standing towards the east, she will address to the Most High words such as these: 'Have I been idle, O so-called God, in erasing Thy face from the earth? See what I have done to Thee, and Thou hast not been able to touch even one hair on my head. Wait a little, and I shall pull down the firmament and ascend up to Thee, and we shall see who is the stronger.'

Then the Lord in great anger will stretch out His hand. He will seize his strong scythe and cut the earth from under the city, and order the waters to swallow it up. With a great crash the waters will well forth and raise the city to a great height, spinning it like a millstone, and then they will cast it down and sink it in the abyss. In this way will our city come to an end.

Next, St Andrew considers the problem whether, upon the destruction of the kingdom of the gentiles, the Jews will be gathered in Jerusalem and allowed to rule until the end of the seventh millennium. He is inclined to believe that they will be gathered, but to be punished instead of being rewarded. Epiphanius, however, is not interested in the fate of the Jews. 'Leave these things aside', he says 'and tell me, O father, whether St Sophia will be swallowed up together with the city, or whether, as some people affirm, it will be suspended in the air by an invisible force.' 'What say you, child?' answers the saint. 'When the whole city sinks, how will St Sophia remain? Who will have need of it? Surely, God does not dwell in temples made by hand. The only thing that will remain will be the column in the Forum, since it contains the Holy Nails. The ships that sail by will be moored to this column. For forty days the city will be mourned, and then the Empire will be given to Rome, Sylaion and Thessalonica, but only for a short time, since the end will be in sight. That same year God will open the Caspian Gates, and the impure nations, seventy-two kingdoms of them, will pour over the whole earth. They will eat human flesh and drink human blood; even dogs, mice and frogs will they consume with pleasure. The sun will turn to blood and the moon will be darkened. The inhabitants of Asia will then flee to the Cyclades and there they will mourn for 660 days. Finally, the Antichrist will arise from the tribe of Dan. He will not be born naturally, but God will release him from Hell and fashion an unclean body for him. His advent will be announced by Elijah, Enoch and St John the Evangelist. The Antichrist will kill them and make a terrible war on God. Blessed are those who will suffer for the faith in those days.' Naturally, the Antichrist will be defeated and dragged back to Hell. The trumpet will sound, God will appear on Sion and the Judgement will take place.

Such is the blood-curdling prospect described by St Andrew the Fool. It is a potpourri of elements which, by now, will have become familiar to the reader. Setting aside various touches that are typical of the Byzantine mentality (disapproval of music and games, a horror of sexual relations and incest in particular), we may note that the Arabs are regarded as the principal enemy without being, apparently, greatly feared. St Andrew does not foresee a period of Arab supremacy: on the contrary, they will be speedily defeated. Yet the subjugation of the foe does not open up a period of happiness and tranquillity. The sum total of prosperous years that may be expected on earth adds up to forty-five; the rest will be a tale of unrelieved carnage and destruction. We may also note the narrowness of Andrew's geographical outlook: he is aware of certain peripheral cities like Rome, Thessalonica and Sylaion whose inhabitants will escape the calamities taking place at the centre of history, but, essentially, he is concerned only with the fate of Constantinople. And in Constantinople it is the relics of the saints and of the Passion, rather than the churches or the icons, that constitute the principal object of God's concern.

We have been taught to regard the second half of the tenth century as marking the apogee of medieval Byzantium, yet even in those days of military success many people remained deeply pessimistic. The historian Leo the Deacon, who decided to chronicle for the sake of posterity all the terrible things that he had witnessed, was not even sure that there would be a posterity: God might decide to halt there and then the 'ship of life'.[15] A little earlier Nicetas David the Paphlagonian had been able to show, by means of a somewhat obscure computation, that the world would end in 1028. From the 'cosmic week' only six hours and eight minutes were left: the proposition that the end of the days was at hand was so obvious that it needed no demonstration, and was confirmed by the foolishness of emperors, the corruption of magistrates, and the utter unworthiness of bishops and monks.[16] Ordinary people, however, did not compute. They looked instead at the enigmatic monuments of their city, the statues, the triumphal arches and columns upon which were depicted scenes of warfare and captivity. These, they were convinced, had been made by ancient 'philosophers' who foretold thereby the fall of Constantinople and the end of the world. They even thought for a time (presumably after Igor's raid of 941) that the city was destined to be captured by the Russians.[17]

We need not follow step by step the further development of Byzantine eschatological thinking. In the Comnenian period it was affirmed that Constantinople would not attain the age of a thousand years, so that it would fall before 1324, reckoning from the date of its foundation.[18] The same period produced a set of dynastic prophecies which later circulated under the name of the Emperor Leo the Wise (886–912) and were to serve as the prototype of the Papal prophecies attributed to Joachim of Floris. These foretold a succession of five emperors, to be followed by a division of the Empire and then its resurgence.[19] At the close of the twelfth century there appeared to be a growing preoccupation with the 'liberator king', the one we have already met in the Life of St Andrew the Fool – the king who was destined to reign thirty-two years and defeat the Ishmaelites: Isaac II Angelus (1185–95) fancifully identified himself with this figure.[20] Understandably, when Constantinople had fallen to the Crusaders and the Empire had been dismembered, the myth of the 'liberator king' assumed even greater relevance: it is a constant motif in the great efflorescence of oracular writing that occurred in the latter part of the thirteenth century, partly as a reaction to the betrayal of the Orthodox faith by the Emperor Michael VIII Palaeologus at the Council of Lyon (1274). Here is a typical prophecy of this time which shows how, once again, traditional elements have been re-interpreted to fit a changing reality.

> Thus saith the Lord Almighty: 'Woe to thee, City of seven hills, when the sceptre of the angels [meaning the dynasty of the Angeli] shall reign in thee! Constantinople will be surrounded by camps and will fall without resistance [in 1203]. An infant will now reign in the City [the young Alexius IV]. He will lay his hands on the holy sanctuaries and give the sacred vessels to the sons of perdition [Alexius was forced to confiscate church plate to repay the Crusaders and the Venetians]. Then the sleeping serpent will awake, smite the infant and take his crown. The fair-haired nation will rule in Constantinople sixty-five years [actually fifty-seven].

So far it has been past history; now prophecy begins. The northern nations will march down and fight a great war with the southern nations. The streets of Constantinople will be flooded with blood. This punishment being deemed sufficient, an old, shabbily dressed man will be found in the right-hand side of Constantinople (possibly a reference to the imprisoned legitimate Emperor John IV Lascaris). The angels will crown him in St Sophia and give him a sword, saying, 'Take courage, John, and vanquish the enemy!' He will defeat the Ishmaelites and drive them to the 'lone tree' (i.e. to the end of the world). On his return the treasures of the earth will be revealed and all men will become rich. He will reign thirty-two (or, in some versions, twelve) years. He will foresee his own death, go to Jerusalem and hand his crown over to God. After him will reign his four sons, one in Rome, one in Alexandria, one in Constantinople, and one in Thessalonica. They will fight between themselves and will be destroyed. Then a foul woman will reign in Constantinople. She will profane the churches, in punishment for which the city will be flooded, and only the Dry Hill (the Xerolophos or seventh hill) will be left projecting from the water. Now Thessalonica will rule for a short time, but she, too, will be flooded as well as Smyrna and Cyprus. Then the Antichrist will reign three and a half years, and he will exalt the Jews and rebuild the Temple of Jerusalem. God will withhold the rain and burn the earth to a depth of thirteen cubits. The heavens will open up and Christ will come in his glory.[21]

One more date for the end of the world was left in reserve, namely the end of the seventh millennium which, by the Byzantine reckoning, corresponded to 1492 AD. As the inhabitants of Constantinople saw the steady advance of the Ottoman Turks, they could not help believing that this time all the signs were pointing unmistakably to the final catastrophe. This note was insistently sounded, amongst others, by the popular preacher Joseph Bryennius. The leader of the anti-Latin party at Constantinople, Gennadius Scholarius, was convinced that the world would end in 1493–4 (he counted from 5506 BC), and it was probably this belief that caused him to accept from Mehmed the Conqueror the task of leading the Orthodox community. For the earthly contest was nearly over and the heavenly rewards in sight. The only thing that mattered now was to keep one's faith untainted. Blessed are they that keep their faith during the last tribulations.[22]

Why had the city fallen? This was the agonizing question that the Greek survivors kept asking themselves while desperately trying to ransom their relatives and establish working relations with their new masters. A clergyman, writing on 29 July 1453 – exactly two months after the disaster – pleads with a friend in the town of Ainos (modern Enez): 'I entreat you, my good Sir, to send me the book of St

Methodius of Patara, either an old copy or a newly written one, if you happen to have it. Please don't neglect to do so because I have great need of it. I also beg you to send me, if you can find it, some dried fish roe.'[23] The fateful year 1492 came and went. The world continued to exist.

The final drama of human history which God 'by His inscrutable judgement' kept on postponing was to be the Second Coming, and we may pause to enquire how this was expected to take place. We shall here follow the exact vision of this event contained in the Life of Basil the Younger (tenth century) whose disciple, by the name of Gregory, was transported to heaven and given, so to speak, a special 'preview'. From his elevated vantage point Gregory first saw a city built of gold and precious stones. It was as big as the circle of the firmament; its walls were three hundred cubits high and it had twelve gates, all securely closed. This was the New Zion which Christ had built after His incarnation as a resting place for His apostles and prophets. After certain preparations had been made by angels, an aperture opened in the heavens and a column of fire descended to earth. At the same time an angel was sent to Satan (the Antichrist) who had reigned three years on earth. The angel held a fiery scroll on which was inscribed a missive from the Lord ordering Satan to wipe clean all the evil and corruption he had caused and then depart to Hell. Then the archangel Michael and twelve other angels sounded their trumpets and the dead arose. They all looked alike, in other words there was no difference between men and women, no sign of age, and even infants were transformed into adults. Some, however, had resplendent faces and luminous inscriptions on their brows expressing their respective qualities, while the sinners were covered with filth and dung, with mud and ashes or with the scales of leprosy, each according to his sin. There were also some who resembled animals – those were the idolaters who had never heard of Christ or Moses. The sinners, like the just, were identified by inscription, and among them were the heretics – Arians, Manichees, Paulicians, Iconoclasts, Jacobites and many others. At that point the Lord's throne was prepared: it did not rest on earth, but floated in the air, and next to it was set up a cross at the sight of which the Jews and the Ishmaelites were seized with fear. Four contingents of angels took up their stand at the four cardinal points and another four contingents at the four corners of the earth. Then Christ appeared in a cloud and the righteous sprouted wings and met Him in the air. As Christ sat on His throne, the earth was rejuvenated and the firmament made new: the stars vanished since their place was now taken by the saints, and the sun disappeared since Christ was the new sun. Instead of the ocean, a fiery river was made to flow all round. Then the angels stationed to the west rounded up all the idolaters and all those who had had no knowledge of God and cast them into the fiery flow. All that remained to be judged were the Israelites, the Christians and those members of 'the nations' who had not worshipped idols. The just were now placed to the right of Christ and the sinners, an overwhelmingly bigger group, to the left. From the time of Adam to that of Abraham only one in twenty thousand or one in forty thousand was saved; from Abraham to the Incarnation one in a thousand or even one in ten thousand; and from the time of Christ's predication onwards one in three or one in four.

Christ now led all the righteous in procession to the Heavenly City. The Virgin Mary came first, then John the Baptist, the apostles, the martyrs and confessors, the prophets and good kings of the Jews, and so forth. Among the larger groups of the just were the poor in spirit, the mourners, the merciful, the peacemakers, those who had been persecuted and those who had kept their virginity. The smallest groups included members of 'the nations' who had lived before Christ's advent, the holy fools, the righteous judges, and those who had kept their marriage unsullied.

It was now time to deal with the sinners. First, they were separated by periods (from Adam to the Flood, from Noah to Moses, and so on) and then by categories. Once again, each category is listed with an indication of its relative size – an interesting commentary on Byzantine life. The biggest group of all, made up of both clergy and laity, was that of the profligate (asôtoi): those were the persons who used to ride on horses and fat mules, who bought many garments, invested in luxurious houses and country estates, the drunkards, fornicators and adulterers. They were followed by many monks who had displayed indifference, laziness, avarice and disobedience – in fact, we are told that nearly the entire race of monks had sunk into a hopeless decline in the latter stages of human history. Other big groups were the magicians, the pederasts and sodomites, the thieves (almost infinite in number), the wrathful, the envious, the garrulous, and, of course, the heretics and the Jews (except those who had followed the law of Moses before the Incarnation). Thanks to the intervention of the Virgin Mary, two groups of medium size were, at the last moment, rescued from damnation and given abodes – not, indeed, in the heavenly Jerusalem, but in its less desirable suburbs. Those were the unbaptized children of Christians and those who had been neither good nor bad.

The next step was the investiture of the righteous conducted by Christ in a huge church situated within the Heavenly City. Thrones, crowns and purple vestments were conferred on the saints in the same manner that the Byzantine emperor bestowed dignities on his officials. The investiture was followed by a liturgical service, and the service by a spiritual banquet. Finally, all the righteous settled down to their new and eternal routine. An 'upper kingdom' was established to the east of the City as a habitation for Christ, the Virgin Mary, John the Baptist and those saints who had sufficiently strong wings to travel thither; the rest remained in the City which was provided with houses, churches, chapels, gardens and other amenities. In short, not so much a New Jerusalem as a New Constantinople.[24]

The outline we have given of Byzantine ideas about the future of mankind and the Second Coming shows, for all the gradual reinterpretations they underwent, a remarkably close adherence to their biblical origins. It would be a mistake to relegate such ideas to the realm of fantasy and old wives' tales: for, apart from Holy Scripture itself, hardly any other category of literature was as avidly read by the ordinary man as oracular texts. They provide a key to the understanding of the Byzantine mentality and, as such, are worthy of the historian's attention. They prove, in the first instance, that no lasting happiness or fulfilment was expected on earth. The purpose of 'the last days' was to subject the Christians to a series of cruel tests so as to separate the elect from the sinners. Since the Messiah had already come, there could be no messianic age in the future. St John's Revelation, the only biblical book that looks forward to a thousand years of happiness before the end of the world, did not enjoy canonical status in Byzantium and was not, therefore, taken into account in this respect. Another striking feature of Byzantine prophecy concerns the absence of any national spirit. Admittedly, the geographical scope of the oracles tended to shrink until it was practically limited to the destinies of Constantinople, but that was merely a sign of myopia. Preoccupied with their own troubles, the inhabitants of the diminished Byzantine State did not have the vision to embrace the whole of mankind. The fulfilment of their longings consisted in the simultaneous destruction of both the westerners and the Ishmaelites (now identified with the Turks). Even so, the 'liberator king' would not usher in a period of national revival; while avenging Byzantine grievances, he would introduce the end of the world. It was only after the fall of Constantinople, indeed a long time after, that the liberator, the emperor 'who had been asleep' or 'turned to marble', assumed the role of a national hero who would drive the Turk out of Constantinople, replace the cross on the dome of St Sophia and establish a Greek state.

CHAPTER 12

THE IDEAL LIFE

How was life to be conducted on earth in view of the impending end of the world? Following Christ's advent mankind had reached its maturity, and that meant that stricter standards of behaviour were in force than had been acceptable under the previous dispensation. In the times of the Old Testament a measure of licence had been allowed. Noah may have been a just man and perfect in his own generation, but he would no longer be accounted perfect now. Then it was sufficient to observe the Law; now admittance to Heaven was barred unless one exceeded the righteousness of the scribes and the Pharisees (Mt. 5. 20). Not only murder, as had been the case earlier, but even wrath and abusive language were now cause for perdition; not only adultery, but even a lustful glance cast at a woman; not only perjury, but the swearing of all oaths.[1]

To achieve perfection a man had to sell all his possessions, distribute the proceeds to the poor and renounce the world, materially as well as spiritually – in short, to become a monk. Since, however, the majority of people were too weak or too indolent to follow this difficult path, a method of living in society was laid down. Its basic principle was that of order (*kosmos*, *taxis*, *eutaxia*). God compacted the universe in an orderly manner and it was His wish that human life should be led in the same spirit.[2] By observing the principle of divinely appointed order both in social relations and in our private sphere we conform to the harmony of the universe: life on earth, with all of its inherent imperfections, assumes some resemblance to life in Heaven.

Just as the universe is ruled monarchically by God, so mankind is governed by the Roman emperor. The incarnation of Christ, as we have already pointed out, was providentially timed to coincide with the setting up of the Roman empire which put an end to the dissensions and wars, that is, the disorder caused by the sharing of power between

218

several autonomous states (*polyarchia*).[3] Not only did God ordain the existence of the Empire, He also chose each individual emperor, which was why no human rules were formulated for his appointment. That did not mean that the emperor was always a good man: God in His wisdom might deliberately select a bad emperor so as to punish humanity for its sins.[4] The alternatives to legitimate imperial governance were usurpation (*tyrannis*) and anarchy. A *tyrannos* was one who attempted to make himself emperor in opposition to God's will and consequently failed; for, if he succeeded, God must have been on his side, and he ceased to be a usurper. Absence of sole authority or mob rule (*dêmokratia*) was tantamount to confusion.

God rules mankind by inspiring fear of Hell and promising reward in Heaven,[5] in other words with a stick and a carrot. Likewise, the emperor governs his subjects through fear: his enemies are thrown in prison, banished, disciplined by the whip, deprived of their eyesight or of their life. Even innocent people 'serve him in trembling': they may be sent into battle or given unpleasant tasks, but no one dares to disobey.[6] It is preferable, of course, for the emperor to rule over willing subjects, and to do so he should manifest certain qualities that are also shared by God. Above all, he should be man-loving (*philanthrôpos*). While remaining awesome by reason of his authority, he should make himself loved by the exercise of beneficence. Generosity and leniency are especially appropriate to the emperor, but he must also insist on due observance of the law (*eunomia*). In his own person he must be self-restrained, circumspect, resolute in action and slow to anger. His unique position is, however, defined, first and foremost, by his relation to God, the only being of whom he stands in need. His greatest ornament is, therefore, piety (*eusebeia*).[7] He is, by definition, faithful in Christ (*pistos en Christô*) and Christ-loving (*philochristos*), these attributes being expressed in his titulature, as was also that of being victorious (*nikêtês, kallinikos*), since victory was granted to him in return for his piety.

The emperor was holy (*hagios*) and in his portraits was usually represented wearing a nimbus. His palace was likewise sacred, a *domus divina*, surrounded by a protective zone of 'apartness' (*nam imperio magna ab universis secreta debentur*).[8] When he appeared in public, this was done through the medium of ceremonial which was a reflection of the harmonious working of the universe and was itself synonymous with order (*taxis*).[9] His subjects communicated with him by means of acclamations which were rhythmical and repetitive as in the divine liturgy, and when received in audience prostrated themselves on the ground. What the emperor was to his subjects, God was to the emperor. We accordingly find, from about the seventh century onwards, representations of the earthly emperor performing the same act of *adoratio* or *proskynêsis* before the enthroned Christ.

Was the emperor also a priest, a second Melchisedek? It must be admitted that his position with regard to the Church was not clearly thought out at the time of Constantine's conversion and remained to the end somewhat ambiguous: a precise boundary between *imperium* and *sacerdotium* was not drawn, a fact that often led to a conflict of jurisdiction. It may be fair to say, however, that whereas the emperor never exercised the priestly function of offering the eucharistic sacrifice and did not, as a rule, define religious dogma, he was regarded as being ultimately responsible for maintaining the purity of the faith, convoking ecumenical councils of the Church and enforcing the conversion of heretics. Probably the most emphatic statement of episcopal versus imperial authority in an official Byzantine document is to be found in the law code of Basil I, believed to have been inspired by the patriarch Photius. The patriarch of Constantinople is described therein as 'the living image of Christ', and his purpose as the preservation of the Orthodox people, the conversion of heretics and even urging the infidel to become 'imitators' of the true faith.[10] Yet Leo VI, Basil's successor, legislated on purely ecclesiastical matters and even chided his patriarch for not taking a more active role in affairs that concerned him.[11]

In theory the emperor ruled all men or, at any rate, all Orthodox Christians. The existence of pagan rulers did not infringe this postulate for, as long as pagans remained unconverted, they were outside the main sphere of divine Providence, but if they embraced Orthodox Christianity, they acknowledged *ipso facto* the emperor's ultimate authority. This may have been a plausible approximation of the truth in the Early Byzantine period when the structure of imperial ideology was put together, but it became less and less tenable as other, independent Christian states came into being during the Middle Ages. The fiction of the 'family of princes' in which the Byzantine emperor occupied the position of seniority was accordingly put into circulation and carefully fostered by the prescriptions of court protocol. It is a curious commentary on Byzantine inability to rethink their principles that the imperial myth was still propounded in the late fourteenth century when the Empire was limited to the territory of Constantinople.

The emperor's authority was transmitted to the magistrates

(*archontes*) he appointed. It is worth observing that the term *archôn*, which has no precise English equivalent, denoted all persons invested with command – military, civil and, in some cases, even ecclesiastical. The duty of subjects to obey their *archontes* was explicitly stated in the Bible: 'For there is no power, but of God: the powers that be are ordained of God. Whosoever therefore resisteth the power, resisteth the ordinance of God' (Rom. 13. 1–2). The necessity of such obedience for the sake of order (*eutaxia*) and in deference to him that appointed the magistrate, who was ultimately God acting through the emperor, was stressed by the Fathers of the Church.[12] Besides, everyone knew that powerful persons were like big fishes that swallowed little fishes: nothing was to be gained by opposing them.[13]

The position of the clergy and especially that of bishops in the scheme of ideal life was both honourable and onerous. Ordained, as had been Joshua, by the imposition of hands, the priest alone had the faculty of administering baptism, forgiving sins and performing the liturgical sacrifice. His task was to instruct his flock and to protect the poor, and to instruct not only by means of words, but also by example. Since he was everyone's servant, he had to be humble; since his shortcomings were evident to all, he had to lead a blameless life. He needed to be experienced, patient and vigilant; to know whom to goad and whom to bridle, whom to praise and whom to reprimand. Although his dignity was exalted – indeed, as the spirit surpasses the body, so the priesthood is greater than earthly authority – he had to remember that in the end he would give accounts for his stewardship and, like all men, ran the risk of eternal damnation.[14]

Next to the clergy, judges, teachers and physicians occupied posts of peculiar responsibility. The judge was close to being an *archôn*, since he determined the fate of litigants in his court. He had need of prior training and great intelligence. Above all, he had to keep in his mind the image of true justice like a marksman who shoots an arrow at a target, and treat everyone equally, be he friend or stranger, rich or poor – something that, alas, did not often happen. Oblivious to appearances, he had to look into the secret places of the heart and was enjoined to display the princely virtue of mercy (*philanthrôpia*) and to temper fear with leniency.[15] The teacher, like the bishop, was required to set a good example. Being in possession of a gift, he was obligated to give abundantly of it to those wishing to learn, but, in so doing, he often had to use the rod.[16] Physicians appear to have been less highly regarded: the Lives of saints are full of references to their uselessness and cupidity, and it was openly admitted that instead of healing the patient, they often made him worse. Even so, the experienced doctor played a necessary role which was both physical and moral: he knew how to apply a treatment gradually so as to produce the greatest good, how to administer a bitter medicine in a cup coated with honey, and how to instil hygienic habits into healthy persons by exhibiting to them the terrifying implements of his craft.[17]

Among ordinary members of society, soldiers and farmers were the most useful. The role of soldiers was to keep the peace, for which they were well rewarded by means of donatives. It was their duty, as stressed by St John the Baptist (Lk. 3. 14), to be content with their stipend and not to cause any trouble.[18] The soldier's life was not as difficult as that of the farmer who had to toil constantly in heat and cold, to leave his bed at an early hour and to defend his isolated hut. The soil he tilled was often thin and stony, but if he succeeded in making it bear fruit, his joy was greater than if he had cultivated a fertile field.[19] Merchants, on the other hand, pursued a profession that readily led to wrongdoing. There was much scope for dishonesty in buying and selling, while borrowing and lending at interest was an unmitigated evil. It was our duty not to turn away from anyone who wanted to borrow from us (Mt. 5. 42), but to exact interest was forbidden. A man burdened with a loan had no joy in life and no rest in sleep. He saw his creditor in his dreams, he hated the days and the months that brought him closer to the date of repayment. Loans were the cause of mendacity, ingratitude and perjury. It was infinitely better to be content with one's own means, no matter how paltry, than to have recourse to another man's money.[20] As for craftsmen, they practised certain useful techniques that had been invented once and for all, not so much by the human mind as by divine help. It was vain to trouble oneself with a view to their further perfection.[21]

Slaves, who formed the lowest element of society, had an absolute duty, repeatedly stressed in the Bible, of obeying their masters even if the latter were cruel. The institution of servitude was itself an evil, the consequence of Ham's sin (Gen. 9. 25), and it was praiseworthy to manumit one's inherited slaves, yet to live entirely without them was hardly practicable. A gentleman was well advised to wash his own feet and to be generally self-sufficient. He did not need a servant to hand him his clothes or to accompany him to the bath, but it was unthinkable for a free man to cook.[22] On the other hand, it was unseemly for an ordinary fellow to buy a slave for the sake of display. In general, masters were urged to treat their slaves humanely and not to beat them.

It cannot be doubted that Christianity introduced a measure of clemency into social relations, especially with regard to slavery. The Lives of saints repeatedly stress the fact that all men were made of the same clay and castigate cruel masters. Occasionally a plea is also made for a redistribution of wealth. Thus, Agapetus in the sixth century remarks that the rich and the poor 'suffer similar harm from dissimilar circumstances; the former burst from excess, while the latter are destroyed by hunger'. He accordingly urges the emperor to take some of the surplus from the rich and give it to the poor so as to achieve greater equality.[23] By continually stressing the Christian's obligation to give alms the Church obtained the same result more efficaciously and on a wider scale than any government intervention might have done. At the same time it has to be admitted that no fundamental reform of society was advocated, the more so since merit resided in voluntary action. If wealth in itself had been an evil, we would not all wish to find repose in Abraham's bosom, seeing that Abraham had been a rich man, the master of three hundred and eighteen domestic servants.[24] Granted, the origin of unequal distribution lay in injustice: God gave equally to all men in the same manner that the emperor's public domain was available to all. No dispute or litigation occurred over the use of baths, streets or marketplaces, whereas people were constantly suing one another over private property. Since, however, wealth was inherited from father to son and it was impossible to trace it back to its original act of injustice, all that mattered was for its current holder to use it wisely and to share it among the needy.[25]

Liberality was enjoined on all, but that did not mean that the order of society, in which everyone had his appointed place, needed changing. Two biblical texts were repeatedly quoted in this connection: 'Let every man abide in the same calling wherein he was called' (1 Cor. 7. 20) and 'Remove not the ancient landmark which thy fathers have set' (Prov. 22. 28). The revolutionary, the subverter of order (*neôteristês*) attracted universal condemnation. Besides, the powerful and the rich were sufficiently punished by changes of fortune to which the poor were immune, and ultimate equality was brought about by death. 'When we see an *archôn* dying, then we behold a great mystery. He whom all the condemned used to fear is now dragged away like a condemned man; he who used to chain prisoners is now tried like a prisoner.'[26]

A special group within society, independent of all social classes, consisted of the monks. It is instructive in this connection to examine the choice of biblical quotations which St John Damascene considered as applying to the monastic life:[27] all of them were addressed to the entire Christian community, for example: 'Whosoever he be of you that forsaketh not all that he hath, he cannot be my disciple' (Lk. 14. 33); 'You cannot serve God and mammon' (Lk. 16. 13); 'No man that warreth entangleth himself with the affairs of this life' (11 Tim. 2. 4); and so forth. As we have already stressed in Chapter 5, the monk was a layman. He was the perfect Christian, the true philosopher; which meant that, ideally speaking, all Christians should have become monks. Why, then, was it necessary for them to withdraw from the world? Because everyday life was full of distraction (*perispasmos*) and turmoil which clouded the mirror of the soul and made it incapable of reflecting the divine light; because the perturbed mind could not attain that release from care (*amerimnon*) that was the mark of perfection. It followed from this that the solitary life was preferable to the communal life. Quietude (*hêsychia*) was requisite for purging the soul; it served to assuage desire, anger, sorrow and fear, and render those 'wild beasts' more amenable to the power of reason. By a strange paradox, however, the monk made himself all the more vulnerable to attacks by the devil because he was the devil's chief foe. He was the one who 'put on the whole armour of God' and took up the struggle, 'not against flesh and blood, but against principalities, against powers, against the rulers of the darkness of this world, against spiritual wickedness in high places' (Eph. 6. 11–12). But if he had vanquished his own passions, he had the strength to withstand all demonic assaults.

We can now understand why the question of the monk's 'social usefulness' never arose in the Byzantine world. It was perfectly obvious that the man who had attained mastery over the powers of darkness and had won God's confidence was the most useful member of the community and guaranteed the wellbeing both of his own district and the Empire as a whole. His mission was primarily internal, not external; and only after he had won his own spiritual struggle was he in a position to fulfil his wider purpose. We may add that while the unworthy priest was nevertheless able to carry out his sacerdotal duties, the unworthy monk was absolutely useless.

The same code of morality applied to monks and laymen. While it may be an exaggeration to say that virtue was seen almost exclusively in negative terms, it is undeniably true that Late Antiquity and a good part of the Middle Ages were characterized by an obsessive revulsion from the material world, and this not only among Christians. How else can one explain the success of the Manichaeans? The human soul was visualized as a citadel that had to be vigilantly guarded against external attack. Its weakest points were its gates which were five in number, corresponding to the five senses. The first gate, that of speech, needed to be fortified by the braces and cross-bars consisting in the constant recitation of Holy Scripture: in this way all undesirable entrants would be excluded. The second gate was that of hearing: it was essential not to admit through it any idle gossip or anything unseemly. The third gate, that of smell, had to be bolted in the face of all sweet scents which had the effect of slackening the 'tension' of the soul. The gate of sight was particularly exposed; hence it was important to see as few women as possible and avoid the theatre. The proper function of sight was to behold the beauties of nature. The fifth gate, that of touch, had to be guarded against soft clothing, comfortable beds and contact with other human bodies. It was not, however, sufficient to keep watch at the gates; the citizens living within the citadel of the soul had to observe 'stringent and fearsome laws' and to obey their own 'magistrates'.[28] Equally negative prescriptions applied to the morality of the body. A man had to abstain from fornication, drunkenness and gluttony, a woman from the use of perfume and artificial adornment. The body required only such care as was sufficient for the preservation of health.[29]

Among the many vices and failings to which human beings are prone, some were viewed with a degree of reprobation that may appear to us rather bizarre. It is not perhaps surprising that in a period when foodstuffs were generally in short supply, gluttony should have been considered a grave sin, but it is not so evident to us that it leads to impure desires and licentiousness and is the gateway to all evil. Yet such was the prevalent opinion, and it was held that just as smoke drives away bees, so the glutton drives away from himself the grace of the Holy Spirit.[30] Outspokenness (*parrhêsia*) was also regarded as a great failing as was the sin to which monks were particularly subject, namely indifference of boredom (*akêdia*). On the other hand, mourning (*penthos*) was considered a virtue, especially necessary for monks, but commendable in everyone. Strangest of all is the condemnation of laughter: 'It is generally forbidden to Christians to laugh, and particularly to monks.'[31] Christ, it seems, had never laughed. At the most, one could allow oneself to smile as did the Syrian saint Julian Sabas when he heard news of the death of Julian the Apostate.[32]

Anti-feminism was a fundamental tenet of Byzantine thinking until the sporadic introduction of western ideas of romantic love in about the twelfth century. The sight of a woman, we are told, is like a poisoned arrow: the longer the poison remains in the soul, the more corruption it produces.[33] There was, of course, such a thing as a virtuous woman: it was the one who never showed her face to a stranger.[34] Generally, however, she was a crawling worm, the daughter of mendacity, the enemy of peace. The catalogue of her vices and weaknesses is endless: she was frivolous, garrulous and licentious. Above all, she was addicted to luxury and expense. She loaded herself with jewellery, powdered her face, painted her cheeks with rouge, scented her garments and thus made herself into a deadly trap to seduce young men through all their senses. No amount of wealth was sufficient to satisfy a woman's desires. Day and night she thought of nothing but gold and precious stones, of purple cloth and embroidery, of ointments and perfumes. Were it not for sexual desire, no man in his right mind would wish to share his house with a woman and suffer the consequent injuries, in spite of the domestic services she performed. That is why God, knowing her contemptible nature, provided her from the beginning with the weapon of sexuality.[35]

Oblivious to the sorrows that awaited them, Byzantine men continued to marry and, in so doing, they had the grudging support of St Paul. In the early days of human history, those described in the Old Testament, marriage had been directed to procreation so greatly esteemed by the Jews. Now, however, that 'things were waning and reaching their ultimate end', such considerations no longer applied.[36] Besides, the earth was sufficiently populated, and the idea that the human race would be extinguished by universal continence was quite unjustified. The multiplication of the species was due entirely to God and the one occasion when it had been almost totally obliterated, by the Flood, was brought about by licentiousness, the opposite of continence. Procreation being no longer essential, the main purpose of marriage was to protect men from promiscuity. Marriage was meant to be a 'harbour of chastity', a jetty that broke the waves of desire. It was necessary for the weak, but an obstacle to the strong who knew how to tame the fury of nature by means of fasting and vigils. If, however, matrimony was to achieve this laudable end, it was necessary for parents to have their boys married as early as possible and, in any case, before they had made a career for themselves or obtained posts in the emperor's service. For if marriage was delayed a young man would have recourse to prostitutes and develop a taste for laughter, flippant speech and indecorous behaviour. A woman of good family would refuse to satisfy such yearnings with the result that the bridegroom would begin neglecting her after a couple of nights.[37]

No matter what precautions were observed, marriage was a source of endless turmoil. It was a kind of mutual enslavement, made only worse if the spouses were of unequal fortune. It destroyed tranquillity by the presence of children and by financial worries. If a man sought an escape by involving himself in civic activity, he would inevitably be soiled by sin: he would get irritated at his fellow-citizens, endure insults, adopt insincere postures. The evils of a second marriage were correspondingly greater: unseemly in itself, it created discord in the family so that even the ashes of the departed spouse became a source of envy.

To make a bad situation more tolerable, stringent rules had to be applied to the conduct of a household. No sentimentality was to be lavished on children, who had to be purged from the start of the sin of vanity. It was bad enough for girls to wear jewellery, but quite abominable for little boys to have long hair and to be adorned with necklaces and ear-rings. The model boy, such as might one day become a saint, had the gravity of an old man (*puer senex*): he never played games and never consorted with his fellow schoolchildren for fear of being contaminated by their evil ways. The father's authority in the household was paramount, but he was urged not to enforce it by beating his children: harsh words and reproaches were more efficacious. The only valid reason for refusing obedience to one's father was a determination to respond to a higher call: a boy who decided to become a monk was justified in running away from a prearranged marriage. For as Heaven was to earth and angels were to men, so virginity was to marriage. Its superiority was proved by the fact that it was prized only by the Christian Church: Jews avoided it and pagans viewed it with puzzlement. Admittedly, virginity was also practised by certain heretics like the Manichaeans, but 'the chastity of heretics is worse than all debauchery'.[38] Like fasting, virginity was not an absolute good in itself but was made good by our intention. Frustrated by the presence of worldly cares, it required us to be pure both in body and in spirit. It was the surest means of rising above the mire of earthly life.

While the family was the basic cell of human existence, certain demands were also made by the community which often happened to be a city. We have already commented on the vitriolic attacks launched by churchmen on one of the main amenities of Late Antique urban life, namely the theatre, but their disapprobation was not limited to that institution: the city as a whole was evil. If we consult St John

227

Damascene once again, we discover that the relevant section in his anthology is entitled 'Concerning the city filled with impiety', and that it is made up in its entirety of critical passages, starting with Psalm 55. 9 ('I have seen violence and strife in the city') and going on to the castigations of Nahum, Zephaniah, Hosea, Isaiah, Jeremiah, Ezekiel, St Basil and St Gregory of Nazianzus.[39] Not one kind word for the *polis*. The city was the setting of dances and jests, of taverns, baths and brothels. Women went about with uncovered heads. Everything about them was indecent: their speech, their gestures, their costume, their hair-style, the movement of their limbs and the sidelong glances they cast. Young men, too, such as were to be seen in the city, simulated effeminacy and let their hair grow long.[40] Indeed, people went so far as to decorate their boots. And what about the marketplace with its displays of gold and precious stuffs?[41] Even Jerusalem, the Holy City, was no better than the others, for every kind of temptation was present in it: soldiers' barracks, prostitutes, mimes, buffoons and such a throng of both sexes 'that what you might wish to avoid in part elsewhere, here you are obliged to suffer in its entirety'.[42] If virtue was scarce in the cities, it was more plentiful in the countryside. 'How often', remarks St Symeon the Fool, 'have I seen local peasants coming into the city to take communion! They were purer than gold in their kindness, their artlessness, and because they eat their own bread in the sweat of their brow.'[43]

What then was a Christian to do in urban surroundings? If he needed recreation, he could take a walk in a garden, by a stream or a lake; he could listen to the song of cicadas or visit a suburban martyr's shrine where bodies were restored to health and souls edified. He could even try, in spite of everything that has been said above, to enjoy his family. Did not some barbarians once remark that Romans invented the pleasures of the theatre because they had neither wives nor children?[44] Above all, of course, a Christian was to go to church – not only on Sundays and other feast days, but as often as possible and at least two hours a day. What, indeed, could be pleasanter than attendance at church? Instead of diabolical songs and dancing whores, it provided the warbling of the Prophets, the chanting of the Seraphim, the words of the Gospel. Christ was there, lying on the altar table, the Holy Spirit was in attendance. The church was like a calm harbour in the midst of turmoil. Yet people had to be cajoled to go there. They found the service boring, and only the reputation of a famous preacher would draw them to church in their hundreds. But after applauding the sermon as in a theatre, they did not even bother to remain for the liturgy of the faithful.

Walking in gardens, listening to the song of cicadas and attending church – all of that could be done just as well in a village as in a city. In spite of the fact that the *ecclesia Christi* drew its resources, its leaders and its rhetoric from the cities, its message was fundamentally anti-urban. It abhorred not only the theatres and the baths, the music and the dances, the council chamber and the law court, but the very fact of people coming together in public, whereas they ought to have stayed at home. And so, when the cities collapsed, the dream of the Church must have come true. If St Basil had been able to come back to life and visit the *kastron* of Caesarea in the ninth or tenth century, he would have found no theatres, no mimes or buffoons and no women walking about with uncovered heads. He would have seen that everyone remained at home and assembled only to go to church. Not even a famous preacher was needed to draw them there; in all likelihood there was no preacher at all. St Basil ought to have been pleased; but then, perhaps, his discerning eye might have told him that the devil's work was still flourishing in spite of the changed circumstances.

We have been lectured so often about the penetration of Christianity by Hellenism that we tend to overlook a very basic fact: the scheme of Christian life, as propounded by the Fathers of the fourth century and maintained throughout the Byzantine period, was the antithesis of the Hellenic ideal of the *polis*. Deeply rooted as it was in the Bible, the Christian scheme was also a reflection of the authoritarian and regimented order of the Later Empire. It was founded on absolute monarchy, social rigidity and servility. It regarded the material world, the world of the flesh, with an almost Manichaean horror. It also mirrored the instability of the times by likening the virtuous man to a fortified citadel. While we need not imagine that the average Byzantine lived in complete conformity with the propaganda of the Church, there is no mistaking the effect of a message that was repeated from century to century. A consideration of Byzantine literature will reveal its traces in more than one respect.

PART THREE

THE LEGACY

CHAPTER 13

LITERATURE

As we have indicated in Chapter 1, the multinational Empire of New Rome did not express itself only in Greek. Many of its inhabitants spoke and wrote in other languages. If, therefore, we define Byzantine literature as that of an Empire and a civilization, we ought to include under this heading, in addition to its principal Greek constituent, a considerable body of writing in Latin, Syriac, Coptic, Church Slavonic, even Armenian and Georgian. We shall not do so here, but it is useful to remember that in confining ourselves to Greek we shall be disregarding an intricate pattern of reciprocal influences that manifested itself not only in the migration of texts, but also in linguistic and mental habits.

Greek Byzantine literature, in other words everything that was written in Greek between the fourth and the fifteenth centuries, strikes us immediately by its sheer bulk. Exactly how extensive it is no one appears to have calculated. Let us say at a very rough guess that it would fill two to three thousand volumes of normal size. A part of it – though by now not a very big nor a very interesting part – still remains unpublished, which is to say that it is available only in manuscript; and a considerable portion of it is lost – quite high for the Early period, lower for the Middle period and altogether small for the Late period.

It would be interesting to know in terms of percentages the content of Byzantine literature, but again the calculation has not been made. That the overwhelming mass of it is of a religious nature is at once obvious: hagiography alone accounts for some 2,500 items.[1] Next to hagiography we may place sermons, liturgical books (including liturgical poetry), theology, devotional treatises, commentaries on the Bible and the Fathers and much else besides. By contrast, the secular element is very restricted: all the historians could be accommodated in about a hundred volumes, and the same goes for epistolographers. Lexica and other compendia, commentaries on ancient authors, scientific and pseudo-scientific treatises might account between them for some two hundred volumes. As for secular poetry, it would probably fit into thirty volumes. Most discussions of Byzantine literature have been based on a very small sample of the total output.

It would be unfair to judge Byzantine literature by the criterion of the aesthetic pleasure it affords to the modern reader. If we fail to be captivated or moved by it, this is largely because our literary taste is diametrically opposed to that of educated Byzantines. We appreciate originality, while they prized the cliché; we are impatient of rhetoric, while they were passionately fond of it; we value concision, while they were naturally inclined to elaboration and verbiage. Let us, for the moment, suspend judgement and attempt to gain some understanding of Byzantine literature in its historical setting. To do so we must take several factors into account.

The first concerns the development of the Greek language. To the average classical scholar Greek appears frozen at two stages, the epic (Homer, Hesiod) and the literary Attic of the fifth and fourth centuries BC. Its subsequent evolution, including what is usually termed New Testament Greek, is considered a decadent phase. Like all living languages, however, Greek underwent a continuous development in phonology, morphology, syntax and vocabulary, the decisive shift occurring in the Hellenistic period when Greek became a medium of international communication. This is not the place to describe these changes in detail, but we must note one factor that was to have lasting consequences, namely the disappearance of the quantity of vowels (long and short by nature or by position) whose place was taken by the tonic accent. As a result, the prosodic patterns on which ancient Greek poetry had been based became unintelligible. At the same time or somewhat later many other changes took place: diphthongs ceased to be pronounced, the dual, the middle voice, the optative, the dative case all went out of normal use, etc. To the extent that we know it, ordinary spoken Greek of the Byzantine period was much closer to modern than to ancient Greek.

Notwithstanding the disapproval of classical scholars, there was nothing inherently bad about these changes. Though lacking many of the nuances of ancient Greek, the spoken language could have been raised to a literary level. Besides, many churchmen actively championed the use of lowly speech and rejected 'the fine style of the

Hellenes' which they compared to the proverbial honey that drips from the mouth of a whore. They argued that to cultivate the epic and iambic metres was not only childish; it was an insult to Christ and the apostles.[2] Such advice went unheeded. For better or for worse the tradition of the schools prevailed. And so there developed not so much a *diglossia*, a double language, as a whole tier of linguistic levels. Attic was reserved for belles-lettres. This was not the Attic of the fifth century BC, but that of the Atticists of the Roman imperial period, and the more recherché the better. Then there was the language of the Bible and the liturgy which corresponded to the *koinê* of the Hellenistic period. Finally, there was common speech which had already moved a considerable distance from the *koinê*. Between these three basic levels infinite gradations were possible. The sophisticated author, unless he was constantly on his guard, naturally slipped into unclassical usages. The 'middle-brow' author would often try, no matter how unsuccessfully, to raise his tone to that of his betters. The 'low-brow' author would strive to attain the idiom of the Church. The linguistic chaos was even worse than we imagine, since the editions we use have been subjected to a process of correction. It is only when we consult the manuscripts of works that were not considered as 'classics' that we realize how much variation was allowed.

It was generally admitted that a classical style was not conducive to clarity and had, perforce, to be abandoned in technical treatises, although an apology for so doing was usually called for. Thus, Constantine Porphyrogenitus, in introducing his *De administrando imperio*, finds it necessary to say: 'I have not been studious to make a display of fine writing or of an Atticizing style, swollen with the sublime and lofty, but rather have been eager by means of everyday and conversational narrative to teach you those things of which I think you should not be ignorant.'[3] Likewise in the Preface to the *Book of Ceremonies*: 'With a view to making our text clear and intelligible, we have used a popular and simple style and those very words and names which in current speech have long been attached to each thing.'[4] We need not look for a better illustration of the Byzantine attitude to language and style. To call a spade a spade was sometimes necessary, but was not elegant; calling it by its classical name yielded far greater pleasure. There was a place for 'display' literature and a place for ordinary writing. The sublime and the lofty belonged exclusively to the former.

Inasmuch as Attic was a dead language, the continued use of it had both a literary and a social dimension. On the literary side all that need be said is that very few Byzantine authors succeeded in handling it creatively (Psellus is a notable exception). The rest who aspired to Attic struggled hard with their optatives and their pluperfects, never quite sure how to form the augment, what to do with the particle *an*, whether to use the double 's' or the double 't'. It is perhaps surprising that, on the whole, they managed as well as they did, but it is futile to look for literary merit in their stilted compositions. What is perhaps more significant in a historical perspective is that a knowledge of Attic was the badge of an élite – not necessarily that of the rich and the powerful, not always that of the imperial court, but of an élite nevertheless. As we explained in Chapter 6, access to the ancient language was conditional on a rhetorical education which, after the disaster of the seventh century, was limited to a small group of prospective civil servants and clergymen. The literature they produced was that of a coterie: no one else could understand it.

There can be no doubt that 'ecclesiastical' Greek was the main medium of Byzantine literature exclusive of belles-lettres and, in one form or another, may account for as much as 80 per cent of it. Since it was used in church, it must have been understandable to a considerable segment of the population, yet it was never forged into a sensitive tool of expression. There was something inherently flat and prosaic about it. 'Middle-brow' writers striving for a richer effect tended to pile adjective upon adjective, to line up a string of nearly synonymous phrases or else to entangle their constructions with such comical results as *hosoi ... tên apotagên tautên dia tês pros tous en tê kata Christon hêlikia proêkontas ebebaiôsan hypotagês* (literally, 'those who this renunciation through the towards those in the according to Christ stature pre-eminent have confirmed submission'), by which assemblage of words Gregory Palamas tried to describe those monks who confirmed their renunciation of the world by submitting to spiritual fathers.[5] The high incidence of paratactic constructions, which Greek seems to have inherited from the Semitic world, produced a pervasive monotony, and considerable ambiguity was introduced by an indiscriminate use of the third person pronoun (or adjective). When Theophanes writes of the Emperor Nicephorus that, 'having mounted a most gentle and tame horse, by God's providence he threw him and broke his right foot',[6] it is hard enough to understand who did what to whom. But what are we to make of this sentence in the *Life of St Pachomius*: 'taking bread from him, the janitor gave it to him so as to restore him according to his injunction that he might be healed'?[7]

236

As for the everyday speech of the people, it was not, unfortunately, deemed worthy of being written down. For the Early and Middle Byzantine periods we know it only from a few snippets of dialogue like that between the circus fans and Justinian's herald,[8] from a few lines of popular verse and the evidence of papyri and inscriptions. As we shall see presently, the emergence of the demotic into literature had to wait until the twelfth century.

The second factor we have to consider is one to which we have already alluded, namely the existence of a literary public. In the Early Byzantine period the curial class of the provincial cities formed such a public, though it was doubtless diminishing: Procopius could still claim that he was read throughout the Empire.[9] But as the cities declined, the reading public also vanished. It is certainly no accident that polite literature ceased to be produced. We are greatly indebted to the small band of educated civil servants and clergymen who presided over the transmission of the antique heritage in the ninth and tenth centuries, but we cannot describe them as constituting a sufficient forum for the production of a literature whose aim was to entertain and to please. Only when the cities revived in about the eleventh century were more favourable conditions once again introduced: this is fully confirmed by the writings that have come down to us. Take one example, that of the erotic novel, an antique genre that had died in the third century AD and suddenly re-appeared in the Comnenian period. It is true that the four specimens we possess[10] are unbelievably tedious, but we are not now concerned with their slender literary merit. The important consideration is that such works, whose only purpose was to amuse and titillate, began to be composed once again, indeed by prominent poets. That they addressed themselves to an educated audience is obvious from the style they adopted and the great abundance of learned reminiscences they introduced, sometimes playfully; that they had some success is indicated by the number of manuscripts in which these novels are preserved. Perhaps they were meant in the first instance for oral recitation at the literary salons whose existence in Constantinople is attested in the eleventh and twelfth centuries. In any case, the sphere of polite literature was expanding: no longer limited to a professional coterie, it now reached a segment of the aristocracy. The efforts of Michael Psellus to make learning available in a palatable form (often versified) for various noble personages may be seen in the same light. We should not imagine, of course, that this new public was either large or that it extended beyond the major centres of Constantinople and

Thessalonica. Once created, however, it did not cease to exist until the end of the Empire, and it formed the backdrop against which later Byzantine literature ought to be viewed.

The third factor we ought to take into account concerns the availability of books. In Chapter 6 we have already alluded to the high cost and scarcity of parchment, the material on which Byzantine books were normally written from the seventh century onwards when the supply of Egyptian papyrus was cut off. But even before the loss of Egypt to the Empire a book was by no means a cheap item. An anecdote told by John Moschus concerns a very poor monk in Palestine who was eager to own a New Testament. Although a colleague offered him a copy free of charge, he was unwilling to accept it as a gift and went to work as a labourer in Jerusalem. He was paid 9 *folles* a day, spent almost nothing on food, and after a time accumulated 3 *solidi*, which was the price of the New Testament.[11] Since 1 *solidus* was equivalent to 180 *folles*, our monk would have had to put in 60 working days, not taking into account his living expenses. In modern British terms the price of a New Testament would thus have been in excess of £300. For the same sum of money, as we have seen, one could buy a donkey, which was probably a poor man's major investment.

The production of a longer manuscript, especially one that had to be copied to order, was, of course, a much more expensive affair. To quote only one example, the famous *codex Clarkianus* of Plato, commissioned by Arethas of Caesarea, a good-quality manuscript of 424 folios, cost 13 *solidi* for transcription and 8 for parchment, the equivalent of two years' wages of a manual worker. In modern British terms that would be about £3,000. No matter how one translates these figures into modern equivalents, it is obvious that the possession of books was possible only for the rich and for endowed institutions. A gentleman of means might have owned, say, twenty volumes; somewhat more if he happened to inherit a family library that was added to from generation to generation. The monastery founded in the eleventh century by Michael Attaleiates, a rich and cultivated man, was originally given twenty-eight books, increased to seventy-nine after the founder's death.[12] The famous monastery of St John on Patmos at the time of its greatest prosperity (1201) owned 330 volumes; but that was the result of more than a century of book collecting by an establishment which numbered at the time 150 monks and which had benefited from repeated imperial benefactions.[13]

The cost of books was directly related to the use to which they were put. A professional scholar, who often had recourse to borrowing, would need a number of school textbooks as well as exemplars of ancient prose and poetry into which he could dip to embellish his own writings. An average gentleman of means would have little use for pagan authors; he would prefer some patristic literature or perhaps some books that would satisfy his curiosity concerning the wondrous structure of Creation, such as the *Physiologus*, a chronicle or two, and, of course, an interpretation of dreams. Reading was a laborious business and was meant primarily for edification, not amusement. Here is the advice that Cecaumenus, a retired general, gives to a young man destined for a military career:

When you are free and not busy with a commander's duties, read books, both histories and Church writings. Do not say, 'What benefit is there for a soldier from ecclesiastical books?', for you will profit greatly from them. If you pay sufficient attention, you will reap from them not only doctrines and edifying stories, but also gnomic, moral and military precepts. Indeed, almost the entire Old Testament is concerned with strategy. From the New Testament, too, the assiduous reader will derive many precepts for the mind.

And again: 'Read a great deal and you will learn a great deal. Persevere, even if you do not understand, for after you have read a book several times, you will receive discernment from God and you will understand it.' And once more:

When you have taken a book, read it in private. After you have read a little, do not start counting pages or choosing passages you like best and reading only those. Nay, you should start from the cover where the text begins and read the book until not a single word is left, and in this way you will profit greatly. For it is the trait of a superficial person not to read a whole book twice or three times, but to pick some snippets out of it for the sake of chatter.[14]

It would probably be a mistake to think that the contents of a private library (except that of a professional scholar) differed very markedly from those of a monastic library. In confirmation of this we may glance at the testament of the Cappadocian nobleman Eustathius Boilas (1059) whom we have already had occasion to mention. Boilas built a private church somewhere in the region of Edessa and dedicated to it various items of plate as well as a surprisingly large collection of books, eighty in all.[15] They may be analysed as in the following table.

It is an instructive list, especially as it refers to a fairly distant province. Unfortunately, we are not told how Boilas came to acquire these books. Since he was not himself a cultivated man, one may

Biblical	10
Liturgical	33
Patristic	12
Desert Fathers	3
Apocrypha (*Testament of the Twelve Patriarchs*)	1
Hagiography	4
Christian miscellanies (*Pandektês, Melissa*)	2
Canon law	3
Secular (1 lawbook; 1 dreambook; 1 Aesop; 1 Georgius Pisides; 2 chronicles; 1 Alexander romance; 1 Achilles Tatius; 1 grammar; 1 *Persica*)	10
Indeterminate	2

suspect that this was a family library, accumulated over a span of several generations and intended in large part to serve the needs of a private church. A former Boilas may have gone to school at Constantinople, hence the grammar, the Aesop and the Achilles Tatius. Two characteristics are especially worth noting. With the one exception of Pisides (probably the poem *De opificio mundi*), not a single 'high-brow' Byzantine author was represented. Secondly, there were practically no recent works, except for the *Melissa* (a miscellany of edifying passages said to date from the eleventh century) and the Life of St Michael Maleinus (d. 961). This disregard of contemporary or near-contemporary literature was typical of the Byzantine world.

What then was the purpose of literary composition? Certainly, no Byzantine author had the ambition or the pretension of equalling the classics – I mean not so much the classics of pagan Antiquity as the Christian classics – St John Chrysostom, the two Gregories, St Basil, Synesius. Those stood on a special podium and, judging by the number of preserved manuscripts, were read more than any other authors. The task of the epigones was to chronicle recent events lest those fell into oblivion (a preoccupation often expressed), to record the lives of contemporary saints, to digest the doctrine and moral teaching of the Fathers and to produce all kinds of useful handbooks. Not surprisingly, the Byzantines showed little interest in their own literature and none whatever in the biography of their writers, which is why we know so little about them. It was deemed sufficient to say in the title that so-and-so had been deacon of St Sophia, or bishop of Synnada, or *protospatharios*, in other words to place him in the hierarchy.[16] The part of 'fine' literature was limited, as our chapter on education might have suggested, to rhetorical display. It seems that much of this ornate production was meant for oral recitation, not only speeches and sermons, but also letters, Lives of saints written in the high style, even perhaps chapters of histories. After the recitation had taken place and the orator had received the applause of his friends, the text was apt to be forgotten, unless the author himself or a member of his coterie took the trouble to copy it as an exemplar worthy of imitation. But even if it was copied, it did not circulate widely. Most such texts have survived in a single manuscript. This accounts for the 'timelessness' of Byzantine literature, in the sense that each generation of writers did not build upon the experience and ideas of the previous generation, but rather stood in a constant relation to their distant models. The proof of the matter, as every student of Byzantine philology knows, is that a text not firmly attributed to an identifiable author and lacking any clear historical reference is almost impossible to date. Examples are plentiful and often embarrassing – and I am not speaking only of pastiches, such as the Pseudo-Lucianic dialogues or the Leptinean Orations, long considered to be by Aelius Aristides (second century AD), but now known as the work of Thomas Magister (fourteenth century).[17] Letters by Isidore of Pelusium (fifth century) have been attributed by a reputable scholar to the patriarch Photius (ninth century), and it is still a matter of dispute whether the Greek version of *Barlaam and Joasaph* is by St John Damascene (eighth century) or, as appears more likely, a work of the eleventh century. It has even been argued that one historical text, namely *The Capture of Thessalonica* by John Caminiates, was composed not soon after 904, as has been assumed by everyone, but in the early fifteenth century.[18] Such uncertainty would not have been possible had the style of Byzantine literature shown a consistent development.

After these preliminary observations, we shall consider three genres of writing, each relating to a different linguistic level. A word of apology is perhaps required for the omission from our survey of liturgical poetry. No one will deny that the hymns of Romanus the Melode, in particular, those of Cosmas of Maiuma, Andrew of Crete and John Damascene to a lesser extent, display a felicity of phrase and depth of feeling that are generally lacking in nearly all other works of Byzantine poetry, yet it would be misleading to treat them simply in poetic terms. An understanding of hymnography requires some knowledge of its liturgical function, its musical structure and its Semitic background; above all, it calls for a mental attitude that the modern reader is not likely to possess.

Our first sample concerns historiography, undeniably one of the greatest achievements of Byzantine letters. We shall not be speaking here of the chronicle which we have already discussed in Chapter 10. A 'history' belonged to a different genre: it was written in ancient Greek, imitated ancient models and gave a connected rather than a purely chronological account of events. It sought to explain the why and the how, 'for the body of history is indeed mute and empty if it is deprived of the causes of actions'.[19] It was also a branch of rhetoric, often shading into the laudation or the invective and normally including both the fictitious speech and the ethnographic excursus. Perhaps the most remarkable feature of Byzantine historiography is its continuity: though most of the histories of the fourth and fifth centuries have perished, we do have an almost uninterrupted sequence from the sixth century to the fifteenth. Procopius, who described the wars of the Emperor Justinian, was continued by Agathias for the years 552-9, Menander Protector (of whom only fragments survive) for the span 559-82 and Theophylact Simocatta for 582-602. The disastrous reign of Phocas marked an interruption, but the story was picked up at a later date by the patriarch Nicephorus who covered the period 602-769. For the following half century, down to 813, we are entirely dependent on the chronicler Theophanes, but history revives with Genesius (813-86) and the Continuators of Theophanes (813-961), succeeded by Leo the Deacon (959-76) and Michael Psellus (976-1078), the last overlapping with Michael Attaleiates (1034-79) and Nicephorus Bryennius (1070-9). For the Comnenian period we have Anna Comnena's *Alexiad* (1069-1118), continued by John Cinnamus (1118-76) and Nicetas Choniates (1118-1206); for the Nicene exile George Acropolites (1203-61); for the age of the Palaeologi George Pachymeres (1261-1308), Nicephorus Gregoras (1204-1359) and the memoirs of the Emperor John Cantacuzenus (1320-56), finally Laonicus Chalcocondyles (1298-1463) and the eulogizer of the Turkish conqueror, Michael Critobolus (1451-67).

Naturally, not all of these historians were of equal merit, and some of them, like the patriarch Nicephorus, were little more than paraphrasers of chronicles into an archaic language. Yet a great many of them were not only accomplished writers, but also men of affairs who had a first-hand knowledge of the events they were describing, and several were emperors or members of the imperial family. This circumstance lends to Byzantine historiography a measure of authority and immediacy it would not have possessed had it been delegated to professional men of letters.

In many respects the greatest of Byzantine historians and certainly the one best known today is Procopius of Caesarea, although we probably admire him more for the broad sweep of his narrative, his objectivity and accuracy than for the profundity of his views or his purely literary qualities. In style and approach he modelled himself on Thucydides without, however, imitating the Athenian's complexity. He was a fastidious author and at times – as in describing the last stages of Ostrogothic resistance in Italy – was able to convey a sense of tragic grandeur. In other respects he was less successful. His digressions are not always well timed, as when he interrupts an account of early Persian history with a ludicrous anecdote about a 'swimming' oyster that was pursued by a shark,[20] and his character sketches are not well drawn. Even in the case of the general Belisarius, whom he had served as assessor on several campaigns and must have known intimately, he does not manage to paint a lifelike portrait of the man.[21] The lofty detachment Procopius assumes in his *History of the Wars* and his apparent scepticism with regard to Christianity are largely stylistic traits. Whether they are wholly stylistic may well be doubted. In a work intended for wide circulation under Justinian's autocratic rule detachment was the most prudent attitude to adopt for a man who, like Procopius, did hold strong political views that did not coincide with those of the emperor. But even in the *Wars* his disapproval of Justinian's policies may be read between the lines. As to his religious attitude, it is worth reflecting on the oft-quoted passage concerning the doctrinal dispute between Catholics and Monophysites:

I know well the matter of the controversy, but shall refrain from mentioning it; for I consider it a mark of insane folly to investigate the nature of God and of what kind it may be. Indeed, I believe that man has no exact comprehension even of human affairs, far less of anything that pertains to the nature of God. I shall, therefore, remain silent on these things without incurring any danger, with the sole object that matters held in reverence should not be disbelieved. For my part, I would not express any view about God except that He is altogether good and holds the world in His power. But let each man, whether

243

he is a priest or a layman, say whatever he thinks he knows concerning these matters.[22]

Adherence to classical models is hardly a sufficient explanation of this carefully worded yet curiously ambiguous statement. Does Procopius mean to imply that an exposition of Catholic (or Monophysite) doctrine on the nature of God would result in discrediting it? And what sort of danger does he wish to avoid?

The perennial problem associated with Procopius is that a man of his undoubted gifts and seeming integrity should have composed within the span of about one decade three works of completely different spirit, to wit the objective and stately *Wars*, the scurrilous *Secret History* and the unashamedly encomiastic *Buildings*. It has been conjectured that the last, which describes in terms of superlative praise Justinian's vast programme of construction, was occasioned by some promotion or mark of favour that the author may have received from the emperor. But what of the *Secret History*? Since it was not meant for publication, the chances are that it expresses faithfully Procopius' personal views or, at any rate, the views he held at a particular stage of his career. Yet, of the three works, this is the one we have the greatest trouble in accepting. We are amused by the scabrous account of Theodora's youth, but wearied by the unremitting invective against all the acts of Justinian's policy. Even Belisarius, represented in the *Wars* as a courageous, resourceful yet modest man, is here portrayed as a pitiful weakling. Strangest of all is the author's apparent conviction, stated without any hint of irony, that the emperor was a demon in human form. It is unlikely that this was meant as a joke, and we are left wondering whether Procopius under his mask of cultivated scepticism was not as superstitious as most of his contemporaries.

After Procopius there was a marked decline in historical writing. His successor Agathias, who was a lawyer by profession and a poet by inclination, had no experience of public affairs and no commitment to the objectivity of history which he regarded as being akin to poetry and as serving mainly a moral purpose.[23] A further degradation is discernible in the sententious work of Theophylact, after whom there was a prolonged interruption in the practice of historiography. Its revival (setting aside the rather feeble effort of the patriarch Nicephorus) had to wait until the middle of the tenth century when the patronage of Constantine Porphyrogenitus resulted in two histories stretching back to 813, the point at which the chronicler Theophanes laid down his pen.

The anonymous Continuators of Theophanes are superficially indebted to both classical and Early Byzantine models and deserve some
praise for delineating the Iconoclastic emperors in colours that are not
exclusively black, but about nine parts black and one part grey. If some
germs of humanism may be detected in this slight concession to objectivity, it must be pointed out that the Continuators were dominated by
both theological and dynastic prejudice. They were court historians
charged with perpetuating in acceptable prose the official version of
events.

Skipping over another century and the sober History of Leo the
Deacon, we find ourselves confronted by a masterpiece whose
originality is all the more striking in as much as it is not explicable in
terms of a prior development. The *Chronographia* of Michael Psellus
cannot even be assigned to any established genre, for it is not so much a
history as a private memoir. Traditionally, the historian's person was
kept in the background: after introducing himself in the prologue (for
example, 'My name is Agathias, my place of origin is Myrina, my father
was Memnonius,' and so on), he could, if need be, make occasional
appearances to say that he had seen this or that with his own eyes. Not
so Psellus: he constantly prattles about himself, about his studies, his
intellectual achievements, his retirement to a monastery, the spell he
cast on successive emperors, and so forth. Warfare, the customary stuff
of histories, does not especially interest him and he often bypasses it. He
manages, for example, to tell the story of Basil II without once mentioning the subjugation of Bulgaria. What does interest him is court gossip
and especially the description of human motives and human character.
The *Chronographia* is a veritable portrait gallery. What is more, character is seen to change. Basil II (whom Psellus had not known) develops
under the pressure of events from a voluptuary into a stern, suspicious
and irascible man. We can readily visualize him dressed in modest
clothes, speaking more like a peasant than a gentleman, twirling his
thinning beard or else placing his hands on his hips. Romanus III,
whom Psellus despised, changes as a result of illness. The handsome
but uncultivated Michael IV, whom the ageing Empress Zoe took on as
a lover, becomes a serious and conscientious ruler as soon as he mounts
the throne. Every major character that is introduced is made memorable by both a moral and a physical description: the frivolous Constantine VIII (we learn with surprise that he was also an accomplished
cook), Zoe and Theodora, the eunuch John who was more feared in his
cups than when he was sober, the ruddy and jovial Constantine IX

245

Monomachus, and many more. And as for psychological observation, it is enough to read the one paragraph describing the guilty aversion with which Michael IV, now stricken with epilepsy, regarded his imperial spouse.[24]

Of course, Psellus had classical models, and he facilitates our task by naming them himself (Demosthenes, Isocrates, Aelius Aristides, Plutarch, etc.).[25] But the same models had been available to Constantine Porphyrogenitus and the Continuators of Theophanes and they made what use of them they thought appropriate. The problem does not lie there, but rather in the fact that Psellus displays a sensibility and a keenness of observation that had been previously lacking. Unless we ascribe these traits solely to his personal genius, we have to look for a broader explanation which may perhaps be found in the rise of an urban bourgeoisie to which Psellus himself belonged. Indeed, he did not stand alone; and although none of his contemporaries left an oeuvre of equal variety, it is not difficult to detect in them glimmers of what can only be called a lay spirit. Witness the remarkable poem in which Christopher of Mitylene satirizes the collecting of dubious relics,[26] a poem, incidentally, that had once been ascribed to the iconoclastic period.

It is a sad commentary on the taste of the Byzantine public that the *Chronographia* of Psellus should have come down to us in a single manuscript. Yet it was certainly used, even plagiarized, by later historians, notably Bryennius, Anna Comnena and Zonaras. And it may be said that after Psellus the qualities of personal observation and a lifelike portrayal of character were not lost. They are very evident in the *Alexiad*, a work that is often disingenuous, but vivid and full of psychological insight in addition to being thoroughly researched. They are equally to the fore in the remarkable History of Nicetas Choniates. It is fitting that the end of the imperial epoch of Byzantium (for Nicetas witnessed the catastrophe of 1204) should have been recorded by an author who combined all the traditional tricks of artful rhetoric with a newly found humanity, open-mindedness and scepticism.[27]

Our second sample will concern hagiography which, as we have already indicated, probably represents the largest single genre of Byzantine literature. Under this heading it is customary to group a wide range of texts whose common denominator is that they refer to personages who enjoyed a liturgical commemoration, both Christian saints and biblical figures: biographies of saints, shorter anecdotes, accounts of martyrdom, of posthumous miracles, of the invention and translation of relics, stories about icons, apocalypses, etc. The form of presentation varies a great deal as does the linguistic level. The most interesting specimens are, however, written in standard, 'ecclesiastical' Greek.

The oldest form of Christian hagiography was the *passio* (the account of a martyr's trial and death), but this was already a thing of the past when the Byzantine period began. The two main forms that will concern us are the short anecdote and the full-dress Life. Both appeared almost simultaneously in the milieu of Egyptian monasticism, and this was no accident since the monk was the martyr's successor. Simple stories of how Father Patermuthius could sail through the air and go through closed doors, how Father Helles crossed a river on the back of a crocodile, how St Macarius healed the cubs of a hyena, circulated by word of mouth and were then collected in books that were called *paterica* or *gerontica*. We have already referred in Chapter 5 to some of the better known collections of this kind. Apart from relating the supernatural deeds wrought by monks, the anecdotes laid stress on moral precepts, memorable dicta and the particular discipline (*ergasia*) pursued by this or that ascete. Since we are dealing here with a literature that was oral in origin, it was naturally subject to fluctuation and repetition: the same or similar stories would become attached to different saints. The golden age of *paterica* extends from the late fourth to the seventh century. Always couched in a fairly popular idiom, they possess considerable charm, but also an unavoidable monotony.

The earliest extended Life is that of St Antony by Athanasius of Alexandria (*c.* 360 AD) to which ample reference has already been made. Since a saint's Life (*bios* or very often *bios kai politeia*, meaning life and conduct) was intended as a laudation rather than as a critical biography, it was natural that it should have become modelled on certain prescriptions that had been elaborated for this purpose in the schools of rhetoric. What these prescriptions were we can discover from the handbook of Menander who is here concerned with the laudation of a ruler (*basilikos logos*). You will start, he says, with a proem in which you will express your embarrassment at undertaking a task of such magnitude. After the proem you will mention the ruler's place of origin (*patris*). If he happens to have been born in a famous city, you will praise it; if not, you may be able to magnify the nation to which he belonged. You will go on to his family (*genos*): if it was glorious, you will elaborate on this topic, if not, you will omit it. Next will come the birth and any miraculous signs that may have accompanied it (if none occurred, you should not hesitate to invent a few); physical appearance, upbringing, education with particular emphasis on the young paragon's learning ability (naturally, he surpassed all his school-fellows), endowments, and so on to his adult deeds, suitably subdivided by categories and virtues.[28]

Mutatis mutandis these potted rules were applied to celebrating Christian saints. Certain headings, of course, were no longer relevant, such as physical beauty, deeds of war, naval battles, and so on, but the rest could be used to considerable advantage. There developed accordingly a hagiographic *schema* which, in the case of a monastic saint, ran more or less as follows. In the proem the author admitted his incompetence to celebrate the merits of Saint X. He had, however, been bidden to do so by his superior (abbot or bishop) and dared not disobey, in spite of the lowliness of his mind and the rusticity (*agroikia*) of his diction. So he started with the saint's place of origin: the latter's true *patris* was, of course, the Heavenly Jerusalem, but he happened to have been born in city or village Y which, even if it had been quite obscure, acquired thereby immortal renown. The saint's parents were, almost invariably, rich and noble (*endoxoi*) and his birth was usually foretold in a dream or accompanied by other signs. When old enough to go to school, he avoided the company of other boys. He either completely spurned all classical learning or else imbibed only as much of it as he considered necessary, although his natural aptitude was extraordinary. Upon attaining adolescence, the saint refused the marriage that had been arranged for him by his loving parents and withdrew to a neighbouring monastery. For several years he executed with complete humility the most menial tasks and showed exemplary zeal in fasting and prayer. When he had attained the required fortitude and impassibility, he withdrew to an isolated cell or to the desert. His victories over the demons, acts of healing and prophecy filled the remainder of his life. At length, the priesthood would be bestowed on him, but he would normally refuse all offers of a bishopric. He would foresee his own death and expire peacefully at an advanced age. Lastly, his sanctity would be confirmed by posthumous miracles, a few of which were usually set down as were also the day and month of the saint's demise.

One of the advantages of such a *schema* was that it could be applied to any monastic saint concerning whom nothing definite was known save for his name, place of origin and date of his liturgical commemoration. A great many Lives (not only of monks, but also of martyrs, bishops, etc.) are thus nothing but a string of clichés; others are not only fictitious in themselves, but also concern saints who probably never existed; and a few are fictitious though they refer to saints who happened to be quite well documented (such as St Epiphanius of Salamis). Setting aside such dubious products, there remains a considerable residue of Lives that are, in the main, reliable. Many of them were written by a saint's disciple or by a man of a later generation who was nevertheless able to tap sources of oral information. They abound in precise and picturesque detail which is all the more valuable to the historian since formal histories are deficient in this respect. Indeed, Lives of saints are often our best source for recreating the day-to-day ambiance of Byzantine villages and towns, and there is, fortunately, a long string of excellent texts starting with the Life of Porphyry, bishop of Gaza, by Mark the Deacon (fifth century), going on to that of St Hypatius by Callinicus, those of St Euthymius and St Sabas by Cyril of Scythopolis (an author noted for his accuracy), that of St Symeon the younger stylite, of St Theodore of Sykeon, St Symeon the Fool and St John the Almsgiver and a great many more. The Iconoclastic period produced a spate of interesting Lives (notably that of St Stephen the Younger), and hagiography continued to flourish until the eleventh century, when a decline may be observed.

Not only the authentic, but even some of the fictitious Lives may still be read with pleasure and amusement. Their main deficiency from our viewpoint, however, is that they never convey a sense of a saint's psychological development, even though they are explicitly concerned with his spiritual progress. Since the saint is a paragon of virtue from his earliest childhood and has no negative aspects, we know in advance that he will remain the same throughout his earthly existence. He will never succumb to temptation and never err, except from an excess of zeal or acting on a false report. This predictability was as much appreciated by the Byzantine public as is that of the Western movie by a modern cinema audience; for there can be no doubt that hagiography provided not only edification, but also wish-fulfilment. Medieval men, living in a real world of fear, uncertainty and disease, needed their heroes who routed demons, put physicians to shame and never wavered in their purpose.

The saints' Lives that we consider the most appealing were written in a simple language, sometimes verging on the vernacular, but more often reflecting the normal linguistic usage of the Church. The need of communicating to an uneducated audience was not always overlooked. Leontius of Neapolis (seventh century) makes this point in the Preface

to the Life of St John the Almsgiver: 'The consideration that especially
roused me to this task was that I should tell the tale in the pedestrian,
unadorned and lowly style that belongs to me so that the ordinary
unlettered man might derive benefit from my words.'[29] This approach,
however, was not destined to last. In the Middle Byzantine period it
was felt that naïve hagiographers had not attained to the dignity of their
subject: 'Some actions [of the saints] they distorted, while in other
respects, being unable to set down what was appropriate, they
described the saints' virtue in an inelegant manner. They did not lay
down a good argument, nor did they adorn it with beautiful words.' As
a result, the Lives of saints became an object of ridicule and the
audience was repelled by their slovenly style.[30] The task of re-
composing the hagiographic heritage of earlier centuries was first
undertaken in about 900 AD by Nicetas the Paphlagonian who tackled
about fifty Lives without, however, gaining much acclaim. A few
decades later Symeon the Metaphrast, possibly at the instigation of
Constantine Porphyrogenitus, carried out a more thorough revision.
He paraphrased about 135 Lives, kept another dozen unchanged, and
published the entire collection in ten volumes arranged in the order of
the calendar. His effort won widespread acceptance and about seven
hundred manuscripts of the Metaphrastic *menologium* have survived,
which means that a great number of churches and monasteries adopted
it for liturgical use.

The Metaphrast wrote in a 'proper' Greek, by no means as contorted
as that of Nicetas the Paphlagonian. Some contemporary critics found
him insufficiently sophisticated, but others praised him for having
followed a middle course and succeeded in both pleasing the cultivated
public by the variety and beauty of his style and making himself
understood by the uneducated. In the eyes of Michael Psellus the
Methaphrast's achievement was greater than 'all Hellenic
scholarship'.[31] This strange judgement brings us to the core of the
Byzantine attitude to literature. Granted that the Metaphrast wrote
acceptable Greek, what he did in effect was to take a corpus of texts that
had all the liveliness and the particularity of a given milieu and reduce
them to a set of clichés. He suppressed concrete detail and paraphrased
inelegant terms. Were a martyr's answers to his torturers insufficiently
resolute? He improved on them. Was a monk's discipline related in too
naïve a manner? He elevated it to the required level. It may be an
exaggeration to say that the Metaphrast spelled the death of Greek
hagiography, but he certainly contributed to its emasculation while

also causing the disappearance of many earlier texts which he paraphrased. It is amusing to note that in the twelfth century the patriarch
Nicholas Muzalon ordered the destruction of a Life of St Paraskeve the
Younger on the grounds that it had been written 'by some peasant' in
ordinary language.[32]

We must resist the temptation of going to the opposite extreme and
assuming that anything written in a popular language is *ipso facto*
endowed with literary merit. The validity of this reservation is demonstrated by our third sample which concerns Byzantine literature in the
vernacular. Ever since the Romantic movement the few works in question have attracted considerable attention and have earned a place in
the normal curriculum of modern Greek studies. They are certainly of
interest to the philologist as well as to the social historian, but it must be
admitted that as literature they are pretty disappointing.

Probably the earliest literary works in the vernacular are the so-
called Prodromic poems which seem to date from the first half of the
twelfth century.[33] They are attributed to the court poet Theodore
Prodromos, hence their traditional name. The attribution is disputed
and it is not even certain whether we are dealing with the outpourings of
several authors or of a single person who assumes different disguises.
Written in popular fifteen-syllable verse (*stichos politikos*), the poems
take the form of complaints addressed to the Emperors John ii and
Manuel i as well as to another member of the Comnenian family. In one
case we are introduced to a henpecked husband, in another to the father
of a large family who cannot make ends meet on his modest stipend, in
the third to a poor monk who is treated harshly by his abbot, in the
fourth to a starving intellectual (already quoted by us in Chapter 3).
The milieu is that of the urban middle class and the author's main
preoccupation is with his stomach. He tries to be funny by introducing
scenes of slapstick comedy and by coining bizarre hybrid words
(perhaps as a parody of archaizing poets), but the humour is spoilt by a
tone of monotonous servility and by a tedious repetitiveness.

The growing ascendancy of western fashions over the aristocracy of
the Late Byzantine period, if not over the public at large, is reflected in a
number of romances of chivalry in the vernacular of which five are
preserved, ranging in date from the twelfth or thirteenth century to the
fifteenth. Only one of the five, namely *Callimachus and Chrysorrhoe*,[34] can
be ascribed to a known author, who was Andronicus Palaeologus,
cousin of the Emperor Andronicus ii. The date of its composition is thus
c. 1300 AD. Precise western models have been identified for two of the

five, namely *Phlorios and Platzia Phlore* (a version of the widely diffused *Floire et Blancheflor*) and *Imberios and Margarona* (from the French *Pierre de Provence et la belle Maguelonne* or a precursor of the same). That is practically all the factual information we have at our disposal concerning these curious poems.

Unlike the learned love romances of the twelfth century to which we have already alluded, the romances of chivalry do not have a bogus classical setting: here we are transported to a distinctly medieval world of brave knights, fair maidens, witches, dragons and impregnable castles. In the poem which is probably the earliest and also the most attractive, namely *Belthandros and Chrysantza*,[35] the geography is real enough. The hero, who is the younger son of the Byzantine emperor, quits his home, crosses Asia Minor which is in Turkish hands, is ambushed in a mountain pass in the Taurus range, reaches Tarsus and the borders of Cilician Armenia and then goes on to Antioch where he falls in love with the Latin King's daughter Chrysantza. All the indications are perfectly appropriate to the twelfth or the first half of the thirteenth century. The only element of fantasy is the Castle of Love situated ten days' journey from Tarsus, but there were several romantic castles in Cilicia that the author might have heard about. What interests us here, however, is not the geography, but the cultural climate of the poem. Belthandros is clearly Bertrand, while his father, the Emperor, is called Rodophilos, which sounds rather like Rudolf. The fair-haired hero has no hesitation in becoming the liegeman (*lizios*) of the King of Antioch. He is a great hunter and fighter and totally lacking in religious feeling. In fact, he does not scruple to go through a form of marriage with his beloved's maidservant, a marriage solemnized by the patriarch of Antioch. The Castle of Love with its allegorical statues is certainly alien to the Byzantine tradition, whatever its origin may be. Most remarkable, however, is the poet's attitude to love. Contrary to all Byzantine precedent, the young protagonists freely engage in premarital sex and, after crossing a swollen stream, are left to wander stark naked for several days. Only when a Byzantine ship chances to pick them up is the unclothed princess entrusted to the care of a eunuch. The same prurience pervades the more fantastic and rather more tedious poem of *Callimachus and Chrysorrhoe*. The heroine is first discovered hanging naked by her hair in the Dragon's Castle, and after she has been rescued, the Prince Charming loses little time in consummating his passion after a bath *à deux*. This mild form of pornography had, of course, nothing to do with the Greek 'folk': it represented the daydreams of an aristocracy won over by western mores, but not sufficiently sensitive to the literary qualities of the western romances they were imitating from afar. *Belthandros* has a few good lines and relatively little padding; *Callimachus* is nearly all verbiage.

If we have not mentioned so far the much more meritorious epic or rather romance of *Digenes Akrites* (the Borderer of Double Stock), it is because of the difficulty of assigning it to a specific level of literary production.[36] It is based on heroic tales of the eastern border, the disputed land between Byzantium and the Arabs in the ninth and tenth centuries. By the time the poem was composed, the tales in question had become pretty blurred, but modern research has succeeded in identifying several historical personages and events, not all of the same period, but belonging to various layers, one of which was certainly associated with the Paulician wars and another with the Byzantine reconquest in the following century. If scholars have had less success in tracing the literary ancestry of the poem, it is certainly not for lack of trying. Numerous theories have been presented, none of them fully convincing. The main difficulty stems from the fact that we possess five divergent Greek versions as well as fragments of a Russian version. The reconstruction of the original *Digeneid* which, according to some scholars, dated, at least in part, from the years 934–44, involves, therefore, a considerable element of conjecture. Opinion is also divided as to whether the hypothetical *Digeneid* was written in a popular or, as seems more likely, in a literary language. The most satisfactory and consistent of the Greek versions, that of Grottaferrata (nearly four thousand lines long), cannot be earlier than the mid-eleventh century and is certainly the work of an author possessed of some education, for he knew not only the Bible and some patristic tags, but also the romances of Achilles Tatius and Heliodorus. The popularity of such ancient romances in the eleventh century is attested by Michael Psellus,[37] and we have seen that a copy of Achilles Tatius existed in the library of Eustathius Boilas located in Osrhoene, in other words in the very region where the *Digeneid* appears to have been composed.

The Grottaferrata *Digenes* is made up of two tales of different origin and date, that of the Arab emir who marries a Byzantine noblewoman and converts to Christianity, and that of his son Basil Digenes Akrites. Basil grows up to become a kind of border baron, carries off the lovely Eudocia Doukaina whom he weds, and spends his life fighting reivers (*apelatai*) and wild animals. He finally builds for himself a splendid palace by the river Euphrates and dies there while still in the flower of his youth. Basil is not a Byzantine general, but an independent lord, a hero of superhuman strength and prowess who repeatedly routs whole armies single-handed. It is hazardous to pronounce on the literary qualities of a poem which we perceive rather dimly through its various redactions. In the Grottaferrata text the diction is often prosaic and there is rather too much moralizing. The action, too, tends to be obscure or inconsistent. For example, we are informed towards the end (vii, 201ff.) that Digenes had subjugated the Arabs and brought peace to Roman lands, whereas nothing of the kind had been mentioned before. In a story that is otherwise lacking in supernatural elements it is surprising to be suddenly confronted with a serpent that has assumed human form and then sprouts three heads. The warlike Maximô, descended from the Amazons whom Alexander the Great had brought from the land of the Brahmans, cuts a strange figure in a world that is, but for her, peopled by real men and women. And the hero's infidelities, though excused at some length, are poorly integrated into the plot. In spite of its many blemishes, *Digenes Akrites* does, however, give us a glimpse of a truly heroic milieu that contrasts strongly with the anaemic fantasies of the chivalry romances.

The few samples we have given do not form, of course, a sufficient basis for passing judgement on Byzantine literature as a whole, though it may be hoped that they convey something of its flavour. To a modern observer this literature appears deficient in many respects. It contains reams of verse, but almost no poetry and no dramatic works. It has irony, often heavy-handed, but practically no humour. With very few exceptions, it is not concerned with love, other than sacred or parental love. It has no ribaldry and no *joie de vivre*. Byzantine literature is solemn, even sombre, in tone and is probably at its best when describing death, disasters and the instability of human existence.

It is customary to argue that the greatest achievement of Byzantine men of letters lay not in the creation of original works, but in the preservation of the classical heritage. That the major proportion of ancient Greek literature that is still extant has come to us via Byzantium is an undeniable fact. It is also true to say that preservation was not a passive process: it implied the collecting of books, their copying and editing. It necessitated the writing of commentaries, the compilation of glossaries and encyclopaedias. The *Bibliotheca* of Photius, the Greek Anthology, the *Excerpta* of Constantine Porphyrogenitus, the *Souda*, the Homeric commentaries of Eustathius represent great feats of scholarship as do the endeavours of the Palaeologan philologists like Maximus Planudes and Demetrius Triclinius. Why is it, then, that the Byzantines, who lavished so much attention on the pagan classics, never comprehended their spirit? The blame has been laid on the Church, or monkishness, on autocracy. I do not believe that any of these factors is sufficient to explain the peculiar imperviousness of the medieval mind to a set of ideas and values it considered alien, wicked and obsolete. It may be more fruitful, therefore, to seek an answer in some of the considerations that have been offered at the beginning of this chapter. Fundamental shifts in mental attitudes seldom occur without corresponding changes in social structure. Byzantine society could have been transformed, and the generation of Psellus gives us some reason for supposing that its intellectual habits, including its relation to the classics, might have evolved in a new direction. Unfortunately, events decided otherwise.

CHAPTER 14

ART AND ARCHITECTURE

It is fair to say that art is the one portion of the Byzantine heritage that exerts upon us an immediate appeal. This statement would not have been true a hundred years ago, and if it is true today, this is because our own aesthetic taste has moved away from naturalism in the direction of partial or even total abstraction. As Robert Byron wrote in 1930, 'Of the numerous European cultures whose monuments our taste considers great, Byzantine representational art was the first to discover that principle of interpreting, instead of reproducing, perceived phenomena, which in our time has come to underlie all artistic expression.'[1] For entirely different reasons Byzantine artefacts were also greatly prized in the Middle Ages. The Arab scholar al-Djahiz (ninth century), while remarking that the Byzantines had neither science nor literature, is very appreciative of their woodwork, sculpture and textiles. 'The ancient Greeks', he concludes, 'were men of learning, while the Byzantines are artisans.'[2]

As distinct from its appreciation, which is now widespread, a proper understanding of Byzantine art in its development and in its connection with historical and social factors has not yet been fully achieved. For this there are many reasons. In the first place, Byzantine art, like Byzantine literature, was undeniably very conservative. Since it evolved at a slow pace, the dating of its *oeuvre* is seldom an easy matter, especially in view of the fact that the great majority of objects and buildings bear no dates. Secondly, Byzantine art was anonymous and impersonal. In the art of western Europe, at any rate since the late Middle Ages, individual personalities attract much of our attention, so that the history of European art does not concern itself merely with the evolution of forms: it is also the story of persons who lived known lives, who introduced innovations, who expressed their opinions on art, who exerted an influence on other known artists. Nothing of the kind applied to Byzantine art. In Byzantium artists were regarded as craftsmen and no interest was felt in recording their names or their personalities. The first and the only Byzantine painter who is known to us as an individual is Theophanes the Greek, active in Russia in the late fourteenth and early fifteenth centuries. As to architects, none is mentioned by name after Anthemius and Isidore, the builders of Justinian's St Sophia. Our third difficulty derives from the virtual absence of Byzantine artistic criticism, the lack of a literature that might have discussed or evaluated works of art in terms that were not purely rhetorical. Our last and perhaps most serious difficulty stems from the fact that Byzantine art is preserved only in fragments. The devastation to which most Byzantine lands have been subjected over the centuries has not only swept away a major part of Byzantine artistic creation, but has also determined what one may call the pattern of preservation. The destruction of monuments has been more systematic in the centre of the Empire, in Constantinople, Asia Minor and Thrace than along the periphery as, for example, in Italy, Greece, Yugoslav Macedonia, parts of Syria and Cyprus. From this it follows that Byzantine art is better known in its provincial than in its metropolitan manifestations. Another aspect of the destruction is that it affected secular monuments more seriously than religious ones since, after the Ottoman conquest, churches had a chance of remaining in the hands of Christian communities or else were sometimes preserved by being converted into mosques. A further outcome of the destructive process is the relative importance of the minor arts in the remaining corpus of Byzantine artistic production. Whereas buildings and mural decorations were knocked down, portable objects of value, such as goldsmiths' work, enamels, ivory carvings and illuminated manuscripts, tended to migrate to western Europe where they have survived in cathedral treasuries and museums.

In addition to these objective difficulties, further obstacles have been erected by those very scholars who in the past hundred years have done so much to discover and record the *disjecta membra* of Byzantine art. I do not mean to belittle their achievement. Great strides have been made both in archaeological exploration and in the study of portable artefacts. In 1886–91 one of the creators of Byzantine art history, N. P. Kondakov, published in French translation his *Histoire de l'art byzantin considéré principalement dans les miniatures*. The limitation expressed in the title was due to the fact that at the time very little indeed was known of Byzantine monumental painting. Today this is no longer the case: extensive series of frescoes and mosaics have been found throughout the

Balkans, in Russia, in Cappadocia, Pontus, the Caucasus and Cyprus. Similar or even greater advances have been made in other fields. But while our knowledge has grown enormously, and continues to grow, it should be admitted that the interpretation of the accumulated data has not always proceeded in sensible directions. Too much effort has been spent on debating unreal issues: whether, for example, the origins of Byzantine art should be sought in the East or in the West, and if in the East, whether the decisive impulses came from Alexandria or Antioch or Mesopotamia or somewhere in central Asia. All kinds of 'schools' have been invented and various undocumented objects have been attributed now to one school, now to another. A succession of 'renaissances' has been postulated. What has not been sufficiently perceived is that Byzantine art followed very much the same line of development as Byzantine literature and, indeed, all other manifestations of Byzantine culture. In the following brief survey we shall attempt to present it, as much as possible, in a historical perspective.

In speaking of Early Byzantine or Early Christian art (which comes almost to the same thing) we must remember that we mean the art of the Later Roman Empire adapted to the needs of the Church. It may be that the opposition of the Early Christians to artistic representation has been unduly exaggerated by historians; even so, it cannot be said that they had an artistic programme. The teaching of Jesus, unlike that of Mani, was not conveyed with the help of pictures. The problem of a Christian art was first posed at the time of Constantine's conversion, when the emperor himself, his relatives and members of the higher clergy (who, as we have seen, suddenly found themselves very rich) began setting up splendid churches. For their architectural form a formula was quickly discovered (indeed, it may have pre-existed): this was the basilica, a rectangular colonnaded hall with an elevated dais or *bema* at one end. Adapted from a type of building that was widely used in the Roman world for a variety of judicial, commercial, military and ceremonial purposes, the Christian basilica was designed to satisfy the requirements of the *synaxis*: the spacious nave housed the congregation, while the raised *bema* was for the clergy, with the bishop's chair placed in the centre. A table was provided for the eucharistic sacrifice and another for the offerings of the faithful. While the architectural shell of the church did not create any inherent difficulty, the reverse was true of decoration.

To be sure, even before the reign of Constantine, Christians had adopted certain pictorial formulas such as we see in the earliest catacomb decorations, on sarcophagi and in the Chapel of Dura-Europos on the Euphrates. Executed in the current style of Roman painting and sculpture, these were little vignettes illustrating with the utmost economy a number of key episodes of the Old and New Testaments that were connected with the themes of salvation and life after death. These vignettes, often cryptic as to their meaning, were not, however, suited to decorate the enormous expanses of wall that were offered by the lavish foundations of the Constantinian period. At first, no satisfactory solution appears to have been found. The abbreviated compositions of catacomb art were retained and enriched with elaborate framing motifs; for the rest, 'neutral' subjects were introduced from the secular repertory, such as scenes of hunting and fishing or simply great masses of vegetal scrolls. That is what we find in the very few surviving monuments of mid-fourth-century decoration, for example in the mausoleum of S. Costanza in Rome and the mausoleum, possibly of Constans I, at Centcelles near Tarragona. It was only, it seems, towards the end of the century that a more rational approach to church decoration was found in the use of biblical cycles, sequences of more or less elaborate illustrations which were justified as affording instruction to the illiterate. The changeover to a narrative Christian art is documented in a letter of St Nilus of *c.* 400 AD,[3] but the earliest surviving monument incorporating the new approach is S. Maria Maggiore in Rome (*c.* 445 AD).

This brings us to the topic of Christian iconography which was to play such an important part in the history of Byzantine art. Already in the third to fourth centuries we find a fair degree of consistency in the representation of biblical scenes and this in monuments widely separated in space: the Fall of Man, the Sacrifice of Isaac, the Crossing of the Red Sea are rendered at Dura-Europos in a form recognizably similar to that in the catacombs of Rome. In the case of Old Testament pictures it is probable that their iconography was derived from Jewish sources, perhaps from illustrated biblical manuscripts. The situation was naturally different in the case of the New Testament which acquired its canonical form only towards 200 AD. Representations of Christ's miracles are already found in the third century, though in very schematic form, but a fuller elaboration of New Testament iconography appears to have been achieved only in the fourth and fifth centuries. The earliest surviving example of an extensive New Testament cycle in a monumental context is in the Church of S. Apollinare Nuovo at Ravenna (*c.* 500 AD); the earliest extant illustrated manuscripts of the Gospels are of the sixth century: the codex Rossanensis, the Sinop fragment (now in Paris) and the Syriac Rabula codex (now in Florence). What is significant for the subsequent history of Byzantine art is that complete cycles of both Old Testament and New Testament illustration, whatever their precise origin and date, had been established in an authoritative form by about 500 AD at the latest. There is evidence to show that hagiographic cycles were also elaborated between the fourth and sixth centuries to decorate the walls of martyrs' shrines. This whole body of pictorial material, of which so little survives today, must have played the same part in the Middle Ages as did patristic literature with regard to later theologians and preachers. It provided a standard of reference and a set of clichés.

The artistic achievement of the fourth and fifth centuries lay in the creation of an art which was Christian in content and purpose. This period also coincided with a stylistic trend that was independent of Christianity and may best be described as a provincialization of Graeco-Roman art. The antecedents of this development may be found as far back as the first and second centuries AD, for example in Palmyrene funerary sculpture and in the pagan paintings and carvings of Dura-Europos. Predominance of ornament, increasing loss of the third dimension, frontality of human figures, disregard for scale – these are the traits that are particularly noticeable in much of the provincial work of the late imperial period. The maintenance of classical standards depended on enlightened patronage and a tradition of high-level craftsmanship: both were shattered by the civil wars and economic crisis of the third century. Fourth-century legislation attests to the scarcity of architects and skilled craftsmen whose recruitment had to be encouraged by means of state scholarships and the granting of various immunities.[4] Such measures, even under the best conditions, require a period of time before they bear fruit, whereas the ambitious building programme of Constantine and his successors called for an immediate supply of all kinds of craftsmen in great numbers. The result was jerrybuilding and a kind of decoration that, for all its pretentiousness, revealed very clearly the provincialism and incompetence of its creators. The porphyry 'Tetrarchs' in Venice, which are now known to have been brought from Constantinople, offer a good illustration of what was considered appropriate by way of imperial portraiture in the Constantinian period.

Along with the decline of traditional craftsmanship went a mounting demand for ostentation, pomp and glitter. Here the imperial court set the tone: the theatrical setting, the marble and mosaic, the purple hangings, the solemn ritual of audiences, entrances and exits, the extravagant richness of clothing. There was an art of imperial propaganda with its own iconography: the emperor always triumphant, bigger than life-size, frozen in an immobile pose, receiving tribute, distributing honours, trampling on the necks of the enemy, presiding over public games. What was appropriate to the earthly emperor was equally appropriate to Christ, and so the art of the Church did not hesitate to borrow from the pre-existing art of the court. The Good Shepherd in the mausoleum of Galla Placidia at Ravenna is no longer dressed as a shepherd: He wears a purple tunic with gold stripes. In the Church of S. Pudenziana in Rome (c. 400 AD) Christ, in splendid costume, is enthroned in a semicircular exedra and receives the acclamation of the apostles. Elsewhere He tramples on the asp and the basilisc as the emperor trampled on prostrate enemies, or He receives from His disciples and saints the offering of gold crowns. We notice in art a mounting use of glitter until the background of compositions becomes a solid mass of gold, as in the cupola mosaic of the rotunda at Thessalonica, possibly of the mid-fifth century.

If the art of the fourth and fifth centuries may be viewed in terms of a degradation of the classical style, such a standard is no longer adequate for judging the art of Justinian's epoch. At a date not far removed from 500 AD there occurred an aesthetic change. We are not yet in a position to explain how or why it came about, but there are indications that the new style was introduced deliberately and in the highest circles of society. The development of ornamental sculpture and of the capital in particular provides a good illustration of this phenomenon. It should be explained that the marble quarries of Proconnesus in the Sea of Marmora carried on at the time a brisk export business and that ready-made items, such as capitals, parapet slabs, pulpits and so on were shipped to all parts of the Empire, including the West. Whoever designed these pieces, they were regarded as high-quality stuff and certainly set the newest fashion in many distant lands. Until well into the fifth century the State ateliers of Proconnesus adhered to the traditional capital types, namely the Corinthian (or composite) and the Ionic. No matter how unclassical the acanthus leaves and the volutes became, the basic forms were kept. But from about 500 AD onwards we find an entirely new form, the impost capital, decorated with an over-all pattern, sometimes deeply undercut and looking like lace on a dark background. A whole new vocabulary of ornament appears at this time and the best place to study it is in the recently excavated Church of St Polyeuctus at Istanbul (c 524–7).[5] It was a very large church (about fifty metres square) and probably domed, but the superstructure has completely disappeared leaving only its foundations and a great number of carved elements in Proconnesian marble. The latter show the most bewildering variety of ornament: peacocks with outspread tail, stylized palm trees, palmettes of the Sassanian type, vine scrolls, basket-work, vases with strange vegetal forms growing out of them. The total effect must have been overwhelmingly opulent and probably not entirely harmonious; in any case, it represented a conscious break with the classical tradition. There are two important facts to remember about St Polyeuctus: it was commissioned by the Princess Anicia Juliana, one of the most aristocratic and possibly the richest woman then living at Constantinople; and it was built less than a decade before St Sophia.

The architects and decorators of St Sophia (532–7) could not but have been aware of St Polyeuctus, and they seem to have chosen a more restrained approach. There is no need to give an account of Justinian's mighty cathedral: it has been described and discussed often enough. Furthermore, the building has come down to us almost intact. The visitor need only remember that the original dome was lower than the present one by some twenty feet so that the curvature of the ceiling formed a more continuous canopy and produced a more daring effect; and that the interior illumination was stronger than today's since the side-walls (*tympana*) of the nave appear to have been pierced by huge windows. He should also make allowance for the vast expanse of gold mosaic (now preserved only in fragments) and the splendour of the furnishings, all reveted with sheets of silver – the chancel screen, the ciborium over the altar table, the curving seats for the clergy in the apse, the monumental pulpit in the middle of the nave. As we contemplate the empty shell today, we cannot help observing that St Sophia, too, is fundamentally an unclassical building. The faint suggestion of basilical form is the principal concession to tradition, but the interior vistas curve in strange ways; the columns are of different sizes and proportions; the upper order has consciously been made not to line up with the lower; the capitals are of the undercut impost type; and the original mosaic decoration, as far as we can tell, was entirely non-figural and imitated the effect of shimmering silks enlivened with abstract patterns. Eighteenth-century observers were not entirely mistaken in describing St Sophia as 'Gothick'.

There are other signs of a deliberate break with the past in the Justinianic period. While the basilica still remained the commonest type of church in the provinces, prestige buildings tended more and more to be domed, like S. Vitale at Ravenna (c. 530–45) and St Sergius and St Bacchus at Constantinople (c. 531–36). The tessellated pavement, which had been practically *de rigueur* in Early Byzantine churches, was replaced in St Sophia by large marble slabs; it was not destined to be revived in later centuries. The horizontal entablature makes its last appearance in St Sergius and St Bacchus. As to monumental painting, it is difficult to discern a clear trend in such works as still exist. Perhaps the closest approximation to the art of the capital is provided by the apse mosaic of the Transfiguration on Mount Sinai which dates from the last years of Justinian's reign. With its solid gold background and angular figures suspended in space, it produces an effect of hypnotic abstraction.

It may be said, therefore, that a distinctly Byzantine style had come into being by the sixth century without, however, entirely displacing what was left of the classical tradition. If the Mount Sinai mosaic, with its complete elimination of landscape, was 'progressive', those of S. Vitale, Ravenna, were conservative: for, in the latter monument, the compositions in the presbytery still strive for naturalism. The figures are solid and they have a 'real' setting of sky, rocks and trees. Even the more formal portraits of Justinian and Theodora are meant to suggest an action that is occurring in three-dimensional space. We may not realize at first that Justinian and his entourage are represented walking rather than standing still, but we cannot help noticing that the procession is taking place indoors, under a coffered ceiling. The co-existence of the old and the new, of naturalism (no matter how clumsily rendered) and abstraction was the product of a society that itself showed similar contrasts. The historian Procopius, who was imbued with the ideals of Antiquity, and John of Amida, whose outlook was essentially medieval, lived in the same world.

The fusion of the two opposites does not appear to have been achieved in the century and a half that separates Justinian's death from the outbreak of Iconoclasm, though it must be pointed out that this long period is very poorly known in its artistic manifestations. It is the view of some scholars that the age in question was marked by the growing importance of icons, and in this they are supported by the evidence of texts. It is tempting, therefore, to place in the late sixth and seventh centuries the small number of preserved icons in encaustic, especially the splendid specimens of Mount Sinai, which seem to express the same intensity of religious feeling that we find in contemporary stories of miracles worked by icons. Unfortunately, these remarkable paintings are undated and it is quite conceivable that some of them may go back to the time of Justinian. There is no reason, however, to doubt the seventh-century date of an oft-quoted example of the 'iconic' style, the mosaic of St Demetrius flanked by donors in the same saint's church at Thessalonica. The celestial patron who delivered his city from barbarian attack rises here in all his incorporeal and motionless majesty, suitably emphasized by the rigid geometry of his luminous ceremonial costume. However, were the Byzantines themselves sensitive to the distinction we draw between the naturalistic and the 'iconic' manners? A reading of the relevant texts suggests that they were not. In their eyes an icon was a real portrait which fully conveyed the physical aspect of the holy personage represented. We must quote in this connection Canon 82 of the Quinisext Council (692).[6] In censuring the old custom of representing Christ in the guise of a lamb and recommending that He should be, instead, depicted in human form, it opposes the symbol (*typos*) to the image. The symbol, it argues, had been appropriate to the Old Dispensation when the Truth could be shown only through faint signs and shadows, whereas the New Dispensation needed no symbol: Truth and Grace were there for all to see in Christ's human form. The same idea was later repeated and elaborated in the Synodicon of Orthodoxy of 843. To regard, therefore, Byzantine religious art as symbolic reveals a grave misunderstanding: on the contrary, it sought to be explicit, literal, even realistic.

The simultaneous survival of the Hellenistic tradition of naturalism is documented by a number of examples belonging to the secular sphere. Here we should mention in the first place the pavement mosaic of the imperial palace of Constantinople which, if archaeological evidence is to be trusted, must be later than the time of Justinian. This pavement formed the border of a vast colonnaded courtyard and comprised a variety of vignettes disposed on a white background. The subject-matter is drawn from rural life: animal hunts, peasants tilling the earth, children's games, a mother giving suck, a fisherman, a bear killing a lamb, a monkey climbing a tree, etc. The rendering of human figures, animals and trees is so remarkably vivid, the colouristic effects so varied and subtle, that many scholars have insisted on ascribing the mosaic to a much earlier period. The palace pavement is not, however, an isolated example of the survival of classicism: another is provided by a considerable number of silver plates that continued to be produced until about the middle of the seventh century and can be accurately dated thanks to the hallmarks they bear. Not only are these objects antique in style: many of them are decorated with subjects drawn from pagan mythology, such as Meleager and Atalanta, Poseidon, Silenus and maenads.

As the Early Byzantine Empire came to an end, it left, therefore, a complex and unassimilated legacy made up, on the one hand, of a somewhat degraded classicism and, on the other, of a more abstract and decorative style. It is important to understand that these did not correspond to the secular and religious spheres, respectively. On the contrary, a measure of classicism was permanently embedded in the corpus of biblical and hagiographic illustration that had reached, as we have seen, a canonical form by the beginning of the sixth century. This explains the fact, rather puzzling at first sight, that in the later Byzantine period the highest degree of classicism is associated with traditional religious subject matter.

The history of Byzantine art from about 650 until about 850 is pretty much of a blank. Some inferences concerning the art of Constantinople at the turn of the eighth century may perhaps be drawn from the mosaics and frescoes, now preserved only in fragments, executed in Rome by Pope John VII (705–07). The artistic standard of imperial gold coinage was actually improved, in direct imitation of fifth- and sixth-century types, under Constantine IV, especially in his last years (681–5), and maintained on a good level under Justinian II, the first emperor to have placed an image of Christ on his coins. These manifestations need not surprise us since they correspond to the brief period of euphoria and consolidation following the failure of the Arab attack on Constantinople.

The impact of Iconoclasm on art has to be gauged more on the basis of textual evidence than on that of extant monuments. There was certainly widespread destruction of earlier works bearing religious representations: portable icons were burnt, mural paintings and mosaics scraped off or whitewashed, liturgical plate melted down, illuminated manuscripts mutilated. We must not imagine, of course, that this destruction was carried out with the systematic ruthlessness of a modern police state. For example, we are surprised to hear that some mosaics and paintings in the patriarchal palace of Constantinople, the very nerve-centre of Iconoclasm, were removed as late as 768, some forty years after the promulgation of the ban.[7] At Thessalonica the mosaics of St Demetrius do not appear to have been disturbed, while the apse mosaic of the Monê Latomou (Hosios David) in the same city was concealed behind a protective covering. In general, it would seem that the destruction was most severe in Constantinople and Asia Minor, in other words in areas that were under effective government control, less so in outlying provinces. The Iconoclasts did not succeed in eradicating all trace of Early Christian religious art in the East, but they certainly diminished its volume.

In evolving a substitute form of church decoration, the Iconoclasts relied on 'neutral' motifs. In the famous Church of the Blachernae at Constantinople they put up pictures of trees and various animals, including cranes, crows and peacocks surrounded by scrolls of ivy leaves; in doing so they were accused by their opponents of turning God's house into a fruit shop and an aviary.[8] Thus, consciously or unconsciously, they returned to the kind of decoration that had been applied to churches in the fourth century. The Iconoclasts also gave added emphasis to the symbol of the cross. In the Church of St Irene at Constantinople, rebuilt after the earthquake of 740, a plain cross on a stepped base occupies the semidome of the apse; it is the same device that Iconoclastic emperors used consistently on their coinage. Similar crosses also existed in the apses of St Sophia at Thessalonica and the Dormition church at Nicaea (destroyed in 1922); in both cases the cross was later replaced by a figure of the Virgin and Child. A number of rustic chapels in Cappadocia and elsewhere display a non-figural decoration consisting of crosses and a variety of ornamental motifs including animals and plants. These have often been attributed to the Iconoclastic period, although in most cases their dating is quite uncertain.

While objecting to the use of human figures in religious art, the Iconoclasts are known to have tolerated and even encouraged secular representations such as those of hunts and hippodrome scenes. An example of this was provided by a monument called the Milion, a monumental arch at Constantinople that marked the starting point of the great highway running across the Balkan peninsula. This monument had been decorated with pictures of the six ecumenical councils which were removed by Constantine V and replaced by a representation of his favourite charioteer.[9] Secular subjects also figured prominently in the splendid buildings that were put up in the palace by the Emperor Theophilus: pictures of shields and other weapons, of animals, trees and men picking fruit are specifically mentioned.[10] A similar distinction between religious and secular art was maintained by the Umayyad caliphs of Damascus: while the representation of every living being, even animals, was excluded from mosques, the palaces of princes were freely decorated in painting, mosaic and sculpture with effigies of rulers and courtiers, pictures of hunts and banquets, of musicians and even of nude women. As long as the caliphate remained in Syria the art of the Arab court and that of the Iconoclastic emperors seem to have flowed in parallel channels.

The most significant contribution of the Iconoclastic period to the development of Byzantine art lay, however, in the formulation of an exact theory and justification of religious painting. For a whole century the best minds of Byzantium were bent on this problem; and while the writings of the Iconoclastic theoreticians have been destroyed, those of their Orthodox opponents – of the patriarchs Germanus and Nicephorus, of St John Damascene and St Theodore the Studite – fill many volumes. The debate was conducted on a theological and philosophical plane and centred on questions such as scriptural and patristic authority, the relation between image and archetype (the person represented on it), and, especially, the admissibility of representing Christ who was both God and man. The conclusion that was finally reached was that one was entitled to portray such holy personages as had actually appeared on earth in visible form: Christ since He was a complete man, the saints, and even angels since they manifested themselves in human shape on various occasions; but not God the Father or the Holy Trinity. It was also stated that the image differed from its archetype as to 'essence' or 'substance' (*ousia*), but was identical as to 'person' (*hypostasis*). It was like the impression of a signet ring or the reflection in a mirror. In other words, the icon was considered to be a true and exact portrait.

An inescapable consequence of this definition was the immutability of iconographic types: the artist was not at liberty to alter the accepted features of this or that saint. But the definition also implied something else, namely the validity of iconographic types. In the entire literature of the Iconoclastic period no one, if I am not mistaken, thought of posing the practical question: How do we know the icon is a likeness? What evidence, for example, do we have that St Peter had a hooked nose and curly grey hair? Even if he had, is it sufficient to depict a man with a hooked nose and curly grey hair to obtain the exact likeness of St Peter? The inability of the Byzantines to ask such questions and to see the problem of the icon in terms other than theological ones reveals a general truth about their artistic intuition. Theirs was an art unconcerned with the individual and the particular. A few major differentiations, such as colour of hair, length and shape of beard, details of costume and authenticating inscription were considered sufficient to establish identity. No wonder, then, that Byzantine art never produced real portraiture.

The restoration of icon-worship between 780 and 814 was too transitory to leave any lasting results. It was only after the final liquidation of Iconoclasm in 843 that a major effort was made to recreate religious art. The task could not have been easy since the tradition of sacred painting had been disrupted. To be sure, the fairly tolerant régime of Michael II and Theophilus could not prevent a few determined men from surreptitiously painting icons or illustrating manuscripts, but even so, when the painter Lazarus (one of the very few we happen to know by name) was apprehended in this kind of activity, he was subjected to physical torture and imprisonment.[11] There was, however, a wide gulf between such small-scale work as could be carried out in secret and the formation of regular ateliers capable of redecorating the vast churches of Constantinople. The task was so great that its accomplishment had to be spread over about half a century: in St Sophia the first figural mosaic, that of the Virgin and Child in the apse which is still extant, was made in 867; the Church of St Sergius and St Bacchus was redecorated between 867 and 877, that of the Holy Apostles between 867 and 886, that of the Virgin Mary of the Source (outside the walls of Constantinople) some time before 879. Besides, a number of new churches were being built and these, too, required painted decoration. The second half of the ninth century must have been a time of intensive activity for Byzantine artists.

Many of the formulae adopted after 843 were destined to remain in use for the next three hundred years if not longer. In ecclesiastical architecture the domed building was now firmly established. As compared to the churches of Justinian's time, those of the ninth and later centuries were distinctly small. In fact, Byzantine architects were never to build again on a large scale – something worth pondering on. The double-shell design, like the one of St Sophia, was abandoned in favour of a more unified interior. Constantinople gave preference to the cross-in-square plan, where the central dome was carried on four free-standing columns, a form that we first encounter in Bithynian monasteries towards the end of the eighth century. There was a tendency to multiply domes, as already in the Nea Ekklêsia (New Church) dedicated by Basil I in 880, which had five, presumably one in the centre and one over each of the four corners of the square. The exterior remained at first rather stark, as in the Early Byzantine period, but progressively became enlivened with engaged pilasters and arcading, thus producing a more plastic effect. There also developed a preference for taller, less squat silhouettes. From about the eleventh century onwards brick began to be used to form ornamental patterns on the exterior, but this applied more to the provinces than to Constantinople.

The treatment of the interior remained, in principle, as it had been in the Early Byzantine period. The vertical surfaces of the walls were covered with marble slabs of different colours up to the springing of the arches and vaults, which was marked by a projecting cornice; the space above the cornice was decorated with mosaic. In more modest churches the same effect was imitated in paint. Shallow ornamental carving, usually heightened with paint and gilding, was applied to the cornice, to parapet slabs, door and window frames, and especially to the *templon*, the open marble screen separating the presbytery from the nave. It is difficult today to recapture the extraordinary, if rather excessive, richness of such interiors, since all surviving Byzantine churches of this period have suffered mutilation: Hosios Loukas in Greece and San Marco in Venice come perhaps closest to conveying the total effect that was intended.

It was in mosaic decoration that Byzantine artists achieved their greatest success. There is reason to believe that a formula for such decoration adapted to contemporary architecture was evolved in the ninth century, but no reasonably complete specimen of it is preserved that is earlier than the eleventh. In St Sophia, Constantinople, the figural mosaics executed from 867 onwards can only be described as inserts, splendid in themselves, but inevitably at odds with the immensity of their architectural setting. In St Sophia, Thessalonica, the mosaics of the ninth century are probably limited to the Ascension in the dome. To find a mosaic decoration embracing the whole interior of a church we have to go to Hosios Loukas (early eleventh century), to Nea Monê on Chios (1042–56) and Daphni near Eleusis (*c.* 1100). Earlier examples are known to us only through the evidence of texts.

Despite their differences, these decorations have many common features. Most importantly, the arrangement of subjects is hierarchical. A normal disposition of the Middle Byzantine period (we are not referring here to any specific monument) runs more or less as follows.

The highest part of the church, the centre of the dome, is reserved for the Divinity, usually in the form of Christ Pantocrator (the ruler of the universe): this is a bust of Christ enclosed in a circular medallion. Christ is sometimes surrounded by his angelic bodyguard of archangels, seraphim and cherubim. The second place of honour – the semidome of the apse – is reserved for the Virgin Mary who is usually flanked by the archangels Michael and Gabriel. Below Christ and His retinue come the apostles and prophets; below the Virgin is placed the Communion of the Apostles as well as figures of clerical saints, i.e. bishops (St John Chrystostom, St Basil, St Athanasius, the two St Gregorys, etc.) and deacons (St Stephen, St Lawrence, etc.) who are thus made, as it were, to participate in the liturgy that was celebrated within the presbytery. The four pendentives supporting the dome were traditionally occupied by the four Evangelists. The zone of the barrel vaults above the cornice afforded space for a cycle of New Testament scenes. Any remaining wall surface in the nave was assigned to single figures of 'secular' saints, often grouped by categories, such as holy warriors (George, Demetrius, the two Theodores, and so on), physicians (Cosmas, Damian, Panteleemon), monks (Antony, Arsenius, Euthymius) or martyrs. The general principle of this arrangement remained in force until the end of the Byzantine Empire; indeed, it has been retained by the Orthodox Church to this very day.

To say that a decorative scheme such as we have described forms a *civitas Dei* would be a truism, since every Christian church strives, in one way or another, to represent God's Kingdom. What distinguishes the Byzantine system from, say, the Romanesque and the Gothic is that the *civitas Dei* has been restricted to one main idea: the New Dispensation. It is not a *speculum mundi*: we do not find in Byzantine church decoration any allegories of virtues and vices, any signs of the zodiac, any labours of the months, any liberal arts, any vignettes of trades and crafts. What the Byzantines called 'outside knowledge' has been kept out. Even the Old Testament has been excluded save for the figures of the prophets whose function it was to announce the Incarnation. Once again we are led back to the Quinisext Council and the Synodicon of Orthodoxy: the shadows and symbols of the old order have been made unnecessary by the one supreme reality, God's coming among men by the agency of the Virgin Mary. The Byzantine *civitas Dei* is the New Testament and the choir of Christian saints.

Another feature of Byzantine church decoration from the ninth to the twelfth century is the restriction of the narrative element. Instead of the lengthy cycles of Early Christian art, the story of the New Testament has been condensed to a limited number of key episodes, a kind of liturgical calendar composed of the major feasts, beginning with the Annunciation (usually on the piers flanking the presbytery) and ending with the Dormition of the Virgin (on the west wall of the nave). Such selectivity was consonant with the architectural form of the Middle Byzantine church. As long as the vertical wall surfaces were covered with marble, there was hardly any room in the nave for more than a dozen figural compositions, provided these were represented on a reasonably large scale.

Considering Middle Byzantine church decoration from a formal point of view, we are struck first of all by the elimination of 'picture space'. Elements of landscape and architecture have been removed as much as possible and replaced by a uniform gold background. In some compositions such as the Nativity, the Baptism and the Entry into Jerusalem, the setting could not be entirely eliminated and was conveyed by a number of simple props as on the modern stage. One cross was all that was needed for the Crucifixion. In the Anastasis (Harrowing of Hell) the aspect of the underworld could be conveyed by a small dark chasm filled with miscellaneous hardware (the locks and bolts of Hell) and two sarcophagi from which the elect emerged. In the Annunciation the house of the Virgin could be omitted, leaving only the two protagonists. In the Washing of the Feet (as at Hosios Loukas) two stools and a washbasin were the only props required.

The absence of natural perspective, which is another feature of Byzantine art, is directly traceable to the Early Christian period. The size of figures in a composition depends more on their hierarchical importance than on their position in space. Consider, for example, the beautiful Nativity at Daphni: the Virgin Mary and Joseph are placed on the same plane, yet the Virgin is distinctly bigger than her husband. The angels are about the same size as Joseph, although they are standing at a considerable distance, behind a mountain; two of them even manage to stretch their arms over the mountain which consequently appears like a papiermâché object about three feet high. Reverse or merely inconsistent perspective is regularly applied to pieces of furniture such as thrones which appear narrower at the front than at the back and whose seat usually tilts forward at an inclined plane, a phenomenon that is already observable in the fifth-century mosaics of S. Maria Maggiore. Distance is no longer indicated by gradations of colour, nor is there a uniform source of illumination. Figures cast no shadows. In spite of these anti-illusionistic devices, individual human figures remain at times surprisingly antique. The reason for this lies, we believe, in the extraordinary tenacity of the iconographic tradition of biblical illustration. The training of the Byzantine artist involved the faithful reproduction of formulas which, as we have seen, went back to the period of the Later Roman Empire. For the same reason all biblical figures retained their antique garb consisting of tunic and *chlamys*: contemporary Byzantine costume was not used. Here we are faced with a broader problem which has been the subject of prolonged discussion, namely the relation of Byzantine art to ancient art, and we must pause briefly to examine it.

In the opinion of many recent scholars, the history of Byzantine art was punctuated by a number of renaissance movements, of which the most important are acknowledged to have been the so-called Macedonian Renaissance and the Palaeologan Renaissance. The first of these takes its name from the Macedonian dynasty and is believed, on rather shaky evidence, to have reached its height in the reign of Constantine VII Porphyrogenitus. It should be said at once that the Macedonian Renaissance is not reflected in any extant work of mural painting or mosaic; its imprint is felt only in the minor arts, especially in illuminated manuscripts and carved ivories.

In the field of manuscript illumination the most important 'renaissance works' are the Paris Psalter (Parisinus gr. 139), the Bible of the patrician Leo in the Vatican (Reginensis gr. 1), the Joshua rotulus, also in the Vatican (Palatinus gr. 431), and the Stavronikita Gospels (monastery of Stavronikita on Mount Athos, cod. 43). The Paris Psalter is probably the most striking of these manuscripts, so we may stop to consider the famous miniature representing Isaiah's prayer. Outwardly this is very antique. The prophet is flanked by two personifications, that of Dawn in the form of a putto, and that of Night, a svelte figure holding a billowing veil, who seems to be descended from some ancient Hecate or Selene. And yet the general effect is somehow unsatisfactory. The figures are lined up without any feeling for composition or scale, the drawing is false in places (especially in the case of Dawn), the strip of ground fails to recede, and its terminal line is awkwardly masked by flowering shrubs. Or consider the Anointing of David in the Reginensis gr. 1 (dating from about 940). Here again there is a superficial air of antiquity, but the architecture in the background makes little sense, the figure of Clemency has her left hand growing directly out of her elbow, and David's six brothers are provided with only two pairs of legs. The Joshua rotulus, a unique example of continuous strip illustration, exhibits the same mixture of antique personifications, 'Pompeian' settings and partly misunderstood figural drawing. All three manuscripts reproduce traditional Old Testament iconography and are more or less faithful copies of originals of the Early Byzantine period. To what extent the copies departed from their lost originals it is now almost impossible to determine; but even if there has been some adaptation, this does not amount to a genuinely creative phenomenon. Pseudo-classical rather than classical, the illuminated manuscripts of the Macedonian Renaissance reflect the artificial and anaemic antiquarianism of court circles.

Very similar observations may be made regarding the ivory carvings of the Macedonian period. Single figures have occasionally something of the quality of ancient statuary, as in the panel representing the apostles John and Paul (now at Venice), the companion relief of Andrew and Peter at Vienna, the Harbaville triptych in the Louvre and so on. The classicism never extends, however, beyond individual figures. In the Romanus ivory of the Cabinet des Médailles, made in or about 945, Christ is in the antique manner, while the imperial pair are like stuffed dummies, and the furniture is rendered in reverse perspective. Narrative compositions may have offered recourse to 'pictorial relief' in the Hellenistic manner, but the opportunity was not seized. Consider, for example, the plaque of the Forty Martyrs in the Berlin Museum. The subject, which must have gone back to an Early Byzantine original, represents the saints freezing to death in a lake. By varying the height of the relief, the carver could have achieved an illusion of depth, yet he chose not to do so. The figural work is fine, but it is of uniform depth, with the result that the saints seem to be piled up in a heap. What is particularly instructive in the domain of Byzantine ivories is that we find the least classicism of style precisely where we might have expected to find the most, namely in the group of caskets decorated with mythological and other secular subjects, of which the Veroli casket in the Victoria and Albert Museum is an outstanding example. The figures on these objects always appear as obese, cavorting pygmies, completely lacking the elegance and repose which, in the realm of ivories, characterizes Christian saints, and those alone.

It is, therefore, quite misleading to call the Macedonian Renaissance a return to Antiquity. Had Byzantine artists been eager to imitate classical art, there would have been no shortage of models within their reach. Constantinople itself was a museum of ancient statuary assembled for purposes of urban decoration between the fourth and the sixth centuries; the country, too, was full of classical remains. To take but a single instance, Hadrian's great temple at Cyzicus with its wealth of sculpture was still standing in the fifteenth century, when it was described by Cyriac of Ancona, yet no Byzantine seems to have paid the slightest attention to it. Indeed, the aim of the Macedonian Renaissance, in art as in literature, was a return not to pagan antiquity, but to the period when the Christian Empire had been great, just as the political aim of the Macedonian emperors was the restoration of Justinian's realm. Such bits and pieces of Early Christian art as had survived the Iconoclastic troubles were imitated for the benefit of emperors and courtiers, but there was no assimilation of classical values. The movement, as we have said, appears to have been restricted to the minor arts; significantly, no attempt was made to create major sculpture in stone or bronze, not even imperial statues. By the end of the tenth century the court renaissance had died out. It may have left some imprint on figure drawing in the succeeding period, but it did not deflect Byzantine art from its natural course.

What may be called the mature phase of Byzantine art falls roughly between the years 1000 and 1150, during the period of urban resurgence. This art had a wide radiation beyond the confines of the Empire: Byzantine craftsmen were called to Kiev and Novgorod, to Monte Cassino, Palermo and Cefalù. Byzantine influence was entering Italy through Venice, through Sicily and through the imperial territories situated in the south of the peninsula. Farther north, particularly in Germany, the diffusion of the Byzantine style was effected at a somewhat later date (from about the end of the twelfth century) and mostly by means of portable works such as illuminated manuscripts.

In the realm of architecture the eleventh century saw more activity than any previous period since the fall of the Early Byzantine Empire. It also showed some originality. Unfortunately, we know very little about the great imperial foundations at Constantinople whose extravagance is censured by Psellus, for example the monastery of the Virgin Peribleptos built by Romanus III and that of St George of Mangana commissioned by Constantine IX. It may be conjectured that they provided models for contemporary monuments in Greece, such as Hosios Loukas, Nea Monê and Daphni, all three of which share a new form, that of the octagonal interior space covered by a dome on squinches. Since this form almost certainly came from Armenia, Byzantine architects must have been willing to accept inspiration from

ABOVE Church of St John built by the patrician Studius, Istanbul, *c.* 453 AD.

BELOW Church of Qalb-Loseh, Syria, *c.* 460 AD.

The standard form of Early Byzantine churches is that of the basilica – an elongated, timber-roofed hall terminating in an apse. The nave is usually separated from the aisles by rows of marble columns, but in Syria these are often replaced by masonry piers.

ABOVE Dome mosaic of the Rotunda, Thessalonica, probably mid-fifth century.

BELOW Mosaics of Sant'Apollinare Nuovo, Ravenna, early sixth century.

The pictorial art of the Early Byzantine Church may be divided into the symbolic and the narrative. The former trend is represented in the Rotunda of Thessalonica, where a number of martyrs stand frontally before opulent architectural backdrops. Sant'Apollinare Nuovo has the earliest extant New Testament cycle in a monumental context.

ABOVE Studius Basilica, Istanbul, capital of porch, *c.* 453 AD.

ABOVE RIGHT St Sophia, Istanbul, capital of gallery, *c.* 532 AD.

BELOW San Marco, Venice, capital from St Polyeuctus, Constantinople, *c.* 524–7 AD.

BELOW RIGHT Piazza San Marco, Venice, one of the two 'Pilastri Acritani' from St Polyeuctus, Constantinople, *c.* 524–7 AD.

The style of architectural sculpture underwent a radical change in the early years of the sixth century. The acanthus capital of Corinthian or composite form gave way to the impost capital with surface decoration of a highly fanciful character. This is one instance of a deliberate rejection of the classical tradition.

St Sophia, Istanbul, interior, 532–7 AD. The greatest of Byzantine churches, St Sophia combines elements of the basilica with those of 'centralized' planning, the latter clearly predominating. The mighty dome, rebuilt several times, produces an impression of overwhelming grandeur.

ABOVE Monastery of St Catherine, Mount Sinai, Transfiguration mosaic, 550–1 or 565–6 AD.

BELOW San Vitale, Ravenna, Abraham's Hospitality and the Sacrifice of Isaac, 540–7 AD.

Both are narrative compositions, but whereas the artist of San Vitale clings to a tradition of naturalism, that of Mount Sinai has eliminated all traces of a natural setting in favour of an abstract effect.

LEFT Monastery of St Catherine, Mount Sinai, icon of the Virgin and Saints, sixth or seventh century.

BELOW St Demetrius, Thessalonica, mosaic of St Demetrius and Donors, seventh century.

The icon sought to bring the worshipper into immediate contact with the realm of the saints who were represented in a hieratic and immobile pose.

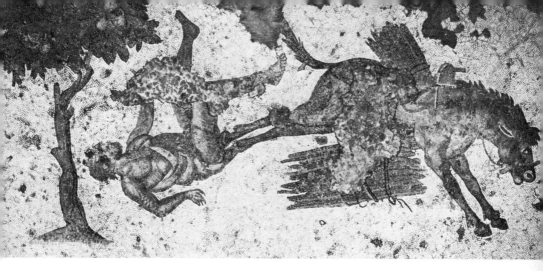

ABOVE Great Palace pavement, Istanbul, perhaps of the late sixth century.

BELOW Leningrad, Hermitage Museum, plate with maenad, 613–30 AD.

The survival, until the middle of the seventh century, of a repertory of classical, even pagan, subject-matter is apparent in luxury goods, especially silver vessels, many of which are dated by the hallmarks they bear.

ABOVE Great Mosque, Damascus, mosaic in courtyard, 705–12 AD.

LEFT St Sophia, Istanbul, mosaics of south-west room of gallery (*rinceau* of the late sixth century and cross of *c.* 769 AD).

The non-figural mosaics of the Damascus mosque give us some inkling of the art that was probably practised under the Iconoclastic emperors who banned religious representations.

ABOVE St Irene, Istanbul, mosaic cross in apse,
after 740 AD.

RIGHT Church of the Dormition (destroyed) at
Iznik (Nicaea), mosaic in apse (Virgin Mary of the
ninth century replacing a cross of the Iconoclastic
period).

The Iconoclasts laid emphasis on the cult of the
cross which they substituted for images of saints.
The cross in St Irene is one of the few remaining
works of this period that survived the redecoration
of churches after 843 AD.

ABOVE Church of the Myrelaion (Bodrum Camii), Istanbul, exterior, *c.* 930 AD.

BELOW Church of St Panteleimon, Nerezi, near Skopje, 1164 AD.

Byzantine churches of the Middle period were of relatively small size and elaborately decorated inside, while the exterior was left fairly plain. A central dome was almost *de rigueur*, and often there were as many as five.

ABOVE Hosios Loukas,
Phocis, Greece, mosaic
of the Anastasis in
narthex, first half of
eleventh century.

LEFT Hosios Loukas,
mosaic of the Washing of
the Feet in narthex, first
half of eleventh century.

ABOVE Daphni, near Eleusis, Greece, mosaic of the Nativity, end of eleventh century.

The artistic development of the eleventh century may be gauged from a comparison of these two famous monuments. The brutal schematism of Hosios Loukas yields to a more 'humanistic' style which, nevertheless, adheres to Byzantine conventions of perspective and relative scale.

Vatican Library, Cod. Reg. Gr. 1 (the Leo Bible), the Anointing of David, *c.* 945
AD. The artistic movement that has been called with some exaggeration the
Macedonian Renaissance manifested itself in the reproduction of Late Antique or
Early Byzantine models in luxury products.

Museo Archeologico, Venice, ivory of St John and St Paul, tenth century.

OIAΓIOITECCAPAKONTA

As in the field of manuscript illumination, the impact of the Macedonian Renaissance on ivory carving is most noticeable in works of a religious nature. Despite its mythological subject-matter, the Veroli casket falls short of recapturing a classical style.

ABOVE Ehemals Staatliche Museen, Berlin-Dahlem, ivory of the Forty Martyrs, tenth century.

BELOW Victoria and Albert Museum, London, the Veroli casket, tenth or early eleventh century.

ABOVE St Sophia, Ohrid, the Apostles of the Ascension, *c.* 1040 AD.

BELOW St Panteleimon, Nerezi, near Skopje, the Deposition from the Cross, 1164 AD.

Liberating itself from the imitation of earlier styles, Byzantine painting found its distinctive idiom in the eleventh and twelfth centuries.

The last phase of
Byzantine painting
before the conquest of
Constantinople by the
Crusaders was marked
by an exaggerated
mannerism which
became almost grotesque
in the hands of
provincial artists.

ABOVE Monastery of St Catherine, Mount Sinai, Annunciation icon, late twelfth century.

Sopoćani, Yugoslavia, the Dormition of the Virgin, *c.* 1265 AD. The classical monumentality achieved in the best work of the mid-thirteenth century soon gave way to a more expressive, yet fussier and more crowded manner.

Kariye Camii (Christ of the Chora), Istanbul, the Virgin entrusted to Joseph, *c.*
1315–21 AD. By the first quarter of the fourteenth century Palaeologan painting had
already passed its peak and was moving into a mannerist phase, seen at its most
elegant in the mosaics and frescoes of the Kariye Camii.

Peribleptos, Mistra, the Entry into Jerusalem, late fourteenth century. Byzantine painting of the late fourteenth and fifteenth centuries appears very backward by Italian standards. It was, nevertheless, developing towards a greater awareness of natural detail when it was interrupted by the Turkish conquest.

ABOVE OPPOSITE Church of St Catherine, Thessalonica, late thirteenth or early fourteenth century.

BELOW OPPOSITE Church of Pantanassa, Mistra, detail of east side, 1428 AD.

The ecclesiastical architecture of the Palaeologan period strove, on a small scale, to achieve elegant and picturesque effects through extensive use of arcading, brickwork arranged in decorative patterns, and even carving of foreign inspiration.

ABOVE Tekfur Sarayi (Palace of the Porphyrogenitus), Istanbul, late thirteenth century.

BELOW Palace of the Despots, Mistra, thirteenth to fifteenth centuries.

The few remaining palace structures of the Palaeologan period show a clear debt to the West, especially to Italy.

distant lands. They also carried their own expertise abroad in undertaking such major projects as St Sophia at Kiev and the rebuilding of the Church of the Holy Sepulchre at Jerusalem.

We have already indicated some of the salient features of the painting of this period without, perhaps, sufficiently stressing its stylistic originality. Work of the ninth and tenth centuries often looks as if it had been reproduced from much earlier models without any creative transformation, whereas that of the eleventh century has more of a distinctive stamp. It has moved away from classicism towards a calligraphic and two-dimensional approach that is sometimes decorative and elegant (as in many illuminated manuscripts), at other times forceful and severe. The line rather than modelling plays an increasingly important part. Drapery sometimes assumes a life of its own with a turbulence that is not justified by the motion of the figure. Eddies of concentric folds are applied to the chest and buttocks and the end of the *chlamys* often flutters as if it were swept by a strong wind. While it is not easy to arrange the surviving works in a strict evolutionary sequence, it may be said that a pictorial *koinê* was elaborated during this period, a kind of vernacular that Byzantine artists understood and used over a large geographical area.

The middle of the twelfth century marks another turning point and the beginning of a more rapid development of Byzantine painting. The new tendencies may be seen in the decoration of Nerezi, dated 1164, in Yugoslav Macedonia. This is work of the highest quality commissioned by a member of the imperial family – Alexius Comnenus, grandson of the Emperor Alexius I. The frescoes of Nerezi are highly stylized, yet charged with a dramatic intensity. We notice here certain phenomena that were to be continued and exaggerated in the next half-century: agitation of drapery that tends to form serpentine folds, composition of figures in terms of groups (as in the Deposition from the Cross, where the Virgin and John the Evangelist bend forward to uphold Christ's drooping body, thus forming a kind of arch), and a device whereby human figures are enclosed within the outline of hills which echo the shapes of the bodies (as in the Lamentation and the Transfiguration). The next stage of evolution, marked by a growing turbulence of movement and drapery, unification of compositions, and an increased emphasis on architectural backdrops, may be seen in the vast mosaic ensemble of Monreale, executed in the seventies and eighties of the twelfth century by an atelier that was in touch with the latest trends at Constantinople. And so we are brought to the last stage of Byzantine painting before 1204, represented for us by a number of small provincial churches: Kurbinovo on Lake Prespa (1191), the Anargyroi at Kastoria (undated), and Lagoudera in Cyprus (1192). A beautiful icon of the Annunciation on Mount Sinai exemplifies the same style with greater elegance, and may, therefore, have been made at Constantinople. The style in question is truly *fin de siècle*: the figures, elongated and contorted, are covered with a welter of serpentine folds, and, at times, a web of gold striations. At Lagoudera, complex architectural forms are used for backdrops, although their rendering remains two-dimensional. The Sinai icon exhibits, rather surprisingly, a stream flowing in the foreground: its waters are inhabited by herons, ducks, fish and octopi, all drawn at an absurdly small scale as compared to the human figures, but showing nevertheless a new interest in picturesque detail.

The impression, suggested by the above monuments, of an artistic upheaval between about 1150 and 1200 is confirmed from other sources. 'Major' sculpture, which had been in abeyance for several centuries, appears to have been revived or, at any rate, some thought was given to reviving it: the Emperor Andronicus I, we are told, was about to set up his own statue in bronze when he was toppled from the throne.[12] The range of secular art was enlarged: the canonist Balsamon (died *c*. 1195) reports that rich men had in their houses pictures of erotic subjects and figural carvings in stucco.[13] Most significant of all was the emergence of the artist as an individual. The foremost painter of this period was one Eulalios who took part in the redecoration of the Church of the Holy Apostles at Constantinople, and is said to have included his own portrait, dressed in his everyday costume, in a representation of the Women at the Sepulchre[14] – an altogether amazing liberty by Byzantine standards. Two other painters named Chênaros and Chartoularis enjoyed favour at court.[15] In 1200 the Russian pilgrim Antony of Novgorod mentions a contemporary painter of great talent, a certain Paul who was responsible for an elaborate rendering of Christ's Baptism in St Sophia.[16] It is also in the same half-century that painters' 'signatures' (inscriptions in which the painter is named) begin to appear in monumental art. The earliest instance, if we are not mistaken, is in the Church of the Nativity at Bethlehem where in 1169 a new set of mosaics was made by the artists Ephraem and Basil. In 1183 one Theodore Apseudes signed the wall-paintings in the hermitage of St Neophytus in Cyprus. Though always exceptional, painters' signatures become relatively more frequent from this time onwards.

The history of Byzantine art in the thirteenth century and, more particularly, in the period 1204–61, has not yet been satisfactorily unravelled. We may suppose that a great number of artists fled from Constantinople and found employment at various Orthodox courts: in the first instance at the Greek courts of Nicaea, Trebizond and Arta, perhaps also at the Serbian and Bulgarian courts. It is a great pity that we should know nothing definite about the art of Nicaea which was the centre of the most dynamic of the three Greek principalities and has, therefore, a strong claim to have played a leading role in artistic development. Some light on this topic may possibly be cast if the blackened paintings in the ruined church of St Sophia at Nicaea are ever cleaned. All we can say at present is that the most remarkable monuments of thirteenth-century Byzantine painting are situated in Yugoslavia – we are referring in particular to Mileševo (c. 1230–6) and Sopoćani (c. 1265). Unfortunately, we know nothing of the truly great artists who decorated these two churches. In both cases an unusual attempt has been made to imitate mosaics in paint for, instead of the normal blue backgrounds, we find yellow backgrounds (originally gilded) covered with a fine grid of dark lines. The style of these two decorations, while showing some contact with Early Christian models, is particularly remarkable for its sense of volume. Human figures, especially at Sopoćani, are statuesque and are placed in front of architectural backgrounds seen in three-quarter view – houses, exedras, colonnades, with pieces of drapery looped round columns or extended from one structure to another, in other words forms traceable to the art of Late Antiquity. The same tendencies are also apparent in the recently cleaned frescoes of St Sophia at Trebizond (c. 1250), thus showing that we have before us a phenomenon not confined to Serbia, but common to the whole Byzantine world.

The last creative effort of Byzantine art is represented by Palaeologan painting which, foreshadowed as it is at Sopoćani, makes its appearance almost simultaneously with the recovery of Constantinople from the Latins (1261). The radiation of this style, though not as wide as that of the Comnenian, was nevertheless considerable: it is found throughout the Balkans, in parts of Asia Minor and, at a somewhat later date, in Russia. This is clear evidence of the cultural prestige enjoyed by Byzantium even at a time of profound political weakness.

The most famous example of the Palaeologan style is offered by the mosaics and frescoes of St Saviour in the Chora (Kariye Camii) at Constantinople, executed in c. 1315–21 at the behest of Theodore

Metochites, Finance Minister and later Prime Minister of the Emperor Andronicus II. This monument may serve, therefore, to define the characteristics of the new art. What strikes us first of all – and this applies to all Palaeologan churches – is the multiplication of pictures and their small scale. Compared to Byzantine art of the eleventh and twelfth centuries, the narrative element has been greatly increased. At Kariye Camii we have in the two nartheces alone (the decoration of the nave has almost completely disappeared) a cycle devoted to the life of the Virgin which originally consisted of twenty episodes, a cycle of the infancy of Christ in fourteen episodes, and a cycle of the ministry of Christ which consisted of at least thirty-two scenes. Since we are dealing here with a fairly small space, the general effect is one of extreme pictorial overcrowding. In other Palaeologan decorations, such as that of Dečani (c. 1348) in Serbia, the number of scenes is even greater: one has the impression that all the walls are crawling with figures.

The effect of overcrowding is further increased by the fact that the backgrounds of all narrative compositions, instead of being left relatively plain, have been encumbered with a variety of architectural forms. This produces a certain illusion of depth, but the handling of the third dimension is always contradictory and, to our eyes, confusing. As a rule, the action takes place on a kind of narrow stage which is delimited at the back by a wall having a number of projecting wings or pavilions. Instead of there being a single point of vision, however, there are usually several: in the same picture one building may be seen from above and another from below, one from the right and another from the left. Nor is an attempt ever made to produce an illusion of interior space as Duccio and Giotto had done a few years before the execution of the Kariye Camii decoration: even when a scene is meant to take place indoors, the ceiling is always omitted.

The 'theatre sets' of Palaeologan painting are peopled with elongated figures that tend to have very small heads and feet (the latter are often badly connected at the ankle), thick middles and swollen calves. They are wrapped in ample garments that fall or flutter in a cascade of folds usually terminating in a sharp tongue. While their anatomical structure is uncertain, the figures have considerable relief owing to the use of bright highlights. The colour scheme is very rich and often exhibits bold juxtapositions, such as of blue and purple. The expression of the faces is pensive, sweet and almost sentimental: the sternness of earlier Byzantine painting has disappeared.

When the mosaics of the Kariye Camii first attracted the attention of specialists, about a hundred years ago, they could be compared only to the works of Cavallini, Giotto and Duccio. A little later the similar church decorations of Mistra came to be known, and so there arose the question of *Orient ou Occident?* – of the relative priority of the Italian and Byzantine Renaissances, a question on which a great deal of ink has been spilt. Today, the number of Palaeologan decorations available to study is very large indeed, and many of them are considerably earlier than the Kariye Camii, which is seen as representing a somewhat academic and decadent phase of the style. The relationship of Palaeologan painting, which we now recognize as being of indigenous growth, to that of Italy remains elusive, and while we can speak of a general parallelism between the two, the number of specific borrowings made by Byzantine painters from the West is remarkably small. This is not surprising when we remember that this period in Byzantium was dominated by hostility towards the Latins and Roman Catholicism. Instead of turning to the West, Byzantine painters went back to their own past and found models, largely, it would seem, among the classicizing manuscripts of the tenth century which were themselves copies of much earlier manuscripts of the fifth and sixth centuries. To speak, therefore, of a Palaeologan Renaissance is rather misleading in that the term 'renaissance' implies an enlargement of horizons and a liberation of the spirit, whereas Palaeologan art bespeaks an antiquarian involution.

The manner of the first half of the fourteenth century was capable of further development. It could move in the direction of a more intense spiritualization, as it did in the work of that supremely great master, Theophanes the Greek, who was active at Novgorod and Moscow between 1378 and 1405; or it could move towards greater 'laicization' by absorbing details of contemporary life and costume, by making compositions more picturesque, as in the charming frescoes of Ravanica (*c.* 1375–85) and Manasija (1406–18) in Serbia and those of the Peribleptos (late fourteenth-century) and Pantanassa (1428–45) at Mistra. The political collapse of Byzantium prevented, however, either of these promising trends from further development on home ground. It was now in Russia that the Byzantine artistic heritage, transformed by a different intuition, was to bear its richest fruit, while in Venetian-occupied Crete it was blended with the Italian Renaissance and Mannerism.

The architecture of the Palaeologan period, though not as significant as the painting, has considerable charm of its own. Here the debt to the West is at times more noticeable. The Parigoritissa at Arta (*c.* 1290) has the appearance of an Italian palazzo and contains carved archivolts in a manner that is purely western. A number of secular buildings, such as the so-called Tekfur Saray at Istanbul (late thirteenth century), the palaces of Mistra and Trebizond, have the same cubic, multi-storeyed form, and the latter two have ogival windows. The majority of Palaeologan churches are, however, in a purely Byzantine tradition. They are distinguished by their tall silhouettes, by the breaking up of surface planes and by an extravagant use of exterior ornament: the Church of the Holy Apostles at Thessalonica (*c.* 1315) is a good example of this. In fact, the exteriors are rather more arresting than the interiors which, because of the added height, do not convey that impression of a unitary vaulted space – the celestial canopy of earlier Byzantine churches. Looking into the dome of a Palaeologan church is like looking into an inverted pit. And so the relation that had prevailed in earlier centuries between architecture and painted decoration has been finally disrupted: on the part of the architecture, because the ceiling and the upper parts of the walls are seen at too steep an angle; on the part of the painting, because each picture has become an entity in itself.

To conclude this rapid survey of Byzantine art, we may be allowed a few general reflections. Undoubtedly, our view of this art is very fragmentary and unbalanced. If more of its secular *oeuvre* had been preserved, we would surely have found greater variety and openness to influences from outside. We are told, for example, that the Emperor Theophilus was so enchanted with reports he had heard of the palaces of Baghdad that he strove to imitate them;[17] and that a hall in the Seljuq style, complete with stalactites and glazed tiles, was erected in the imperial palace in the mid-twelfth century.[18] And speaking of glazed tiles, it is only in the past forty or fifty years that their extensive use in Byzantine wall decoration has come to be acknowledged, though we still have some trouble in visualizing the intended effect. There was also much movement of imported objects, such as Islamic metalwork, silks and rock crystal, that certainly exerted some influence on Byzantine taste. In fact, in some of the minor arts, including textiles and pottery, it is often very difficult to distinguish Byzantine from other Near Eastern products.

Limited as we largely are to the conservative sphere of Byzantine religious art, and prejudiced as we are by our admiration for classical

Antiquity, we are apt to lay too much stress on the antique tradition. We have tried to suggest that just as Byzantine writers had no real comprehension of ancient Greek literature, so Byzantine artists had no interest in classical art of the pagan period, either Greek or Roman. What they knew of Antiquity filtered down to them through the canon of biblical and hagiographic illustration and they repeatedly reverted to early exemplars of it. In so doing, however, Byzantine artists of the Middle Ages could not help paraphrasing the models they imitated, and it is in this selective paraphrase that much of the beauty of Byzantine art resides. Whereas Early Christian art tended to be ostentatious and, if judged by classical standards, incompetent, Byzantine art infused into the old forms its distinctive spirituality and elegance. It forsook naturalism without falling into total abstraction and always retained a certain understanding of the draped human figure. It took over a tradition of bright polychromy and turned it into a palette of superb richness and harmony that was later inherited by the Venetians. To be sure, it was an art of clichés, but its primary function was to express a message that never varied: the timeless re-enactment of the Christian drama, the presence of the Heavenly Kingdom, the mediation of the saints. Within these limits it succeeded admirably.

APPENDIX. CHRONOLOGICAL LIST OF BYZANTINE EMPERORS

Constantine I (sole rule)	324–37	Justinian II (again)	705–11
Constantius II	337–61	Philippicus	711–13
Julian	361–3	Anastasius II	713–15
Jovian	363–4	Theodosius III	715–16
Valens	364–78	Leo III	716–40
Theodosius I	379–95	Constantine V	740–75
Arcadius	395–408	Leo IV	775–80
Theodosius II	408–50	Constantine VI	780–90
Marcian	450–7	Irene	790
Leo I	457–74	Constantine VI (again)	790–7
Leo II	474	Irene (again)	797–802
Zeno	474–5	Nicephorus I	802–11
Basiliscus	475–6	Stauracius	811
Zeno (again)	476–91	Michael I Rhangabe	811–13
Anastasius I	491–518	Leo V	813–20
Justin I	518–27	Michael II	820–9
Justinian I	527–65	Theophilus	829–42
Justin II	565–78	Michael III	842–67
Tiberius I Constantine	578–82	Basil I	867–86
Maurice	582–602	Leo VI	886–912
Phocas	602–10	Alexander	912–13
Heraclius	610–41	Constantine VII	913–59
Constantine III and Heraclonas	641	Romanus I Lecapenus	920–44
		Romanus II	959–63
Constans II	641–68	Nicephorus II Phocas	963–9
Constantine IV	668–85	John I Tzimiskes	969–76
Justinian II	685–95	Basil II	976–1025
Leontius	695–8	Constantine VIII	1025–8
Tiberius II	698–705	Romanus III Argyrus	1028–34
		Michael IV	1034–41

Michael V	1041–2	*At Nicaea*	
Zoe and Theodora	1042	Theodore I Lascaris	1204–22
Constantine IX		John III Ducas	
Monomachus	1042–55	Vatatzes	1222–54
Theodora (again)	1055–6	Theodore II Lascaris	1254–8
Michael VI	1056–7	John IV Lascaris	1258–61
Isaac I Comnenus	1057–9		
Constantine X Ducas	1059–67	Michael VIII	
Romanus IV Diogenes	1068–71	Palaeologus	1258–82
Michael VII Ducas	1071–8	Andronicus II	
Nicephorus III		Palaeologus	1282–1328
Botaneiates	1078–81	Andronicus III	
Alexius I Comnenus	1081–1118	Palaeologus	1328–41
John II Comnenus	1118–43	John V Palaeologus	1341–91
Manuel I Comnenus	1143–80	John VI Cantacuzenus	1347–55
Alexius II Comnenus	1180–3	Andronicus IV	
Andronicus I Comnenus	1183–5	Palaeologus	1376–9
Isaac II Angelus	1185–95	John VII Palaeologus	1390
Alexius III Angelus	1195–1203	Manuel II Palaeologus	1391–1425
Isaac II (again) and		John VIII Palaeologus	1425–48
Alexius IV Angelus	1203–04	Constantine XI	
Alexius V Murtzuphlus	1204	Palaeologus	1449–53

ABBREVIATIONS IN THE NOTES

AB	*Analecta Bollandiana*
BZ	*Byzantinische Zeitschrift*
Cod. Just.	*Codex Justinianus*, ed. P. Krueger = *Corpus iuris civilis*, ii (Berlin, 1929)
Cod. Theod.	*Codex Theodosianus*, ed. Th. Mommsen (Berlin, 1905). English trans. by C. Pharr, *The Theodosian Code* (Princeton, 1952)
CSHB	*Corpus scriptorum historiae byzantinae* (Bonn, 1828–97)
DOP	*Dumbarton Oaks Papers*
Joannou, *Discipline*	P.-P. Joannou, *Discipline générale antique (IVᵉ–IXᵉ s.)*, i/1, i/2 (Grottaferrata, 1962)
JRS	*Journal of Roman Studies*
Just. Nov.	*Justiniani Novellae*, ed. R. Schoell and W. Kroll = *Corpus iuris civilis*, iii (Berlin, 1928)
PG	*Patrologia graeca*, ed. J. P. Migne (Paris, 1857–66)
PL	*Patrologia latina*, ed. J. P. Migne (Paris, 1844–80)
PO	*Patrologia orientalis* (Paris, 1907–)
REB	*Revue des études byzantines*
ROC	*Revue de l'Orient chrétien*
TM	Centre de Recherche d'Histoire et Civilisation de Byzance, *Travaux et mémoires*
Zepos, *Jus*	J. and P. Zepos, *Jus graeco-romanum* (Athens, 1931)

NOTES

CHAPTER I PEOPLES AND LANGUAGES

1 Honigmann, E. (ed.), *Le Synekdèmos d'Hiéroklès et l'opuscule géographique de Georges de Chypre* (Brussels, 1939).
2 Ed. J. Rougé (Paris, 1966).
3 See Cosmas Indicopleustes, *Christian Topography*, Prologue, ed. W. Wolska-Conus, i (Paris, 1968), 255–7.
4 P. J. Alexander, *The Oracle of Baalbek* (Washington, D.C., 1967), 14.
5 Procopius, *Secret History*, xxiii. 24.
6 Gregorii I *Registrum epistularum*, vii. 27, *Monumenta Germaniae historica, Epist.*, i/1 (Berlin, 1887), 474.
7 P. Van den Ven (ed.), *La Vie ancienne de S. Syméon Stylite le jeune*, i (Brussels, 1962), ch. 189, p. 168.
8 H. Pétré (ed.), *Itinerarium Aetheriae*, xlvii. 3–4 (Paris, 1948), 260–2.
9 Jerome, *Adv. Rufinum*, ii. 22; iii. 6, *PL* xxiii, 446A, 462A.
10 L. Clugnet, 'Vie et récits de l'abbé Daniel de Scété,' *ROC*, v (1900), 71.
11 *Pratum spirituale*, *PG* lxxxvii/3, 2884, 2909, 2976, 3004, 3017. Cf. Evagrius, *Historia ecclesiastica*, ed. J. Bidez and L. Parmentier, i. 7 (London, 1898), 13.
12 Procopius, *Wars*, vi. 21. 39.
13 Procopius, *Secret History*, xviii, 13.
14 *Ibid.*, xviii, 20–1.
15 Procopius, *Buildings*, iv. 4. 3.
16 E. de Stoop (ed.), *Vie d'Alexandre l'Acémète*, §§27, 43, *PO* vi, 678, 692.
17 *Vita Theodosii Coenobiarchae*, ix, *PG* cxiv, 505C.
18 Antoninus of Piacenza, *Itinerarium*, ed. P. Geyer, *Itinera hierosolymitana* (Vienna, 1898), §37, p. 184.
19 E. Schwartz (ed.), *Acta Conciliorum Oecumenicorum*, iii (Berlin, 1940), 70, 146, etc.
20 E. Stein, 'Introduction à l'histoire et aux institutions byzantines,' *Traditio*, vii (1949–51), 154. For estimates of the population of Egypt, Syria and Asia Minor see A. C. Johnson, F. M. Heichelheim and T. R. S. Broughton, in T. Frank (ed.), *An Economic Survey of Ancient Rome*, ii (Baltimore, 1936), 245 ff.; iv (1938), 158, 815–16.

21 *The Third Part of the Ecclesiastical History of John Bishop of Ephesus*, trans. R. Payne Smith (Oxford, 1860), 432–3.

22 P. Lemerle, 'La chronique improprement dite de Monemvasie,' *REB*, xxi (1963), 9–10.

23 Theophanes, *Chronographia*, ed. C. de Boor (Leipzig, 1883), A.M. 6183, 365.

24 *Ibid.*, A.M. 6180, 6184, pp. 364–6.

25 Nicephorus Patriarcha, *Opuscula historica*, ed. C. de Boor (Leipzig, 1880), 68–9.

26 *Ibid.*, 66; Theophanes, *Chronographia*, A.M. 6237, 6247, 6270, pp. 422, 429, 452.

27 Leo VI, *Tactica*, *PG* cvii, 969A.

28 P. Lemerle, 'La chronique improprement dite', 10.

29 *Life of St Nikon Metanoeite*, ed. S. Lampros, *Neos Hellênomnêmon*, iii (Athens, 1906), 194.

30 Constantine Porphyrogenitus, *De Cerimoniis*, *CSHB*, i, 666, 669.

31 Anna Comnena, *Alexiad*, xv. 2. 4, ed. B. Leib, iii (Paris, 1945), 192.

32 Nicetas Choniates, *Historia*, ed. J.-L. van Dieten (Berlin, 1975), 16.

33 John Climacus, *Scala paradisi*, *PG* lxxxviii, 721.

34 Leo Grammaticus, *Chronographia*, *CSHB*, 307–8.

35 F. Dvorník (ed.), *La Vie de S. Grégoire le Décapolite* (Paris, 1926), 54.

CHAPTER 2   SOCIETY AND ECONOMY

1 Leontius of Neapolis, *Life of St Symeon the Fool*, ed. L. Rydén (Uppsala, 1963), 128.

2 Ibn Khordâdhbeh, *Bibliotheca geographorum arabicorum*, ed. M. J. de Goeje, vi (Leiden, 1889), 81; V. Minorsky, 'Marvazi on the Byzantines', *Annuaire de l'Inst. de Philol. et d'Histoire Orientales et Slaves*, x (1950), 460.

3 Cf. H. Ahrweiler, 'Un discours inédit de Constantin VII Porphyrogénète,' *TM*, ii (1967), 399.

4 H. Beckh (ed.), *Geoponica*, praef. 6 (Leipzig, 1895), 2.

5 Constantine VII, *Nov.* viii, praef. in Zepos, *Jus*, i, 222.

6 Leo VI, *Tactica*, *PG* cvii, 796A.

7 Anon., *On Strategy*, i–iii, *Griechische Kriegsschriftsteller*, ed. H. Köchly and W. Rüstow, ii/2 (Leipzig, 1855), 42ff.

8 Zosimus, *Historia nova*, ii. 34.

9 R. Keydell (ed.), *Historiae*, v. 13. 7 (Berlin, 1967), 180.

10 John Lydus, *De magistratibus*, ed. R. Wünsch (Leipzig, 1903), i. 28.

11 John of Ephesus, *Lives of the Eastern Saints*, ed. E. W. Brooks, *PO* xvii, 158–9.

12 John Chrysostom, *In Matth. hom.* lxvi, *PG* lviii, 630.

13 A.-J. Festugière (ed.), *Léontios de Néapolis: Vie de Syméon le Fou et Vie de Jean de Chypre* (Paris, 1974), 255ff.

14 *Just. Nov.*, xl, praef. 1.

15 A.-J. Festugière (ed.), *Life of St John the Almsgiver* (Paris, 1974), 378.

16 A.-J. Festugière (ed.), *Vie de Théodore de Sykéôn*, i (Brussels, 1970), ch. 78.

17 *Heraclii Nov.* in Zepos, *Jus*, i, 28–30.

18 *Just. Nov.*, iii. 1.

19 *The Sixth Book of the Select Letters of Severus Patriarch of Antioch*, trans. E. W. Brooks, ii/1 (London, 1903), i. 8 and 17, pp. 43, 64–5.

20 G. Pasquali (ed.), *Epist.* xxv (Berlin, 1925), 79.

21 John Moschus, *Pratum spirituale, PG* lxxxvii/3, 2998C.

22 A.-J. Festugière (ed.), *Life of St John the Almsgiver*, 387.

23 *The Syriac Chronicle Known as that of Zachariah of Mitylene*, trans. F. J. Hamilton and E. W. Brooks (London, 1899), vii. 6, p. 166.

24 A.-J. Festugière (ed.), *Life of St John the Almsgiver*, 392.

25 *Cod. Theod.*, xiv. 20.

26 *Chronicon Paschale, CSHB*, i, 593.

27 A.-J. Festugière (ed.), *Life of St John the Almsgiver*, 367.

28 John Moschus, *Pratum, PG* lxxxvii/3, 2980D.

29 Mark the Deacon, *Life of Porphyry*, ed. H. Grégoire and M.-A. Kugener (Paris, 1930), ch. 6, p. 6.

30 Procopius, *Secret History*, iv. 31.

31 John Lydus, *De magistratibus*, iii. 26–8.

32 *In Matth. hom.* lxvi, *PG* lviii, 630.

33 John Chrysostom, *De inani gloria et de educandis liberis*, ed. A.-M. Malingrey (Paris, 1972), §§13–15.

34 *Doctrina Jacobi nuper baptizati*, ed. N. Bonwetsch, *Abh. Kön. Ges. d. Wiss. Göttingen*, Phil.-hist. Klasse, Neue Folge, xii/3 (1910), 90.

35 John Chrysostom, *De inani gloria*, ed. A.-M. Malingrey, §70.

36 G. Tchalenko, *Villages antiques de la Syrie du nord* (Paris, 1953), i, 377ff.

37 *Cod. Just.*, xi. 52. 1.

38 *Ibid.*, xi. 48. 21.

39 Cecaumenus, *Strategicon*, ed. G. G. Litavrin, *Sovety i rasskazy Kekavmena* (Moscow, 1972), §20, p. 152.

40 Lectantius, *De mortibus persecutorum*, ed. J. Moreau, vii (Paris, 1954), 84ff.

41 N. Bonwetsch (ed.), *Doctrina Jacobi*, 90–1.

42 Gregory of Nyssa, *Contra Eunomium, PG* xlv, 260–1; Sozomen, *Historia ecclesiastica*, ed. J. Bidez and G. C. Hansen, iii. 15. 8 (Berlin, 1960), 126–7.

43 J. B. Bury, *The Imperial Administrative System in the Ninth Century* (London, 1911), 20.

44 Ed. W. Ashburner in *Journal of Hellenic Studies*, xxx (1910), 85–108; xxxii (1912), 68–95.

45 M.-H. Fourmy and M. Leroy, 'La Vie de S. Philarète,' *Byzantion*, ix (1934), 113.

46 Methodii *Vita S. Theophanis Confessoris*, ed. V. V. Latyšev, *Mémoires de*

287

l'Acad. des Sciences de Russie, VIIIᵉ, sér., Classe hist.-philol., xiii/4 (1918), 3ff.

47 Theophanes Continuatus, *CSHB*, 227–8, 316–21.

48 Can. 14 in Joannou, *Discipline*, i/1, 316.

49 J. Becker (ed.), *Legatio Constantinopolitana*, 3rd ed., lxiii (Hanover and Leipzig, 1915), 210–11.

50 *Vie de S. Luc le Stylite*, ed. F. Vanderstuyf, *PO* xi, 208.

51 Constantine Porphyrogenitus, *De administrando imperio*, ed. Gy. Moravcsik and R. J. H. Jenkins (Washington, D.C., 1967), ch. 22/79, p. 98.

52 Theophanes Continuatus, *CSHB*, 76.

53 Theophanes, *Chronographia*, ed. C. de Boor, A.M. 6211, p. 400.

54 Pseudo-Symeon, *Annales*, along with Theophanes Continuatus, 684; George the Monk, *ibid.*, 836.

55 Theophanes Continuatus, *CSHB*, 399.

56 Constantine Porphyrogenitus, *De thematibus*, ed. A. Pertusi (Vatican, 1952), 91.

57 N. G. Svoronos, 'Le cadastre de Thèbes,' *Bulletin de correspondance héllénique*, lxxxiii (1959), 74–5.

58 Michael Attaliates, *Historia*, *CSHB*, 218ff.

59 D. I. Polemis, *The Doukai* (London, 1968), 3.

60 J. Mavrogordato (ed.), *Digenes Akrites*, i. 265ff. (Oxford, 1956), 18.

61 Texts in Zepos, *Jus*, i, 198ff., 222ff., 240ff., 249ff., 262ff.

62 *Ibid.*, 256.

63 *Ibid.*, 215.

64 Nicetas Choniates, *Historia*, ed. J.-L. van Dieten, 208–9.

65 Cecaumenus, *Strategicon*, ed. G. G. Litavrin, §§4, 6, pp. 124–6, 130..

66 P. Lemerle, *Cinq études sur le XIᵉ siècle byzantin* (Paris, 1977), 49ff.

67 Anna Comnena, *Alexiad*, xii. 12. 1, ed. B. Leib, iii, 125.

68 *The Russian Primary Chronicle*, trans. S. H. Cross and O. P. Sherbowitz-Wetzor (Cambridge, Mass., 1953), 64ff.

69 J. Nicole (ed.), *Le Livre du Préfet* (Geneva, 1893); trans. by E. H. Freshfield, *Roman Law in the Later Roman Empire* (Cambridge, 1938). Both reprinted in I. Dujčev (ed.), *To eparchikon biblion* (London, 1970).

70 N. Oikonomides, 'Quelques boutiques de Constantinople au Xᵉ siècle,' *DOP*, xxvi (1972), 345ff.

71 Michael Psellus, *Chronographia*, ed. E. Renauld, i (Paris, 1926), 96, 102.

72 *Ibid.*, i, 132.

73 *Ibid.*, ii, 145.

74 Cecaumenus, *Strategicon*, ed. G. G. Litavrin, §3, p. 124.

CHAPTER 3   THE DISAPPEARANCE AND REVIVAL OF CITIES

1 *Expositio totius mundi*, xxvi, xxxv, xxxviii, xlix.

2 G. Garitte (ed.), *La prise de Jérusalem par les Perses* (Louvain, 1960), 50–3.

3 Procopius, *Buildings*, vi. 6. 14–16.

4 *Miracula S. Artemii*, ed. A. Papadopoulos-Kerameus, *Varia graeca sacra* (St Petersburg, 1909), 26.

5 John Chrysostom, *De inani gloria*, ed. A.-M. Malingrey, §4.

6 *De Lazaro*, ii, *PG* xlviii, 986; *De Lazaro*, vi, *PG* xlviii, 1034–5.

7 *In epist. I ad Thess.*, v, *PG* lxii, 428.

8 *In Matth. hom.*, xxxvii, *PG* lvii, 427.

9 *In Matth. hom.*, vi, *PG* lvii, 71–2.

10 *In illud, Salutate Priscillam, PG* li, 188.

11 Fr. 1, C. Müller (ed.), *Fragmenta historicorum graecorum*, iv (Paris, 1851), 201–2.

12 Ed. L. Rydén (Uppsala, 1963).

13 Priscus, fr. 8, *Fragmenta hist. graec.*, ed. C. Müller, iv, 78.

14 Procopius, *Buildings*, iv, 1, 31.

15 Theodoret, *Epist.*, ed. Y. Azéma (Paris, 1955), vii, xv, xxxiii (xxix), etc., pp. 79, 86, 98, etc.

16 *The Chronicle of Joshua the Stylite*, trans. W. Wright (Cambridge, 1882), 17–43.

17 Malalas, *Chronographia*, *CSHB*, 422.

18 Procopius, *Secret History*, vii.

19 A. Cameron, *Circus Factions* (Oxford, 1976).

20 Procopius, *Wars*, ii. 23. 1.

21 *Hist. eccles.*, iv. 29.

22 Procopius, *Wars*, ii. 22. 1.

23 Procopius, *Secret History*, xviii. 44.

24 *Ibid.*, xxiii. 19–21.

25 *Miracula S. Demetrii*, i. 10, *PG* cxvi, 1261ff.

26 Anna Comnena, *Alexiad*, xiv. 2–3, ed. B. Leib, iii, 178.

27 *Miracula S. Demetrii*, *PG* cxvi, 1337A.

28 Theophanes, *Chronographia*, ed. C. de Boor, A.M. 6180, p. 364.

30 F. Dvorník, *La Vie de S. Grégoire le Décapolite* (Paris, 1926), 59.

31 Ibn Khordâdhbeh, *Bibl. geogr. arab.*, ed. M. J. de Goeje, vi, 77–80.

32 Theophanes, *Chronographia*, A.M. 6287, p. 469.

33 H. Grégoire, 'Inscriptions historiques byzantines,' *Byzantion*, iv (1927–8), 438.

34 G. E. Bates, *Byzantine Coins*, Archaeological Exploration of Sardis, Monograph 1 (Cambridge, Mass., 1971), 6–7.

35 Ibn Khordâdhbeh, *Bibl. geogr. arab.*, ed. M. J. de Goeje, vi, 84.

36 *Epist.* 47 in J. Darrouzès, *Epistoliers byzantins du Xᵉ siècle* (Paris, 1960), 246.

37 K. Horna, 'Das Hodoiporikon des Konstantin Manasses,' *BZ*, xiii (1904), 339.

38 O. Seeck (ed.), *Notitia dignitatum* (Berlin, 1876), 229–43.

39 Procopius, *Secret History*, xxii. 17.

40 Nicephorus, *Opuscula historica*, ed. C. de Boor, 64.

41 Theophanes, *Chronographia*, A.M. 6238, p. 423.

42 *Miracula S. Artemii*, ed. A. Papadopoulos-Kerameus, *Varia graeca sacra*, 26.

43 Theophanes, *Chronographia*, A.M. 6232, p. 412.

44 *Ibid.*, A.M. 6247, p. 429.

45 *Ibid.*, A.M. 6258, p. 440.

46 Th. Preger (ed.), *Scriptores originum Constantinopolitanarum*, i (Leipzig, 1901), 19ff.

47 Theophanes Continuatus, *CSHB*, 321ff.

48 P. Lemerle, 'La chronique improprement dite de Monemvasie,' *REB*, xxi (1963), 10.

49 Theophanes Continuatus, *CSHB*, 339.

50 P. Noailles and A. Dain (eds.), *Les Novelles de Léon VI le Sage* (Paris, 1944), novel 4, novel 15, pp. 21ff., 59ff.

51 Ed. G. G. Litavrin, §§3, 39, 51, pp. 124, 202, 220.

52 D.-C. Hesseling and H. Pernot (eds.), *Poèmes prodromiques en grec vulgaire* (Amsterdam, 1910), 72ff.

53 G. Moravcsik, 'Barbarische Sprachreste in der Theogonie des Johannes Tzetzes,' *Byzantinisch-neugriechische Jahrbücher*, vii (1928–9), 352ff.; reprinted in same author's *Studia byzantina* (Budapest, 1967), 283ff.

54 Villehardouin, *La conquête de Constantinople*, ed. E. Faral, i (Paris, 1938), chs. 128, 192, pp. 131, 195.

55 *Embassy to Tamerlane*, trans. G. le Strange (London, 1928), 87ff.

CHAPTER 4 DISSENTERS

1 *Cod. Theod.*, xvi. 1. 2; *Cod. Just.*, i. 1. 1.

2 *Cod. Theod.*, xvi. 2. 16.

3 *Just. Nov.*, cxxxvii, praef.

4 *Confessio rectae fidei*, *PG* lxxxvi, 1013A. Cf. *Cod. Just.*, i. 1. 5.

5 *Cod. Theod.*, xvi. 5. 28.

6 Mark the Deacon, *Life of Porphyry*, ed. H. Grégoire and M.-A. Kugener, chs. 11, 19, pp. 11, 16.

7 See J. B. Segal, 'Pagan Syriac Monuments in the Vilayet of Urfa,' *Anatolian Studies*, iii (1953), 107–12.

8 John of Ephesus, *Lives of the Eastern Saints*, *PO* xviii, 681; Michael the Syrian, *Chronique*, ed. J.-B. Chabot, ii/2 (Paris, 1902), 207–8.

9 *Lives of the Eastern Saints*, *PO* xvii, 229ff.

10 See, for example, Callinicus, *Life of St Hypatius*, ed. G. J. M. Bartelink (Paris, 1971), 74, 80.

11 So, for example, J. C. Lawson, *Modern Greek Folklore and Ancient Greek Religion* (Cambridge, 1910).

12 Trullan Council, can. 61, 62, 65 in Joannou, *Discipline*, i/1, 196ff., 203.

13 *Just. Nov.*, xlv, praef. The earlier legislation may be found in *Cod. Theod.*, xvi. 8.

14 *Just. Nov.*, cxlvi.

15 Malalas, *Chronographia*, *CSHB*, 433; *The Chronicle of John, Bishop of Nikiu*, trans. R. H. Charles (London–Oxford, 1916), 142.

16 On these events see I. Shahîd, *The Martyrs of Najrân* (Brussels, 1971).

17 Sebeos, *Histoire d'Héraclius*, trans. F. Macler (Paris, 1904), 63.

18 G. Garitte (ed.), *La prise de Jérusalem*, 17–18.

19 'S. Georgii Chozebitae Vita,' *AB*, vii (1888), 134.

20 F. Dölger, *Regesten der Kaiserurkunden des oströmischen Reiches*, i (Munich–Berlin, 1924), no. 206.

21 Theophanes *Chronographia*, ed. C. de Boor, A.M. 6214, p. 401; Michael the Syrian, *Chronique*, trans. J.-B. Chabot, ii/3, 489–90.

22 Can. 8 in Joannou, *Discipline*, i/1, 261–3.

23 Theophanes Continuatus, *CSHB*, 341–2.

24 *The Itinerary of Benjamin of Tudela*, trans. M. N. Adler (London, 1907), 10ff.

25 *De haeresibus*, *PG* xciv, 677ff.

26 *Cod. Theod.*, xvi. 5. 9.

27 A. Adam, *Texte zum Manichäismus* (Berlin, 1954), no. 56.

28 Procopius, *Secret History*, xxii. 25.

29 Theophanes, *Chronographia*, ed. C. de Boor, A.M. 6214, p. 401.

30 *The Homilies of Photius*, trans. C. Mango (Cambridge, Mass., 1958), 279ff.

31 *Hist. eccles.*, ed. J. Bidez and L. Parmentier, ii. 5, p. 53.

32 *Ibid.*, iii. 14, pp. 111ff.

33 Michael the Syrian, *Chronique*, trans. J.-B. Chabot, ii/3, 412–13.

34 Constantine Porphyrogenitus, *De administrando imperio*, ed. Gy. Moravcsik and R. J. H. Jenkins, ch. 50, p. 237.

35 Theophanes, *Chronographia*, ed. C. de Boor, A.M. 6270, p. 452.

36 *Vita S. Pancratii*, ed. A. N. Veselovskij, 'Iz istorii romana i povesti,' *Sbornik Otdel. Russk. Jazyka i Slov. Imper. Akad. Nauk*, xl/2 (1886), 90.

37 Theophanes, *Chronographia*, A.M. 6275, pp. 456–7.

38 *The Homilies of Photius*, trans. C. Mango, 302ff.

39 *Nov.* 15, ed. P. Noailles and A. Dain, 59–61.

40 Peter the Sicilian, ed. Ch. Astruc *et al.*, in 'Les sources grecques pour l'histoire des Pauliciens d'Asie Mineure,' *TM*, iv (1970), 59, §157.

41 J. Darrouzès, *Epistoliers byzantins du Xe siècle*, 275.

42 *Le Traité contre les Bogomiles de Cosmas le Prêtre*, trans. H.-Ch. Puech and A. Vaillant (Paris, 1945), 85–6.

43 *Ibid.*, 93–4.
44 J. Gouillard, 'Le Synodicon de l'Orthodoxie,' *TM*, ii (1967), 183ff.
45 Anna Comnena, *Alexiad*, xiv. 8, ed. B. Leib, iii, 177ff.
46 Procopius, *Secret History*, xi. 26.
47 Nicephorus, *Antirrheticus* iii, *PG* c, 501B.
48 Peter the Sicilian, ed. Ch. Astruc *et al.*, in 'Les sources grecques', 53, §139.
49 *Confessio rectae fidei, PG* lxxxvi, 993C.
50 Theodore Studite, *Epist.*, ii. 155, *PG* xcix, 1481–5.

CHAPTER 5   MONASTICISM

1 *Vita S. Antonii*, chs. 3–4, *PG* xxvi, 844–5.
2 See, for example, *The Oxyrhynchus Papyri*, ii (London, 1899), nos. 251–3.
3 *Vita S. Antonii*, ch. 14, col. 865.
4 A. Boon, *Pachomiana latina* (Louvain, 1932), 3ff.
5 *Praecepta*, §49, *ibid.*, p. 25.
6 J. B. Pitra, *Iuris ecclesiastici graecorum historia et monumenta*, i (Rome, 1864), 487ff.
7 *Epistula Ammonis*, in F. Halkin (ed.), *S. Pachomii vitae graecae* (Brussels, 1932), §2, p. 97.
8 *The Longer Rule, PG* xxxi, 925C.
9 *PG* xxxi, 905ff.
10 H. Delehaye, *Les saints stylites* (Brussels, 1923), 1–94.
11 *Cod. Theod.*, xvi, 3. 1 and 2.
12 John Chrysostom, *Adv. oppugnatores vitae monast.*, *PG* xlvii, 320–2.
13 A.-J. Festugière (ed.), *Vie de Théodore de Sykéôn* (2 vols., Brussels, 1970).
14 See his Life, ed. L. Rydén; Evagrius, *Hist. eccles.*, ed. J. Bidez and L. Parmentier, iv. 34.
15 *Just. Nov.*, v.
16 Text (unsatisfactory) in *PG* lxxxvii/3, 2852ff. French trans. by M.-J. Rouet de Journel, *Le Pré Spirituel* (Paris, 1946).
17 Ed. E. W. Brooks, *PO* xvii, xix.
18 Theophanes, *Chronographia*, ed. C. de Boor, A.M. 6262, p. 445.
19 See especially his *Testamentum*, *PG* xcix, 1817ff.
20 *Hypotypôsis*, §25, *ibid.*, 1713A.
21 Zepos, *Jus*, i, 213.
22 *Ibid.*, 249ff.
23 *Ibid.*, 267–9.
24 See especially John of Antioch, *De monasteriis laicis non tradendis*, *PG* cxxxii, 1117ff.
25 See P. Lemerle *et al.* (eds.), *Archives de l'Athos* (founded by G. Millet) (Paris, 1937–).

26 See especially the *Treatise on Confession* in K. Holl, *Enthusiasmus und Buss-gewalt beim griechischen Mönchtum* (Leipzig, 1898), 110ff.

27 *De emendanda vita monastica* in T. L. F. Tafel, *Eustathii opuscula* (Frankfurt, 1832; reprinted Amsterdam, 1964), 215ff.

28 I. P. Tsiknopoullos (ed.), *Kypriaka typika* (Nicosia, 1969), 1ff.

29 Neophytus, *Typicon, ibid.*, 69ff. For a discussion of his life see C. Mango and E. J. W. Hawkins, 'The Hermitage of St. Neophytos and its Wall Paintings,' *DOP*, xx (1966), 122ff.

30 *Hagioreitikos tomos* in P. Chrêstou *et al.* (eds.), *Grêgoriou tou Palama syngramata*, ii (Thessaloniki, 1966), 568–9.

31 J. Lefort (ed.), *Actes d'Esphigménou = Archives de l'Athos*, vi (Paris, 1973), no. 12, pp. 89–90.

32 See N. Oikonomidès, 'Monastères et moines, lors de la conquête ottomane', *Südost-Forschungen*, xxxv (1976), 1ff.

CHAPTER 6   EDUCATION

1 H. Rabe (ed.), *Hermogenis opera* (Leipzig, 1913), 1ff.

2 See L. Petit, *Les étudiants de Libanius* (Paris, 1957).

3 *Ibid.*, 170.

4 'Oration of Constantius' (355 AD), in Themistius, *Orationes*, ed. G. Downey and A. F. Norman, 20d–21a, vol. iii (Leipzig, 1974), 125. English trans. in G. Downey, 'Education and Public Problems as Seen by Themistius,' *Trans. Amer. Philol. Assoc.*, lxxxvi (1955), 295.

5 *Cod. Theod.*, xiv. 9. 3 = *Cod. Just.*, xi. 19. 1.

6 *Cod. Theod.*, xv. 1. 53; vi. 21. 1.

7 *Const. apost.*, i. 6, ed. F. X. Funk, *Didascalia et Constitutiones apostolorum* (Paderborn, 1905), 13–15.

8 *Vita S. Antonii*, chs. 20, 73, *PG* xxvi, 873, 945.

9 C. A. Trypanis (ed.), *Fourteen Early Byzantine Cantica* (Vienna, 1968), strophe 17, pp. 36–7.

10 Socrates, *Hist. eccles.*, iii. 16. Cf. Sozomen, *Hist. eccles.*, v. 18.

11 John Chrysostom, ed. A.-M. Malingrey, *De inani gloria*, §§39, 52.

12 N. G. Wilson (ed.), *On the Value of Greek Literature* (London, 1975).

13 M.-A. Kugener (ed.), *PO* ii, 7ff.

14 *Cod. Just.*, i. 5. 18. 4. Cf. i. 11. 10. 2.

15 F. Nau, 'L'Histoire ecclésiastique de Jean d'Asie,' *ROC*, ii (1897), 481–2.

16 Malalas, *Chronographia, CSHB*, 491.

17 Procopius, *Secret History*, xxvi. 5.

18 T. Gaisford (ed.), *Georgii Choerobosci dictata*, iii (Oxford, 1842).

19 See W. Bühler and C. Theodoridis, 'Johannes von Damaskos *terminus post quem* für Choiroboskos,' *BZ*, lxix (1976), 397ff.

20 Can. 71 in Joannou, *Discipline*, i/1, 208–9.

21 Zachariä von Lingenthal (ed.), *Collectio librorum juris graeco-romani ineditorum* (Leipzig, 1852), 11.

22 Theophanes, *Chronographia*, ed. C. de Boor, A.M. 6218, p. 405.

23 H. Berbérian, 'Autobiographie d'Anania Širakaci,' *Revue des études arméniennes*, N.S., i (1964), 189–94.

24 *Vita Tarasii*, ed. I. A. Heikel, *Acta Societatis Scientiarum Fennicae*, xvii (Helsingfors, 1899), 423.

25 *Scriptor incertus de Leone*, along with Leo Grammaticus, *CSHB*, 350.

26 Theophanes Continuatus, *CSHB*, 185ff.

27 Genesius, *CSHB*, 98.

28 *Anthol. Palatina*, xv. 36–8. Cf. R. Aubreton, 'La translittération d'Homère,' *Byzantion*, xxxix (1969), 13–34.

29 P. Matranga, *Anecdota graeca* (Rome, 1850), 555–6.

30 Theophanes Continuatus, *CSHB*, 446.

31 R. Browning, 'The Correspondence of a Tenth-Century Byzantine Scholar,' *Byzantion*, xxiv (1954), 397–452; R. Browning and B. Laourdas, 'To keimenon tôn epistolôn tou kôdikos B.M. 36749,' *Epetêris Hetairias Byzantinôn Spoudôn*, xxvii (1957), 151–212.

32 See P. Lemerle, 'La Vie ancienne de S. Athanase l'Athonite,' *Le Millénaire du Mont Athos, 963–1963*, i (Chevetogne, 1963), 59ff.

33 See novel of Constantine ix, *Iohannis Euchaitorum metropolitae quae ... supersunt*, ed. J. Bollig and P. de Lagarde (Göttingen, 1882), no. 187, pp. 195–202; A. Salač (ed.), *Novella constitutio saec. XI medii* (Prague, 1954).

34 Psellus, *Chronographia*, ed. E. Renauld, i, 135–8.

35 F. I. Uspenskij, 'Deloproizvodstvo po obvineniju Ioanna Itala v eresi,' *Izvestija Russk. Arkheol. Instit. v Konstantinopole*, ii (1897), 1–66.

36 J. Gouillard, 'Le Synodikon de l'Orthodoxie,' *TM*, ii (1967), 57–61.

37 Anna Comnena, *Alexiad*, v, 8, ed. B. Leib, ii, 32ff.

38 Pseudo-Lucian, *Timarion*, ed. R. Romano, §43–4 (Naples, 1974), 88–9.

39 J. Darrouzès, *Recherches sur les 'offikia' de l'Eglise byzantine* (Paris, 1970), 71ff.

40 R. Browning, 'A New Source on Byzantine–Hungarian Relations in the Twelfth Century,' *Balkan Studies*, ii (Thessaloniki, 1961), 173–214.

41 A. Pignani, 'Alcuni progimnasmi di Niceforo Basilace', *Rivista di studi bizantini e neoellenici*, N.S., viii/ix (1971/2), 295–315.

42 P. Lemerle, 'Elèves et professeurs à Constantinople au Xᵉ siècle,' Acad. des Inscr. et Belles-Lettres, Lecture faite dans la séance ... du 28 Nov. 1969, p. 11.

43 *Reg. brev.*, question 292, *PG* xxxi, 1288.

CHAPTER 7   THE INVISIBLE WORLD OF GOOD AND EVIL

1 *Synaxarium ecclesiae Constantinopolitanae*, ed. H. Delehaye, *Propylaeum ad Acta Sanctorum Novembris* (Brussels, 1902), 107ff.

2 *Iohannis Euchaitorum ... quae ... supersunt*, ed. J. Bollig and P. de Lagarde, p. 31.

3 Can. 35 in Joannou, *Discipline*, i/2, 144–5.

4 *Interpret. epist. ad Coloss.*, *PG* lxxxii, 613.

5 So, for example, Pseudo-Caesarius, i. 48, *PG* xxxviii, 917.

6 Th. Preger (ed.), *Scriptores originum Constantinopolitanarum*, i (Leipzig, 1901), 86.

7 *PG* cxi, 692.

8 Pantoleon diaconus, *Miracula S. Michaelis*, in F. Halkin (ed.), *Inédits byzantins d'Ochrida, Candie et Moscou* (Brussels, 1963), 150.

9 See C. Walter, 'Two Notes on the Deesis,' *REB*, xxvi (1968), 311–36.

10 See N. H. Baynes, 'The Supernatural Defenders of Constantinople,' *AB*, lxvii (1949), 165ff.; reprinted in *Byzantine Studies and Other Essays* (London, 1955), 248ff.

11 See J. Ebersolt, *Sanctuaires de Byzance* (Paris, 1921), 54ff.

12 See N. H. Baynes, 'The Finding of the Virgin's Robe', *Annuaire de l'Inst. de Philol. et d'Hist. Orient. et Slaves*, ix (1949), 87ff.; reprinted in *Byzantine Studies*, 240ff.

13 G. Anrich, *Hagios Nikolaos* (2 vols., Leipzig, 1913–17).

14 See H. Delehaye, *Les légendes grecques des saints militaires* (Brussels, 1909), 103ff.; id., *Les origines du culte des martyrs* (Brussels, 1933), 228–9; P. Lemerle, 'Saint-Démétrius de Thessalonique', *Bulletin de correspondance héllénique*, lxxvii (1953), 660ff.; M. Vickers, 'Sirmium or Thessaloniki?', *BZ*, lxvii (1974), 337ff.

15 *PG* lxxxvii/3, ch. 180, col. 3052.

16 *Vita S. Basilii iunioris*, ed. S. G. Vilinskij, *Zapiski Imp. Novorossijskago Universiteta*, vii (Odessa, 1911), 318ff.

17 *Miracula S. Artemii*, ed. A. Papadopoulos-Kerameus, *Varia graeca sacra*, 19, 29.

18 See E. Peterson, 'Zur Bedeutungsgeschichte von *parrêsia*', *R. Seeberg Festschrift*, i (Leipzig, 1929), 283ff.; G. J. M. Bartelink, 'Quelques observations sur *parrêsia* dans la littérature paléo-chrétienne', *Graecitas et latinitas christianorum primaeva*, suppl. 3 (Nijmegen, 1970), 5ff., 155ff.

19 *Vita S. Basilii iunioris*, ed. S. G. Vilinskij, *Zapiski Imp. Nov. Univ.*, vii, 344–5.

20 J. Goar, *Euchologion sive rituale graecorum* (Paris, 1647), 730–1.

21 Anrich, *Hagios Nikolaos*, i, 12ff.

22 A.-J. Festugière (ed.), *Vie de Théodore de Sykéôn*, i, §8, 16, 26a, 43.

23 *Ibid.*, §44 (cf. 114–16), 118, 161.

24 *Vita S. Andreae sali*, §90, *PG* cxi, 732.

25 *Vita S. Basilii iunioris*, ed. A. N. Veselovskij, *Sbornik Otdelenija Russkago Jazyka i Slov. Imp. Akad. Nauk*, liii (1891), suppl., 7.

26 *Vita S. Antonii*, §9, 28, *PG* xxvi, 857, 888.

27 *Ibid.*, §65, *PG* xxvi, 935.

28 *Life of St Symeon the Fool*, ed. L. Rydén, 141. Cf. A.-J. Festugière (ed.), *Life of St John the Almsgiver*, 395–6 and notes, 613–17.

29 *Vita S. Basilii iunioris*, ed. A. N. Veselovskij, *Sbornik Otdelenija Russkago Jazyka i Slov. Imp. Akad. Nauk.*, xlvi (1889), suppl., 19ff.

30 Pseudo-Macarius Alexandrinus, *De sorte animarum*, PG xxxiv, 388ff.

31 L. Petit, X. A. Sideridès and M. Jugie (eds.), *Oeuvres complètes de Georges Scholarios*, i (Paris, 1928), 505ff. Cf. Symeon of Thessalonica, *Responsa ad Gabrielem Pentapolitanum*, PG clv, 841ff.

CHAPTER 8   THE PHYSICAL UNIVERSE

1 See Philostorgius, *Historia ecclesiastica*, iii. 9–10.

2 R. Arnaldez (ed.), *De opificio mundi* (Paris, 1961), §15–16, 29, 45–6, 56, 58.

3 *Ad Autolycum*, ii. 13ff.

4 Ed. S. Giet (Paris, 1950).

5 This mistaken view may be traced back to Aristotle, *Meteorologica*, 352b.

6 *Bibliotheca*, cod. 223, ed. R. Henry, iv (Paris, 1965), especially pp. 42–3.

7 PG lvi, 429ff.

8 PG xxxviii, 852ff. Cf. R. Riedinger, *Pseudo-Kaisarios* (Munich, 1969).

9 Ed. W. Wolska-Conus (3 vols., Paris, 1968–73); trans. J. W. McCrindle, *The Christian Topography of Cosmas, an Egyptian Monk* (London, 1897). See also W. Wolska-Conus, *La Topographie Chrétienne de Cosmas Indicopleustès* (Paris, 1962).

10 Ed. W. Wolska-Conus, i, 255–7; trans. J. W. McCrindle, 2.

11 *Bibliotheca*, cod. 36, ed. R. Henry, i (Paris, 1959), 21–2.

12 See E. K. Redin, *Khristianskaja Topografija Koz'my Indikoplova po grečeskim i russkim spiskam*, i (Moscow, 1916).

13 The connection between Cosmas Indicopleustes and the Byzantine iconography of the Last Judgement is discussed by D. V. Ainalov, *The Hellenistic Origins of Byzantine Art*, trans. E. and S. Sobolevitch (New Brunswick, N.J., 1961), 33ff.

14 See A. Grabar, 'Le témoignage d'une hymne syriaque sur l'architecture de la cathédrale d'Edesse', *Cahiers archéologiques*, ii (1947), 54ff.

15 Ed. L. G. Westerink (Nijmegen, 1948), §120ff.

CHAPTER 9   THE INHABITANTS OF THE EARTH

1 Basil, *Homil.* viii in S. Giet (ed.), *Hexaemeron*, 440; Severianus of Gabala, *De mundi creatione orat.* iv, PG lvi, 458.

2 Basil, *ibid.*, 431ff.

3 Severianus, *De mundi creatione orat.* v, PG lvi, 481.

4 *Id.*, *Orat.* vi, *ibid.*, 484.

5 Basil, *Homil.* vii in S. Giet (ed.), *Hexaemeron*, 402ff.

6 *Id., Homil.* viii in S. Giet (ed.), *Hexaemeron*, 446ff.

7 Ed. F. Sbordone (Milan, 1936), §1, 4, etc.

8 *Hist. eccles.*, iii. 11.

9 W. Wolska-Conus (ed.), *Christian Topography*, iii, 315ff.

10 John Damascene, *De draconibus, PG* xciv, 1600.

11 Cecaumenus, *Strategicon*, ed. G. G. Litavrin, *Sov. i rassk. Kekavmena*, 678.

12 J. Bidez, *Deux versions grecques inédites de la Vie de Paul de Thèbes*, Recueil de travaux publiés par la Fac. de Philos. et Lettres de Gand, fasc. 25 (1900), 12ff.

13 Moschus, *Pratum spirituale*, ch. 184, *PG* lxxxvii/3, 3056.

14 *Acta Sanctorum*, July, iii (1723), 605–6.

15 *Pratum spirituale*, ch. 107, *PG* lxxxvii/3, 2965ff.

16 Photius, *Bibliotheca*, cod. 223.

17 *PG* xxxviii, 980ff.

18 *Antiquitates judaicae*, i. 5–6.

19 Fullest version in *Chronicon Paschale, CSHB*, i, 46ff. See also Epiphanius, *Adversus haereses, PG* xlii, 160; *id., Ancoratus*, §113, *PG* xliii, 220ff.; W. Wolska-Conus (ed.), *Topographie Chrétienne*, i, 329ff.; Georgius Syncellus, *CSHB*, i, 82ff. Cf. A. von Gutschmid, *Kleine Schriften*, v (Leipzig, 1894), 240ff., 585ff.

20 *Expositio totius mundi*, ed. J. Rougé, 110ff. A similar Greek text is A. Klotz (ed.), 'Hodoiporia apo Edem tou Paradeisou achri tôn Rhomaiôn', *Rheinisches Museum für Philologie*, lxv (1910), 606ff. For the Georgian version see Z. Avalichvili, 'Géographie et légende dans un récit apocryphe de S. Basile', *ROC*, xxvi (1927–8), 279ff.

21 W. Wolska-Conus (ed.), *Topographie Chrétienne*, ii, 133ff.; Georgius Syncellus, *CSHB*, i, 94.

22 Anastasius Sinaita, *Quaestiones, PG* lxxxix, 764.

23 *Ibid.*, 708.

24 R. À. Lipsius and M. Bonnet (eds.), *Acta apostolorum apocrypha*, ii/1 (Leipzig, 1898), 46–7, 65; ii/2 (1903), 37, 100.

25 See F. Dvornik, *The Idea of Apostolicity in Byzantium and the Legend of the Apostle Andrew* (Cambridge, Mass., 1958), 138ff.

26 Sozomen, *Hist. eccles.*, ed. J. Bidez and L. Parmentier, ii. 6–14. On this topic see W. H. C. Frend, 'The Missions of the Early Church, 180–700 AD', *Religion Popular and Unpopular* (London, 1976), viii.

27 *The Syriac Chronicle known as that of Zachariah of Mitylene*, trans. F. J. Hamilton and E. W. Brooks (London, 1899), xii, 7, p. 329ff.

28 Ed. W. Wolska-Conus, i, 503ff.

29 *Syriac Chronicle of Zachariah of Mitylene*, trans. F. J. Hamilton and E. W. Brooks, xii, 7, pp. 331–2.

30 Anastasius Sinaita, *Quaestiones, PG* lxxxix, 484.

31 *Ibid.*, 521, 732–3.

32 *The Homilies of Photius*, trans. C. Mango (Cambridge, Mass., 1958), 107.

33 Manuel II Palaeologus, *Dialoge mit einem 'Perser'*, ed. E. Trapp (Vienna, 1966), 55ff.

CHAPTER 10   THE PAST OF MANKIND

1 *Pratum spirituale*, ch. 87, *PG* lxxxvii/3, 2944–5.

2 On the end of consular dating see E. Stein, 'Post-consulat et *autokratoreia*', *Mélanges Bidez* (Brussels, 1933–4), 869ff.

3 See especially his *Contra Apionem*.

4 *Ad Autolycum*, iii. 24ff.

5 On this subject see V. Grumel, *La chronologie*, Traité d'études byzantines, ed. P. Lemerle, i (Paris, 1958).

6 What follows has been culled from several chronicles, in particular those of Malalas, Syncellus and Georgius Monachus.

7 Georgius Monachus, ed. C. de Boor, 78–9, 224ff. Cf. Eusebius, *Demonstratio evangelica*, iv. 8. 1.

8 K. Buresch, *Klaros. Untersuchungen zum Orakelwesen des späteren Altertums* (Leipzig, 1889), 111–12.

CHAPTER 11   THE FUTURE OF MANKIND

1 P. J. Alexander, *The Oracle of Baalbek* (Washington, D.C., 1967), 14, 25, 53–5.

2 F. Macler, 'Les apocalypses apocryphes de Daniel', *Rev. de l'histoire des religions*, xxxiii (1896), 288ff.

3 Malalas, *Chronographia*, *CSHB*, 408–9; *Chronicon Paschale*, *CSHB*, i, 610–11; John Moschus, *Pratum spirituale*, ch. 38, *PG* lxxxvii/3, 2888–9.

4 viii. 13; xii. 19–32. Cf. B. Rubin, 'Der Fürst der Dämonen', *BZ*, xliv (1951), 469ff.; *id.*, 'Der Antichrist und die "Apocalypse" des Prokopios von Kaisareia', *Zeitschr. der Deutschen Morgenländischen Gesellschaft*, cx (1961), 55ff.

5 Agathias, *Historiae*, v. 5, ed. R. Keydell, 169–70.

6 Theophylactus Simocatta, *Historiae*, ed. C. de Boor, i. 2 (reprinted Stuttgart, 1972), 43.

7 *Ibid.*, v. 15, pp. 216–17.

8 Theophanes, *Chronographia*, ed. C. de Boor, A.M. 6119, pp. 327–8.

9 *Ibid.*, A.M. 6127, p. 339.

10 The Greek text is V. M. Istrin (ed.), *Otkrovenie Mefodija Patarskago i apokrifičeskija Videnija Daniila* (Moscow, 1897), Texts, 5ff. The Latin version is E. Sackur (ed.), *Sibyllinische Texte und Forschungen* (Halle, 1898), 57ff. Cf. M. Kmosko, 'Das Rätsel des Pseudomethodius', *Byzantion*, vi (1931), 273ff.

11 Theophanes, *Chronographia*, A.M. 6169, p. 356.

12 H. Usener, 'De Stephano Alexandrino', *Kleine Schriften*, iv (reprinted Osnabrück, 1965), 276.

13 First Vision of Daniel, ed. A. Vassiliev, *Anecdota graeco-byzantina* (Moscow, 1893), 33ff.

14 *PG* cxi, 852ff.; L. Rydén, 'The Andreas Salos Apocalypse', *DOP*, xxviii (1974), 197ff.

15 Leo Diaconus, *Historia*, *CSHB*, 4.

16 L. G. Westerink, 'Nicetas the Paphlagonian on the End of the World', *Essays in Memory of B. Laourdas* (Thessaloniki, 1975), 177ff.

17 Th. Preger (ed.), *Scriptores originum Constantinopolitanarum*, ii (Leipzig, 1907), §47. Cf. §§50, 73, 79.

18 John Tzetzes, *Epistulae*, ed. P. A. M. Leone (Leipzig, 1972), 88; *id.*, *Historiae*, ed. P. A. M. Leone (Naples, 1968), 370–1.

19 *PG* cvii, 1129ff. Cf. C. Mango, 'The Legend of Leo the Wise', *Zbornik radova Vizantološkog Instituta*, vi (Belgrade, 1960), 59ff.

20 Nicetas Choniates, *Historia*, ed. J.-L. Van Dieten (Berlin, 1975), 355.

21 V. M. Istrin (ed.), *Otkrovenie Mefodija Patarskago*, 135ff. Cf. A. Vassiliev (ed.), *Anecdota graeco-byzantina*, 43ff.

22 L. Petit, X. A. Sideridès and M. Jugie (eds.), *Oeuvres complètes de Georges Scholarios*, iv (1935), 511–12. Cf. i (1928), 211; iii (1930), 94, 288, 383, etc.

23 J. Darrouzès, 'Lettres de 1453', *REB*, xxii (1964), 91.

24 *Vita S. Basilii iunioris*, ed. Veselovskij, *Sbornik Otdelenija Russkago Jazyka i Slov. Imp. Akad. Nauk.*, xlvi, suppl., 12ff.

CHAPTER 12   THE IDEAL LIFE

1 John Chrysostom, *De virginitate*, §83, *PG* xlviii, 594.

2 J. Nicole (ed.), *Book of the Prefect*, Proem (Geneva, 1893), 13.

3 Eusebius, *Praeparatio evangelica*, i. 4. 3ff.

4 Anastasius Sinaita, *Quaestiones*, *PG* lxxxix, 476.

5 John Chrysostom, *De inani gloria*, ed. A.-M. Malingrey, §67.

6 Theodore the Studite, *Parva catechesis*, ed. E. Auvray (Paris, 1891), 16.

7 Agapetus, *Capita admonitoria*, *PG* lxxxvi/1, 1164ff.

8 *Cod. Theod.*, xv. 1. 47.

9 Constantine Porphyrogenitus, *De Cerimoniis*, Proem, ed. A. Vogt, i (Paris, 1935), 1–2.

10 *Epanagoge*, tit. *3* in Zepos, *Jus*, ii, 242.

11 P. Noailles and A. Dain (eds.), *Les Novelles de Léon VI le Sage*, novel 17, 63ff.

12 See the quotations collected by John Damascene, *Sacra Parallela*, ed. M. Lequien, alpha, tit. 21 (Paris, 1712), ii, 358–9.

13 Antiochus monachus, *Pandectes*, ch. 37, *PG* lxxxix, 1549.

14 John Damascene, *Sacra Parallela*, ed. M. Lequien, epsilon, tits. 17–18, ii, 509ff.; *Parallela Rupefucaldina*, *ibid.*, 779ff.

15 *Ibid.*, delta, tit. 18–19, p. 440ff.

16 *Ibid.*, delta, tit. 11, p. 435.

17 *Ibid.*, iota, tit. 5, p. 557.

18 *Ibid.*, sigma, tit. 15, p. 688.

19 *Ibid.*, gamma, tit. 5, p. 405.

20 *Ibid.*, delta, tit. 9, p. 430ff.

21 Diodorus of Tarsus quoted by Photius, *Bibliotheca*, cod. 223, ed. R. Henry, iv, 34.

22 John Chrysostom, *De inani gloria*, ed. A.-M. Malingrey, §70.

23 *Capita admonitoria*, §16, *PG* lxxxvi/1, 1169.

24 John Chrysostom, *In inscriptionem altaris*, §2, *PG* li, 69.

25 John Chrysostom, *In epist. 1 ad Timoth. hom.* xii, *PG* lxii, 562–3.

26 Anastasius, *On the Departed*, in C. A. Trypanis (ed.), *Fourteen Early Byzantine Cantica* (Vienna, 1968), 63.

27 John Damascene, *Sacra Parallela*, ed. M. Lequien, mu, tit. 10, ii, 609ff.

28 John Chrysostom, *De inani gloria*, ed. A.-M. Malingrey, §23ff.

29 John Chrysostom, *In epist. 1 ad Timoth. hom.* iv, *PG* lxii, 524.

30 Antiochus, *Pandectes*, ch. 4, *PG* lxxxix, 1444.

31 *Ibid.*, ch. 95, col. 1721. See discussion in I. Hausherr, *Penthos*, Orientalia Christiana Analecta, 132 (Rome, 1944), 109ff.

32 Theodoret, *Historia religiosa*, ed. P. Canivet and A. Leroy-Molinghen, ii. 14, vol. i (Paris, 1977), 224–6.

33 Antiochus, *Pandectes*, ch. 17, *PG* lxxxix, 1480.

34 Moschus, *Pratum spirituale*, ch. 78, *PG* lxxxvii/3, 2933.

35 John Chrysostom, *Contra eos qui subintroductas habent*, §5, *PG* xlvii, 502.

36 Eusebius, *Demonstratio evangelica*, i. 9. 1–4.

37 John Chrysostom, *In epist. 1 ad Thess. hom.* v, *PG* lxii, 426; John Chrysostom, *De inani gloria*, ed. A.-M. Malingrey, §81.

38 John Chrysostom, *De virginitate*, §5, *PG* xlviii, 537.

39 John Damascene, *Sacra Parallela*, ed. M. Lequien, pi, tit. 31, ii, 670–1.

40 John Chrysostom, *In Matth. hom.* xxxvii, *PG* lvii, 426.

41 John Chrysostom, *In Kalendas*, *PG* xlviii, 954, 960.

42 Jerome, *Epist.* lviii, *PL* xxii, 582.

43 Leontius of Neapolis, *Life of St Symeon the Fool*, ed. L. Rydén, 167.

44 John Chrysostom, *In Matth. hom.* xxxvii, *PG* lvii, 428.

CHAPTER 13   LITERATURE

1 See F. Halkin, *Bibliotheca hagiographica graeca*, 3rd ed. (3 vols., Brussels, 1957); F. Halkin, *Auctarium bibl. hagiogr. graecae* (Brussels, 1969).

2 Nilus, *Epist.* 49, *PG* lxxix, 220.

3 Ed. Gy. Moravcsik and R. J. H. Jenkins (Washington, D. C., 1967), ch. 1, p. 48.

4 Ed. A. Vogt, i (Paris, 1935), 2.

5 P. Chrêstou *et al.* (eds.), *Grêgoriou tou Palama syngramata*, ii (Thessaloniki, 1966), 568.

6 Theophanes, *Chronographia*, ed. C. de Boor, A.M. 6295, p. 479.

7 L. Th. Lefort, *Les Vies coptes de Saint Pachôme* (Louvain, 1943), xliif.

8 Theophanes, *Chronographia*, ed. C. de Boor, A.M. 6024, pp. 181ff.

9 Procopius, *Wars*, viii. 1. 1.

10 R. Hercher (ed.), *Erotici scriptores graeci*, ii (Leipzig, 1859), 161–577.

11 *Pratum spirituale*, ch. 134, *PG* lxxxvii/3, 2997.

12 F. Miklosich and J. Müller (eds.), *Acta et diplomata graeca medii aevi*, v (Vienna, 1887), 324ff.; W. Nissen *Die Diataxis des Michael Attaleiates von 1077* (Jena, 1894), 86ff.

13 Ch. Diehl, 'Le trésor et la bibliothèque de Patmos au commencement du 13ᵉ siècle', *BZ*, i (1892), 496ff.

14 Cecaumenus, *Strategicon*, ed. G. G. Litavrin, §§21, 46, 63, pp. 154, 212, 240.

15 P. Lemerle, *Cinq études sur le XIᵉ siècle byzantin* (Paris, 1977), 24f.

16 See the valuable observations of L. G. Westerink, *Nicétas Magistros: Lettres d'un exilé* (Paris, 1973), 9ff.

17 F. W. Lenz, 'On the Authorship of the Leptinean Declamations ...', *American Journal of Philology*, lxiii (1942), 154ff.

18 A. P. Kazhdan, 'Some Questions Addressed to the Scholars who Believe in the Authenticity of Kaminiates' "Capture of Thessalonica"', *BZ*, lxxi (1978), 301ff.

19 Theophanes Continuatus, *CSHB*, 167.

20 Procopius, *Wars*, i. 4. 17ff.

21 Procopius, *Wars*, vii. 1. 5–15.

22 Procopius, *Wars*, v. 3. 6–9.

23 Agathias, *Historiae*, ed. R. Keydell, Proem, 12 and i. 7, pp. 6, 18–19.

24 Ed. E. Renauld, i, 63.

25 J. F. Boissonade (ed.), *On the Characteristics of Certain Writings*, along with *De operatione daemonum* (Nürnberg, 1838), 50ff.

26 E. Kurtz (ed.), *Die Gedichte des Christophoros Mitylenaios* (Leipzig, 1903), no. 114.

27 See the perceptive analysis of Nicetas by A. P. Kazhdan, *Kniga i pisatel' v Vizantii* (Moscow, 1973), 82ff.

28 L. Spengel, *Rhetores graeci*, iii (Leipzig, 1856), 368ff.

29 A.-J. Festugière (ed.), *Néapolis: Vie de Syméon Léontios de le Fou et Vie de Jean de Chypre*, 344.

30 Psellus, *Encomium Metaphrastae*, in E. Kurtz and F. Drexl (eds.), *Scripta minora*, i (Milan, 1936), 100.

31 *Ibid.*, 101.

32 H.-G. Beck, *Kirche und theologische Literatur im byzant. Reich* (Munich, 1959), 640.

33 D.-C. Hesseling and H. Pernot (eds.), *Poèmes prodromiques en grec vulgaire* (Amsterdam, 1910).

34 M. Pichard (ed.), *Le Roman de Callimaque et de Chrysorrhoé* (Paris, 1956).

35 E. Legrand (ed.), *Bibliothèque grecque vulgaire*, i (Paris 1880), 125ff. All five romances are conveniently accessible in E. Kriaras, *Byzantina hippotika mythistorêmata*, Basikê bibliothêkê, ii (Athens, 1955).

36 J. Mavrogordato (ed.), *Digenes Akrites*, with English trans., not always reliable (Oxford, 1956). A more elaborate edition has been attempted by E. Trapp, *Digenes Akrites: Synoptische Ausgabe der ältesten Versionen* (Vienna, 1971).

37 J. F. Boissonade (ed.), *On the Characteristics of Certain Writings*, 48.

CHAPTER 14   ART AND ARCHITECTURE

1 *The Birth of Western Painting* (London, 1930), 25.

2 See Ch. Pellat, 'Al-Ǧāhiz: Les nations civilisées et les croyances religieuses', *Journal asiatique*, cclv (1967), 71.

3 *PG* lxxix, 577ff.

4 *Cod. Theod.*, xiii, 4. 1 and 4.

5 See preliminary reports by R. M. Harrison and N. Firatli, in *DOP*, xix (1965), 230ff.; xx (1966), 222ff.; xxi (1967), 273ff.; xxii (1968), 195ff.

6 Joannou, *Discipline*, i/1, 218–20.

7 Nicephorus, *Opuscula historica*, ed. C. de Boor, 76.

8 *Vita S. Stephani iunioris*, *PG* c, 1120.

9 *Ibid.*, 1172.

10 Theophanes Continuatus, *CSHB*, 139ff.

11 *Ibid.*, 102ff.

12 Nicetas Choniates, *Historia*, ed. J.-L. Van Dieten, 332.

13 G. A. Rallês and M. Potlês, *Syntagma tôn theiôn kai hierôn kanonôn*, ii (Athens, 1852), 545–6.

14 Nicholas Mesarites, *Description of the Church of the Holy Apostles*, ed. with English trans. by G. Downey, xxviii. 23, *Trans. of the American Philos. Society*, N.S., xlvii/6 (1957), 855ff.

15 A. Maiuri, 'Una nuova poesia di Teodoro Prodromo', *BZ*, xxiii (1920), 399f.

16 Ch. Loparev (ed.), *Kniga palomnik* (St Petersburg, 1899), 17.

17 Theophanes Continuatus, *CSHB*, 98f.

18 Nicholas Mesarites, *Die Palastrevolution des Johannes Komnenos*, ed. A. Heisenberg (Würzburg, 1907), 44f.

BIBLIOGRAPHY

INTRODUCTION

The best handbook of Byzantine history is G. Ostrogorsky, *History of the Byzantine State*, 2nd ed. (Oxford, 1968) translated by J. Hussey from the 3rd ed. of the same author's *Geschichte des byzantinischen Staates* (Munich, 1963). The older work by A. A. Vasiliev, *History of the Byzantine Empire*, 2nd ed. (Madison, Wisc., 1952) remains useful in some respects. For a wider geographical coverage, including countries adjacent to Byzantium, see *The Cambridge Medieval History*, i (1911) and ii (1913) down to 717 AD, and iv, pt 1 (1966) for the period 717–1453.

The early part of Byzantine history down to the death of Justinian I (565) has been treated in detail by J. B. Bury, *History of the Later Roman Empire* (2 vols., London, 1923) and more exhaustively, by E. Stein, *Histoire du Bas-Empire* (2 vols., Paris–Brussels–Amsterdam, 1949–59). We lack an equally well documented account of the remainder of Byzantine history. Among many monographs devoted to individual reigns and longer periods, the following deserve mention:

J. B. Bury, *History of the Later Roman Empire from Arcadius to Irene* (2 vols., London, 1889).
P. Goubert, *Byzance avant l'Islam*, i, ii/1, ii/2 (Paris, 1951–65).
A. Lombard, *Constantin V, empereur des Romains* (Paris, 1902).
J. B. Bury, *History of the Eastern Roman Empire from the Fall of Irene to the Accession of Basil I* (London, 1912).
A. Vogt, *Basile Ier, empereur de Byzance* (Paris, 1908).
S. Runciman, *The Emperor Romanus Lecapenus and his reign* (Cambridge, 1929).
A. Rambaud, *L'Empire grec au Xe siècle: Constantin Porphyrogénète* (Paris, 1870).
A. Toynbee, *Constantine Porphyrogenitus and his World* (London, 1973).
G. Schlumberger, *Un empereur byzantin au Xe siècle. Nicéphore Phocas* (Paris, 1890).
——, *L'épopée byzantine à la fin du Xe siècle*, 3 vols. (Paris, 1896–1905).

F. Chalandon, *Les Comnène*, i. *Essai sur le règne d'Alexis Ier Comnène* (Paris, 1900).

——, *Les Comnène*, ii. *Jean II Comnène et Manuel I Comnène* (Paris, 1912).

D. M. Nicol, *The Last Centuries of Byzantium, 1261–1453* (London, 1972).

For the Byzantine splinter states:

M. J. Angold, *A Byzantine Government in Exile. Government and Society under the Laskarids of Nicaea* (London, 1975).

D. M. Nicol, *The Despotate of Epiros* (Oxford, 1957).

W. Miller, *Trebizond, the Last Greek Empire* (London, 1926).

D. A. Zakythenos, *Le despotat grec de Morée*, 2nd ed. (2 vols., London, 1975).

Among numerous books devoted to Byzantine civilization and culture, the most comprehensive is L. Bréhier, *Le monde byzantin*, ii, *Les institutions de l'Empire byzantin* (Paris, 1949) and iii, *La civilisation byzantine* (Paris, 1950). See also *The Cambridge Medieval History*, iv, pt 2 (1967). More modern and incisive in his approach is A. Guillou, *La civilisation byzantine* (Paris, 1974). The following are also worthy of note:

N. H. Baynes and H. St. L. B. Moss (eds.), *Byzantium. An Introduction to East Roman Civilization* (Oxford, 1948).

H.-G. Beck, *Das byzantinische Jahrtausend* (Munich, 1978).

Ch. Diehl, *Byzance: Grandeur et décadence*, 2nd ed. (Paris, 1926); English trans., *Byzantium: Greatness and Decline* (Brunswick, N. J. 1957) with a good bibliography by P. Charanis.

H. W. Haussig, *Kulturgeschichte von Byzanz*, 2nd ed. (Stuttgart, 1966); English trans., *A History of Byzantine Civilization* (London, 1971).

H. Hunger, *Reich der neuen Mitte: Der christliche Geist der byzantinischen Kultur* (Graz, 1965).

A. P. Každan, *Vizantijskaja kul'tura* (Moscow, 1968); German trans. *Byzanz und seine Kultur* (Berlin, 1973).

A. P. Rudakov, *Očerki vizantijskoj kul'tury po dannym grečeskoj agiografii* (Moscow, 1917; reprinted London, 1970).

S. Runciman, *Byzantine Civilization* (London, 1933).

The determined reader may also be able to extract much useful information from Ph. Koukoules, *Byzantinôn bios kai politismos* (5 vols., Athens, 1948–52).

CHAPTER I PEOPLES AND LANGUAGES

There does not exist any comprehensive work on the peoples of the Byzantine Empire. For the Early period a good deal of information may be found in A. H. M. Jones, *The Cities of the Eastern Roman Provinces*, 2nd ed. (Oxford, 1971). For a survey based on hagiographical sources and limited to the eastern provinces see A. P. Rudakov, *Očerki vizantijskoj kul'tury* (reprinted London, 1970), 45ff. There are some good general remarks in E. Stein, 'Introduction à l'histoire et aux institutions byzantines', *Traditio*, vii (1949–51), 154ff. A number of relevant studies by P. Charanis have been reprinted in his *Studies on the Demography of the Byzantine Empire* (London, 1972).

Greek, Latin and native languages

G. Bardy, *La question de langues dans L'Eglise ancienne* (Paris, 1948).

G. Dagron, 'Aux origines de la civilisation byzantine. Langue de culture et langue d'état', *Rev. historique*, ccxli (1969), 23–56.

R. MacMullen, 'Provincial Languages in the Roman Empire', *Amer. Journal of Philol.*, lxxxvii (1966), 1–17.

P. Peeters, *Le tréfonds oriental de l'hagiographie byzantine* (Brussels, 1950).

H. Zilliacus, *Zum Kampf der Weltsprachen im oströmischen Reich* (Helsingfors, 1935).

Asia Minor

K. Holl, 'Das Fortleben der Volkssprachen in Kleinasien in nachchristlicher Zeit', *Hermes*, xliii (1908), 240–54.

W. M. Ramsay, 'The intermixture of Races in Asia Minor', *Proc. of the British Acad.*, vii (1915–16), 359–422.

L. Robert, *Noms indigènes dans l'Asie Mineure gréco-romaine* (Paris, 1963).

S. Vryonis, Jr., *The Decline of Medieval Hellenism in Asia Minor* (Berkeley–Los Angeles, 1971), 42ff.

Syria and Palestine

F. Altheim and R. Stiehl, *Die Araber in der alten Welt*, i (Berlin, 1964).

M. Avi-Yonah, *The Holy Land from the Persian to the Arab Conquests* (Grand Rapids, Mich., 1966), 212ff.

——, *The Jews of Palestine* (Oxford, 1976).

R. Dussaud, *La Pénétration des Arabes en Syrie avant l'Islam* (Paris, 1955).

F. Nau, *Les Arabes chrétiens de Mésopotamie et de Syrie* (Paris, 1933).

Egypt

H. I. Bell, 'Hellenic Culture in Egypt', *Journal of Egyptian Archaeol.*, viii (1922), 139ff.

——, *Egypt from Alexander the Great to the Arab Conquest* (Oxford, 1948).

E. R. Hardy, *Christian Egypt: Church and People* (New York, 1952).

R. MacMullen, 'Nationalism in Roman Egypt', *Aegyptus*, xliv (1964), 179ff.

Th. Papadopoullos, *Africanobyzantina. Byzantine Influences on Negro-Sudanese Cultures* (Athens, 1966).

North Africa

P. Brown, 'Christianity and Local Culture in Late Roman Africa', *JRS*, lviii (1968), 85–95.

305

C. Courtois, *Les Vandales et l'Afrique* (Paris, 1955).

——, 'Saint Augustin et le problème de la survivance du punique', *Rev. africaine*, xciv (1950), 259–82.

M. Simon, 'Punique ou berbère?', *Ann. de l'Inst. de Philol. et d'Hist. Orient. et Slaves*, xiii (1953), 613–29.

Italy and Sicily

L. Bréhier, 'Les colonies d'orientaux en Occident au commencement du moyen-âge', *BZ*, xii (1903), 1–39.

P. Charanis, 'On the Question of the Hellenization of Sicily and Southern Italy during the Middle Ages', *Amer. Hist. Rev.*, lii (1946), 74–86.

A. Guillou, *Régionalisme et indépendance dans l'Empire byzantin au VIIe siècle* (Rome, 1969), 77ff.

G. Rohlfs, *Scavi linguistici nella Magna Grecia* (Rome, 1933).

——, *Nuovi scavi linguistici nella antica Magna Grecia* (Palermo, 1972).

L. Ruggini, 'Ebrei e orientali nell'Italia settentrionale fra il IV e il VI secolo d. Cr.', *Studia et documenta historiae et Juris* (Pontif. Inst. Utriusque Juris), xxv (1959), 186–308.

E. Sestan, 'La composizione etnica della società in rapporto allo svolgimento della civiltà in Italia nel sec. VII', *Caratteri del sec. VII in Occidente = Settimane di studio del Centro ital. di studi sull'alto medioevo*, v/2 (Spoleto, 1958), 649–77.

Balkans

V. Beševliev, *Untersuchungen über die Personennamen bei den Thrakern* (Amsterdam, 1970), 69ff.

D. Detschew, *Die Thrakischen Sprachreste* (Vienna, 1957).

V. Georgiev, 'The Genesis of the Balkan Peoples', *Slavonic and East European Rev.*, xliv (1965–6), 285–97.

N. G. L. Hammond, *Migrations and Invasions in Greece and Adjacent Areas* (Park Ridge, N. J., 1976).

P. Lemerle, 'Invasions et migrations dans les Balkans depuis la fin de l'époque romaine jusqu'au VIIIe siècle', *Rev. historique*, ccxi (1954), 265–308.

I. I. Russu, *Die Sprache der Thrako-Daker* (Bucharest, 1969).

V. Velkov, 'Les campagnes et la population rurale en Thrace aux IVe–VIe siècles', *Byzantinobulgarica*, i (1962), 31–66.

Some developments after the sixth century

P. Charanis, 'The Chronicle of Monemvasia and the Question of the Slavonic Settlements in Greece', *DOP*, v (1950), 141–66.

——, 'Ethnic Changes in the Byzantine Empire in the Seventh Century', *DOP*, xiii (1959), 25–44.

——, *The Armenians in the Byzantine Empire* (Lisbon, 1963).

R. J. H. Jenkins, *Byzantium and Byzantinism*, Lectures in Memory of Louise Taft Semple (Cincinnati, 1963), 21ff.

P. Lemerle, 'La chronique improprement dite de Monemvasie', *REB*, xxi (1963), 5–49.

M. Vasmer, *Die Slaven in Griechenland*, Abhandlungen d. Preuss. Akad. d. Wiss., Philos.-hist. Kl., 1941, Nr. 12.

CHAPTER 2 SOCIETY AND ECONOMY

Early Period

All the essential information may be found in A. H. M. Jones, *The Later Roman Empire, 284–602* (3 vols., Oxford, 1964), and, in a more condensed form, in the same author's *The Decline of the Ancient World* (London, 1966).

Administration, Taxation and the Army

D. van Berchem, *L'armée de Dioclétien et la réforme constantinienne* (Paris, 1952).

A. Déléage, *La capitation du Bas-Empire* (Mâcon, 1945).

R. Grosse, *Römische Militärgeschichte von Gallienus bis zum Beginn der byzantinischen Themenverfassung* (Berlin, 1920).

R. Guilland, *Recherches sur les institutions byzantines* (2 vols., Berlin–Amsterdam, 1967).

J. Karayannopulos, *Das Finanzwesen des frühbyzantinischen Staates* (Munich, 1958).

R. MacMullen, *Soldier and Civilian in the Later Roman Empire* (Cambridge, Mass., 1963).

J. Maspéro, *Organisation militaire de l'Egypte byzantine* (Paris, 1912).

G. Rouillard, *L'administration civile de l'Egypte byzantine*, 2nd ed. (Paris, 1928).

The Church

J. Gaudemet, *L'Eglise dans l'Empire romain (IVᵉ–Vᵉ siècles)* (Paris, 1959).

A. H. M. Jones, 'Church Finance in the Fifth and Sixth Centuries', *Journal of Theological Studies*, xi (1960), 84–94.

M. Kaplan, *Les propriétés de la Couronne et de l'Eglise dans l'Empire byzantin siècles)* (Paris, 1976).

M. V. Levčenko, 'Cerkovnye imuščestva V–VII vekov v Vostočno-Rimskoj imperii', *Vizantijskij Vremennik*, N.S., ii (1949), 11–59.

E. Wipszycka, *Les ressources et les activités économiques des églises en Egypte du IVᵉ au VIIIᵉ siècle* (Brussels, 1974).

Trade and Supplies

H. Antoniadis-Bibicou, *Recherches sur les douanes à Byzance* (Paris, 1963).

R. S. Lopez, 'The Role of Trade in the Economic Readjustment of Byzantium in the Seventh Century', *DOP*, xiii (1959), 67–85.

J. Rougé, *Recherches sur l'organisation du commerce maritime en Méditerranée sous l'Empire romain* (Paris, 1966).

N. V. Pigulewskaja, *Byzanz auf den Wegen nach Indien* (Berlin, 1969).

J. L. Teall, 'The Grain Supply of the Byzantine Empire, 330–1025', *DOP*, xiii (1959), 87–139.

Social Classes

R. Ganghoffer, *L'évolution des institutions municipales en Occident et en Orient au Bas-Empire* (Paris, 1963).

L. Harmand, *Libanius, Discours sur les patronages* (Paris, 1955).

R. MacMullen, 'Social Mobility and the Theodosian Code', *JRS*, liv (1964), 49–53.

——, *Enemies of the Roman Order* (Cambridge, Mass., 1967).

A. F. Norman, 'Gradations in Later Municipal Society', *JRS*, xlviii (1958), 79–85.

E. Patlagean, *Pauvreté économique et pauvreté sociale à Byzance, 4ᵉ–7ᵉ siècles* (Paris–The Hague, 1977).

Monetary System, Prices and Wages (All Periods)

A. R. Bellinger and P. Grierson, *Catalogue of the Byzantine Coins in the Dumbarton Oaks Collection and in the Whittemore Collection* (3 vols. in 5 parts, Washington, D.C., 1966–73).

P. Grierson, 'Coinage and Money in the Byzantine Empire, 498–ca. 1090', in *Moneta e scambi nell'alto medioevo*, Settimane di studio del Centro Italiano di studi sull'alto medioevo, viii (Spoleto, 1961), 411–53.

——, 'Byzantine Coinage as Source Material', *Proceedings of the XIIIth Internat. Congress of Byzantine Studies, Oxford, 1966* (London, 1967), 317–33.

M. F. Hendy, 'On the Administrative Basis of the Byzantine Coinage, *c.* 400–*c.* 900 and the Reforms of Heraclius', *University of Birmingham Historical Journal*, xii (1970), 129–54.

——, *Coinage and Money in the Byzantine Empire, 1081–1261* (Washington, D.C., 1969).

C. Morrisson, *Catalogue des monnaies byzantines de la Bibliothèque Nationale* (2 vols., Paris, 1970).

G. Ostrogorsky, 'Löhne und Preise in Byzanz', *BZ*, xxxii (1932), 293–333.

System of the 'Themes'

W. E. Kaegi, 'Some Reconsiderations on the Themes (Seventh–Ninth Centuries)', *Jahrbuch der Österr. Byzant. Gesellschaft*, xvi (1967), 39–53.

J. Karayannopulos, *Die Entstehung der byzantinischen Themenordnung* (Munich, 1959).

A. Pertusi, 'La formation des thèmes byzantins', *Berichte zum XI. Internat. Byzantinisten-Kongress* (Munich, 1958), i.

Middle Period. Administration

J. B. Bury, *The Imperial Administrative System in the Ninth Century* (London, 1911).

H. Glykatzi-Ahrweiler, 'Recherches sur l'administration de l'Empire byzantin aux IXe–XIe siècles', *Bulletin de Correspondance Hellénique*, lxxxiv (1960), 1–111.

N. Oikonomidès, *Les Listes de préséance byzantines des IXe et Xe siècles* (Paris, 1972).

Society, Landholding and Taxation

H.-G. Beck, 'Byzantinisches Gefolgschaftwesen', Bayerische Akad. der Wissenschaften, Philos.-hist. Kl., *Sitzungsberichte*, 1965, no. 5.

——, 'Senat und Volk von Konstantinopel', *ibid.*, 1966, no. 6.

C. M. Brand, 'Two Byzantine Treatises on Taxation', *Traditio*, xxv (1969), 35–60.

P. Charanis, *Social, Economic and Political Life in the Byzantine Empire* (collected papers) (London, 1973).

F. Dölger, *Beiträge zur Geschichte der byzantinischen Finanzverwaltung besonders des 10. und 11. Jahrhunderts* (Munich–Berlin, 1927; reprinted Hildesheim, 1960).

J. Ferluga, 'La ligesse dans l'Empire byzantin', *Zbornik Radova Vizant. Instituta*, vii (Belgrade, 1961), 97–123.

P. Lemerle, 'Esquisse pour une histoire agraire de Byzance', *Revue historique*, ccxix/1 (1958), 32–74, 254–84; ccxix/2 (1958), 43–94.

——, 'Recherches sur le régime agraire à Byzance: La terre militaire à l'époque des Comnènes', *Cahiers de civilisation médiévale*, ii (1959), 265–81.

——, *Cinq études sur le XIe siècle byzantin* (Paris, 1977).

R. Morris, 'The Powerful and the Poor in Tenth Century Byzantium: Law and Reality', *Past and Present*, no. 73 (1976), 3–27.

G. Ostrogorsky, *Pour l'histoire de la féodalité à Byzance* (Brussels, 1954).

——, *Quelques problèmes d'histoire de la paysannerie byzantine* (Brussels, 1956).

——, 'Pour l'histoire de l'immunité à Byzance', *Byzantion*, xxviii (1958), 55–106.

——, 'La commune rurale byzantine', *Byzantion*, xxxii (1962), 139–66.

——, 'Agrarian Conditions in the Byzantine Empire in the Middle Ages' in *Cambridge Economic History of Europe*, ed. M. M. Postan, 2nd ed. (Cambridge, 1966), 205–34.

——, 'Die Pronoia unter den Komnenen', *Zbornik Radova Vizant. Instituta*, xii (1970), 41–54.

——, 'Observations on the Aristocracy in Byzantium', *DOP*, xxv (1971), 1–32.

N. Svoronos, *Etudes sur l'organisation intérieure, la société et l'économie de l'Empire byzantin* (collected papers) (London, 1973).

——, 'Remarques sur les structures économiques de l'Empire byzantin au XIe siècle', *TM*, vi (1976), 49–67.

S. Vryonis, 'Byzantium: The Social Basis of the Decline in the XIth Century', *Greek, Roman and Byzantine Studies*, ii (1959), 159–75.

P. A. Yannopoulos, *La société profane dans l'Empire byzantin des VIIe, VIIIe et IXe siècles* (Louvain, 1975).

Prominent Families

A. Bryer, 'A Byzantine Family: The Gabrades', *University of Birmingham Historical Journal*, xii (1970), 164–87.
I. Djurić, 'Porodica Foka', *Zbornik Radova Vizant. Instituta*, xvii (1976), 189–296.
A. P. Každan, *Social'nyj sostav gospodstvujuščego klassa Vizantii XI–XII vekov* (Moscow, 1974).
D. M. Nicol, *The Byzantine Family of Kantakouzenos (Cantacuzenus), ca. 1100–1460* (Washington, D.C., 1968).
A. Papadopulos, *Versuch einer Genealogie der Palaiologen, 1261–1453* (Munich, 1938).
D. I. Polemis, *The Doukai. A Contribution to Byzantine Prosopography* (London, 1968).

Late Period

P. Charanis, 'On the Social Structure and Economic Organization of the Byzantine Empire in the Thirteenth Century and Later', *Byzantinoslavica*, xii (1951), 94–153.
H. Glykatzi-Ahrweiler, 'La politique agraire des empereurs de Nicée,' *Byzantion*, xxviii (1958), 51–66, 135–6.
A. Laiou-Thomadakis, *Peasant Society in the Late Byzantine Empire* (Princeton, 1977).
D. M. Nicol, *Church and Society in the Last Centuries of Byzantium* (Cambridge, 1979).
I. Ševčenko, 'Alexios Makrembolites and his "Dialogue between the Rich and the Poor"', *Zbornik Radova Vizant. Instituta*, vi (1960), 187–228.
——, 'Society and Intellectual Life in the Fourteenth Century', *Actes du XIVe Congrès Internat. des Etudes Byzantines*, i (Bucharest, 1974), 69–92.

CHAPTER 3   THE DISAPPEARANCE AND REVIVAL OF CITIES

General

D. Claude, *Die byzantinische Stadt im 6. Jahrhundert* (Munich, 1969).
F. Dölger, 'Die Frühbyzantinische und byzantinisch beeinflusste Stadt', *Atti del 3° Congr. Internaz. di Studi sull'Alto Medioevo*, 1956 (Spoleto, 1959), 65–100; reprinted in same author's *Paraspora* (Ettal, 1961), 107–39.
A. H. M. Jones, *The Greek City from Alexander to Justinian* (Oxford, 1940).
——, *Cities of the Eastern Roman Provinces*, 2nd ed. (Oxford, 1971).
A. P. Každan, 'Vizantijskie goroda v VII–XI vekakh', *Sovetskaja Arkheologija*, xxi (1954), 164–83.

E. Kirsten, 'Die byzantinische Stadt', *Berichte zum XI. Intern. Byzant. Kongress* (Munich, 1958), v/3.

G. L. Kurbatov, *Osnovnye problemy vnutrennego razvitija vizantijskogo goroda v IV–VII vekakh* (Leningrad, 1971).

G. Ostrogorsky, 'Byzantine Cities in the Early Middle Ages', *DOP*, xiii (1959), 45–66.

R. Stillwell (ed.), *The Princeton Encyclopedia of Classical Sites* (Princeton, N.J., 1976).

Constantinople

H.-G. Beck, 'Konstantinopel. Zur Sozialgeschichte einer frühmittelalterlichen Hauptstadt', *BZ*, lviii (1965), 11–45.

—— (ed.), *Studien zur Frühgeschichte Konstantinopels* (Munich, 1973).

G. Dagron, *Naissance d'une capitale. Constantinople et ses institutions de 330 à 451* (Paris, 1974).

D. Jacoby, 'La population de Constantinople à l'époque byzantine', *Byzantion*, xxxi (1961), 81–110.

R. Janin, *Constantinople byzantine*, 2nd ed. (Paris, 1964).

——, *La géographie ecclésiastique de l'Empire byzantin*, i/3. *Les églises et les monastères* [de Constantinople], 2nd ed. (Paris, 1969).

A. van Millingen, *Byzantine Constantinople* (London, 1899).

W. Müller-Wiener, *Bildlexikon zur Topographie Istanbuls* (Tübingen, 1977).

Asia Minor

C. Foss, 'The Persians in Asia Minor and the End of Antiquity', *English Hist. Rev.*, xc (1975), 721–47.

——, *Byzantine and Turkish Sardis* (Cambridge, Mass., 1976).

——, 'Archaeology and the "Twenty Cities" of Byzantine Asia', *Amer. Journal of Archaeol.*, lxxxi (1977), 469–86.

—— 'Late Antique and Byzantine Ankara', *DOP*, xxxi (1977), 29–87.

F. W. Hasluck, *Cyzicus* (Cambridge, 1910).

G. de Jerphanion, *Mélanges d'archéologie anatolienne* (Beirut, 1928).

J. Keil, *Ephesos. Ein Führer durch die Ruinenstätte und ihre Geschichte*, 5th ed. (Vienna, 1964).

G. Kleiner, *Die Ruinen von Milet* (Berlin, 1968).

W. Müller-Wiener, 'Mittelalterliche Befestigungen in südlichen Jonien', *Istanbuler Mitteilungen*, xi (1961), 5–122.

P. D. Pogodin and O. F. Vul'f (Wulff), 'Nikomedija', *Izvestija Russk. Arkheol. Inst. v Konstant.*, ii (1897), 77–184.

L. Robert, 'Sur Didymes à l'époque byzantine', *Hellenica*, xi–xii (1960), 490–504.

Mesopotamia, Syria, Palestine

J. and J. Ch. Balty (eds.), *Apamée de Syrie. Bilan des recherches archéologiques, 1965–8* (Brussels, 1969); *Bilan des recherches archéologiques, 1969–71* (Brussels, 1972).

J. W. Crowfoot *et al.*, *The Buildings at Samaria* (London, 1942).

G. Downey, *A History of Antioch in Syria from Seleucus to the Arab Conquest* (Princeton, N.J., 1961).

A. J. Festugière, *Antioche païenne et chrétienne* (Paris, 1959).

C. T. Fritsch (ed.), *Studies in the History of Caesarea Maritima*. The Joint Expedition to Caesarea Maritima, i (Missoula, Mont., 1975).

G. Goossens, *Hiérapolis de Syrie* (Louvain, 1943).

C. H. Kraeling (ed.), *Gerasa, City of the Decapolis* (New Haven, 1938).

J. H. W. G. Liebeschuetz, *Antioch. City and Imperial Administration in the Later Roman Empire* (Oxford, 1972).

P. Petit, *Libanius et la vie municipale à Antioche au IVe siècle après J.-C.* (Paris, 1955).

J. Sauvaget, *Alep* (Paris, 1941).

J. B. Segal, *Edessa, the Blessed City* (Oxford, 1970).

G. Tchalenko, *Villages antiques de la Syrie du Nord* (3 vols., Paris, 1953–8).

H. Vincent and F. M. Abel, *Jérusalem*, ii. *Jérusalem nouvelle* (Paris, 1914–26).

Greece

Ch. Bouras, 'Houses and Settlements in Byzantine Greece', *Shelter in Greece*, ed. O. B. Doumanis and P. Oliver (Athens, n.d.), 30–52.

M. Chatzidakis, *Mystras*, 2nd ed. (Athens, 1956).

P. Lemerle, *Philippes et la Macédoine orientale à l'époque chrétienne et byzantine* (Paris, 1945).

R. L. Scranton, *Corinth*, xvi. *Mediaeval Architecture* (Princeton, N.J., 1957).

G. A. Soteriou, 'Hai christianikai Thêbai tês Thessalias', *Archaiol. Ephêmeris*, 1929, 1–158.

O. Tafrali, *Topographie de Thessalonique* (Paris, 1913).

——, *Thessalonique au quatorzième siècle* (Paris, 1913).

——, *Thessalonique des origines au XIVe siècle* (Paris, 1919).

H. A. Thompson, 'Athenian Twilight, AD 267–600', *JRS*, xlix (1959), 61–72.

I. N. Travlos, *Poleodomikê exelixis tôn Athênôn* (Athens, 1960).

Balkans

B. Aleksova and C. Mango, 'Bargala: A Preliminary Report', *DOP*, xxv (1971), 265–81.

V. Beševliev, 'Les cités antiques en Mésie et en Thrace à l'époque du haut moyen âge', *Etudes balkaniques*, v (1966), 207–20.

R. F. Hoddinott, *Bulgaria in Antiquity* (London, 1975).

E. Kitzinger, 'A Survey of the Early Christian Town of Stobi', *DOP*, iii (1946), 81–161.

V. Popović (ed.), *Sirmium*, i (Belgrade, 1971).

Serdica, i. *Matériaux et recherches archéologiques* (Sofia, 1964).

V. Velkov, *Cities in Thrace and Dacia in Late Antiquity* (Amsterdam, 1977).

Coin Finds

G. Bates, *Byzantine Coins*, Archaeol. Exploration of Sardis, Monograph 1 (Cambridge, Mass., 1971).

P. Charanis, 'The Significance of Coins as Evidence for the History of Athens and Corinth in the Seventh and Eighth Centuries', *Historia*, iv (1955), 163–72.

J. M. Harris, 'Coins Found at Corinth', *Hesperia*, x (1941), 143–62.

D. M. Metcalf, 'The Slavonic Threat to Greece *c*. 580: Some Evidence from Athens', *Hesperia*, xxxi (1962), 134–57.

M. Thompson, *The Athenian Agora*, ii. *Coins from the Roman through the Venetian Period* (Princeton, N.J., 1954).

CHAPTER 4   DISSENTERS

General

P. Brown, 'Religious Coercion in the Later Roman Empire: The Case of North Africa', *History*, xlviii (1963), 283–305.

N. G. Garsoian, 'Byzantine Heresy. A Reinterpretation', *DOP*, xxv (1971), 85–113.

J. Gouillard, 'L'hérésie dans l'Empire byzantin des origines au XIIe siècle', *TM*, i (1965), 299–324.

A. H. M. Jones, 'Were Ancient Heresies National or Social Movements in Disguise?', *Journal of Theol. Studies*, x (1959), 280–98; reprinted in *The Roman Economy*, ed. P. A. Brunt (Oxford, 1974), 308–29.

Pagans

G. Boissier, *La fin du Paganisme*, 4th ed. (Paris, 1903).

J. Geffcken, *Der Ausgang des griechisch-römischen Heidentums* (Heidelberg, 1929); English trans., *The Last Days of Greco–Roman Paganism* (Amsterdam, 1978).

P. de Labriolle, *La réaction païenne. Etude sur la polémique antichrétienne du Ier au VIe siècle* (Paris, 1948).

A. Momigliano (ed.), *The Conflict between Paganism and Christianity in the Fourth Century* (Oxford, 1963).

Jews

J. Parkes, *The Conflict of the Church and the Synagogue* (London, 1934).

A. Sharf, *Byzantine Jewry from Justinian to the Fourth Crusade* (London, 1971).

J. Starr, *The Jews in the Byzantine Empire, 641–1204* (Athens, 1939).

Manichaeans

A. Adam, *Texte zum Manichäismus* (Berlin, 1954).

P. Brown, 'The Diffusion of Manichaeism in the Roman Empire', *JRS*, lix (1969), 92–103.

F. C. Burkitt, *The Religion of the Manichees* (Cambridge, 1925).

H.-C. Puech, *Le Manichéisme. Son fondateur, sa doctrine* (Paris, 1949).

Monophysites

R. Devreesse, *Le patriarcat d'Antioche depuis la Paix de l'Eglise jusqu'à la conquête arabe* (Paris, 1945).

L. Duchesne, *L'Eglise au VIᵉ siècle* (Paris, 1925).

W. H. C. Frend, *The Rise of the Monophysite Movement* (Cambridge, 1972).

E. Honigmann, *Evêques et évêchés monophysites d'Asie antérieure au VIᵉ siècle* (Louvain, 1951).

J. Lebon, *Le monophysisme sévérien* (Louvain, 1909).

J. Maspéro, *Histoire des patriarches d'Alexandrie* (Paris, 1923).

Iconoclasts

P. J. Alexander, *The Patriarch Nicephorus of Constantinople* (Oxford, 1958).

E. Bevan, *Holy Images* (London, 1940).

A. Bryer and J. Herrin (eds.), *Iconoclasm* (Birmingham, 1977).

A. Grabar, *L'iconoclasme byzantin. Dossier archéologique* (Paris, 1957).

E. Kitzinger, 'The Cult of Images in the Age before Iconoclasm', *DOP*, viii (1954), 83–150.

E. J. Martin, *A History of the Iconoclastic Controversy* (London, 1930).

Medieval dualist heresies

P. G. Ficker, *Die Phundagiagiten* (Leipzig, 1908).

N. G. Garsoian, *The Paulician Heresy* (The Hague, 1967).

P. Lemerle, 'L'histoire des Pauliciens d'Asie Mineure d'après les sources grecques', *TM*, v (1973), 1–144.

M. Loos, *Dualist Heresy in the Middle Ages* (Prague, 1974).

D. Obolensky, *The Bogomils* (Cambridge, 1948).

H.-Ch. Puech and A. Vaillant, *Le Traité contre les Bogomiles de Cosmas le Prêtre* (Paris, 1945).

S. Runciman, *The Medieval Manichee* (Cambridge, 1947).

CHAPTER 5   MONASTICISM

General

G. Bardy, 'Les origines des écoles monastiques en Orient', *Mélanges J. de Ghellinck*, i (Gembloux, 1951), 293–309.

P. Brown, 'The Rise and Function of the Holy Man in Late Antiquity', *JRS*, lxi (1971), 80–101.

P. Charanis, 'The Monk as an Element of Byzantine Society', *DOP*, xxv (1971), 61–84.

D. J. Chitty, *The Desert a City* (Oxford, 1966).

A. J. Festugière, *Les moines d'Orient*, I–IV (Paris, 1959–65).

I. Hausherr, *Penthos*, Orient. Christ. Analecta, 132 (Rome, 1944).

——, *Direction spirituelle en Orient autrefois*, *ibid.*, 144 (Rome, 1955).

P. de Meester, *De monachico statu iuxta disciplinam byzantinam* (Vatican, 1942).

Egypt

P. van Cauwenberg, *Etude sur les moines d'Egypte depuis le Concile de Chalcédoine (451) jusqu'à l'invasion arabe (640)* (Paris–Louvain, 1914).

H. G. Evelyn White, *The Monasteries of the Wâdi 'n Natrûn* (3 vols., New York, 1926–33).

K. Heussi, *Der Ursprung des Mönchtums* (Tübingen, 1936).

O. Meinardus, *Monks and Monasteries of the Egyptian Deserts* (Cairo, 1962).

H. E. Winlock and W. E. Crum, *The Monastery of Epiphanius at Thebes* (New York, 1926).

Syria and Palestine

P. Canivet, *Le monachisme syrien selon Théodoret de Cyr* (Paris, 1977).

S. Vailhé, 'Répertoire alphabétique des monastères de Palestine', *ROC*, iv (1899), 512–42; v (1900), 19–48, 272–92.

A. Vööbus, *History of Asceticism in the Syrian Orient* (2 vols., Louvain, 1958–60).

Constantinople, Asia Minor, Greece

E. Amand de Mendieta, *L'ascèse monastique de Saint Basile* (Maredsous, 1949).

——, *La presqu' île des caloyers: le Mont Athos* (Bruges, 1955).

G. Dagron, 'Les moines en ville. Le monachisme à Constantinople jusqu'au Concile de Chalcédoine (451)', *TM*, iv (1970), 229–76.

J. Gribomont, 'Le monachisme au IVe siècle en Asie Mineure: de Gangres au Messalianisme', *Texte und Untersuchungen zur Gesch. der altchristlichen Literatur*, lxiv (1957), 400–15.

J. Leroy, 'La réforme studite', Orient. Christ. Anal., 153 (1958), 181–214.

B. Menthon, *L'Olympe de Bithynie* (Paris, 1935).

Le Millénaire du Mont Athos, 963–1963 (2 vols., Chevetogne, 1963–4).

D. M. Nicol, *Meteora. The Rock Monasteries of Thessaly*, 2nd ed. (London, 1975).

D. Papachryssanthou, 'La vie monastique dans les campagnes byzantines du VIIIe au XIe siècle: Ermitages, groupes, communautés', *Byzantion*, xliii (1973), 158–80.

J. Pargoire, 'Les débuts du monachisme à Constantinople,' *Rev. des questions historiques*, N.S., xxi (1899), 67–143.

315

Monastic Properties

H. Ahrweiler, 'Charisticariat et autres formes d'attribution de fondations pieuses aux Xᵉ–XIᵉ siècles', *Zbornik Radova Vizant. Inst.*, x (1967), 1–27.

P. Charanis, 'Monastic Properties and the State in the Byzantine Empire', *DOP*, iv (1948), 53–118.

J. Darrouzès, 'Dossier sur le charisticariat', *Polychronion, Festschrift F. Dölger* (Heidelberg, 1966), 150–65.

P. Lemerle, 'Un aspect du rôle des monastères à Byzance: Les monastères donnés à des laïcs, les charisticaires', *Comptes rendus de l'Acad. des Inscriptions et Belles-Lettres*, 1967, 9–28.

CHAPTER 6   EDUCATION

General

L. Bréhier, 'L'enseignement classique et l'enseignement religieux à Byzance', *Rev. d'hist. et de philos. religieuses*, xxi (1941), 34–69.

F. Fuchs, *Die höheren Schulen von Konstantinopel im Mittelalter* (Leipzig, 1926).

W. Jaeger, *Early Christianity and Greek Paideia* (Cambridge, Mass., 1961).

P. Lemerle, *Le premier humanisme byzantin* (Paris, 1971).

H.-I. Marrou, *Histoire de l'éducation dans l'antiquité*, 6th ed. (Paris, 1965); English trans., *A History of Education in Antiquity* (London, 1956).

Early Period

Alan Cameron, 'The End of the Ancient Universities', *Cahiers d'histoire mondiale*, x (1966–7), 653–73.

——, 'The Last Days of the Academy at Athens', *Proc. of the Cambridge Philol. Society*, No. 195 (1969), 7–29.

P. Collinet, *Histoire de l'Ecole de droit de Beyrouth* (Paris, 1925).

G. Downey, 'Education in the Christian Roman Empire', *Speculum*, xxxii (1957), 48–61.

——, 'The Emperor Julian and the Schools', *Classical Journal*, liii (1957), 97–103.

M. L. W. Laistner, *Christianity and Pagan Culture in the Later Roman Empire* (Ithaca, N.Y., 1951).

P. Petit, *Les étudiants de Libanius* (Paris, 1957).

M. Richard, *'Apo phônês'*, *Byzantion*, xx (1950), 191–222.

A. Vööbus, *History of the School of Nisibis* (Louvain, 1965).

L. G. Westerink (ed.), *Anonymous Prolegomena to Platonic Philosophy* (Amsterdam, 1962).

Middle and Late Periods

H.-G. Beck, 'Bildung und Theologie im frühmittelalterlichen Byzanz', *Polychronion, Festschrift F. Dölger* (Heidelberg, 1966), 69–81.

R. Browning, 'The Correspondence of a Tenth-Century Byzantine Scholar', *Byzantion*, xxiv (1954), 397–452.

——, 'The Patriarchal School at Constantinople in the Twelfth Century', *Byzantion*, xxxii (1962), 167–202; xxxiii (1963), 11–40.

——, 'Enlightenment and Repression in Byzantium in the Eleventh and Twelfth Centuries', *Past and Present*, No. 69 (1975), 3–23.

P. Gautier (ed.), *Michel Italikos, Lettres et discours* (Paris, 1972).

P. Lemerle, *Cinq études sur le XIᵉ siècle byzantin* (Paris, 1977), 195ff.

I. Ševčenko, *Etudes sur la polémique entre Théodore Métochite et Nicéphore Choumnos* (Brussels, 1962).

P. Speck, *Die kaiserliche Universität von Konstantinopel* (Munich, 1974).

P. E. Stephanou, *Jean Italos, philosophe et humaniste*, Orient. Christ. Anal., 134 (1949).

W. Wolska-Conus, 'Les écoles de Psellos et de Xiphilin sous Constantin IX Monomaque', *TM*, vi (1976), 223–43.

——, 'L'école de droit et l'enseignement du droit à Byzance au XIᵉ siècle: Xiphilin et Psellos', *TM*, vii (1979), 1–107.

CHAPTER 7   THE INVISIBLE WORLD OF GOOD AND EVIL

W. Bousset, 'Zur Dämonologie der späteren Antike', *Archiv für Religionswissenschaft*, xviii (1915), 134–73.

A. Delatte and C. Josserand, 'Contribution à l'étude de la démonologie byzantine', *Mélanges J. Bidez* (Brussels, 1934), 207–32.

P. Ioannou, 'Les croyances démonologiques au XIᵉ siècle à Byzance', *Actes du VIᵉ Congrès Internat. d'Etudes Byzant., Paris, 1948*, i (Paris, 1950), 245–60.

——, *Démonologie populaire – démonologie critique au XIᵉ siècle. La Vie inédite de S. Auxence par M. Psellos* (Wiesbaden, 1971).

J. Michl, art. 'Engel IV' and 'Engel VII', *Reallexikon für Antike und Christentum*, v (Stuttgart, 1962), 109ff., 243ff.

P. Perdrizet, *Negotium perambulans in tenebris. Etudes de démonologie gréco-orientale* (Strasbourg, 1922).

J. Turmel, 'Histoire de l'angélologie des temps apostoliques à la fin du Vᵉ siècle', *Rev. d'hist. et de litt. religieuses*, iii (1898), 289–308, 407–34, 533–52.

——, 'L'angélologie depuis le faux Denys l'Aréopagite', *ibid.*, iv (1899), 217–38, 289–309, 414–34, 537–62.

CHAPTERS 8 AND 9   THE PHYSICAL UNIVERSE and THE INHABITANTS OF THE EARTH

C. R. Beazley, *The Dawn of Modern Geography*, i (London, 1897).

F. E. Robbins, *The Hexaemeral Literature. A Study of the Greek and Latin Commentaries on Genesis* (Chicago, 1912).

S. Sambursky, *The Physical World of Late Antiquity* (London, 1962).

J. O. Thomson, *History of Ancient Geography* (Cambridge, 1948).

D. S. Wallace-Hadrill, *The Greek Patristic View of Nature* (Manchester, 1968).

W. Wolska, *La Topographie Chrétienne de Cosmas Indicopleustès* (Paris, 1962).

CHAPTER 10   THE PAST OF MANKIND

H. Gelzer, *Sextus Julius Africanus und die byzantinische Chronographie* (2 vols., Leipzig, 1880–5).

V. Grumel, *La chronologie*, Traité d'études byzantines, ed. P. Lemerle, i (Paris, 1958).

R. L. P. Milburn, *Early Christian Interpretations of History* (London, 1954).

J. Sirinelli, *Les vues historiques d'Eusèbe de Césarée pendant la période prénicéene* (Paris, 1961).

CHAPTER 11   THE FUTURE OF MANKIND

P. J. Alexander, 'Historiens byzantins et croyances eschatologiques', *Actes du XII͘ Congrès Internat. d'Etudes Byzant.*, ii (Belgrade, 1964), 1–8.

——, 'Medieval Apocalypses as Historical Sources', *Amer. Hist. Rev.*, lxxiii (1968), 997–1018.

——, 'Byzantium and the Migration of Literary Works and Motifs', *Medievalia et humanistica*, N.S., ii (1971), 47–68.

W. Bousset, *Der Antichrist* (Göttingen, 1895); English trans., *The Antichrist Legend* (London, 1896).

Ch. Diehl, 'De quelques croyances byzantines sur la fin de Constantinople', *BZ*, xxx (1929–30), 192–6.

V. Istrin, *Otkrovenie Mefodija Patarskago i apokrifičeskie Videnija Daniila* (Moscow, 1897).

F. Macler, 'Les apocalypses apocryphes de Daniel', *Rev. de l'hist. des religions*, xxxiii (1896), 37–53, 163–76, 288–319.

C. Mango, 'The Legend of Leo the Wise', *Zbornik Radova Vizant. Inst.*, vi (Belgrade, 1960), 59–93.

G. Podskalsky, *Byzantinische Reichseschatologie* (Munich, 1972).

L. Rydén, 'The Andreas Salos Apocalypse', *DOP*, xxviii (1974), 197–261.

E. Sackur, *Sibyllinische Texte und Forschungen* (Halle, 1898).

A. Vasiliev, 'Medieval Ideas of the End of the World, West and East', *Byzantion*, xvi (1942–3), 462–502.

CHAPTER 12   THE IDEAL LIFE

The only study which, to my knowledge, attempts to cover much the same ground as this chapter is A. Guillou, 'Le système de vie enseigné au VIII͘ siècle dans le monde byzantin', *I Problemi dell'Occidente nel sec. VIII =*

Settimane di studio del Centro ital. di studi sull'alto medioevo, xx (Spoleto, 1973), i, 343–81.

The extensive bibliography on the Byzantine conception of the Empire and the imperial office may be found in H. Hunger (ed.), *Das byzantinische Herrscherbild* (Darmstadt, 1975), 415ff.

Some important works on this topic are:

F. Dölger, *Byzanz und die europäische Staatenwelt* (Ettal, 1953).

F. Dvornik, *Early Christian and Byzantine Political Philosophy* (2 vols., Washington, D.C., 1966).

A. Grabar, *L'empereur dans l'art byzantin* (Paris, 1936).

H. Hunger, *Prooimion. Elemente der byzantinischen Kaiseridee in den Arengen der Urkunden* (Vienna, 1964).

E. von Ivánka, *Rhomäerreich und Gottesvolk* (Freiburg–Munich, 1968).

G. Ostrogorsky, 'Die byzantinische Staatenhierarchie', *Seminarium Kondakovianum*, viii (1936), 41–61; reprinted in same author's *Zur byzantinischen Geschichte* (Darmstadt, 1973), 119–41.

—— 'The Byzantine Emperor and the Hierarchical World Order', *Slavonic and East European Review*, xxxv (1956–7), 1–14.

O. Treitinger, *Die oströmische Kaiser- und Reichsidee nach ihrer Gestaltung im höfischen Zeremoniell* (Jena, 1938; reprinted Darmstadt, 1969).

For the monastic ideal see Bibliography of Chapter 5.

Numerous monographs devoted to the Fathers of the Church, individually or collectively, discuss their doctrine of Christian morality. See, for example, S. Giet, *Les idées et l'action sociale de Saint Basile* (Paris, 1941); and A. Puech, *Saint Jean Chrysostome et les moeurs de son temps* (Paris, 1891).

CHAPTER 13 LITERATURE

The famous textbook by K. Krumbacher, *Geschichte der byzantinischen Literatur*, 2nd ed. (Munich, 1897) has now been superseded by:

H.-G. Beck, *Kirche und theologische Literatur im byzantinischen Reich* (Munich, 1959).

——, *Geschichte der byzantinischen Volksliteratur* (Munich, 1971).

H. Hunger, *Die hochsprachliche profane Literatur der Byzantiner* (2 vols., Munich, 1978).

Some general discussions and appreciations

H.-G. Beck, 'Antike Beredsamkeit und byzantinische Kallilogia', *Antike und Abendland*, xv (1969), 91–101.

——, 'Das literarische Schaffen der Byzantiner', Österr. Akad. d. Wiss., Philos.-hist. Kl., *Sitzungsberichte*, 294, 4 Abh. (Vienna, 1974).

H. Hunger, 'Aspekte der griechischen Rhetorik von Gorgias bis zum Untergang von Byzanz', *ibid.*, 277/3 (Vienna, 1972).

R. J. H. Jenkins, 'The Hellenistic Origins of Byzantine Literature', *DOP*, xvii (1963), 37–52.

A. P. Každan, *Kniga i pisatel' v Vizantii* (Moscow, 1973).

G. L. Kustas, 'The Function and Evolution of Byzantine Rhetoric', *Viator*, i (1970), 55–73.

——, *Studies in Byzantine Rhetoric* (Thessaloniki, 1973).

C. Mango, *Byzantine Literature as a Distorting Mirror*, Inaugural Lecture (Oxford, 1975).

Development of the Greek Language

R. Browning, *Medieval and Modern Greek* (London, 1969).

——, 'The Language of Byzantine Literature', *Byzantina kai Metabyzantina*, ed. S. Vryonis, Jr, i (Malibu, 1978), 103–33.

R. M. Dawkins, 'The Greek Language in the Byzantine Period', in *Byzantium. An Introduction to East Roman Civilization*, ed. N. H. Baynes and H. St. L. B. Moss (Oxford, 1953), 252–67.

S. Kapsomenos, 'Die griechische Sprache zwischen Koine und Neugriechisch', *Berichte zum XI. Internat. Byzantinisten-Kongress* (Munich, 1958), ii/1.

E. Kriaras, 'Diglossie des derniers siècles de Byzance', *Proceedings of the XIIIth Internat. Congress of Byzant. Studies, Oxford, 1966* (London, 1967), 283–99.

S. B. Psaltes, *Grammatik der byzantinischen Chroniken* (Göttingen, 1913).

D. Tabachovitz, *Etudes sur le grec de la basse époque* (Uppsala, 1943).

There does not exist as yet a proper dictionary of medieval Greek. C. Ducange's famous *Glossarium ad scriptores mediae et infimae graecitatis* (Lyon, 1688; many reprints) is still in many ways the best. For the Early period see G. W. H. Lampe, *Lexicon of Patristic Greek* (Oxford, 1961–8). E. A. Sophocles, *Greek Lexicon of the Roman and Byzantine Periods* (Boston, 1870) is generally unsatisfactory and extends only to 1100 AD. For the vernacular language of the Late Byzantine period see E. Kriaras, *Lexiko tês mesaiônikês hellênikês dêmôdous grammateias, 1100–1669* (Thessaloniki, 1968–).

Books, Libraries and Scholarship

R. Browning, 'Byzantine Scholarship', *Past and Present*, No. 28 (1964), 3–20.

Byzantine Books and Bookmen. A Dumbarton Oaks Colloquium (Washington, D.C., 1975).

G. Cavallo (ed.), *Libri, editori e pubblico nel mondo antico* (Rome–Bari, 1975), 83ff.

A. Dain, *Les manuscrits*, 2nd ed. (Paris, 1964).

R. Devreesse, *Introduction à l'étude des manuscrits grecs* (Paris, 1954).

K. A. Manaphês, *Hai en Kônstantinoupolei bibliothêkai autokratorikai kai patriarchikê* (Athens, 1972).

L. D. Reynolds and N. G. Wilson, *Scribes and Scholars* (Oxford, 1968), 44ff.

Historiography

An indispensable guide to Byzantine historical texts is Gy. Moravcsik, *Byzantinoturcica*, 2nd ed., i (Berlin, 1958). Some further studies are:

Averil Cameron, 'The "Scepticism" of Procopius', *Historia*, xv (1966), 466–82.

——, *Agathias* (Oxford, 1970).

Averil and Alan Cameron, 'Christianity and Tradition in the Historiography of the Late Empire', *Classical Quarterly*, N.S., xiv (1964), 316–28.

M. E. Colonna, *Gli storici bizantini dal IV al XV secolo* (Naples, 1956).

R. J. H. Jenkins, 'The Classical Background of the Scriptores post Theophanem', *DOP*, viii (1954), 13–30.

Ja. N. Ljubarskij, *Mikhail Psell. Ličnost' i tvorčestvo* (Moscow, 1978).

B. Rubin, art. 'Prokopios von Kaisareia', *Paulys Realencyclopädie der class. Altertumswiss.*, xxiii/1 (1957), 273–599.

Hagiography

G. da Costa-Louillet, 'Saints de Constantinople aux VIIIᵉ, IXᵉ et Xᵉ siècles', *Byzantion*, xxiv (1955), 179–263, 453–511; xxv–xxvii (1957), 783–852.

——, 'Saints de Sicile et d'Italie méridionale aux VIIIᵉ, IXᵉ et Xᵉ siècles', *Byzantion*, xxix–xxx (1960), 89–173.

——, 'Saints de Grèce aux VIIIᵉ, IXᵉ et Xᵉ siècles', *Byzantion*, xxxi (1961), 309–69.

H. Delehaye, *Les légendes grecques des saints militaires* (Paris, 1909).

——, *Les passions des martyrs et les genres littéraires* (Brussels, 1921).

——, *Les saints stylites* (Brussels, 1923).

——, *Cinq leçons sur la méthode hagiographique* (Brussels, 1934).

E. Patlagean, 'Ancienne hagiographie byzantine et histoire sociale', *Annales: Economies, sociétés, civilisations*, xxiii (1968), 106–26.

I. Ševčenko, 'Hagiography of the Iconoclast Period' in *Iconoclasm*, ed. A. Bryer and J. Herrin (Birmingham, 1977), 113–31.

Vernacular literature

M. Jeffreys, 'The Nature and Origins of Political Verse', *DOP*, xxviii (1974), 141–95.

M. and E. Jeffreys, 'Imberios and Margarona', *Byzantion*, xli (1971), 122–60.

B. Knös, *Histoire de la littérature néogrecque* (Stockholm, 1962).

M. I. Manoussacas, 'Les romans byzantins de chevalerie et l'état présent des études les concernant', *REB*, x (1952), 70–83.

Digenes Akrites

G. Huxley, 'Antecedents and Context of *Digenes Akrites*', *Greek, Roman and Byzantine Studies*, xv (1974), 317–38.

N. Oikonomidès, 'L' ''épopée'' de Digenis et la frontière orientale de Byzance aux Xe et XIe siècles', *TM*, vii (1979), 375–97.

A. Pertusi, 'La poesia epica bizantina et la sua formazione', *Atti del Convegno Internaz. sul tema: 'La poesia epica et la sua formazione'* (Rome, 1970), 481–544.

L. Polites, 'L'épopée byzantine de Digénis Akritas', *ibid.*, 551–81.

CHAPTER 14   ART AND ARCHITECTURE

General

J. Beckwith, *The Art of Constantinople. An Introduction to Byzantine Art* (London, 1961).

——, *Early Christian and Byzantine Art*, Pelican History of Art (Harmondsworth, 1970).

Ch. Delvoye, *L'art byzantin* (Paris, 1967).

A. Grabar, *Martyrium* (3 vols., Paris, 1946).

——, *L'art de la fin de l'antiquité et du moyen âge* (collected papers) (3 vols., Paris, 1968).

——, *Les voies de création en iconographie chrétienne* (Paris, 1979).

C. Mango, *The Art of the Byzantine Empire, 312–1453. Sources and Documents* (Englewood Cliffs, N.J., 1972).

Reallexikon zur byzantinischen Kunst, ed. K. Wessel and M. Restle (Stuttgart, 1963–   ).

W. F. Vollbach and J. Lafontaine-Dosogne, *Byzanz und der christliche Osten*, Propyläen Kunstgeschichte 3 (Berlin, 1968).

Early period

B. Brenk, *Spätantike und frühes Christentum*, Propyläen Kunstgeschichte, Supplementband 1 (Berlin, 1977).

F. W. Deichmann, *Ravenna, Hauptstadt des spätantiken Abendlandes* (2 vols. in 3 parts, Wiesbaden, 1969–75).

A. Grabar, *Le premier art chrétien (200–395)* (Paris, 1966).

——, *L'âge d'or de Justinien. De la mort de Théodose à l'Islam* (Paris, 1966).

E. Kitzinger, 'Byzantine Art in the Period between Justinian and Iconoclasm', *Berichte zum XI. Internat. Byzantinisten-Kongress* (Munich, 1958), iv/1.

——, *Byzantine Art in the Making* (London, 1977).

C. R. Morey, *Early Christian Art*, 2nd ed. (Princeton, 1953).

Middle and Late Periods

Art et société à Byzance sous les Paléologues, Actes du Colloque organisé par
l'Association Internat. des Etudes Byzantines à Venise en sept. 1968
(Venice, 1971).

O. Demus, *Byzantine Art and the West* (New York, 1970).

A. Grabar, *Byzance. L'art byzantin du moyen âge* (Paris, 1963).

G. de Jerphanion, *Une nouvelle province de l'art byzantin. Les églises rupestres de
Cappadoce* (4 vols., Paris, 1925–42).

G. Millet, *Monuments byzantins de Mistra* (Paris, 1910).

Architecture

H. C. Butler, *Early Churches in Syria*, ed. E. B. Smith (Princeton, 1929).

R. Krautheimer, *Early Christian and Byzantine Architecture*, Pelican History of
Art, 2nd ed. (Harmondsworth, 1975).

J. Lassus, *Sanctuaires chrétiens de Syrie* (Paris, 1947).

C. Mango, *Byzantine Architecture* (New York, 1976).

Sculpture

A. Grabar, *Sculptures byzantines de Constantinople (IVᵉ–Xᵉ siècle)* (Paris, 1963).

——, *Sculptures byzantines du moyen âge (XIᵉ–XIVᵉ siècle)* (Paris, 1976).

J. Kollwitz, *Oströmische Plastik der theodosianischen Zeit* (Berlin, 1941).

Monumental Painting and Mosaics

H. Belting, C. Mango and D. Mouriki, *The Mosaics and Frescoes of St. Mary
Pammakaristos (Fethiye Camii) at Istanbul* (Washington, D.C., 1978).

O. Demus, *Byzantine Mosaic Decoration* (London, 1948).

——, *The Mosaics of Norman Sicily* (London, 1950).

——, 'Die Entstehung des Paläologenstils in der Malerei', *Berichte zum XI.
Internat. Byzantinisten-Kongress* (Munich, 1958), iv/2.

E. Diez and O. Demus, *Byzantine Mosaics in Greece. Hosios Lucas and Daphni*
(Cambridge, Mass., 1931).

R. Hamann-MacLean and H. Hallensleben, *Die Monumentalmalerei in Serbien
und Makedonien* (Giessen, 1963).

V. Lazarev, *Feofan Grek i ego škola* (Moscow, 1961).

——, *Old Russian Murals and Mosaics* (London, 1966).

——, *Storia della pittura bizantina* (Turin, 1967).

D. Levi, *Antioch Mosaic Pavements* (2 vols., Princeton, 1947).

C. Mango, *Materials for the Study of the Mosaics of St. Sophia at Istanbul*
(Washington, D.C., 1962).

P. A. Underwood, *The Kariye Djami* (4 vols., New York–Princeton,
1966–75).

T. Velmans, *La peinture murale byzantine à la fin du moyen âge* (Paris, 1977).

Icons

W. Felicetti-Liebenfels, *Geschichte der byzantinischen Ikonenmalerei*
(Olten–Lausanne, 1956).

323

G. A. and M. Soteriou, *Icônes du Mont-Sinaï* (2 vols., Athens, 1956–8).

K. Weitzmann, *The Monastery of St. Catherine at Mount Sinai. The Icons*, i (Princeton, 1976).

K. Weitzmann, M. Chatzidakis, K. Miatev, S. Radojčić, *Frühe Ikonen* (Vienna–Munich, 1965).

Illuminated Manuscripts

H. Belting and G. Cavallo, *Die Bibel des Niketas* (Wiesbaden, 1979).

H. Buchthal, *The Miniatures of the Paris Psalter* (London, 1938).

H. Buchthal and H. Belting, *Patronage in Thirteenth-Century Constantinople. An Atelier of Calligraphy and Book Decoration* (Washington, D.C., 1978).

J. Leroy, *Les manuscrits syriaques à peintures* (2 vols., Paris, 1964).

K. Weitzmann, *Byzantinische Buchmalerei des 9. und 10. Jahrhunderts* (Berlin, 1935).

——, *The Joshua Roll. A Work of the Macedonian Renaissance* (Princeton, 1948).

——, *Illustrations in Roll and Codex*, 2nd ed. (Princeton, 1970).

——, *Studies in Classical and Byzantine Manuscript Illumination* (Chicago, 1971).

Other Minor Arts

A. V. Bank, *Prikladnoe iskusstvo Vizantii IX–XII vekov* (Moscow, 1978).

E. Cruikshank Dodd, *Byzantine Silver Stamps* (Washington, D.C., 1961).

R. Delbrueck, *Die Consulardiptychen und verwandte Denkmäler* (2 vols., Berlin, 1929).

A. Goldschmidt and K. Weitzmann, *Die byzantinischen Elfenbeinskulpturen des zehnten bis dreizehnten Jahrhunderts* (2 vols., Berlin, 1930–4).

A. Grabar, *Les ampoules de Terre Sainte (Monza, Bobbio)* (Paris, 1958).

——, *Les revêtements en or et en argent des icones byzantines du moyen âge* (Venice, 1975).

W.-F. Volbach, *Elfenbeinarbeiten der Spätantike und des frühen Mittelalters*, 3rd ed. (Mainz, 1976).

K. Wessel, *Die byzantinische Emailkunst vom fünften bis dreizehnten Jahrhundert* (Recklinghausen, 1967); English trans., *Byzantine Enamels from the 5th to the 13th Century* (Shannon, 1969).

INDEX

Abasgians, the, 17
Acathist Hymn, 131–2
actors, 63–4, 65
administration: civil, 34–5;
    imperial, 36; military, 34;
    municipal, 35; provincial, 34–46
Aetius, heretic, 45
Agathias, historian, 34, 244
agriculture, 43
Alexandria: Church of, 37–8;
    School of, 128, 134
Alexius I Comnenus, Emperor, 53,
    58, 59, 83, 102
Anastasian Long Walls, the, 25
Anastasius I, Emperor, 39, 40, 62,
    89, 96, 203–4
Ancyra, 17, 72, 81
Andrew the Fool, St, 208–11
Andronicus I Comnenus, Emperor,
    276
Andronicus II Palaeologus,
    Emperor, 251
angels, 154–5
animals, 177–9
Anna Comnena, historian, 29, 242
Antioch in Syria, 17, 18, 38, 39, 62,
    96, 128
Antioch in Pisidia, 17
Antony, St, 106–7, 108; Life of,
    105, 164, 247–8; on demons,
    163; on education, 131

Apocalypse, visions of, 204–11,
    214–16
Arabs, the, 1, 4, 19–20, 78, 207
Aramaic (language), 18, 19
archaeology, 4, 6, 7, 38, 43, 69, 81,
    257
architecture: ecclesiastical, 258–81;
    monastic, 118; remaining
    examples of, 257–8; see also under
    churches
archives, 5–6
Arethas, bishop of Caesarea, 140
Argives, the, 24
Arianism, 89
aristocracy, the, 56, 237; rise to
    power of, 51–2; retinues of, 53
arithmetic, 127
Armenian (language), 27
Armenians, the, 15, 26, 29
army, the Byzantine, 26, 27, 49,
    52; Constantine's reforms of, 34;
    in society, 33–4; hierarchy and
    administration of, 34;
    recruitment to, 34; reform of,
    under Heraclius, 46; size of, 34
Artemius, St, 78, 79, 158–9
art, Byzantine: development of,
    256–81; frescoes, 265;
    iconography, 259–60, 267; icons,
    belief in, 98, 264, 268; influence
    of, 274; 'Macedonian

325